1 MONTH OF
FREE
READING

at

www.ForgottenBooks.com

By purchasing this book you are eligible for one month membership to ForgottenBooks.com, giving you unlimited access to our entire collection of over 1,000,000 titles via our web site and mobile apps.

To claim your free month visit:

www.forgottenbooks.com/free276292

ISBN 978-0-331-52392-8
PIBN 10276292

BIENNIAL REPORTS

OF THE

SECRETARY OF STATE,

COMMISSIONERS OF PUBLIC PRINTING,

AND THE

SUPERINTENDENT OF PUBLIC PROPERTY

OF THE

STATE OF WISCONSIN,

For the Fiscal Term Ending September 30, 1894.

MADISON, WISCONSIN:
DEMOCRAT PRINTING COMPANY, STATE PRINTER.
1894.

STATE OF WISCONSIN.

REPORT OF THE SECRETARY OF STATE.

DEPARTMENT OF STATE,
October 10, 1894.

To His Excellency, GEORGE W. PECK,
Governor of the State of Wisconsin.

SIR:—In compliance with the requirements of law, I have the honor to present the biennial report of this department, showing the condition of the several funds, with a complete statement of receipts and disbursements of said funds for the biennial fiscal term closed September 30, 1894.

I have also appended the usual detailed statements and statistical tables deemed of interest to the people of the state.

T. J. CUNNINGHAM,
Secretary of State.

166051

GENERAL STATEMENT.

General Statement.

The aggregate result of the financial transactions during the fiscal years ending Sept. 30, 1893 and 1894, is as follows:

	Balance Sept. 30, 1892.	Receipts for 1893.	Receipts for 1894.	Total.	Disbursements for 1893.	Disbursements for 1894.	Total disbursements for 1893 and 1894.	Balance Sept. 30, 1894.
General Fund	$640,228 12	$1,600,314 84	$2,226,164 24	$4,475,707 20	$1,786,501 55	$1,711,889 94	$3,498,391 49	$977,315 71
TRUST FUNDS.								
School Fund	$1,811 08	$157,779 65	$207,911 45	7902 18	454 50	$211,535 00	$365,789 50	$1,712 68
School Fund income	25,327 83	852,512 87	616 40	1,740,557 10	840,826 07	868,063 42	1,708,889 49	31,667 61
University Fund	1,361 42	6,939 28	10,481 95	18,782 65	8,000 00	11,000 00	9,000 00	*217 35
University Fund income	....	238,325 50	470,073 72	708,399 22	238,325 50	470,073 72	708,399 22	....
Agricultural College Fund	11,264 49	20,435 93	19,511 44	51,211 86	8,827 79	22,400 00	51,227 79	*15 93
Agricultural College Fund income	....	17,390 10	27,828 96	45,219 06	17,390 10	27,828 96	45,219 06	....
Normal School Fund	11,887 50	22,968 28	0,239 52	245,095 30	129,643 50	106,900 00	236,543 50	8,551 80
Normal School Fund Income	86,845 37	311,780 09	162,131 08	473,911 17	311,780 09	162,131 08	473,911 17	....
Drainage Fund	....	30,219 01	21,635 98	138,700 36	92,102 64	30,272 07	122,374 71	16,325 65
Delinquent Tax Fund	475 14	814 02	8,393 92	14,783 08	6,020 46	8,096 74	14,117 20	665 88
Deposit Fund	11,310 91	867 06	....	12,177 97	754 80	138 23	893 03	11,284 94

Fund								
Indemnity Land Fund		15,318 87	13,545 29	28,864 16	15,318 87	13,545 29	28,864 16	
Redemption Fund	35 02	29 50	113 14	177 66				177 66
Ex-State Officers' Judgment Fund								
Manitowoc and Winnebago Swamp Land Fund		177,312 54	250,590 01	427,902 55		427,902 55	427,902 55	
Vilas & Sauk Co. Bounty Land Fund	2,209 90	586 02	220 92	3,016 84		3,016 84	3,016 84	
Wisconsin Farm Mortgage Co. Fund	2,874 38	180 40	450 10	3,504 88				3,504 88
St. C. & L. S. R. R. Trespass Fund	4,546 31			4,546 31		17 50	*17 50	1,528 81
St. C. & L. S. R. R. Fund	2,067 46			2,067 46		2,067 46	2,067 46	
Deposit Fund	408 02			408 02				408 02
Allotment Fund	916 54			916 54				98 54
Totals	$163,341 37	$1,958,559 12	$2,165,843 88	$1,287,744 37	$1,843,244 32	$2,364,988 86	$4,208,233 18	$79,511 19

* Overdrawn.

b—Sec'y.

GENERAL FUND.

This fund embraces all the revenues of the state applicable to the payment of the ordinary expenses of the state government.

The sources from which it is derived are, a tax on civil actions, license of railroad companies, plank road companies, log driving and booming companies, savings, loan and trust companies, telegraph and telephone companies, insurance companies, and hawkers and peddlers; fees received from notaries public and from the various state offices, and from the sale of books and reports.

The expenditures therefrom are authorized by permanent and temporary appropriations, and by the several laws requiring the Secretary of State to audit accounts.

A statement of the transactions of this fund will be found in detail under appendix "A" in this report.

The receipts and disbursements have been as follows:

RECEIPTS.

	1893.	1894.
Railroad companies, sections 1212 and 1213, R. S.........	$1,156,260 75	$1,438,758 66
Telegraph companies, chapter 345, laws 1883, am ch. 332, laws 1887..................	9,657 62	9,935 71
Telephone companies, chapter 345, laws 1883, and ch. 337, laws 1885..................	11,705 71	9,716 29
Sleeping car companies, chapter 358, laws 1883, am. ch. 415, laws 1885..............	1,193 04	1,223 39
From counties for maintaining insane, ch. 298, laws 1881....	139,723 27	153,257 47
From counties for industrial school for boys, ch. 298, laws 1881......................	8,511 81	8,078 53
For fifth normal school, chapter 364, laws 1885..........	9,985 59	10,014 41
For aid to free high schools, sec. 496, R. S., am. by ch. 298, laws 1885.................	49,927 95	50,072 05
From suit tax, sec. 743, R. S..	6,559 00	7,903 00
From peddler licenses, sec. 1772, R. S., am. by ch. 510, laws 1889.................	15,228 17	12,841 95

General Fund.

	1893.	1894.
From insurance licenses, sec. 1219, R. S., am. by ch. 138, laws 1879	$122,651 27	$129,931 05
From loan and trust companies, chapter 263, laws 1891.	1,025 85	1,902 84
From log driving and boom companies, chapter 422, laws 1891	4,187 66	1,579 11
From United States for maintaining inmates W. V. Home	14,711 94	12,662 21
From office fees..............	39,828 36	30,980 07
From interest on general fund balance in banks...........	12,56) 08	14,178 13
From ex-state treasurers' judgments	....	327,902 55
From all other sources......	5,587 77	5,226 82
	$1,609,587 77	$2,226,164 24

Total for two years................................... $3,835,752 01

GENERAL FUND INVESTMENTS.

There has been invested, in pursuance of law, the following amounts, from the general fund during the biennial term ending Sept. 30, 1894:

	1893.	1894.
Loan to state agricultural society.....................	$30,000 00	....
Purchase of E. C. McFetridge mortgage on state fair grounds...................	....	$47,782 03

Total for two years................................... $77,782 03

DISBURSEMENTS.

1. SALARIES AND EXPENSES.

	1893.	1894.
Governor's office..............	$6,800 41	$6,183 00
Secretary's office..............	7,095 88	7,000 00
Treasurer's office	7,095 88	7,000 00
Attorney general's office	4,318 48	5,500 00
State superintendent's office...	5,332 67	5,950 06
Railroad commissioner's office.	5,468 48	4,894 96
Insurance commissioner's office	4,314 68	4,847 54
Superintendent public property	2,027 39	2,000 00
Supreme court....	34,606 50	34,351 75
Circuit courts.....	68,000 00	67,956 20
State historical society.........	9,800 00	9,499 00
State library....	4,426 66	8,770 52
State board of charities and reform.	1,084 40	....
State board of control	18,250 80	18,578 05
	$178,567 18	$177,431 08

Total............................ .... $855,998 26

General Fund.

2. PERMANENT APPROPRIATIONS.

	893.	1894.
Bureau of labor statistics......	$7,974 65	$7,248 47
State board of health...	6,043 80	5,668 80
Fish culture	13,000 00	13,000 00
Dairy and food commission....	7,456 49	7,046 32
Dairy and food commission laboratory....................	286 43	925 67
Land protection	2,532 97	6,148 89
Teachers' institutes............	1,444 60	1,811 54
Appraising Crawford county swamp lands............	99 16	....
	$38,838 10	$41,349 69
Total...........................		$80,187 79

3. LEGISLATIVE EXPENSES.

Lieutenant governor	$1,097 69	$500 00
Senate salaries...............	16,500 00	....
Mileage, 2d special session.	892 40	....
Mileage, regular session...	951 00	....
Employes, 2d special session....................	599 00	... .
Employes, regular session..	22,904 00	....
Assembly salaries	50,500 00	....
Mileage, 2d special session.	2,667 30	....
Mileage, regular session...	3,040 01	... .
Employes, 2d special session	547 00	....
Employes, regular session.	29,003 75	....
Miscellaneous expenses....	760 10	....
Legislative chaplains......	420 00	....
Contesting seats, assembly.	7,093 53	....
Legislative visiting committee...	300 00	....
Printing for legislature ...	6,566 45	105 21
Annotated statutes for legislature.............	1,782 00	... .
Blue book................	8,879 72	100 00
	$154,503 95	$705 21
Total.......		$155,209 16

General Fund.

4. Charitable and Penal Institutions.

	1893.	1894.
State Hospital for insane	$113,833 44	$94,403 65
Northern Hospital for insane	114,098 59	121,686 52
Wisconsin school for deaf	39,497 44	39,938 43
Wisconsin school for blind	33,209 39	25,523 45
Industrial school for boys	57,300 30	54,458 97
States prison	10,813 68	28,829 34
State public school	*40,720 09	37,538 12
	$408,967 93	$402,378 48

Total.. $811,346 41

5. Clerk Hire.

Governor's office	$1,812 47	$1,500 00
Secretary's office	21,260 67	21,310 00
Treasurer's office	10,404 0)	10,159 98
State Superintendent's office	4,428 83	3,913 61
Land office	15,568 56	13,402 15
Supt. Public Property's office	1,500 00	1,520 54
Bureau labor statistics	1,200 00	1,200 (0
	$56,174 53	$53,006 28

Total.. $109,180 81

6. Labor about Capitol.

Engineers and firemen	$5,416 50	$5,682 75
Carpenters	2,512 90	1,980 00
Janitors and messengers	18,866 00	18,944 00
Painters	1,683 33	1,800 00
Police	4,294 00	4,380 00
Nightwatchmen	1,460 00	1,400 00
Laborers	11,653 98	11,504 10
Bookroom attendant	900 00	900 00
Elevator attendant	73) 00	730 00
Storekeeper	730 00	730 00
Steam and gas fitter	821 25	821 25
	$49,067 96	$48,872 10

Total $97,940 06

*Including payments on account of fire loss (ch. 152, laws of 1893) amounting to $5,067.80.

General Fund.

FOR SUNDRY PURPOSES.

	1893.	1894.
Transient labor...............	$15,170 02	$11.289 87
Incidental expenses..........	25,148 33	14,701 26
Printing.....................	25,291 19	22,332 48
Postage......................	7,001 93	5,422 12
Expressage...................	2,568 61	2,347 57
Paper........................	15,467 49	13,737 30
Stationery...................	5,218 94	2,472 54
Gas..........................	5,666 85	3,849 99
Fuel.........................	5,146 85	6,426 24
Treasury agent...............	3,808 04	2,972 72
Compiling war records........	6,305 00	4,510 00
Militia......................	82,459 79	105,469 74
Wisconsin rifle range........	2,204 59	3,942 61
Examiners, state teachers....	517 87	335 37
Examiners, admission to bar..	785 20	577 84
Governor's contingent fund..	2,147 96	572 69
Veterinary surgery...........	5,743 41	4,697 01
Glandered horses slaughtered	1,659 87	1,051 04
State fish and game warden..	2,334 59	3,342 49
Illustrating report agricultural experiment station...	388 40	189 08
Ex-state treasurers' suits.....	8,248 29	25 06
Publishing and advertising...	657 80	1,297 35
Publishing general laws......	42,000 00	100 00
Statistics of crime...........	....	29 60
Publishing private and local laws.....................	478 80	....
Publishing laws in state paper	1,422 60	38 40
Publishing bank reports.....	261 05	246 14
Advertising lands...........	473 95	441 10
Real estate returns..........	1,936 13	1,842 02
Free high schools	47,623 45	47,402 91
Chicamauga committee.......	....	273 50
Presidential electors..........	370 60	....
Maintaining insane in county asylums..................	244,289 18	270,780 30
University summer school....	....	1,000 00
Deaf mute instruction in cities.....................	5,236 10	9,315 37
Circuit court reporters.......	10,112 50	10,160 60
County agricultural societies.	31,203 91	27,374 30
Bounty on wild animals.....	12,778 00	13,068 00
Special appropriations........	208,920 98	266,073 84
Miscellaneous................	69,383 63	128,438 65
	$900,381 90	$988,147 10

Total... $1,888,529 00

SCHOOL FUND.

The School Fund is composed of:

1. Proceeds of lands granted by the United States for support of schools.
2. All moneys accruing to the state by forfeiture or escheat.
3. All penalties for trespass upon school lands.
4. All fines collected in the several counties for breach of penal laws.
5. All moneys paid as an exemption from military duty.
6. Five *per cent.* of net proceeds of sales of United States public lands.

The number of acres of unsold land, the proceeds of which are applicable to this fund, is, 47,381.47.

The cash receipts and disbursements during the last two years have been as follows:

RECEIPTS.

	1893.	1894.	
Sales of land....................	$4,288 00	$2,316 50	
Dues on certificates of sale.....	15,025 46	8,444 87	
Loans, school district and individual........................	89,835 36	56,627 16	
Penalties......................	10 34	6 78	
Fines	16,606 30	22,444 69	
Bonds	30,985 95	54,962 33	
Special loans...................	48,176 15	57,907 88	
United States 5 per cent. on sale of public land................	2,656 37	5,201 74	
Escheat estate of Anna Riley, per J. W. Sales, judge Rock Co. court....................	195 72	....	
	$157,779 65	$207,911 45	
Total.......			$365,691 10

DISBURSEMENTS.

School district loans............	$90,454 50	$119,485 00	
Special loans....................	42,000 00	92,000 00	
Bonds purchased................	21,800 00	....	
Refunded.......................	....	50 00	
	$154,254 50	$211,535 00	
Total..			$365,789 50

School Fund.

The amounts of productive school fund on the 30th day of September, 1893, and 1894, were as follows:

	1893.	1894.
Dues on certificates of sales..................	$110,748 21	$104,988 84
Due on school district and individual loans..	288,741 54	349,495 88
Certificate of indebtedness—state of Wisconsin..	1,568,700 00	1,563,700 00
Ashland county bonds.............	15,000 00	15,000 00
Ashland city bonds...............	36,000 00	30,000 00
Chippewa Falls city bonds.....	20,000 00	20,000 00
Chilton city bonds..........................	7,600 00	7,600 00
Chilton town bonds	17,400 00	17,400 00
Elkhorn school bonds....	10,000 00	8,000 00
Elroy city bonds...	6,350 00	6,350 00
Eau Claire city bonds...............	30,000 00	30,000 00
Fond du Lac school bonds.................. ...	30,000 00	30,000 00
Madison city bonds.....	60,000 00	60,000 00
Milwaukee city bonds........................	303,000 00	266,000 00
Milwaukee city school bonds........	60,000 00	60,000 00
Mineral Point city bonds............	6,000 00	5,000 00
Marathon county bonds.....	32,000 00	24,000 00
Marathon county bonds premium......... ..	614 88	336 72
Oconomowoc city hall bonds.................	2,000 00	....
Oshkosh city bonds..	50,000 00	50,000 00
Oshkosh city sewer bonds..................	21,800 00	21,800 00
Ripon city bonds...........................	6,000 00	4,500 00
Stoughton city bonds	30,000 00	30,000 00
Superior city bonds........................	250,000 00	250,000 00
Superior city bonds premium...	38,090 09	34,905 92
Wausau city bonds	30,000 00	30,000 00
Loan to board of education, city of Madison..	15,000 00	10,000 00
Loan to Barron county......................	10,000 00	8,000 00
Loan to Brown county......................	78,300 00	78,950 00
Loan to Jackson county....................	8,000 00	6,000 00
Loan to Lincoln county....................	4,198 50	....
Loan to Oneida county.....................	3,863 79	30,000 00
Loan to Price county	24,000 00	20,000 00
Loan to Washburn county..........	2,154 80	....
Loan to Winnebago county.....	4,000 00	,0
Loan to city of Berlin......	6,000 00	,0
Loan to city of Chippewa Falls..............	....	0
Loan to city of Green Bay........	85,000 00	4 000 00
Loan to city of Menasha.............	....	35,000 00
Loan to city of Merrill.......	1,180 00	·
Loan to city of Neenah...	8,000 00	8,0
Loan to city of New London.	14,000 00	12,0
Loan to city of Oconto	....	35, 00 00
Loan to city of Rice Lake	1,800 00	1,500 00
Loan to city of Wausau....................	2,000 00	... .
Loan to town of Arcadia....................	10,000 00	8,88 883
Loan to town of Arena....................	500 00	400 00
Loan to town of Ashland...............	3,441 58	2,366 08

School Fund.

	1893.	1894.
Loan to town of Arthur......................	$1,200 00	$600 00
Loan to town of Cleveland, Marathon county	96 48	....
Loan to town of Crandon....................	1,400 00	....
Loan to town of Clinton, Barron county......	600 00	400 00
Loan to town of Day........................	700 00	350 00
Loan to town of Gillett.	200 00	100 00
Loan to town of Hixon, Clark county........	660 00	....
Loan to town of Millston	666 67	....
Loan to town of Mineral Point...............	1,000 00	....
Loan to town of Moscow........	4,542 00	3,785 00
Loan to town of Mosinee....................	600 00	400 00
Loan to town of Maine	2,800 00	2,050 00
Loan to town of Pleasant Valley	2,299 46	1,532 98
Loan to town of Richfield...................	1,875 00	1,100 00
Loan to town of Rolling......................	300 00	200 00
Loan to town of Russell.....	4,000 00	3,500 00
Loan to town of St. Croix Falls..............	1,000 00	750 00
Loan to town of Shell Lake	3,333 33	....
Loan to town of Spooner................	4,500 00	1,000 00
Loan to town of Waldwick..................	9,850 00	8,500 00
Loan to town of Weston	170 00	....
Loan to town of Wood......................	4,000 00	3,000 00
Loan to town of Bloomer...................	200 00	....
Loan to State Agricultural Society...........	90,666 00	90,666 00
Total....	$3,380,672 28	$3,418,750 25

School Fund Income.

SCHOOL FUND INCOME.

The interest received on school fund investments and on the principal due for sales of school lands, and the mill tax on all assessable property in the state (287–1885), constitutes the school fund income.

The amount of this fund in the treasury on the first day of June is annually certified by the Secretary of State to the State Superintendent of Public Instruction, and by him apportioned under the provision of section 554 of the Revised Statutes.

The receipts and disbursements during the last two years have been as follows:

RECEIPTS.

	1893.	1894.
Interest on land certificates and loans...............................	$21,202 90	$24,092 87
Interest on certificates of indebtedness..................	109,301 18	109,616 82
One mill tax	653,057 00	654,943 00
Interest on bonds	48,663 30	48,481 92
Interest on special loans	14,569 93	16,871 80
Interest on school fund in banks...........	3,656 01	8,582 06
Normal school fund income transfer......................	2,062 50	....
Washburn county penalty.....	....	110 08
Refunds......................	....	67 85
	$852,512 87	$862,716 40

Total.. .. $1,715,229 27

DISBURSEMENTS.

	1893.	1894.
Apportionment to counties....	$839,996 17	$867,998 50
Accrued interest..............	653 25	....
Refunded........	176 65	64 92
	$840,826 07	$868,063 42

Total..... ....♦..... ..... $1,708,889 49

University Fund.

UNIVERSITY FUND.

The proceeds of sales of lands granted by the United States to the state of Wisconsin for the support of the State University by acts of Congress, approved June 12, 1838, August 6, 1846, and December 12, 1852, form the University Fund. The principal or capital is productive, drawing interest.

The number of acres of unsold land is 937.4. The cash receipts and disbursements during the last two years have been as follows:

RECEIPTS.

	1893.	1894.	
Sales of land	$59 70	$139 95	
Dues on certificates of sales ...	1,613 00	1,067 00	
Loans, school district and individual....	266 58	275 00	
Bonds........................	1,500 00	3,500 00	
Special loans..................	3,500 00	5,500 00	
	$6,939 28	$10,481 95	
Total... ....,....................................			$17,221 23

DISBURSEMENTS.

Special loans..................	$8,000 00	$6,000 00	
Bonds........................	....	5,000 00	
	$8,000 00	$11,000 00	
Total			$19,000 00

University Fund Income.

The amount of productive University Fund on the 30th day of September, 1893 and 1894, was as follows:

	1893.	1894.
Dues on certificates of sales.	$11,797 00	$10,813 00
Due on loans	625 00	350 00
Due on certificates of indebtedness...........	111,000 00	111,000 00
Eau Claire county bonds....................	10,000 00	10,000 00
Greenwood city bonds.	....	2,500 00
Manitowoc county bonds....................	80,000 00	80,000 00
Vernon county bonds......................	20,000 00	16,000 00
Waupaca county bonds...........	8,000 00	8,000 00
Stoughton city bonds..................	8,000 00	3,000 00
Tomahawk city bonds.....................	8,500 00	7,000 00
Platteville city bonds.	6,000 00	6,000 00
Loan to city of Menomonie.................	4,000 00	2,000 00
Loan to Shawano county.....	9,000 00	7,500 00
Loan to Winnebago county.................	8,000 00	8,000 00
Loan to village of Thorp...........	....	4,000 00
Loan to town of Florence......	....	2,000 00
Loan to board of education, city of Ripon....	....	2,500 00
Total..............................	$229,922 00	$280,663 00

UNIVERSITY FUND INCOME.

This fund is derived chiefly from the annual tax levy authorized by section 390, Revised Statutes, and from the interest on university land certificates and loans, and the 1-8 mill tax on all assessable property in the state, chapter 300, laws of 1885 — with an additional 1-10 mill tax annually for six years, to be used for building purposes — chapter 21, laws of 1891 — and is perpetually appropriated to the support and endowment of the state university by section 389, Revised Statutes. By provision of said section, this entire fund is placed at the disposal of the board of regents by transfer to the treasurer of said board and the detailed record of its expenditures is kept by said treasurer distinct and independent of the accounts of the state.

University Fund Income.

The receipts and disbursements during the last two years have been as follows:

RECEIPTS.

	1893.	1894.
Interest on land certificates and loans	$395 85	$799 46
Interest on certificates of indebtedness	7,758 90	7,781 10
From 9-40 mill tax	146,937 32	147,862 18
Interest on university fund deposited in banks	1,661 52	775 57
United States treasurer, appropriation for experimental station	15,000 00	15,000 00
United States treasurer, appropriation for agricultural college	19,000 00	20,000 00
Secretary board of regents, students' fees, etc	41,558 67	48,738 72
M. M. Jackson, bequest	154 74	25 00
Interest on bonds	4,270 00	3,701 76
Interest on loans	1,088 00	1,294 28
From ex-treasurers' judgments	....	41,936 82
From appropriations, ch. 280, laws 1893	....	140,000 00
From appropriations for agrl. institutes	....	18,000 00
One per cent. railroad and other license fees	....	24,643 07
Washburn county penalty	....	22 31
	$238,325 50	$470,073 72
Total		$708,399 22

DISBURSEMENTS.

Treasurer state university	$238,319 84	$470,039 40
Refunded	5 66	34 32
	$238,325 50	$470,073 72
Total		$708,399 22

Agricultural College Fund.

AGRICULTURAL COLLEGE FUND.

The proceeds of sales of 240,000 acres of land granted by the United States to the state by act of congress, approved July 2, 1862, for the support of an institution of learning, where shall be taught the principles of agriculture and mechanic arts, form the Agricultural College Fund. The number of acres of unsold land is 243.07.

The cash receipts and disbursements during the last two years have been as follows:

RECEIPTS.

	1893.	1894.	
Sales of land................	$62 47	$29 12	
Dues on certificates of sales..	5,329 00	1,329 00	
Bonds........................	13,044 46	16,153 32	
Special loans................	2,000 00	2,000 00	
	$20,435 93	$19,511 44	
Total...			$39,947 37

DISBURSEMENTS.

	1893.	1894.	
Bonds........................	$15,817 50	....	
Special loans................	13,000 00	$22,400 00	
Refunds......................	10 29	....	
	$28,827 79	$22,400 00	
Total..			$51,227 79

Agricultural College Fund.

The amount of productive agricultural college fund on the 30th day of September, 1893 and 1894, was as follows:

	1893.	1894.
Dues on certificates of sales....................	$62,665 00	$61,336 00
Certificates of indebtedness...................	60,600 00	60,600 00
Eau Claire county bonds.	10,000 00	10,000 00
Eau Claire city bridge bonds.................	15,000 00	15,000 00
Eau Claire city bridge bonds premium..	778 04	719 72
Manitowoc county bonds	53,000 00	43,000 00
Grand Rapids bridge bonds......	6,000 00	5,000 00
Board of education, city of Neenah bonds....	3,000 00	....
Black River Falls city bonds.................	20,000 00	20,000 00
Madison city bonds	2,500 00	2,500 00
Milwaukee city bonds.......................	30,000 00	30,000 00
New Richmond city bonds...................	2,000 00	1,500 00
Platteville city bonds......................	5,400 00	3,800 00
Tomahawk city bonds.....................	5,500 00	5,500 00
Loan to town of Colburn..............	2,000 00	2,000 00
Loan to city of Merrill...................	6,000 00	5,000 00
Loan to city of Waupaca....................	....	7,000 00
Loan to town of Hancock.........	4,000 00	3,000 00
Loan to Manitowoc county..................	9,000 00	19,000 00
Loan to Winnebago county...................	4,000 00	4,000 00
Loan to town of Day.........................	....	1,400 00
Loan to town of Minong.....	....	2,000 00
Total.............	$301,438 04	$302,355 72

Agricultural College Fund Income.

AGRICULTURAL COLLEGE FUND INCOME.

The receipts and disbursements during the last two years have been as follows:

RECEIPTS.

	1893.	1894.
Interest on land certificates and loans.....	$4,606 89	$4,802 60
Interest on certificates of indebtedness..................	4,235 89	4,248 11
Interest on bank deposits......	143 28	135 17
Interest on bonds	7,565 54	7,071 68
Interest on special loans	899 00	1,792 30
From ex-treasurers' judgments	....	10,278 48
From Washburn county, penalty.....	....	62
	$17,390 10	$27,828 96

Total............................ .... $45,219 06

DISBURSEMENTS.

	1893.	1894.
Treasurer of state university...	$17,171 48	$27,822 13
Refund for overpayments.....	29 72	6 83
Accrued interest on bonds.....	188 90	....
	$17,390 10	$27,828 96

Total... .... $45,219 06

NORMAL SCHOOL FUND.

This fund consists of one-half of the proceeds of the sales of all swamp and overflowed lands received by the state from the United States under act of congress approved September 28, 1850. The number of acres of unsold land is 212,911.91.

The cash receipts and disbursements during the last two years have been as follows:

RECEIPTS.

	1893.	1894.	
Sales of land	$22,006 53	$12,860 22	
Dues on certificates of sales ...	1,302 00	811 00	
Loans	1,569 50	1,737 50	
Bonds	76,164 14	47,191 48	
Special loans.	14,266 67	40,866 67	
Indemnity fund transfer	7,659 44	6,772 65	
	$122,968 28	$110,289 52	
Total			$233,207 80

DISBURSEMENTS.

	1893.	1894.	
Bonds	$85,643 50	....	
Loans	44,000 00	$106,900 00	
	$129,643 50	$106,900 00	
Total			$236,543 50

The amount of productive Normal School Fund on the 30th day of September, 1893, and 1894, was as follows:

	1893.	1894.
Due on certificates of sales	$11,967 00	$10,197 50
Due on loans	10,210 47	14,260 47
Certificates of indebtedness	515,700 00	515,700 00
Ashland county bonds	45,000 00	45,000 00
Ashland city bonds	22,000 00	22,000 00
Ashland city bonds premium	1,067 80	1,011 60
Chippewa Falls city bonds	85,000 00	85,000 00
Columbus city hall bonds	12,000 00	12,000 00
Columbus school house bonds	6,000 00	5,000 00
Centralia city bridge bonds	2,900 00	1,900 00

c—Sec'y.

Normal School Fund.

	1893.	1894.
Beaver Dam city bonds........................	$12,000 00	$12,000 00
Durand city bonds........................	3,000 00	3,000 00
Edgerton city bonds........................	15,000 00	14,000 00
Eau Claire city bonds........................	10,000 00	10,000 00
Eau Claire city bonds premium............	511 56	476 28
Eau Claire Light Guard Armory bonds.......	10,000 00	10,000 00
Glenwood town bonds........................	10,000 00	10,000 00
Hudson city bonds........................	44,000 00	44,000 00
Kenosha city bonds....	100,000 00	100,000 00
La Crosse city bonds..	10,000 00	10,000 00
Madison city bonds.......	115,000 00	115,000 00
Manitowoc county bonds........................	70,000 00	70,000 00
Milwaukee city bonds.................	240,000 00	226,000 00
Milwaukee city school bonds..................	100,000 00	90,000 00
Menasha city bonds........................	12,250 00	11,250 00
Oshkosh city bonds......	48,000 00	45,000 00
Oshkosh bridge bonds	16,000 00	9,000 00
Plymouth school bonds........................	12,000 00	10,000 00
Portage city bonds	24,000 00	24,000 00
Richland Center water bonds	6,000 00	5,000 00
Taylor county bonds ....,.	1,000 00	....
Viroqua village bonds........................	2,000 00	....
Viroqua dist. No. 5 bonds....................	4,100 00	....
Waushara county bonds....................	5,000 00	4,000 00
Waupaca city bonds........................	3,750 00	3,750 00
Loan to Brown county	17,500 00	15,000 00
Loan to Chippewa county	... .	17,000 00
Loan to Dunn county........................	65,000 00	60,000 00
Loan to Florence county....	9,000 00	6,000 00
Loan to Jackson county	18,000 00	18,000 00
Loan to Lincoln county	1,565 04	11,565 04
Loan to Manitowoc county....................	15,000 00	....
Loan to Oneida county	1,969 91	1,969 91
Loan to Washburn county....................	10,000 00	16,000 00
Loan to Winnebago county	44,000 00	44,000 00
Loan to city of Menasha	6,000 00	4,500 00
Loan to village of Osceola..................	800 00	600 00
Loan to village of Whitefish Bay........ ...	6,000 00	5,400 00
Loan to city of Chippewa Falls...............	12,000 00	9,000 00
Loan to village of Boyd	3,000 00	3,000 00
Loan to Light Horse Squadron...............	30,000 00	30,000 00
Loan to town of Grover......	2,700 00	1,800 00
Loan to town of Worcester..................	1,500 00	1,000 00
Loan to town of Waupaca...	3,000 00	2,000 00
Loan to city of Waupaca	12,500 00	11,500 00
Loan to city of Mineral Point	10,000 00	10,000 00
Loan to city of Phillips	9,333 33	8,666 66
Loan to board of education, city of Madison..	....	40,000 00
Loan to board of education, city of White- water	....	10,000 00
Loan to village of Bloomer....................	....	4,500 00
Loan to city of Cumberland..	....	5,900 00
Loan to town of Pine River..................	....	1,500 00
Total.....................................	$1,811,325 11	$1,827,447 46

NORMAL SCHOOL INCOME.

This fund is derived from the interest on swamp land certificates and loans, and a state tax levy of $10,000 for the fifth normal school, chapter 364, laws of 1885; the 1-20 mill tax for new normal schools, chapter 185, laws of 1893, and is applied to establishing and maintaining normal schools as provided by law. By the provisions of section 394, Revised Statutes, this entire fund is placed at the disposal of the Board of Regents of Normal Schools, by transfer to the treasurer of said board, and the detailed record of its expenditures is kept separate and distinct from the accounts of the state. The receipts and disbursements during the last two years have been as follows:

RECEIPTS.

	1893.	1894.
Interest on land certificates and loans	$1,529 90	$1,840 42
Interest on certificates of indebtedness...................	36,046 95	36,151 05
Interest on bonds	51,118 61	46,166 27
Interest on special loans.......	11,125 40	16,607 23
Interest on normal school fund in banks.... ·	1,624 49	5,789 88
General fund for fifth normal.	10,000 00	10,000 00
Drainage fund under chapter 185, laws 1893	70,989 02	....
Donation for Stevens Point Normal School	50,000 00	....
Donation for Superior Normal School................	65,000 00	....
Platteville Normal, tuition fees.	2,093 40	1,984 15
Whitewater Normal, tuition fees................	2,650 16	2,088 49
River Falls Normal, tuition fees..........	3,223 56	2,416 56
Oshkosh Normal, tuition fees..	4,820 78	5,018 29
Milwaukee Normal, tuition fees	1,578 39	1,761 11
Refunded overpayments	34 43	152 47
General fund transfer for 1-20 mill tax...................	....	32,700 00
Washburn county, penalty	....	5 21
	$311,780 09	$162,131 08

Total.............................. .... $473,911 17

Note.—There was transferred from ex-State Treasurers' Judgment fund to treasurer Board of Normal Regents, and not included in Normal School Fund Income in general statement, found on page iv of this report, the sum of $47,785.20.

Drainage Fund.

DISBURSEMENTS.

	1893.	1894.
Treasurer Board of Normal Regents	$308,854 88	$162,114 80
Refunded........	41 47	16 28
Transfer to school fund income	2,062 50	....
Accrued interest on bonds purchased	821 74	....
	$311,780 09	$162,131 08
Total............		.... $473,911 17

DRAINAGE FUND.

This fund consists of one half the proceeds of sales of all swamp and overflowed lands received by the state from the United States, and is distributed on the 30th day of September, under the provisions of section 254, Revised Statutes, as amended by chapter 264, laws of 1883, among the several counties wherein such lands lie, in proportion to the amount of sales in the respective counties. The moneys so paid are then apportioned by the county clerks to the several towns in their respective counties, and are expended under direction of the town board in draining and reclaiming the swamp lands in such town, and in constructing roads and bridges over such swamp lands. The number of acres of unsold land is 230,439.52.

The cash receipts and disbursements during the last two years have been as follows:

RECEIPTS.

	1893.	1894.
Interest on land certificates....	$145 34	$4,004 48
Sales of land.............	22,306 24	10,748 86
Dues on certificates of sales...	108 00	115 00
General fund, transfer, one half indemnity fund........	7,659 43	6,772 64
	$30,219 61	$21,635 98
Total...		.... $51,854 99

Delinquent Tax Fund.

DISBURSEMENTS.

	1893.	1894.
Apportioned to counties	$21,135 68	$30,191 07
Refunded.........	3 15	81 00
Transfer to normal school fund income... ....;.........	70,939 02	....
Commission on trespass.......	24 79	....
	$92,102 64	$30,272 07
Total.........		$122,374 71

The amount of productive drainage fund on the 30th day of September, 1893 and 1894, was as follows:

	1893.	1894.
	$2,316 00	$2,075 00
Total.		$4,891 00

DELINQUENT TAX FUND.

This fund consists of taxes collected on state lands by the State Treasurer in accordance with the provisions of section 1146, Revised Statutes, and is credited quarterly to the different counties in which the lands are situated. The amounts which have been so received and disbursed are as follows:

RECEIPTS.

	1893.	1894.
Taxes on state lands......	$5,914 02	$8,393 92
Total...		$14,807 94

DISBURSEMENTS.

	1893.	1894.
Apportioned to counties.......	$6,007 41	$8,090 41
Refunded....................	13 05	6 33
	$6,020 46	$8,096 74
Total		$14,117 20

DEPOSIT FUND.

On the sale of land forfeited to the state, and the payment of the amount due the state, and all costs and penalties accrued under the provisions of section 225, of the Revised Statutes, if any balance remain, the amount of such balance is deposited in the State Treasury to the credit of the persons entitled thereto, and is denominated the Deposit Fund.

The transactions therein have been as follows:

RECEIPTS.

	1893.	1894.	
Balances deposited...........	$867 06	....	
Total..			$867 06

DISBURSEMENTS.

	1893.	1894.	
On surplus paid...............	$754 80	$138 23	
Total......			$893 03

ST. CROIX AND LAKE SUPERIOR RAILROAD TRESPASS FUND.

(Chapter 46, Laws of 1869.)

	1894.
Disbursements...	$2,067 46

REDEMPTION FUND.
(Section 228, R. S.)

RECEIPTS.

	1893.	1894.	
Advertising, interest, penalties and fees.....................	$29 50	$113 14	
Total......................................			$142 64

Swamp Land, and Indemnity Funds.

WISCONSIN RAILROAD FARM MORTGAGE LAND COMPANY.

Chapter 235, laws of 1882, authorizes the Commissioners of the Wisconsin Railroad Farm Mortgage Land Company to close up the business of said corporation, and to turn over and to pay to the State Treasurer all its money and bank accounts, and to take his receipt therefor, and at the same time to make its report in writing, to the Secretary of State, of its proceedings under this act. Accordingly the said commissioners paid the sum of $8,935.09 into the Treasury, and deposited with the Secretary of State, the books, together with a list of claimants to whom dividends are yet due with the amount set opposite their respective names.

DISBURSEMENTS

	1894.
To claimants........................	$17 50

MANITOWOC AND CALUMET SWAMP LAND FUND.
(Chapter 352, Laws of 1883.)

RECEIPTS.

	1893.	1894.	
From counties.................	$586 02	$220 92	
Total..............................			$806 94

DISBURSEMENTS.

To counties.. ...	$3,016 84

COLUMBIA AND SAUK CO. INDEMNITY FUND.
(Chapter 90, Laws of 1885.)

RECEIPTS.

	1893.	1894.	
From counties.................	$180 40	$450 10	
Total..........			$630 50

INDEMNITY LAND FUND.

The proceeds of lands sold for indemnifying the state of Wisconsin for swamp lands sold by the United States. The number of acres of land unsold is 37,890.16.

The cash receipts and disbursements during the last two years have been as follows:

RECEIPTS.

	1893.	1894.	
Sales of land.................	$15,318 87	$7,405 21	
Transfer from general fund ...	....	6,140 08	
	$15,318 87	13,545 29	
Total			$28,864 16

DISBURSEMENTS.

	1893.	1894.	
Transfer	$15,318 87	$13,545 29	
Total			$28,864 16

EX-STATE TREASURERS' JUDGMENT FUND.

RECEIPTS.

	1893.	1894.	
From clerk of circuit court, Dane Co., on judgments.....	$177,312 54	$250,590 01	
Total			$427,902 55

DISBURSEMENTS.

Total transferred	$427,902 55

ALLOTMENT FUND.

Section 3, of chapter 190, general laws, 1862, directed the State Treasurer to receive such sums of money as might be placed in his hands by any volunteer making an allotment,

Appropriations.

as provided by the act of congress, approved December 24, 1861, and dispose of the same according to the order and direction of such volunteer. This fund consists of moneys so received by the State Treasurer and yet unclaimed by the beneficiaries named by the volunteers. There having been no payments made from the fund during the year, the account stands as follows:

Balance, September 30, 1892.................	$916 54	
Balance, September 30, 1894.................	....	$916 54

APPROPRIATIONS.

The following table exhibits the balance due on the direct appropriations made to the several charitable and penal institutions of the state for the years 1893 and 1894, the payments therefrom, including the amounts set apart for the salaries and expenses of the State Board of Control, and the balances remaining unexpended at the end of the fiscal year:

	Remaining due on appropriations Sept. 30, 1892.	Appropriations 1893 and 1894, including am't paid by counties.	Paid to Sept. 30, 1894.	Remaining unexpended Sept. 30, 1894.
State Hospital for Insane............	$34,288 79	$213,291 02	$206,785 58	$40,794 23
Northern Hospital for Insane..............	22,905 28	257,306 64	233,189 56	47,023 36
Wisconsin School for Blind..............	3,934 58	68,520 14	58,179 72	9,275 00
Wisconsin School for Deaf..............	20,529 90	81,000 00	80,391 28	21,138 62
Industrial School for Boys..............	32,457 21	108,590 34	115,124 05	25,928 50
State Prison...	648 44	50,000 00	45,486 58	5,161 86
State Public School...	7,402 75	109,000 00	73,297 86	43,104 89
Total....	$122,166 95	$882,708 14	$812,453 63	$192,421 46

STATE DEBT.

The bonded debt of the state, created in 1861–63, for the purpose of carrying on the war for the maintenance of the Union, has now all been paid or converted into certificates of indebtedness to the Trust Funds, except one thousand dollars, which was paid from the General Fund, August 13, 1888.

The distribution of the debt on the 30th *ultimo*, was as follows:

Certificates of indebtedness, school fund.....................	$1,563 700 00
Certificates of indebtedness, normal school fund...	515,700 00
Certificates of indebtedness, university fund................	111,000 00
Certificates of indebtedness, agricultural college fund... ...	60,600 00
	$2,251,000 00

ESTIMATES OF EXPENDITURES AND REVENUES.

In accordance with the requirements of subdivision 13, section 144, Revised Statutes, I append the following detailed estimate of expenditures to be defrayed from the treasury during the years beginning January 1st, 1895, and January 1st, 1896, based on expenses of former years, in which are shown the amounts provided by permanent or temporary appropriations and the amount required to be provided for as before stated.

I also submit a careful estimate of the revenues from which such expenditures are to be defrayed.

Estimate of Expenditures.

EXPENDITURES FOR GENERAL PURPOSES.

Governor's office	$7,000 00
Lieutenant Governor	1,000 00
Secretary of State's office	7,000 00
State Treasurer's office	7,000 00
Attorney General's office	5,000 00
State Superintendent's office	6,000 00
Supreme Court, salaries and reports	84,000 00
Circuit Court, salaries and expenses	67,000 00
State library and librarian	4,000 00
State Historical Society	9,500 00
State Board of Control	18,000 00
State Board of Health	6,000 00
State Militia	90,000 00
Protecting state lands	4,000 00
Insurance Commissioner's office	4,500 00
Railroad Commissioner's office	5,000 00
Commissioner of Labor Statistics	7,000 00
Farmers' Institutes	12,000 00
Fish culture	13,000 00
Fish and Game Warden	3,800 00
Dairy and Food Commission	7,500 00
Circuit Court reporters	10,000 00
One per cent. railroad license fee for State University	12,000 00
Director Washburn Observatory	3,000 00
State Veterinarian	5,000 00
Total	$347,800 00

CLERKS AND EMPLOYES.

Governor's office	$1,800 00
Secretary of State's office	20,000 00
State Treasurer's office	10,000 00
State Land office	13,000 00
Superintendent of Public Property	1,500 00
Compiling War Records	4,000 00
Engineers and watchmen	5,500 00
Janitors and messengers	18,000 00
Laborers about Capitol	25,000 00
State Superintendent's office	4,000 00
	$102,800 00

LEGISLATIVE EXPENSES.

Salaries of Senators	$16,500 00
Salaries of members of Assembly	50,500 00
Mileage	4,000 00
Officers and employes	48,000 00
Printing	7,000 00
Blue Book	10,000 00
Incidentals	10,000 00
	$146,000 00

Estimate of Expenditures.

MISCELLANEOUS.

Publishing laws	$43,000	00
State printing	25,000	00
Paper	10,000	00
Stationery	4,000	00
Postage	6,000	00
Gas and fuel	10,000	00
Agricultural societies	30,000	00
Care of insane in counties	260,000	00
Bounty on wild animals	12,000	00
Contingent expenses	20,000	00
Miscellaneous expenses and appropriations	120,000	00
	$540,000	00

CHARITABLE AND PENAL INSTITUTIONS.

State Hospital for Insane	$95,000	00
Northern Hospital for Insane	110,000	00
Wisconsin School for Blind	30,000	00
Wisconsin School for Deaf	40,000	00
Wisconsin School for Boys	55,000	00
State Prison	10,000	00
State Public School	40,000	00
	$380,000	00

EDUCATIONAL PURPOSES.

One mill tax, School Fund income	$600,000	00
State University	135,000	00
Free high schools	50,000	00
Interest on certificates of indebtedness	157,570	00
Fifth normal school	10,000	00
New normals	30,000	00
Total	$982,570	00

Estimate of Revenues.

REVENUES.

1. Estimated balance in general fund $10,000 00

2. Licenses and fees.

Railway companies, license........................	$1,200,000 00
Insurance companies, license	180,000 00
Telegraph and telephone companies, licenses	20,000 00
Hawkers and peddlers........	15,000 00
State tax on suits	7,000 00
From counties for maintaining insane in state hospitals, and the Industrial School for Boys	158,000 00
Railway car companies....	1,000 00
Miscellaneous sources	70,000 00
Total	$1,601,000 00

3. Taxes authorized by law.

Interest on state indebtedness	$157,570 00
Annual levy for State University	135,000 00
Annual levy for free high schools....................	50,000 00
Annual levy for fifth normal school	10,000 00
Annual levy for new normal schools................	30,000 00
One mill tax for common school income..............	600,000 00
Total	$982,570 00

TAX REDUCTION.

From the foregoing estimates it appears that the receipts of the general fund will be ample to meet the necessary expenses of the state government during the next biennial term. Of the $977,315.71 now on hand in the general fund of the State Treasury, the sum of $742,570 has been transferred to reduce the state tax levy under the following resolution:

WHEREAS, It appears that after reserving sufficient moneys for defraying the entire expense of state government from this date to January first, 1895, there is a surplus in the general fund in the State Treasury of $742,570 derived as follows:

Recovered in judgments from former state treasurers, to the credit of the general fund...................	$327,902 55
Direct war tax refund	89,466 10
Interest from bank deposits on general fund	46,644 78
Railroad and insurance license and office fees	278,556 57

Tax Levy.

and that such surplus without detriment to the public service can be applied as a portion of the state tax levy; now, therefore,

Resolved, That we, the undersigned, Governor, Secretary of State and State Treasurer, in pursuance of Section 1069 a. of Sanborn & Berryman's Annotated Statutes, do hereby apply as a portion of the state tax levy, the sum of $742,570 to be applied as follows:

The one mill tax for the support and maintenance of the Common Schools	$600,000 00
Fifth Normal School tax	10,000 00
State University tax...	132,570 00

Leaving to be levied in accordance with section 1070 of chapter 48 of the Revised Statutes of the state of Wisconsin, the sum of $240,000.00, being $157,570.00 to pay the interest upon the certificates of state indebtedness incurred between the years 1866 and 1886.

For the support and maintenance of Free High Schools............	$50,000 00
For one twentieth mill tax for Normal Schools	30,000 00
For the support and maintenance of the State University..............	2,430 00

IN WITNESS WHEREOF we have hereunto set our hands, and the Great Seal of the State of Wisconsin, this 20th day of July, in the year of our Lord One Thousand Eight Hundred and Ninety-four.

GEO. W. PECK, Governor.

T. J. CUNNINGHAM, Secretary of State.

JOHN HUNNER, State Treasurer.

DETAILS OF REPORT.

For the purpose of easy reference, the full financial details required by law, and such tabular statistics as may' be deemed of interest, are classified as follows:

"A"

Includes detailed statements of the receipts and disbursements of the several funds belonging to the state for the years 1893 and 1894.

"B"

Showing the relative value of real and personal property as assessed by the State Board of Assessment for the year 1894.

"C"

Showing the valuation of taxable property of the several counties of the state, as determined by the State Board of Assessment for the years 1893 and 1894, and the apportionment of the state tax and special charges for said years.

"D"

Abstract of assessment rolls of the several counties as returned to this department for the year 1893, showing the average assessed value of live stock and real estate by counties, and total assessed value of all property in the state.

"E"

Valuation of property in the different counties in the state as fixed by the county boards of supervisors and

---
Details of Report.

---

town assessors, and the amount of state, county, town, city and village taxes levied in 1894. •

"F"

Statement showing for what purposes the county tax was expended in the several counties for the year ending December 31, 1893.

"G"

Statement showing all indebtedness of towns, cities, villages and school districts, December 31, 1893.

"H"

Statement showing all indebtedness of the several counties, December 31, 1893.

"I"

Statement of the principal farm products grown in 1893, and statement of the principal farm products growing at the time of making the annual assessment for the year 1894.

"J"

Report of agricultural societies for 1893.

"K"

Abstracts of marriages, births and deaths reported to this department during the two years ending December 31, 1893.

"*A.*"—*General Fund Receipts for 1893.*

APPENDIX "A."

DETAILED STATEMENT

OF THE

Receipts and Disbursements of the Several Funds

FOR THE

Fiscal Year Ending September 30, 1893.

GENERAL FUND RECEIPTS, 1893.

Counties.	Suit Tax.	Revenues	
Adams.............................	$8 00	$892 12	... .
Ashland	458 00	2,540 6*	....
Barron..........................	31 00	2,451 82	....
Bayfield.........................	34 00	980 48	....
Brown.......................	89 00	4,203 75	....
Buffalo..........................	27 00	2,813 87	....
Burnett	8 00	1,340 50	....
Calumet	21 00	3,223 64	....
Chippewa...	106 00	5,593 15	....
Clark	3 00	2,426 06	....
Columbia........................	93 00	2,849 00	....
Crawford...	20 00	3,742 65	....
Dane............................	180 00	6,596 29	... .
Dodge...........................	24 00	3,591 90	... .
Door	35 00	2,197 01	....
Douglas.........................	322 00	3,233 82	....
Dunn	41 00	2,965 12	....
Eau Claire	185 00	5,876 03	....
Florence........................	10 00	485 02	....
Fond du Lac.....................	99 00	4,081 58	... .
Forest..........................	12 00	248 02	....
Grant...........................	66 00	3,612 33	....
Green...........................	42 00	2,345 00	....

3—Sec'y.

"A."—General Fund Receipts for 1893.

Counties.	Suit Tax.	Revenues.	
Green Lake............................	$41 00	$2,597 27	....
Iowa...................................	68 0	1,407 56	....
Iron	....	....	....
Jackson	101 00	3,490 64	....
Jefferson.............................	41 00	3,564 59	....
Juneau..............................	74 00	4,328 81	....
Kenosha..............................	36 00	3,857 54	....
Kewaunee.............................	30 00	2,709 31	....
La Crosse............................	177 00	3,641 87	....
La Fayette...........................	32 00	4,664 11	....
Langlade.............................	29 00	803 52	....
Lincoln	125 00	1,447 95	....
Manitowoc............................	92 00	3,173 54	....
Marathon.............................	111 00	3,703 67	....
Marinette............................	109 00	2,906 40	....
Marquette............................	5 00	1,867 91	....
Milwaukee............................	1,294 00	12,300 40	....
Monroe...............................	57 00	3,465 61	....
Oconto	64 00	2,797 00	....
Oneida	73 00	608 21	....
Outagamie............................	72 00	3,025 98	....
Ozaukee..............................	45 00	3,897 72	....
Pepin................................	26 00	1,026 12	....
Pierce...............................	44 00	3,885 99	....
Polk	52 00	3,081 15	....
Portage..............................	84 00	2,044 40	....
Price	40 00	830 78	....
Racine	62 00	2,935 53	....
Richland	94 00	3,536 70	....
Rock.................................	169 00	4,401 49	....
St. Croix............................	116 00	4,187 11	....
Sauk	83 00	2,561 19	....
Sawyer...............................	1 00	547 53	....
Shawano	65 00	1,400 67	....
Sheboygan............................	66 00	3,977 29	....
Taylor...............................	24 00	1,394 84	....
Trempealeau..........................	30 00	3,913 82	....
Vernon...............................	68 00	1,999 71	....
Vilas	....	....	....
Walworth.............................	86 00	3,525 57	....
Washburn.............................	....	....	....
Washington...........................	30 00	4,422 21	....
Waukesha.............................	125 00	7,767 68	....
Waupaca	58 00	4,369 12	....
Waushara	24 00	1,798 11	....
Winnebago............................	39 00	5,267 52	....
Wood	49 00	1,774 61	....
Total for fiscal year, Sept. 30, 1893	$6,559 00	$208,148 62	....
Grand total..........................	....	....	$214,707 62

"A."—General Fund Receipts for 1893.

RAILROAD COMPANIES — LICENSE TAX.		
Abbottsford & North Eastern R. R. Co.	$75 90	
Chicago, Burlington & Northern R'y Co.	54,971 33	
Chicago, St Paul, Minneapolis & Omaha R'y Co	148,442 55	
Chicago, Milwaukee & St. Paul R'y Co.	275,105 99	
Chicago, Fairchild & Eau Claire R'y Co.	50 00	
Chippewa & Menomonie River R'y Co.	120 00	
Chicago & Northwestern R'y Co.	288,490 93	
Chicago, Milwaukee & Northern R'y Co.	456 55	
Drummond & South Western R'y Co	46 26	
Duluth Short Line R'y Co	925 25	
Duluth, South Shore & Atlantic R'y Co.	724 75	
Duluth & Winnipeg R'y Co.	57 50	
Eastern Railway Company of Minnesota	11,774 05	
Green Bay, Winona & St. Paul R'y Co.	3,667 52	
Goodyear & Neillsville R'y Co.	94 31	
Kewaunee, Green Bay & Western R'y Co.	164 54	
Kickapoo Valley & Northern R'y Co.	170 00	
Lake Superior Terminal Transfer R'y Co.	65 00	
Milwaukee, Lake Shore & Western R'y Co.	149,625 07	
Milwaukee & Northern R'y Co.	53,709 43	
Milwaukee & Superior R'y Co.	228 70	
Menomonie R'y Co.	25 10	
Milwaukee, Chicago & Bay View R'y Co.	2,270 68	
Minneapolis, St. Paul & Sault Ste. Marie R'y Co.	28,549 08	
Minnesota & Wisconsin R'y Co.	75 00	
Northern Pacific Railway Co	19,723 13	
Oshkosh Transportation Co.	63 16	
Portage & Centralia R'y Co.	150 00	
Prairie du Chien & McGregor R'y Co	1,152 50	
Sault Ste. Marie & Southwestern R'y Co	185 00	
Saint Cloud, Grantsburg & Ashland R'y Co.	312 89	
Winona Bridge R'y Co.	333 40	
Western Range R'y Co	35 00	
Wisconsin and Chippewa R'y Co	30 00	
Wisconsin Central Lines, Northern Pacific, Lessee	114,391 28	
Total	$1,156,260 75	

"A."—General Fund Receipts for 1898.

PALACE CAR COMPANIES — LICENSE TAX.			
Pullman Palace Car Co.	$519 96	.. ..	....
Wagner Palace Car Co...., ...	673 08	....	....
Total......................		$1,193 04	....
TELEGRAPH COMPANIES — LICENSE TAX.			
Western Union Telgraph Co........	$9,283 20	....	....
Grant County Telegraph System....	9 92	....	....
Chicago & Milwaukee Telegraph Co.	66 00	....	....
Chicago, Milwaukee & Lake Shore Telegraph Co.................	232 00	....	....
Postal Telegraph Co........	66 50	....	....
Total......................	....	$9,657 62	....
FIRE INSURANCE COMPANIES — LICENSE TAX.			
Atlas Assurance Co., London, Eng..	$250 38	....	....
American Central Fire Insurance Co.. St. Louis. Mo	361 19	....	....
American Fire Insurance Co., Newark, N. J	245 47	....	....
Ætna Fire Insurance Co., Hartford, Conn	1,674 50	....	....
Allemania Fire Ins. Co., Pittsburg. Pa	212 70	....	....
American Fire Insurance Co., Philadelphia, Pa....	1,668 89	....	....
American Fire Ins. Co , New York, N. Y.................... ...	924 86	....	.........….
Agricultural Fire Ins. Co., Water town, N. Y.	222 70	....	....
Albany Fire Ins. Co., Albany, N. Y.	83 72	. ...	....
American Fire Ins. Co , Boston, Mass................	118 20	....	....
Buffalo German Fire Ins. Co., Buffalo, N. Y	386 43	....	....
British American Assurance Co., Toronto, Can....................	398 11	....	....
British & Foreign Marine Ins. Co , London, Eng	251 17	....	....
Broadway Fire Ins. Co., New York, N. Y...	112 04	....	....
Boylston Fire Ins. Co., Boston, Mass.	306 02	....	....
Commerce Fire Ins. Co., Albany. N. Y .....'................	83 45	....	....
Commonwealth Fire Ins. Co., New York, N. Y	236 73	....	....
Connecticut Fire Ins Co., Hartford, Conn	1,055 99	....	....
Citizens' Fire Ins. Co., Pittsburg. Pa.	296 28	....	....•
Concordia Fire Ins. Co., Milwaukee, Wis................	1,544 55	....	....

"A."—General Fund Receipts for 1893.

Citizens' Fire Ins. Co., New York City, N. Y.	$302 47		
Continental Fire Ins. Co., New York City, N. Y.	1,068 26		
Caledonia Fire Ins. Co., Edinburg, Scotland	585 32		
Concord Fire Ins. Co., Concord, N. H.	97 71		
Commercial Union Ins. Co., London, Eng.	1,875 76		
Detroit Fire & Marine Ins. Co., Detroit, Mich.	301 31		
Delaware Fire Ins. Co., Philadelphia, Pa.	514 31		
Dwelling House Ins. Co., Boston, Mass.	176 54		
Eagle Fire Ins. Co., New York, N.Y.	78 46		
Equitable Fire & Marine Ins. Co., Providence, R. I	209 58		
Fire Association, Philadelphia, Pa.	1,756 56		
Fireman's Fund Ins. Co, San Francisco, Cal	766 45		
Fire Ins. Co., County of Philadelphia, Philadelphia, Pa	160 71		
Farmers' Ins. Co, York, Pa.	360 22		
Firemen's Ins. Co., Newark, N. J.	150 67		
Franklin Fire Ins. Co., Philadelphia, Pa.	209 69		
Greenwich Fire Ins. Co., New York, N. Y.	346 73		
Granite State Fire Ins. Co., Portsmouth, N. H.	302 46		
German Fire Ins. Co., Freeport, Ill.	1,889 94		
Guardian Life & Fire Ins. Co., London, Eng.	382 89		
Germantown Farmers' Mutual Ins. Co., Rockfield, Wis	327 76		
Girard Fire & Marine Ins Co., Philadelphia, Pa	293 95		
German Fire Ins. Co., Peoria, Ill	285 83		
Grand Rapids Fire Ins. Co., Grand Rapids, Mich	276 07		
German-American Ins. Co., New York, N. Y.	2,024 78		
German Fire Ins. Co., Quincy, Ill.	209 22		
German Fire Ins. Co., New York, N.Y	718 79		
German Fire Ins. Co., Pittsburg, Pa	185 95		
Glen Falls Fire Ins. Co., Glen Falls, N. Y.	275 81		
Hartford Fire Ins. Co., Hartford, Conn	2,318 45		
Home Fire Ins. Co., New York, N. Y	2,587 48		
Hanover Fire Ins. Co., New York, N. Y.	604 95		
Hartford Steam Boiler Inspection Co., Hartford, Conn.	286 89		
Herman Farmers' Mutual Ins. Co., Herman, Wis.	164 07		
Hamburg. Bremen Fire Ins. Co., Hamburg, Germany	688 05		

"A."—*General Fund Receipts for 1893.*

Imperial Fire Ins. Co., London, England	$580 77	....	....
Ins. Co., State of Pennsylvania, Philadelphia, Pa	270 07	....	....
Lion Fire Ins. Co., London, England	319 07	....	....
Liverpool, London & Globe Ins. Co. Liverpool, Eng	1,761 15	....	....
London & Lancashire Ins. Co., Liverpool, Eng	1,439 01	....	....
London Assurance Corporation, London, Eng	1,020 64	....	....
Lancashire Fire Ins Co., Manchester, Eng	2,002 41	....	....
Mannheim Fire Ins. Co., Mannheim, Germany	26 43	....	....
Manchester Fire Assurance Co., Manchester, Eng	1,141 93	....	....
Manufacturers' & Merchants' Fire Ins. Co., Pittsburg, Pa	102 56	....	....
Millers' & Manufacturers' Fire Ins. Co, Minneapolis, Minn	241 32	....	....
Millers' National Ins. Co., Chicago, Ill	111,67	....	....
Milwaukee Mechanics' Ins. Co., Milwaukee, Wis	3,204 61	....	....
Manufacturers' & Merchants' Mutual Ins. Co., Rockford, Ill	139 89	....	....
Mechanics' Fire Ins. Co., Philadelphia, Pa	223 55	....	....
Marine Fire Ins. Co., London, Eng.	160 54	....	....
Merchants' Fire Ins. Co., Newark, N. J.	446 92	....	....
Mercantile Fire and Marine Ins. Co., Boston, Mass	152 79	....	....
Mutual Fire Ins. Co. New York, N. Y.	818 73	....	....
Michigan Fire & Marine Ins. Co., Detroit, Mich	563 37	....	....
Merchants' Fire Ins. Co., Providence, R. I.	209 58	....	....
Manufacturers' & Builders' Fire Ins. Co., New York, N. Y.	52 26	....	....
Northern Assurance Co., London, Eng.	668 18	....	....
New York Bowery Ins. Co , New York, N. Y	293 26	....	....
National Fire Ins. Co,, Hartford, Conn	982 77	....	....
North British & Mercantile Ins. Co., London, Eng	1,920 84	....	....
North American Fire Ins. Co., Philadelphia, Pa	2,589 30	....	....
Newark Fire Ins. Co., Newark. N. J.	125 78	....	....
New Hampshire Fire Ins. Co., Manchester, N. H.	410 60	....	....
North Western National Ins. Co., Milwaukee, Wis	1,658 24	....	....
Norwich Union Society, Norwich, Eng	797 40	....	....

"A."—General Fund Receipts for 1893.

Niagara Fire Ins. Co., New York, N. Y.	$1,238 83		
Orient Fire Ins. Co., Hartford, Conn.	924 99		
Oakland Home Fire Ins. Co., Oakland Cal	473 55		
Phoenix Assurance Co., London, Eng	1,085 22		
Phoenix Fire Ins. Co., Brooklyn, N. Y	3,366 66		
Peoples' Fire Ins. Co., Manchester, N. H.	224 12		
Protection Mutual Fire Ins. Co., Chicago, Ill.	48 90		
Pacific Fire Ins. Co., New York, N. Y.	159 73		
Pennsylvania Fire Ins. Co., Philadelphia, Pa.	1,234 49		
Prussian National Fire Ins. Co., Stettin, Germany	305 84		
Phoenix Fire Ins Co., Hartford, Conn	1,571 55		
Queen's Ins. Co. of America, New York	1,304 78		
Royal Ins. Co., Liverpool, England	1,380 82		
Reliance Marine Ins. Co., Liverpool, England	60 25		
Rochester German Ins. Co., Rochester, N. Y.	560 84		
Reading Fire Ins. Co., Reading Pa.	193 06		
Reliance Fire Ins. Co., Philadelphia, Pa.	96 73		
Rutgers Fire Ins. Co., New York, N. Y.	80 15		
Rockford Fire Ins. Co., Rockford, Ill.	1,238 15		
Spring Garden Ins. Co., Philadelphia, Pa.	136 86		
St Paul Fire & Marine Ins. Co., St. Paul, Minn.	792 21		
Security Fire Ins. Co., New Haven, Conn.	488 89		
Scottish Union & National Ins. Co., Edinburg, Scotland	540 77		
Syndicate Fire Ins. Co., Minneapolis, Minn.	321 24		
Standard Marine Ins. Co., Liverpool, England	145 25		
State Investment Ins. Co., San Francisco. Cal	599 79		
State Fire Ins Co., Des Moines, Ia.	375 87		
Springfield Fire & Marine Ins. Co., Springfield, Mass	1,158 46		
Sun Fire Ins. Co., London. England	1,743 12		
Transatlantic Fire Ins. Co., Hamburg, Germany	212 21		
Teutonia Fire Ins. Co , Philadelphia, Pa	29 75		
Traders' Ins. Co., Chicago, Ill	1,047 87		

"A."—General Fund Receipts for 1893.

Union Marine Ins. Co., Liverpool, England	$194 71		
United States Fire Ins. Co., New York, N. Y.	125 04		
United Firemen Ins. Co., Philadelphia, Pa.	111 65		
Union Fire Ins. Co., Philadelphia, Pa.	189 17		
Union Assurance Society, London, England.	153 74		
Westchester Fire Ins. Co., New York, N. Y.	781 20		
Western Assurance Co., Toronto, Canada.	1,745 78		
Williamsburg City Fire Ins. Co., New York. N. Y.	249 70		
Washington Fire Ins. Co., Providence, R. I	535 66		
Total		$84,829 16	

LIFE INSURANCE COMPANIES—LICENSE TAX.

Ætna Life Insurance Co., Hartford, Conn.	$300 00		
Bankers' Life Association, St. Paul. Minn	300 00		
Connecticut Life Ins. Co., Hartford, Conn	300 00		
Equitable Life Association, New York, N. Y.	300 00		
Germania Life Ins. Co., New York, N. Y	300 00		
Home Life Ins. Co., New York, N. Y	300 00		
Hartford Life Annuity Co., Hartford, Conn	300 00		
Life Insurance Clearing Co , St. Paul, Minn	300 00		
Life Indemnity & Investment Co., Sioux City, Ia	300 00		
Mutual Reserve Life Association, New York, N. Y.	300 00		
Metropolitan Life Ins. Co., New York, N. Y	300 00		
Michigan Mutual Life Ins. Co., Detroit, Mich.	300 00		
Mutual Life Ins. Co, New York City, N. Y.	300 00		
Mutual Benefit Life Ins. Co., Newark. N. J.	300 00		
Massachusetts Mutual Life Ins. Co., Springfield. Mass	300 00		
Manhattan Life Ins. Co , New York, N. Y.	300 00		
Northwestern Mutual Life Ins. Co., Milwaukee, Wis	23,136 86		

"A."—General Fund Receipts for 1893.

New England Mutual Life Ins. Co., Boston. Mass	$300 00		
New York Life Ins. Co., New York. N. Y.	300 00		
National Life Ins. Co., Montpelier, Vt	300 00		
Pennsylvania Mutual Life Ins. Co., Philadelphia, Pa	1,059 34		
Phœnix Mutual Life Ins. Co., Hartford, Conn	300 00		
Provident Savings Life Ins. Co., New York, N. Y	300 00		
Providential Life Ins. Co., Newark, N. J.	300 00		
Travelers' Ins. Co., Hartford, Conn.	300 00		
Union Central Life Ins. Co., Cincinnati, Ohio.	300 00		
United States Life Ins. Co., New York, N. Y.	300 00		
Washington Life Ins. Co., New York, N. Y.	300 00		
Total		$31,996 20	
ACCIDENT INSURANCE COMPANIES— LICENSE TAX.			
American Security Co., New York, N. Y.	$29 82		
American Employers' Liability Co., Jersey City. N. J.	293 77		
American Casualty & Security Co , Baltimore. Md	709 37		
American Mutual Accident Ins. Co., Oshkosh, Wis	423 50		
Casualty & Fidelity Co., New York, N. Y.	1,754 72		
Employers' Liability Assurance Corporation, London, Eng	440 08		
Guarantee Ins. Co. of North America, Montreal. Can	17 82		
Lloyds' Plate Glass Ins. Co., New York, N. Y.	140 69		
Masonic Fraternal Accident Assn., Westfield, Mass	100 24		
Mutual Accident Association, N. W., Chicago, Ill	90 90		
Metropolitan Accident Association, Chicago, Ill	180 98		
Metropolitan Plate Glass Co , New York, N. Y.	32 03		
New York Plate Glass Ins. Co., New York. N. Y.	65 61		
New England Mutual Accident Association. Boston, Mass	65 51		
National Accident Society, New York, N. Y	3 10		
Provident Fund Soc.,New York,N.Y.	52 05		

"A."—General Fund Receipts for 1893.

Preferred Masonic Mutual Accident Association, Detroit, Mich	$25 66		
Preferred Mutual Accident Association, New York, N. Y	121 12		
Railway Officials' & Employes' Accident Assn., Indianapolis, Ind ..	159 55		
Standard Life & Accident Ins. Co., Detroit, Mich....	883 68		
United States Mutual Accident Assn., New York, N. Y	287 32		
Total.........................		$5,825 91	
TELEPHONE COMPANIES — LICENSE TAX.			
Duluth Telephone Co....	$416 02		
Wisconsin Telephone Co...........	11,289 69		
Total......................		$11,705 71	
SAVINGS, LOAN AND TRUST COMPANIES—LICENSE TAX.			
Savings, Loan & Trust Co., Madison, Wis......................	$428 42		
Wisconsin Trust Co., Milwaukee, Wis..........................	597 43		
Total......................:		$1,025 85	
LOG DRIVING AND BOOMING COMPANIES — LICENSE TAX.			
Ashland Boom and Canal Co.......	$38 47		
Jas. Barden, booms on American river	43 49		
Black River Improvement Co., La Crosse, Wis.....................	645 50		
East Fork Improvement Co., La Crosse, Wis...................	395 52		
Eagle Dam Co., Milwaukee, Wis...	20 48		
Fish Creek Boom and Log Driving Co., Ashland, Wis	170 30		
Hay Creek Log Driving and Boom Co , La Crosse, Wis	59 90		
Knapp, Stout and Company Co., Menomonie, Wis.....	20 42		
Merrill Boom Co., Merrill, Wis	1,029 94		
Nemadji Boom Co , Superior, Wis..	318 19		
Peshtigo Co., Chicago, Ill.........	703 79		
Pelican Boom Co., Rhinelander, Wis	445 88		
Tomahawk Land and Boom Co., Tomahawk, Wis.................	295 83		
Total......................		$4,187 66	

"A."—General Fund Receipts for 1893.

SUNDRY SOURCES.

Secretary of state, office fees........	$8,299 88	....	....
Secretary of state, notary fees.	2,406 00	....	... .
Land commissioners' fees.,...........	742 98	....	....
Insurance commissioner's fees......	28,378 50	....	....
Superintendent of public property, sales of books and merchandise...	446 75	....	... .
State superintendent, sale of books..	56 75	... .	... .
Income penalty...................	784 71	....	....
United States, by Geo. W. Peck, governor, for care of inmates Wisconsin Vet. Home...	14,711 94	....	....

Refunds.

Unexpended balance special appropriation for State Hospital Insane	$523 20	....	....
Unexpended balance special appropriation for Northern Hospital Insane........................	512 86	....	....
R. G. Thwaites, on salary overpaid..	1 00	....	....
Chicago & Northwestern Railway, on transportation W. N. G........	4 84	....	....
Chicago, Milwaukee & St. Paul, on freight.	72	....	... .
Hon. H. F. Hagemeister, mileage...	6 40	... .	....
Jerry Dobbs, contingent fund......	10 50	....	... .
Wonewoc Reporter, on publishing..	1 20	....	....
Quart -Mast. Gen'l unexpended balance company " L " 2nd Reg.....	619 45	....	....
J. B. Doe, adjutant general, overpayment Co's "A" and " B," 2nd Reg....................	71 54	....	....
Sommers Bros., overpayment......	25 54	....	....
H. N. Moulton, state carpenter, re funded for State Hist. Society shelving...	288 59		
		$57,894 35	....

HAWKERS AND PEDDLERS.

License...........................	$15,228 17	....	....
		$15,228 17	....

MISCELLANEOUS.

Morris Wormser, license, chapter 443, laws 1891	$100 00	....	....
West Salem Banking Co., publishing bank reports	1 00	....	....
J. S Anderson, certified copies re port Banking Co...............	1 50	....	....
J. R. Berryman, librarian, catalogue	3 00	....	....
Treas. United States, H. H. Caton, damages for Fox and Wis River Imp. Co......................	1,140 00	....	....
Democrat Printing Co., settlement on paper....	234 96	....	....

"A."—General Fund Receipts for 1893.

Publishing bank reports........ ...	$658 00	....	....
Librarian supreme court, Index sold.	1 00	....	... .
Marathon county land,sales.	60 00	....	....
Interest on general fund deposited in banks...	12,569 08	....	....
H. S. Kopmeier, certified copies ...	1 37	....	....
Van Dyke & Van Dyke, certified copies	6 00	....	....
Winkler, Flanders, Smith, Bottom, and Vilas, certified copies	1 62	....	....
Northwestern Mutual Life Insurance Co., certified copies.............	6 00	....	....
Wilson & Hopkins, certified copies..	1 74	....	....
W. H. Timlin, certified copies.....	1 25	....	....
Joshua Stark, certified copies......	1 25	....	....
Express on funds...	5 75	... .	....
A. S. Sannier. J. P., fines, chapter 106, laws 1893	8 28	....	....
Geo. Merrill, deputy game warden, fines.............................	1 05	....	....
		$14,802 80	
Total general fund receipts	....	....	$1,609,314 84

"A."—General Fund Disbursements for 1893.

GENERAL FUND DISBURSEMENTS FOR 1893.

FOR SALARIES AND EXPENSES.

Governor's office—

Geo. W. Peck, governor's salary.	$5,068 49	....	....
Charles Jonas, acting governor, salary..........................	110 00	....	....
C. L. Clark, private secretary, salary........	1,621 92	....	....
		$6,800 41	....

Secretary's office —

T. J. Cunningham, secretary of state, salary................ ...	$5,068 49	....	....
T. B. Leonard, assistant secretary of state, salary...........	2,027 39	....	....
		$7,095 88	....

Treasurer's office—

John Hunner, state treasurer, salary......................	$5,068 49	... .	....
F. F. Proudfit, assistant state treasurer, salary...	2,027 39		....
		$7,095 88	....

Attorney General's office—

J. L. O'Connor, attorney general, salary..................... ...	$2,291 09	....	....
J. M. Clancy, asst. attorney general, salary....................	2,027 39	....	....
		$4,318 48	....

State Superintendent's office—

O. E. Wells, state superintendent, salary.....................	$1,100 00	....	....
O. E. Wells, state superintendent, expenses.	397 93	... .	....
C. A. Hutchins, asst. state superintendent, salary................	1,824 66	....	....
C. H Sylvester, insp. free high schools, salary...............	1,350 00	....	....
C. H. Sylvester, insp. free high schools, expenses..............	563 75	....	....
A. R. Green. tooks.............	6 00	....	....
A. C. McClurg & Co., books......	29 19	....	....
Publishers' Weekly, books	5 00	....	....
Binner Engraving Co., engravings	10 94	....	....
State superintendent, drawings and plates.....................	20 20	....	....
Callaghan & Co	25 00	....	....
		$5,332 67	....

"A."—General Fund Disbursements for 1893.

Railroad Commissioner's office—			
Thos. Thompson, commissioner, salary......	$3,041 09	....	....
Thos. Thompson, commissioner, expenses...........	583 17	....	....
J. B. Webb, deputy commissioner, salary..............	1,773 22	....	....
J. B. Webb, deputy commissioner, expenses...............	66 00	.. ..	....
		$5,463 48	....
Insurance Commissioner's office—			
W. M. Root, insurance commissioner, salary.................	$2,791 09	....	....
W. M. Root, insurance commissioner, expenses...............	.. ..	....	....
Ned M. Root, deputy insurance commissioner, salary....... ...	1,523 54	....	....
		$4,314 63	....
Public Property office—			
E v. Briesen, supt. of public property, salary............. .	$2,027 39		
		$2,027 39	....
Supreme Court—			
Wm. P. Lyon, chief justice.......	$5,000 00	....	....
H. S. Orton, associate justice....	5,000 00	....	....
J. B. Cassoday, associate justice..	5,000 00	....	....
John B. Winslow, associate justice	5,000 00	....	....
S. U Pinney, associate justice....	5,000 00	....	....
Clarence Kellogg, clerk, per diem.	485 00	....	....
Clarence Kellogg, clerk, fees... .	227 50	....	....
F. K. Conover, reporter..........	3,000 00	....	....
C. H. Beyler, crier..............	194 00	... .	....
C. H. Beyler, messenger........	900 00	....	....
F. W. Dockery, mess. and copyist	900 00	... .	....
F. D. Reed, mess. and copyist....	900 00	....	....
W. D. Hooker, mess. and copyist.	862 50	....	....
Jos. S. Keyes, proof reader.......	800 00	....	....
J. Fliegler, Jr., proof reader.....	900 00	....	....
Wm. F. Wolfe, messenger........	900 00	....	....
Fred A. Foster, copyist..........	37 50	....	....
		$34,606 50	....
Circuit Courts—			
F. M. Fish, judge of 1st circuit...	$4,000 00	....	....
D. H. Johnson, judge of 2d circuit	4,000 00	....	....
Geo. W. Burnell, judge of 3d circuit......................	4,000 00	....	....
Norman S. Gilson, judge of 4th circuit	4,000 00	....	....
Geo. Clementson, judge of 5th circuit	4,000 00	....	....
A. W. Newman, judge of 6th circuit.................. .	4,000 00	....	....
Chas. M. Webb, judge of 7th circuit............................	4,000 00	....	....
Egbert B. Bundy, judge of 8th circuit...	4,000 00	....	....

"A."—General Fund Disbursements for 1893.

Circuit Court—Continued.			
R. S. Siebecker, judge of 9th circuit	$4,000 00	... .	... .
John Goodland, judge of 10th circuit	4,000 00	.....	....
R. D. Marshall, judge of 11th circuit	4,000 00	....	....
John R. Bennett, judge of 12th circuit	4,000 00	....	
A. Scott Sloan, judge of 13th circuit	4,000 00	....	....
Sam'l D. Hastings, judge of 14th circuit	4,000 00	....	....
J. K. Parish, judge of 15th circuit	4,000 00	....	
Chas. V. Bardeen, judge of 16th circuit	4,000 00	....	....
W. F. Baily, judge of 17th circuit.	4,000 00	....	
		$68,000 00	....
State Historical Society—			
R. S. Thwaites, cor. secretary...	$2,000 00	....	
J. S. Bradley, librarian	1,600 00	....	
Minnie M. Oakley. asst. librarian.	1,200 00	....	
Treasurer appropriation	5,000 00	....	
		$9,800 00	....
State Library—			
J. R. Berryman. librarian	$3,000 00	....	
Callaghan and Co.. books	725 00	....	
Carswell Co., limited. books	285 08	....	
Boston Book Co.. books	555 15	....	
Beauchemin & Fils. books	24 82	....	
Banks & Bros.. books	88 00	....	
Banking Law Journal. books	6 00	....	
Chicago Legal News Co., books...	2 20	....	
T. H. Flood & Co., books	45 50	....	
T. & J. W. Johnson & Co. books..	18 53	....	
Little, Brown & Co., books	32 50	....	
Lawyers Co operative Pub. Co., books	25 00	....	
W. H. Lowdermilk & Co.. books..	4 00	....	
Roswell & Hutchinson. books...	15 50	....	
F. H. Thomas Law Book Co., books	194 05	....	
Edward Thompson & Co., books..	54 00	....	
Frank Shepard. books	30 00	....	
Yale Law Journal. books	2 00	....	
West Publishing Co.. books	159 60	....	
Weekly Law Bulletin and Ohio Law Journal. books	5 00	....	
Columbia Law Times. books	2 50	....	
John Byrne & Co , books.	13 00	....	
Kay & Bros.. books	5 00	....	
Michigan Law Journal, books	2 50	....	
Review Publishing Co., books....	5 00	....	
Stevens & Haynes, books	88 73	....	
Stumpf & Steurer. books .	1 00	....	....
United States Corporation Bureau, books	5 00	....	....

"A."—General Fund Disbursements for 1893.

State Library. - Continued—			
University of Pennsylvania Press, books	$5 00		
North American Review, books...	5 00		
Geo. A. Lewis, books....	10 00		
T. L. Cole, books.	12 60		
		$4,426,66	
State Board Charities and Reform—			
W. W Reed, per diem and expenses from April 1, 1890, to June 30, 1891	$1,034 40	$1,034 40	
Board of Control—			
Clarence Snyder, salary and expenses	$3,973 65		
J. E. Jones, salary and expenses..	2,879 38		
J. L. Cleary, salary and expenses.	2,541 38		
C. D. Parker, salary and expenses.	2,521 45		
J. W. Oliver, salary and expenses.	2,448 71		
W. H. Graebner, salary and expenses	2,644 23		
P. Mulholland, secretary, salary .	1,582 25		
Clint Goodwin, clerk, salary	280 00		
Ida Herfurth, clerk, salary	12 00		
D. S. Comley, secretary, salary...	367 75		
		$18,250 80	
			$178,567 18
PERMANENT APPROPRIATIONS.			
Bureau of Labor Statistics—			
Jerry Dobbs, com., salary	$2,000 00		
Jerry Dobbs, com., expenses	1,250 00		
F. M. Dyer, dep. com., salary...	1,500 00		
John W. Zwaska, factory inspector, salary	1,200 00		
John W Zwaska, factory inspector, expenses	145 48		
John W Zwaska, factory inspector, office rent.	150 00		
S. L. Van Etten, asst. factory inspector, salary	1,000 00		
S. L. Van Etten, asst. factory inspector. expenses	561 30		
Jerry Dobbs, commissioner, books.	43 87		
Jerry Dobbs. commissioner, office rent, factory inspector	125 00		
		$7,974 65	
State Board of Health—			
J. T. Reeve, secretary, expenses of board	$6,043 80		
		$6,043 80	
Fish Culture—			
Treasurer of fish commission, appropriation	$13,000 00		
		$13,000 00	

"A."—General Fund Disbursements for 1893.

Dairy and Food Commission—			
D. L. Harkness, com., salary	$2,496 00		
D. L. Harkness, com., expenses...	545 84		
Geo. S. Cox, dep. com., salary ...	1,800 00		
Geo. S. Cox, dep. com., expenses..	276 16		
Walter A. West, dep. com., salary	1,800 00		
Walter A. West, dep. com., expenses	438 16		
M. J. Cantwell, merchandise.....	61 75		
Madison Gas Co., merchandise....	6 13		
Wm. Owen, gas fitting..........	7 92		
W. J. Park & Sons, merchandise.	• 12 60		
Ramsay & Lerdall, merchandise..	11 98		
		$7,456 49	
Laboratory — Dairy and Food Commission—			
Geo. S. Cox, expenses...........	$246 95		
W. J. Park & Sons, merchandise..	80		
Madison Gas Co., gas..........	6 30		
M. J. Cantwell, merchandise.....	2 50		
Dunning & Sumner, merchandise.	29 88		
		$286 43	
Land Protection—			
Jas. Allen...................	$50 00		
S. W. Blanding...............	559 20		
John Kane	222 05		
Simon J. McNally	24 80		
Martin Page.................	1,327 00		
Jas. Russell	137 80		
O. R. Skaar.................	19 29		
James Whelan................	192 83		
		$2,532 97	
Teachers' Institutes —			
L. D. Harvey.................	$120 76		
J. W. Stearns	1,261 54		
C. H. Sylvester..............	62 30		
		$1,444 60	
Appraising Crawford Co. Swamp Lands.			
W. D Merrell, per diem and expenses............	$99 16		
		$99 16	
			$88,838 10

LEGISLATIVE EXPENSES.

Senators — Mileage 2nd Special Session,1892 —			
Adam Apple...................	$25 00		
Frank Avery..................	8 00		
Paul Bechtner................	16 40		
R. J. Burdge.................	9 60		
P. J. Clawson................	8 20		
Henry Conner	30 00		
Russell C. Falconer...........	8 00		

4—Sec'y.

"A."—*General Fund Disbursements for 1893.*

Senators— Mileage 2nd Special Session, 1892—Continued.			
John Fetzer............................	$52 60	....	....
Fred. W. Horn.....................	22 00	....	....
R. L. Joiner...........	9 40	....	....
John J. Kempf.....................	16 40	....	....
Wm. Kennedy......................	38 00	....	....
Edward J. Kidd....	20 00	....	....
John T. Kingston	88 40	....	....
C. A. Koenitzer..................	17 00	....	....
Herman Kroeger..............	17 00	....	....
Rob't Lees.......... ●	38 00	....	....
Robert J. McBride	30 60	....	....
M. C. Mead......................	29 00	....	....
Wm. Miller......	43 20	....	....
Wm. F. Nash..................	34 00	... .	....
E. W. Persons...................	38 00	....	....
W. H. Phipps.....................	50 40	....	....
Geo W Pratt................	32 40	....	....
H. H. Price...	27 00	....	....
J. C. Reynolds..................	24 60	....	... .
S. B Stanchfield...............	32 00	....	....
Albert Solliday.................	8 20	....	....
Chas. S. Taylor.....	47 00	....	... .
Wm. F. Voss.	8 20	....	....
J. H. Woodnorth.	42 80	....	....
F. T. Yahr.......	26 00		....
		$892 40	....
Assembly—Mileage 2nd Special Session. 1892—			
Chas. H. Anson..................	$20 00	....	....
J. W. Babcock...	18 40	.. ..	....
L. S. Bailey...	52 00	....	....
Edmund U. Baker..............	11 40	....	....
James Bannon....................	29 60	....	....
Frank Howe.......................	31 40	....	.....·.....
Neil Brown......................	40 00	....	....
Ernest L. Bullard	16 80	....	....
Michael E. Burke................	14 00	....	....
D. W. Cheney....................	21 60	....	....
Geo. W. Chinnook.................	52 80	....·......	....
Samuel A. Cook.................	85 00	....	....
P. J Conway......................	40 00	....	....
Chas. Couch	31 80	....	....
Robt. M. Crawford..............	25 00	....	....
Wm. Croll	89 00	....	....
C. A. Davenport....	87 00	....	....
John Dawson.....................	29 60	... .	....
H. J. Desmond	20 00	....	....
Henry B. Dike...................	65 00	....	....
D. J. Dill......................	57 40	... .	....
J. E. Dodge....	21 00	....	....
Thos. W. English.......	9 00	....	....
Edgar Eno..................	22 00	....	....
Wm. Faber.....................	82 40	....	....
W. J. Fiebrantz.................	20 00	....	....
Jos. Filz..........................	49 20	....	....

"*A.*"—*General Fund Disbursements for 1893.*

Assembly—Mileage 2nd Special Session 1892—Continued.

Oscar Finch	$32 40		
W. H. Fitzgerald	25 00		
O. P. Gardner	11 00		
Albert L. Gray	46 00		
Christopher Heim	15 00		
Jos. J. Hogan	23 00		
Albert R. Hall	42 00		
John Horn	20 00		
R. S Houston	27 00		
Jos. R. Henderson	4 00		
H. C. Hunt	10 60		
David Jennings	30 00		
C. Hugo Jacobi	8 00		
Edward Keogh	20 00		
Michael Kruszka	20 00		
Conrad Krez	20 00		
Theo. Knapstein	30 00		
F. C. Kizer	9 80		
August Conrad	24 00		
G. S. Luscher	32 40		
Jay G. Lamberson	11 80		
John Longbotham	21 00		
James Larsin	58 00		
John Leonhardy	40 00		
Ambrose McGuigan	20 00		
Wm. V. McMullen	44 00		
R. J. McGeehan	45 60		
J. J. McGillivray	26 00		
Chas. J. Meloy	20 00		
A. R. Munger	30 00		
Jos. S. Maxon	17 00		
L. H. Mead	75 00		
Chas. W. Moore	45 20		
J. P. Nolan	44 20		
Chas. F. Osborn	20 00		
Brown Olson	27 00		
Thos. O'Connor	40 00		
Jno. J. Oswald	18 00		
C. E. Pierce	27 00		
Wm. Pierron	20 00		
H. C. Putnam	12 40		
Dennis T. Phalen	30 60		
Wm. T. Pugh	36 60		
W. E. Plummer	37 40		
Wm. H. Porter	4 00		
Christian Reuter	8 00		
Louis Rossman	80 00		
O L. Rosenkrans	10 00		
Phillip Schmitz, Jr	20 00		
Wm. Schwefel	9 60		
Henry Schuetz	20 00		
C. E. Smith	13 60		
Joseph Stoppenbach	7 20		
B E. Sampson	16 00		
L. H. Smith	5 00		
E. C. Smith	25 00		

"A."—General Fund Disbursements for 1893.

Assembly—Mileage 2d Special Session 1892 Continued.

J. A. Taylor....	$45 00	....	....
James Tormey......	20 00	....	....
John Tracy............	38 00	....	....
Henry Tarrant....................	9 60	....	....
Clinton Textor..............	64 00	....	....
Ambrose Thompson................	25 00	....	....
O. f Williams............,......	20 00	....	....
C. M. Whiteside.............. ..	55 00	....	....
Jas. W. Watson..................	29 00	....	....
M. J. Warner....................	32 00	....	....
O. O. Wiegand....... .--.... ..	46 50	....	....
John Winans....................,.....	8 00	$2,667 30	....

Senate Employes — 2d Special Session, 1892.

Henrietta Bevitt, enrolling and indexing......	$32 00	....	....
J. A. Barney, sergt. at arms......	55 00	....	....
Mattie M. Fowler, enrolling and indexing	32 00	....	....
Berthold Husting, messenger... .	22 00	....	....
Fred Herman, asst. sergt. at arms	44 00	....	....
Paul Kingston, messenger........	20 00	....	....
Thos. Leary, doorkeeper.........	30 00	....	....
M. L. Lueck, postmaster	40 00	....	....
Edward Malone, bookkeeper	55 00	....	....
Bertha Mayer, enrolling and indexing	32 00	....	....
Sam'l J. Shafer, chief clerk, opening session........	50 00	....	....
Jackson Silbaugh, asst. chief clerk.	55 00	....	....
J. E. Taylor, messenger..........	22 00	....	....
Sam'l J. Shafer, chief clerk, per diem...............	110 00	$599 00	....

Assembly Employes—2d Special Session, 1892.

Ed. Casey, doorkeeper..	$33 00	....	....
Jennie Collins, proofreader.... ..	24 00	....	....
E. D. Doney, asst. chief clerk and bookkeeper.....................	110 00	....	....
G. H. Daubner, doorkeeper......	33 00	....	....
George Hagenon, messenger.....	22 00	....	....
Archie McCoy. messenger.........	22 00	....	....
Willie Mulholland, messenger....	22 00	....	....
Everett Monchau, messenger.....	22 00	....	....
Geo. W. Porth, chief clerk, opening session...............	50 00	....	....
Geo. W. Porth, chief clerk, per diem.....	110 00	....	....
J. A. Venus, asst. sergt. at arms..	44 00	....	....
P. Whalen, sergt. at arms........	55 00	$547 00	....

"G."—General Fund Disbursements for 1893.

Senators— Regular Session 1893.	Salaries.	Mileage.		
Oscar Altpeter	$500 00	$20 00		
Adam Apple	500 00	25 00		
Neal Brown	500 00	57 00		
Chas. Baxter	500 00	18 00		
Paul Bechtner	500 00	16 40		
R. J. Burdge	500 00	10 00		
R. M. Bashford	500 00	20		
Henry Connor	500 00	30 00		
Russell C. Falconer	500 00	8 00		
John Fetzer	500 00	50 00		
Fred. W. Horn	500 00			
Wm. Kennedy	500 00	88 00		
J. T. Kingston, Jr	500 00	83 40		
C. A. Koenitzer	500 00	20 00		
Mich. Kruszka	500 00	20 00		
Robert Lees	500 00	88 00		
Robert J. McBride	500 00	30 60		
Robert J. McGeehan	500 00	38 00		
Levi F. Martin	500 00	45 00		
J. W. Murphy	500 00	20 00		
Wm. F. Nash	500 00	34 00		
Dennis Phalen	500 00	30 60		
Wm. H. Phipps	500 00	50 40		
Geo. W. Pratt	500 00	32 40		
Saml. L. Smead	500 00	29 00		
Albert Solliday	500 00	8 20		
Calvert Spensley	500 00	22 40		
Wm. F. Voss	500 00	8 20		
Thompson D. Weeks	500 00	10 00		
Doyn F. Wescott	500 00	50 40		
Levi Withee	500 00	28 00		
J. H. Woodnorth	500 00	42 80		
F. T. Yahr	500 00	37 00		
	$16,500 00	$951 00		
			$17,451 00	
Members of Assembly, Regular Session, 1893.	Salaries.	Mileage.		
Geo. A. Albert	$500 00	$20 00		
Wm. H. Austin	500 00	20 00		
A. B. Barney	500 00	57 00		
Michael Blenski	500 00	20 00		
Orrin W. Bow	500 00	20 60		
Isaac G. Brader	500 00	2 40		
Henry A. Brauer	500 00	50 80		
John Brill	500 00	42 00		
Henry P. Burdick	500 00	65 00		
M. E. Burke	500 00	30 00		
Wm. A. Cochran	500 00	28 00		
Park J. Conway	500 00	40 00		
B. H. Corcoran	500 00	62 70		
Chas. Couch	500 00	31 80		
Lemuel B. Cox	500 00	32 00		
Wm. Croll	500 00	38 00		
Chas. C. Daily	500 00	57 40		

"A."—General Fund Disbursements for 1893.

Members of Assembly, Regular Session, 1893—Continued.	Salaries.	Mileage.		
Geo. Danielson......	$500 00	$30 60	....	....
John Dassow........	500 00	30 00	....	... ...
Cornelius A. Davenport..............	500 00	37 00	....	....
J. O. Davidson	500 00	28 60	....	....
Frank A. Deleglise...	500 00	57 00	....	... .
Joseph Deuster	500 00	20 00	....	....
Theo. Diekman	500 00	30 40	... .	....
E. A. Edmunds..:...	500 00	51 60	....	....
Neils C. Evans.......	500 00	5 00	....	....
Joseph Filz..........	500 00	49 20	....	....
David Finn..........	500 00	34 00	....	....
Wm. H. Fitzgerald.	500 00	25 00	....	....
Frank L. Frazer.....	500 00	21 00	... .	....
Baldwin M. Fulmer..	500 00	39 00	....	....
John A. Gaynor.....	500 00	27 60	....	....
Benj. F. Goss........	500 00	16 00	....	....
Paul M. Green.......	500 00	7 00	....	....
Christopher Grimm..	500 00	7 00	....	....
Henry F. Hagemeister..............	500 00	46 00	....	....
Albert R. Hall.......	500 00	42 00	....	....
Chas. F. Hanke	500 00	32 00	....	....
John C. Harmon	500 00	45 00	.. ..	....
Chas. W. Heyl... ..	500 00	20	....	....
C. F. A. Hintze......	500 00	20 00	....	....
Chas. Hirschinger...	500 00	9 00	....	....
David L. Holcomb...	500 00	40 00	....	....
Nels Holman........	500 00	4 00	....	....
Emerson D. Hoyt....	500 00	29 00	....	....
Benj. W. Hubbard .	500 00	5 40	....	....
H. C. Hunt	500 00	10 60	....	....
Jacob J. Iverson	500 00	20 00	....	....
C. Hugo Jacobi	500 00	8 00	....	....
Hugh P. Jamison....	500 00	5 00	....	... .
David Jennings.....	500 00	30 00	....	....
Gustav J. Jeske.....	500 00	20 00	....	... ...
Jos B. Johnson.. ..	500 00	13 00	....	....
Edward Keogh, speaker.	1,000 00	20 00	....	....
James Keogh.......	500 00	55 50	....	....
August Konrad	500 00	24 00	....	....
Geo. H. Kroencke...	500 00	27 41	....	....
Jay J. Lamberson..	500 00	11 80	....	....
Louie A. Lange.....	500 00	29 00	....	....
Henry Lebeis.......	500 00	47 80	....	....
Alfred A. Leissring.	500 00	26 60	....	... .
John W Liebenstein	500 00	30 00	....	....
John Longbotham..	500 00	21 00	....	....
Gustav S. Luscher..	500 00	32 40	....	....
R. N. McConnochie..	500 00	13 00	....	....
Frank McDonough..	500 00	65 20	....	....
M. G. McGeehan....	500 00	86 60	....	....
J. J. McGillivray....	500 00	26 00	....	....

"A."—General Fund Disbursements for 1893.

Members of Assembly, Regular Session, 1893—Continued.	Salaries.	Mileage.		
Duncan J. McKenzie	$500 00	$39 00		
Daniel A. Mahoney..	500 00	28 00		
Daniel O. Mahoney..	500 00	30 00		
C. W. Milbrath	500 00	20 00		
Edgar G. Mills......	500 00	68 00		
Peter Nelson........	500 00	20 00		
Wm. O'Neil	500 00	71 00		
Jas. W. Parkinson..	500 00	33 60		
Albert J. Perkins....	500 00	65 20		
Sewell A. Peterson..	500 00	48 40		
Clarence E. Pierce..	500 00	27 00		
Henry C. Putnam...	500 00	13 00		
Chas. E. Quigg......	500 00	20 00		
Peter G. Rademacher	500 00	20 00		
Rip Reukema	500 00	20 00		
Francis Reuschlein...	500 00	24 60		
John Ringle	500 00	57 00		
Bennett E. Sampson.	500 00	30 00		
John Schmidt.......	500 00	18 00		
Phil. Schmitz, Jr....	500 00	20 00		
Wm Schwefel......	500 00	9 60		
J. M. Smith.........	500 00	25 00		
Jno. M. Stack	500 00	32 00		
Frank Suelflohn.....	500 00	20 00		
Lyman W. Thayer..	500 00	26 00		
John Tracy.........	500 00	38 00		
Frank T. Tucker....	500 00	32 40		
Anton Van Der Heiden..	500 00	39 00		
W. P. Wheelihan...	500 00	20 00		
Orrin J. Williams...	500 00	56 00		
Agesilaus O. Wilson.	500 00	8 00		
Jacob Wipf...	500 00	46 00		
	$30,500 00	$3,040 01	$53,540 01	
Senate Employes—				
Sam J. Shafer, chief clerk, opening session		$50 00		
Sam J. Shafer, chief clerk, per diem.....		800 00		
Franklin Bowen, ass't chief clerk.		573 00		
John Arent, night watch....		303 00		
J. A. Adamson, messenger		184 00		
Etta Alford, copyist		94 80		
Emma Allen, copyist......... ...		98 80		
May Armstrong, ass't index clerk.		292 00		
Nic. Brever, gallery attendant....		303 00		
Robert Burk, janitor		303 00		
Martin Baumgaertner, messenger.		203 00		
J. B. Becker, serg't at arms.......		505 00		
Antone Boex, proof reader.......		404 00		
Henrietta J. Bevitte, copyist......		126 65		
S. C. Bass, doorkeeper..........		303 00		
Cliff P. Best, general clerk.......		195 00		

"A."—General Fund Disbursements for 1893.

Senate Employes—

C. F. Bundy, comparing clerk....	$213 00		
Frankie Brown, copyist..........	98 00		
Ruth C. Burton, copyist..........	20 00		
Albert Cavanaugh, messenger....	202 00		
W. F. Collins, clerk judiciary committee......................	404 00		
Sarah Cunningham, copyist... ..	83 00		
Tracy Cooney, copyist............	82 60		
R. Cary, doorkeeper...	303 00		
A. R. Deignon, comparing clerk..	186 00		
Mary Donovan, copyist	20 45		
P T. Diamond, ass't bookkeeper...	340 00		
Bennie Erickson, messenger	202 00		
Jno. D. Fay, night laborer....... .	303 00		
Don Frank, messenger.:	202 10		
Jno. G. Faulds, enrolling clerk....	404 00		
Mattie M. Fowler, gen'l comparing clerk	124 70		
Carl Felker, com room att'd't... .	258 00		
J. M Frey, custodian............	243 00		
Nellie Gates, comparing clerk.....	303 00		
Grace Glennon, copyist.....	20 00		
C. B. Goodwin, copyist....	96 20		
Jno Hayes, messenger..........	202 00		
H. J. Husting, messenger.........	202 00		
Anna Hanrahan, copyist.........	115 90		
Eva Harmon, copyist.	67 90		
Anna Hurley, ruling clerk	285 00		
O. F. Huhn, general clerk	120 00		
R. Huyck, com. room attend't ...	258 00		
J. A. Jacobs, com. room attend't..	258 00		
Lizzie Jahnke, copyist and com paring clerk.....	213 00		
Jesse Knowles, index clerk.......	482 00		
Thos. Kennedy, com. room attend't	303 00		
Bert. Levy, messenger..........	202 00		
Minnie Le Claire, com. on engrossed bills..................	288 00		
Isabella La Mont. copyist........	31 95		
R. J McBride, Jr., clerk com. on incorporations.....	344 00		
James McBrien, asst. enrolling clerk	248 50		
Kathryne McGillan, stenographer jud. com	228 00		
Edward Malone, bookkeeper.....	505 00		
Bertha M. Mayer, copyist.	135 80		
Geo. Malone, custodian engrossing room	204 00		
Alice Monahan, copyist	104 85		
Joseph Mashek, general clerk.....	186 00		
M. Norris, messenger	202 00		
Noel Nash, printing page........	303 00		
J O'Rourke, attendant	303 00		
Thos. O'Hara, asst. engrossing clerk	319 00		

"A."—General Fund Disbursements for 1893.

Senate Employes—Continued.

Kassimer Owocki, asst. sergt.-at arms	$404 00	....	....
E. R. Petherick, general clerk...	303 00	....	....
R. B. Pratt, clerk com. on railroads	344 00	....	....
Lucy A. Pregent, copyist	20 20	....	....
Annette Rasdall, copy holder	303 00	....	....
M. W. Ryan, postmaster	404 00	....	....
Christine Ramsteck, copyist	109 85	....	....
J. W Reed, attendant	303 00	....	....
Adam Schroth, attendant	60 00	....	....
S. M. Sherwood, doorkeeper...	303 00	....	....
Jos. Sims, gen'l clerk.	308 00	....	....
Chas. Seiler, messenger	202 00	....	....
Carl Schneider, document room attendant	404 00	....	....
Jackson Silbaugh, journal clerk..	505 00	....	....
Emma Sturdevant, copyist	98 30	....	....
Lizzie Skinner, copyist	102 80	....	....
Fred Smith, clerk com. on enrolled bills	248 50	....	....
Lydia Selbach, copyist	94 95	....	....
Grace G. Smith, copyist	68 70	....	....
Geo. F. Steele, comparing clerk..	153 00	....	....
Callie Shafer, copyist	50 50	....	....
R. Tuttle, doorkeeper	303 00	....	....
Henry Tierney, messenger	202 00	....	....
F. W. Teske, document clerk	371 00	....	....
Clarice C. Thayer, copyist	88 60	....	....
R E. Taylor, messenger	202 00	....	....
Minnie Van Horn, copyist	107 40	....	....
Arnold Wagoner, asst. postmaster	337 00	....	....
Bert Williams, clerk com. town and co. organization	344 00	....	....
Will N. Wells, engrossing clerk...	404 00	....	....
W. H. Wiebold, clerk, com. on claims	404 00	....	....
B. A. Weatherby, clerk, com. on C. and P. Inst	344 00	....	....
Julia Wirka, copyist	80 50	....	....
Sidna Williams, copyist	26 10		
		$22,904 00	....

Assembly Employes—

Geo. W. Porth, chief clerk, opening session	$50 00	....	....
Geo. W. Porth, chief clerk, per diem	800 00	....	....
St. Andrzejewski, messenger	202 00	....	....
Fred. Ackermann, general clerk..	162 00	....	....
Wm. Amadon, engrossing	120 00	....	....
R. Amadon, engrossing	30 00	....	....
Jacob Beth, wash room attend't...	303 00	....	....
Fred. Bishop, night watchman...	303 00	....	....
Frank Bartlett, proof reader	364 00	....	....
Eddie Ballschmieder, messenger..	202 00	....	....
Thos. Burke, messenger	202 00	....	....

"A."—General Fund Disbursements for 1893.

Assembly Employes--Continued.

J. A. Blackwell, com. room attend't	$303 00	....	....
Walter Boyd, gen'l and enrolling clk......	171 50	....	....
Anna M. Bowe, engrossing......	82 60	....	.. ..
Birdie Burkee, enrolling	60 95	......,'.	....
Ruth C. Burton, engrossing.......	177 05	......·..	....
O. W. Bowe Jr., gen'l clk. and engrossing	94 00	....	....
Blanche Bird, enrolling...........	2 00	....	....
Geo. Coughran, general clerk....	333 00	.. ..	....
James Carrol, general clerk.......	303 00	....	....
Ed. Conway Jr., general clerk....	303 00	....	....
T. E. Chubbuck, doorkeeper......	303 00	....	....
D. C. Clune, com. room attend't.	285 00	....	....
John Conway, messenger.........	202 00	....	....
Louis Carey, messenger.........	202 00	....	....
Wm. S. Croll, com. room attend't	303 00	....	....
C. J. Courtney, custodian engrossing room....................	183 00	....	....
Alex. Coughrane Jr., comparing clerk.....................	111 00	...........·	....
Jennie Collius, enrolling and engr< ss.ng	187 05	.......····	....·.....
Mary E. Chadwick, engrossing...	68 00	....	....
Nellie Cook, engrossing	103 40	....	....·..,..
Ruth B. Croll, enrolling and comparing clk.	213 50	....	....
Lucy Cosgrove, enrolling........	50 95	....	....
E. D. Doney, asst. chief clerk.....	573 00	....	....
Bennie Dodge, messenger	202 00	.... ·	....
Carrie B. Dunning, engrossing....	64 90	....	....
E. E. Depsey, enrolling and engrossing	70 55	... .	....
L. J. Evans, com. room attend't..	306 00	....	....
Wm. Fahrenger, janitor..........	303 00	....	....
Kate Falvey, engrossing..........	86 30	....	....
E. M. Fox, enrolling.............	66 50	....	....
S. D. Goodell, asst. engrossing clerk..................... ...	353 00	....	....
J. J. Gleason, asst. enrolling clerk	307 00	....	....
Arthur Gardner, messenger.......	202 00	....	....
Jos. E. Grassberger, com. room attend't......................	246 00	....	....
E. J. Goetz, printing page	243 00	....	... ...
A Goertz, enrolling clerk	324 00	....	....
Ella Graham, clk. com. on railroads........	312 50	....	....
Mary Good, engrossing........ ..	88 50	....	....
Clint Goodwin, ruling and gen'l clerk	156 00	....	....
W. H. Gillman, gen'l clerk	51 00	....	....
Maggie Gallagher, enrolling	47 55	... .	....·..·
Tillie Grimm, engrossing	68 40	....	....
F. Herman, gallery attend't......	303 00	....	....
St. Hanizeski, doorkeeper	303 00	....	....
Jos. Hartele, com. room attend't.	285 00	....	... .
Jno. F. Harns, com. room attend't	294 00	....	....

"A."—General Fund Disbursements for 1893.

Assembly Employes – Continued.

C. W. Hunt, clk. com. on en- grossed bills	$227 50		
E. L. Hardy, clk. com. on bills third reading	301 00		
W. P. Hyland, clk. com. on town and county organization	312 50		
Mamie Harrison, comparing and enrolling	213 5+		
Aggie Hyland, engrossing and en- rolling	187 05		
Annie Hallagan, enrolling	63 80		
Fannie Jones, engrossing	106 70		
Addie Joachim, enrolling	59 80		
Theo. Knapstein, sergeant-at arms	505 00		
Valentine Klesges, com. room at tendant	237 00		
May Keily, enrolling	66 10		
A. B. Kildow, com. room attend't	174 00		
Chas. A. Leicht, index clerk	482 00		
Casper Lebeis, doorkeeper	303 00		
Bessie Lusk, copy holder	273 00		
Martin Lueck, comparing clerk	102 00		
Minnie Luebkemann, enrolling	77 20		
Maggie Leary, engrossing	100 80		
Ada Lynch, enrolling	70 05		
Emma Lawrence, enrolling	122 65		
Kate Lafferty, enrolling	30.05		
Wm. McMullen.... ..	404 00		
G. T McElroy, asst. postmaster ..	343 50		
Archie McCoy, messenger	202 00		
Thos. McBean, clk. com. on en- rolled bills	252 00		
L. McBean, engrossing	66 00		
J. E. McGinnis, comparing clerk..	60 00		
Wm. Mayworm, bookkeeper	505 00		
Aug. C. Mann, gallery attend't. .	303 00		
Everett Monshau, messenger	202 00		
Byron Moore, flagman	243 00		
Jas. Mellon, comparing clerk	213 00		
Ole Nelson, doorkeeper	303 00		
Geo. Nebel, com. room attend't	285 00		
Elizabeth Neeb, engrossing	171 00		
Jennie Nelson, enrolling	74 00		
Nellie B. Nichols, engrossing	55 00		
J. D. O'Brien, asst. bookkeeper	475 00		
Jno. O'Keif, cloak room attend't.	303 00		
Tom Overland, gen'l and ass't en grossing clerk	229 00		
Grace O'Malley, engrossing clerk.	63 80		
Robt. Plisch, com. room attend't.	246 00		
Nellie Proctor, enrolling	183 10		
Hattie Pier, stenographer judi ciary com....	224 00		
John Pinzger, porter	285 00		
John H. Rooney, asst. sergt. at arms	404 00		

"A."—General Fund Disbursements for 1893.

Assembly Employes—Continued.			
Chas. Reuschlein, comparing and enrolling clerk.................	$290 00	....	....
Wm. Ringle, clerk com. on state affairs......	316 00	....	....
Patrick Ryan, clerk com on corporations.....	316 00	....	....
Elmer Skelley, stationery clerk..	347 00	....	....
Geo. Silbernagel, general clerk...	279 00	....	....
Albert Stoppenbach, general attend't...........	394 00	....	....
Peter Spehn, cloak room attend't.	303 00	....	....
Frank Shealey, messenger.......	202 00	....	....
Frank Sims, messenger...... ...	202 00	....	....
Geo. Sherer, custodian enrolling room	204 00	....	....
E. G. Springer, engrossing.......	100 00	....	....
Mary Sullivan, engrossing........	88 40	....	....
Vina Sylvester, enrolling.......	67 90	....	....
Nellie Skaben, engrossing.......	88 30	....	....
F. M.Shaughnessy, clerk judiciary com..................	396 00	....	....
Nora Sullivan. engrossing........	10 00	....	....
Rose Starck, enrolling...........	43 05	....	....
Hulda Sieker, engrossing........	66 80	....	....
W. J. Taylor, ruling clerk.......	201 00	....	....
W. Temple. asst. index clerk.....	389 00	....	....
Belle Thompson, engrossing......	95 20	....	....
J. A. Venus, document clerk.....	404 00	....	....
L. W Wright, journal clerk	505 00	....	....
J. C. Wright, journal clerk	465 00	....	....
Ulrich Wettstein, document room attend't	404 00	....	....
Jas. Whitty, Jr., messenger......	202 00	....	....
Albert S. White, clerk com. privileges and elections	316 00	....	....
Louis Wolf, comparing clerk.....	123 00	....	....
Cora Warren......	50 00	....	....
		$29,003 75	....
Annotated Statutes for Legislature –			
Callaghan & Co..................	$1,782 00		
		$1,782 00	....
Funeral Expenses, Senator Horn and Assemblyman Mahoney--			
Theo. Knapstein, sergeant-at-arms assembly...	$678 90		
		$678 90	....
Lieutenant Governor—			
Chas. Jonas................,.......	$1,097 69		
		$1,097 69	....
Chaplains for Legislature—			
J. D. Butler..... .-...............	$30 00	....	....
E. E. Bartlett...................	30 00	....	....

"A."—General Fund Disbursements for 1893.

Chaplains for Legislature—Contin'd			
E. C. Effmeyer.....................	$45 00		
Chas. E. Hall	45 00		
W. R. Irish	30 00		
P. B. Knox	30 00		
H. A. Miner......................	30 00		
C. Roehl	45 00		
A. V. C. Schenck.................	30 00		
E. G. Updike	30 00		
H. A. Winter....................	30 00		
A. L Williamson	45 00		
		$420 00	
Contesting Seats—Assembly—			
Frank A. Deleglise..............	$1,034 21		
Jno. O. Davidson...............	703 02		
Jos. Filz.....	891 50		
Jas. Fisher, Jr	440 51		
Benj. F. Goss...................	1,058 38		
Theo. Prochnow.....	954 50		
O. L. Rosenkrans	587 18		
Peter G. Rademacher............	674 72		
Geo. H. Wunderlich....	749 51		
		$7,093 53	
Blue Book—			
Edwin E. Bryant....	$200 (0		
Democrat Printing Co...........	5,594 72		
Milwaukee Litho. & Eng. Co. ..	2,675 00		
W. C. Brawley...................	410 00		
		$8,879 72	
Legislative Visiting Committee—			
A. R. Hall..............	$100 00		
J. M. Smith................. ...	100 00		
F. T. Yahr.....................	100 00		
		$300 00	
Publishing List Legislative Employes—			
Milwaukee Journal Co...........	$31 20		
		$31 20	
Printing for Legislature—			
Democrat Printing Co.:			
Assembly bills and titles........	$1,784 21		
Assembly journal.	701 15		
Assembly slips and calendar....	874 06		
Senate bills and titles.	1,251 26		
Senate journals	543 66		
Senate slips and calendars......	880 60		
Miscellaneous...	531 51		
		$6,566 45	
Wisconsin Telephone Co.—			
Messages........	$50 00		
		$50 00	
Total Legislative Expenses....			$154,503 95

"A."—General Fund Disbursements for 1893.

CHARITABLE AND PENAL INSTITUTIONS.			
State Hospital for Insane—			
Expenses	$113,338 44		
Northern Hospital for Insane—			
Expenses	114,093 59		
Wisconsin School for Deaf—			
Expenses	39,497 44		
Wisconsin School for Blind—			
Expenses	33,209 39		
Industrial School for Boys—			
Expenses	57,300 80		
State Prison—			
Expenses	10,813 68		
State Public School —			
Expenses	40,720 09		
			$408,967 93
CLERK HIRE.			
Governor's Office—			
Werner Pressentin, executive clerk	$1,500 00		
Geo. W. Peck, Jr., clerk	312 47		
		$1,812 47	
Secretary's Office—			
H. G. L. Paul, chief clerk	$600 00		
F. W. Grumm, chief clerk	1,050 00		
Geo. W. Levis, bookkeeper	2,000 00		
C. H Phillips, ass't bookkeeper	1,500 00		
Thomas McBean, ass't bookkeeper	875 00		
A. F. Warden, printing clerk	1,800 00		
W. N. Carter, filing clerk	375 00		
A. N. Altenhofen, filing clerk	1,470 00		
Francis S. Weil, recording clerk	145 67		
Nellie Leonard, warrant clerk	1,035 00		
Isabel C. Schneider, registration clerk	1,380 00		
Julius Bruess, draughtsman	1,495 00		
R. M. Lamp, general clerk	1,067 72		
Henry Lebeis, general clerk	650 00		
Paul O. Husting, mailing clerk	900 00		
M. C. McDougall, stenographer	810 00		
H. J. Lohmar, proof reader	850 00		
Lena Breese, stenographer and proof reader	425 00		
Thomas McBean, compiling clerk	196 00		
Geo. W. Brower, indexing clerk	1,050 00		
Bernard Esser, indexing clerk	650 00		
John J. Thornton, indexing clerk	900 00		
John H. Kernan, indexing clerk	132 28		
J. De LaMotte, indexing clerk	192 00		
J. A. Venus, indexing clerk	212 00		
		$21,260 67	
Treasurer's Office—			
P. McMahon, bookkeeper	$2,100 00		
L. B. Murphy, corresponding clerk	1,800 00		

"A."—General Fund Disbursements for 1893.

Treasurer's Office—Continued.			
Geo. L. Blum, deposit clerk......	$1,800 00		
F. W. Bartz, mailing clerk......	1,850 00		
Robert Henry, messenger........	900 00		
Chas. C. Hunner, messenger......	300 00		
Chas. C. Hunner, clerk.	194 00		
Chas. C. Hunner, night watch...	486 00		
P. S. Reinsch, night watch......	184 00		
Earl E. Hunner, night watch.....	60 00		
W. H. G. Mueller, janitor........	730 00		
		$10,404 00	
State Superintendent's Office—			
J. A. Sheridan, chief clerk.	$1 520 54		
F. A. Hutchins, library clerk.....	1,200 00		
F. A. Hutchins, expenses library			
clerk	188 08		
Anna Lum, stenographer.........	989 97		
. Etta S. Carle, clerk	354 79		
Frances M. Hall, clerk...........	22 50		
S. S. Lamont, clerk.............	63 00		
Florence Norton, clerk..........	90 00		
		$4,428 88	
Land Office—			
W H. Canon, chief clerk........	$1,800 00		
W. H. Canon, clerk to land com-			
missioners	199 92		
O. R. Skaar, asst. chief clerk.....	1,699 92		
H. Schildhauer, book eeper.....	1,699 92		
C. J. M. Malek, patent clerk.....	1,699 92		
L. A. Brace, clerk	1,500 00		
W F. Dockery, clerk........ ...	1,275 00		
Alex. Moran, clerk.............	758 31		
Virgil Borst, clerk.......	758 31		
John Byrne, clerk..............	1,245 00		
Carl Soig, clerk.....	805 00		
W. H. Coyne, clerk.............	700 00		
Geo J. Reinsch, clerk..........	575 00		
Robt. M. Lamp, clerk..........	132 26		
Stella Keenan, stenographer......	720 00		
		$15,568 56	
Public Property Office—			
W. B. Vance, asst. supt. public			
property	$1,500 00		
		$1,500 00	
Labor Statistics—			
Max A. Blumenfeldt, clerk.......	$1,200 00		
		$1,200 00	
			$56,174 53
LABOR ABOUT CAPITOL.			
Engineers and Firemen—			
John Doyle, engineer...........	$1,200 00		
John Butler, asst. engineer......	1,095 00		
John Delaney, fireman.........	821 25		

"A."—General Fund Disbursements for 1893.

Engineers and Firemen—Continued.			
John Davenport, fireman	$821 25	....	....
William Ledwith, fireman.......	821 25	....	....
Harry Meloy. fireman...........	590 25	....	....
Wm. J. Flock, asst. engineer.....	67 50	....	....
		$5,416 50	....
Carpenters—			
H. N. Moulton, state carpenter...	$1,080 00	....	....
Chas. Moll, asst. state carpenter.	532 90	....	....
Jacob Schwehm, asst. state carpenter...................	900 00		
		$2,512 90	....
Painters—			
Charles Dengler...............	$960 00	....	....
Wm. J. Schleicher....	723 33	....	....
		$1,683 33	....
Janitors and Messengers--			
E. E Alford, supreme court.....	$730 00	....	....
H. W. Bolte, bureau of labor statistics	730 00	....	....
Thos. Curley, board of control...	730 00	....	....
Henry Cummings, treasury agent	730 00	.. ..	....
Oscar Dorschel, land office	190 00	....	....
Chas. Ermatinger, art gallery .	730 00	....	....
Frank Erlich, supt. public property	730 00	....	....
Chas. Fauerbach, insurance com.'s office	730 00	....	....
James Glennon, adjt. gen.'s office	730 00	....	....
Frank H. Hubbard, water closet attendant	416 00	....	....
Ida Herfurth, attorney general's office	900 00	....	....
L. W. Joachim. insurance commissioner's office..............	960 00	....	....
John Kappel, historical rooms....	302 00	....	....
Dan Lavin, water closet attendant	302 00	....	....
Henry Lebeis, Jr., secretary of state's office.......	650 00	....	....
Henry L. Lueders, supt. public property office.	1,080 00	... .	....
R. J McCarl, Q M. gen'l office...	730 00	....	....
Joseph Malec, historical rooms....	428 00	....	....
Thomas Mills, law class room.....	730 00	....	....
Peter Nelson, railroad com's office	790 00	....	....
Louis Preuss agricultural rooms..	780 00	....	....
Geo. J. Reinsch, land office.......	424 00	....	....
Oscar Schubert, executive office..	730 00	....	....
John Scanlon, state supt.'s office..	402 00	....	....
Mike Tighe, board of control.. . ..	730 00	....	....
Chas. Todd, D. and F. Com's office.	730 00	.. ..	....
S. H. Tuttle, art gallery..........	670 00	....	....
Will Wells, state supt's office. ...	402 00	....	....
August Wandry, sec. of state's office	730 00	....	....
		$18,866 00	....

"A."—General Fund Disbursements for 1893.

Police—			
Christ Graesen...................	$220 00	....	....
J. H. Holcomb........	780 00	....	....
A. R. Jones	730 00	....	....
Thos. Kingston...................	730 00	....	....
L. Potter.	424 00	....	....
Charles Stevens............	730 00	....	....
James Whitty.	730 00	....	....
		$4,294 00	....
Night Watchmen—			
W. H. Hammersley.......	$730 00	....	....
Iver Jenson...	730 00	....	....
		$1,460 00	....
Laborers—			
James A. Patton, foreman........	$900 00	....	....
C. Amoth.........	660 00	....	....
H. R. Brewer.........	660 00	....	....
Fred Buergin	660 00	....	....
Mrs. Bradley................... ..	167 65	....	....
Felix Dushek	660 00	....	....
Mrs. Ennis	25 95	....	....
Mrs. Erbe.....................	167 10	....	....
Wm. Godenschwager............	730 00	....	....
Mrs. Kelley	147 50	....	....
John Lawlus.....................	660 00	....	....
Mary Lucas.....................	365 00	....	....
Fritz Meibaum	660 00	....	....
Dan McCloskey..................	673 78	....	....
Bridget McKenna	365 00	....	....
John O'Neil	798 00	....	....
August Pengsdorf....	660 00	....	....
Andrew J. Smith................	660 00	....	....
Mrs. Starkweather....	183 00	....	....
Anna Stemple. ....·......	365 00	....	....
Ole Togstad......	660 00	....	....
Frank Vollender	660 00	....	....
Mrs. Wiedenbeck...........	166 00	....	....
		$11,653 98	....
Miscellaneous.—			
C. F. Crane, book room attendant.	$225 00	....	....
M. C. Foley, steam and gas fitter.	821 25	....	....
Peter Hyland, elevator attendant.	730 00	....	....
H. C. Mumbrue, book room attendant	675 00	....	....
Charles McSorley, store keeper..	730 00	....	....
		$3,181 25	....
	... .		$49,067 96
TRANSIENT LABOR.			
M. Aminson......................	$565 94	....	....
Wm. Boorman...	782 50	....	....
J. Barry...........................	660 00	... .	....
J. Bush............................	135 05	....	....
J. D. Bradford	182 09	....	....

5–Sec'y.

"A."—General Fund Disbursements for 1893.

M. Brophy....	$2 95	....	....
Mrs. Augustine Beinewiss..........	92 50	....	....
M. Blankenheim..........	102 38	....	....
W. Behrnd......................	16 44	....	....
J. Brennan.....................	157 67	....	....
Wm. G. Barckhan................	185 00	... .	....
G. Barckhan....................	147 00	....	....
T. Casey......................	300 03	....	....
John Coners...................	89 15	... .	....
Barney Corcoran..............	219 90	....	.. ..
P. Carey......................	1 96	....	....
J. Daley...	150 60	....	....
M. Derenzo...................	14 66	....	....
Frank Dushek.................	6 88	....	....
M. Fury	22 85	....	....
John Fay.....................	186 50	....	....
James Fox....................	3 54	... .	....
A. Gannon	2 95	....	....
M. Gary	233 96	....	....
Thomas Good..................	73 18	....	....
Fred Getz....................	25 49	....	.. ..
John Garity..........	25 49	....	....
W. Hartsmier..........	43 08	....	....
J. Hoffman...................	782 50	....	....
H. Heinrichs.... ....\.........	249 75	....	....
S. Hanson....	655 68	....	....
T. Harrington..	142 32	... .	....
John Howards.................	71 41	....	....
Patrick Hogan.................	54 28	....	....
D. Hogerdy	18 27	....	....
W. Harrington...	27 50	... .	....
C. Hyland....................	94 50	....	....
Edwin Heick	68 68	....	....
W. Haley....................	183 29	....	....
J. Haley......................	12 89	....	....
John Hockey..................	3 93	....	....
N. Heins.....................	189 60	....	....
Nick Imec....................	27 26	....	....
John Kopp	36 49	....	....
John Kennedy.................	31 17	....	....
Fred Klein...................	94 50	....	....
T. Kavanaugh.................	24 51	....	....
H. Kroeger	15 75	....	....
Mrs. Kavanaugh..............	29 00	....	....
Wm. Lamp....................	488 25	....	....
T. Lally.....................:	565 94	....	... .
John Linde...................	239 37	....	.. ..
John Link....................	258 27	....	....
J. Link.......	97 38	....	....
D. McCluskey.................	5 00	....	....
James McGowan	61 11	....	..... • ••
John McCarthy................	14 76	....	....
Chas. McSorley	11 00	....	....
P. McGowan..................	2 95	....	....
H. Mueller...................	488 25	....	....
S. Morrell...................	565 05	....	... .
Aug. Meyer...................	73 95	....	....
Fred N. Moulton..............	625 00	....	....
P. Mibeck	1 77	... .	....

"A."—General Fund Disbursements for 1893.

Mrs. Macken	$ 50	....	....
V. Newman	565 04	....	....
P. Nerney	199 48	... .	
G Noyes........................	14 76	....	....
John O'Neil	2 00	....	....
M. O'Connell....................	58 35	....	....
Mrs. Oehlmiller....	6 00	....	....
J. Parrill.......................	38 25	....	....
J. Purcell	567 72	....	....
P. Phillips...	84 72	....	....
H. Pheney......................	45 49	....	....
T. Quinlan.....................	163 40	....	... .
M. Reynolds	1 96	... .	... .
L. Riker	1 77	....	....
J. Replinger	474 76	....	....
G. V. Roesch	361 70	....	....
Will Ring....	531 10	....	....
P. Ryan	14 67	....	....
L. Roman......................	5 82	... .	....
C. Roman	15 55	....	....
F. Repke.......................	18 31	....	....
C. Reinhold	98	....	....
H. Shott......................	328 38	....	....
Andy Sullivan......	65 44	....	....
G. Schmidt...................	43 02	....	....
W. Snow	14 67	....	....
H. Schmelzkopf	105 75	....	....
J. Scheicher....................	35 75	....	....
John Sullivan...................	26 58	....	....
Henry Sanger	131 63	....	....
Mrs. Starkweather...............	30 50	....	....
Annie Starweather	1 00	....	....
Mrs. Stemple	50	....	.. ....
D. Tranor	140 55	....	....
J. E. Utter....................	18 97	....	....
Mrs Wiedenbeck	3 50	....	....
John Wergin	349 98	....	....
Mrs. Zimmerman	64 05	....	... .
		$15,170 02	....

INCIDENTAL EXPENSES.

Chas Baumbach Co., mdse........	$803 00	....	....
H. Boelte Son, mdse..............	6 25	....	....
Peter Behrend, sprinkling.........	75 00	....	....
Badger Typewriter & Stationery Co. mdse	117 05	... ...	....
Bishoff Bros., mdse and labor.......	206 15	....	....
Francis Bresee mdse...............	33 10	....	....
Brittingham & Hixon, mdse	209 74	....	....
J. H. D. Baker & Co., mdse	47 06	....	....
Blind & Huegel, mdse.............	60	....	....
Blied Bros., mdse	47 90	....	.. ..
Butnam Furnace Co., mdse........	228 72	....	....
L. A. Brace, mdse.................	1 75	....	....
G. Barkhan, labor................	123 00	....	....
Bon Ton store, mdse	2 05	....	....
M. Brahany, mdse	24 75	....	....

"A."—General Fund Disbursements for 1893.

Bross & Quinn....	$9 50	....	....
Conklin & Son. mdse	76 00	....	....
Maurice Coughlin, mdse...........	91 45	....	....
M. J. Cantwell, mdse.............	50 00	....	....
C., M. & St. P. Ry. Co., freight.....	225 40	....	....
C. & N W. Ry. Co., freight........	86 44	....	....
T. A. Chapman Co., mdse...........	188 95	.. ..	....
John H. Clark and Clark's Drug Store, mdse	69 03	....	....
James Conlin, cartage........... ..	11 00	....	....
D. F. Conlin, cartage	84 79	....	....
Clement, Williams & Co., mdse.....	540 70	....	... .
Callaghan & Co , mdse.	83 00	....	....
Consolidated Time Lock Co., opening treasury vault	26 05	....	....
H. Christoffers & Co., mdse	72 49	....	....
M. J. Cantwell, ballot envelopes....	50 00	....	....
Conklin & Son, mdse	427 60	....	....
The Clasp Envelope Co., mdse......	16 75	....	....
A. Cox, mdse	8 00	... .	....
Barney Curren, mdse...	19 00	....	....
Cnare & Coyne, mdse...	14 04	....	....
T. H. Curtiss, labor................	12 13	....	....
H. Christoffers & Co., mdse........	10 49	....	....
John Damm, mdse.................	1 20	....	....
Dunning & Sumner, mdse	8 00	....	....
Thomas Davenport, mdse..........	80 50	....	....
Democrat Printing Co., mdse.......	224 15	....	....
Theo. F. Dresen. repairing clock ...	8 50	....	....
Des Forges & Co., mdse. Board of Control....	18 90	....	....
H. D. Delaney, mdse..........	29 40	....	....
John Delaney, mdse	7 86	....	....
A. B. Denson, labor	85	....	....
Eau Claire Grocery Co., mdse......	21 50	....	....
Four Lakes Light & Power Co., park lights	700 00	....	....
Wm. Frankfurth Hdw. Co.........	204 48	....	....
C. Forter, cartage............	25	....	....
James E. Fisher, mdse.....	11 00	....	....
N. Fredrickson & Sons, mdse.......	4 66	....	....
C. F. Ford. mdse	13 20	....	....
Marshall Field & Co	12 00	....	....
John Greig. mdse........	108 00	....	....
Goldsmith & Co.......	471 95	....	....
Gugler Lith Co., certificates of in corporation....................	142 05	....	.. ..
Goodyear Rubber Co., mdse	41 80	....	....
Gordon & Pannack, architectural designs	20 00	....	....
Gimbel Bros., mdse	510 95	....	....
H. C. Gerling, cartage.............	50	....	....
G. Grim, mdse...................	1 00	....	....
John D Hayes, blacksmithing. .. .	35 71	....	....
Theo. Hoeveler, repairing furniture.	219 40	....	....
L. C. Haley & Bro., mdse..........	89 00	....	....
Jos. Hussey, plumbing........	586 69	....	....

"A."—General Fund Disbursements for 1893.

Hoffmann Keefe Office File Co., mdse. for vaults	$6,612 50		
A. H. Hollister, mdse	10 55		
Hecht & Zummach, mdse	62 63		
Hall & McChesney, mdse	30 00		
J. B. Hoeger & Sons, mdse	422 64		
F. Huels, mdse	10 40		
James W. Harrington, sprinkling	75 00		
Jno. Hutchinson, mdse	172 50		
H. B. Hobbins, insurance	100 00		
John Hunner, cash paid Consolidated Time Lock Co	52 00		
Hale Elevator Co., mdse	211 72		
J. J. Heggins, mdse	3 00		
Jos. Hussey, mdse	195 56		
Joys Bros. & Co., mdse	52 75		
Krehl & Beck, mdse	123 04		
King & Walker Co., mdse	3 94		
Keeley, Neckerman & Kessenich, mdse	92 22		
Geo Kraft, mdse	72 09		
J. Knauber. Lith. Co., mdse	22 00		
Kelling & Klappenbach, mdse	20 63		
James Ledwith, blacksmithing	20 50		
Peter Lahm, cartage	114 85		
James Livesey, mason work	680 94		
John Larson & Co., mdse	89 00		
Lueders & Krouse, mdse	4 50		
Fredr'k Linn & Co., mdse	10 00		
Martin Lyons, blacksmithing	4 80		
Chas McSorley, labor	5 25		
Madison Hardware Co., mdse	237 82		
H. N. Moulton, cash for mdse	38 19		
Madison Water Works, water ex. residence	41 53		
E. Morden, mdse	5 00		
Andrew A. Mayers, mdse	3 28		
Madison Gas Light & Coke Co., mdse	40 02		
W. F. McConnell & Co., mdse	74 55		
Milwaukee Litho. & Engraving Co., mdse	258 50		
J. E Moseley, mdse	7 62		
James Morgan mdse	6 00		
Milwaukee Journal Co., newspaper	3 75		
H. Mooers Co., mdse	4 00		
H. Mann, assignee, mdse	284 83		
Wm. Moll, mdse	7 75		
Manville Covering Co., mdse	140 66		
Milwaukee Paste Co., mdse	17 25		
W. C. McConnell, mdse	57 70		
M. L. Nelson, mdse	113 80		
Newton & Lyons, blacksmithing	1 20		
Chas. H. Naffz, mdse	176 80		
T. A. Nelson, mdse	151 12		
Mrs. J. B. Nye, mdse	1 25		
H. Niedecken, mdse	216 07		
Olson & Jacobson, mdse	249 30		
Wm. Owen, plumbing ex. residence	1 80		

"A."—General Fund Disbursements for 1893.

Wm. Owen. mdse..	$9 77	....	....
J. E O'Keefe Co., mdse	77 45	.. ..	....
R. B. Ogilvie & Co., mdse..........	3,556 06	....	....
Roy Peck, electrical work	5 50	....	....
Chas. Presentin, Sr., repairing clock	3 00	....	....
R. L. Polk & Co., mdse.............	24 00	....	....
C. Preusser Jewelry Co., mdse......	16 00	....	....
Wm. J. Park & Sons, mdse	7 60	....	....
Frank D. Reed, services to Atty.			
General........................	8 10	....	....
Geo. J. Reinsch, mdse	1 73	....	....
Ramsay & Lerdall, mdse	18 09	....	....
B. O. Reily, labor	10 73	....	....
Ramsey & Lerdall, mdse	12 04	....	....
E. S. Reynolds, cartage and freight..	260 51	....	....
Sommers Bros , mdse	53 97	....	....
J. A. Swenson, mdse	23 46	....	....
C. R. Stein & Co., mdse	111 49	....	....
K. F. Steul, cartage	8 00	....	....
August Scheibel, mdse.	506 20	....	....
Fred Sperling, cartage.	9 50	....	.. ..
C. Suhr, cartage	50	....	....
J. W Scott, cartage	15 93	....	....
Sheasby & Smith, mdse	46 25	....	....
L J. Smith, mdse....	11 10	....	....
Spence & Foley, mdse..............	229 40	....	... .
Carl Schmidt, repairing...........	10 80	....	....
Silbernagle & Dean, mdse	205 69	... .	....
Schlimgen & Son, mdse	19 40	....	....
Schwaab Stamp & Seal Co., mdse..	21 80	....	....
W. W. Swinger, mdse..............	4 00	....	....
Sumner & Morris, mdse...	24 60	....	....
G. Scott, mdse.....	8 00	....	....
Edwin Sumner, mdse	3 50	....	....
J. H. Starck & Co., mdse	88 98	....	....
W. K. Stafford & Co , mdse	60, (0	....	... .
Silbernagle & Dean, mdse....	30 45	....	....
J. W. Thomas China Co., mdse... ..	37 75	....:.......	....
Mrs. D. H. Tullis, purchase 6 vols.			
sec'y's reports....	12 00	....	....
Wm. Theiss, mdse,...........	47 25	... .	. ...
Fritz Tente.....	60 00	....	....
Andrus Viall, labor..............	196 00	...:	....
J. G. Wagner, mdse...............	8 40	....	....
C. B. Whitnall, mdse.............	13 10	....	....
Wis. Bank Note & Lith. Co.,			
print'g, state board of control.....	212 10	....	....
West Publishing Co., mdse........	26 00	....	....
F. M. Wootton, assignee Lamont			
& Purcell. mdse	7 10	....	....
Chas. Wehrman, mdse....	3 90	....	... ...
Wyckoff, Seaman & Benedict,			
mdse...	192 00	....	....
Emanuel Weil & Co., mdse........	44 80	....	....
F. H. York, mdse........	65 00	....	....
		$25,148 33	... .

"A."—General Fund Disbursements for 1893.

PRINTING.

Democrat Printing Co.—
Printing blanks for

Governor	$49 29		
Secretary of state	1,062 82		
State treasurer	161 72		
Attorney general	184 98		
State superintendent	1,513 11		
Railroad commissioner	426 73		
Insurance commissioner	160 88		
Supreme court	96 87		
State library	225 50		
State historical society	595 30		
State land office	164 71		
Quartermaster general	83 70		
Adjutant general	239 97		
Supt. of public property	18 11		
Treasury agent	57 12		
State board of control	338 64		
Bureau of labor statistics	77 59		
State veterinarian	4 64		
Brief—State vs Cunningham	45 00		
Brief—State vs. McFetridge	8 00		
State prison	16 98		
State fish and game warden	7 33		

Report of

Secretary of state	$936 98		
State treasurer	221 91		
State agricultural society	1,909 20		
Board of university regents	144 36		
State board of control	640 86		
Adjutant general	66 58		
Normal school regents	107 95		
Proceedings state historical society	1,331 64		
Commissioners of public lands	57 75		
Milwaukee hospital for insane	111 20		
Washburn observatory	202 55		
Several charitable and penal institutions	39 00		
Dairy and food commissioner	1,470 75		
State board of health	402 69		
State oil inspector	38 57		
State superintendent	649 12		
Wisconsin fish commission	110 41		
Railroad commissioner	549 11		
Quartermaster general	50 32		
Wisconsin national guard	218 54		
Bank statements	566 02		
County superintendents to state superintendent	65 62		
List of books, Wis. Auth. world's fair and state historical society	16 30		
Bulletin No. 32 experiment station	388 45		
Insurance commissioner	104 65		

"A."—General Fund Disbursements for 1893.

Democrat Printing Co.—Continued.			
Fish and game laws..............	$10 25	....	....
Assessment laws.........	104 61	....	....
General charter law..............	174 18	....	... .
Laws of special session....... ...	1,875 75	....	....
Laws of 1893	3,872 51	....	....
Report Wisconsin dairymen's association	768 15	....	....
Supplement to election laws	68 45	....	....
Report bureau of labor statistics..	1,184 70	....	....
Election registers.. ....'.	693 78	....	....
Report agricultural experiment station........................	54 80	....	... .'.
Arbor day circulars..............	154 73	....	... .'.
Bibliography of Wisconsin authors	365 81	....	....
		$25,291 19	....

POSTAGE.

Madison Post Office, stamps for—			
Governor.	$219 00	....	....
Secretary of state................	752 00	....	....
State treasurer	463 00	....	....
Land department.......	855 10	....	... .
State superintendent	1,282 00	....	....
Superintendent public property ..	83 00	....	....
Attorney general	35 55	....	....
Railroad commissioner...	106 28	....	....
Insurance commissioner	414 25	....	....
Adjutant general	288 00	....	....
Quartermaster general	105 25	....	....
Supreme court	262 50	....	....
State board of control............	355 80	....	....
State librarian...................	55 00	....	....
State historical society	383 50	....	....
Treasury agent	84 20	... .	....
State agricultural society.........	139 50	....	....
Bureau of labor statistics.......	324 10	....	....
State fish and game warden......	29 50	....	....
Dairy and food commissioner	165 00	....	....
Drawer rent....	152 00	....	....
Werner Presentin, postage for governor.....................	3 00	....	....
		$6,054 03	....

WESTERN UNION TELEGRAPH CO.

Telegrams for—			
Adjutant general	$17 25	....	....
Attorney general	50 30	....	....
Dairy and food commissioner.....	2 60	....	....
Executive office..................	140 60	....	....
Insurance commissioner..........	63 45	....	....
Quartermaster general...........	23 20	....	... .
Railroad commissioner	27 80	... ...	....
Secretary of state	76 25	....	....
State board of control............	23 25	....	....
State land department	75	....	....

"A."—General Fund Disbursements for 1893.

Telegrams for—Continued.

State superintendent........... .	$16 55	... .	....
State treasurer................., ..	15 05	....	....
State treasury agent..	3 75	....	....
Superintendent public property...	1 75	....	....
Bureau of labor statistics........	25	....	....
State librarian	65	....	....
		$463 45	....

WISCONSIN TELEPHONE CO.

Messages for—

Executive office...	$244 40	....	....
Secretary of state .. .'	68 85	....	....
State board of control	70 65	....	....
State treasurer	1 00	....	....
Attorney general...	1 55	....	....
Railroad commissioner...........	50 00	....	....
Supt public property.............	50 00	....	....
		$481 45	....
			$7,001 93

EXPRESSAGE.

American Express Co.—Expressage for—

Attorney general...............	$1 35	....	....
Adjutant general...............	6 35	....	....
Academy of sciences, arts and letters...	30 54	....	....
Bureau of labor statistics........	143 75	....	....
Dairy and food commissioner....	157 48	....	....
Executive office................	9 89	....	... .
Insurance commissioner.........	7 57	....	....
Quartermaster general...........	312 30	....	....
Secretary of state................	512 48	....	....
State treasurer	19 73	....	....
State superintendent.............	177 35	....	... .
State library.....................	6 46	....	....
State land office.....	1 05	....	.'............
Supt. of public property.........	228 49	....	....
State agricultural society	127 55	....	....
State board of control....'.......	28 08	....	....
State historical society.....	5 60	....	..'..........
Railroad commissioner...........	18 34	....	....
		$1,794 36	....

Adams Express Co.—Expressage for—

Attorney general	$ 65	....	....
Adjutant general	1 70	....	....
Academy of sciences, arts and letters	21 21	....	....
Bureau of labor statistics........	41 84	....	....
Dairy and food commissioner....	34 27	....	....
Governor's office.............	1 60	....	....
Insurance commissioner.........	2 53	....	....
Quartermaster general...........	17 83	....	....
Railroad commissioner	1 43	....	....

"A."—General Fund Disbursements for 1893.

*Adams Express Co.—Expressage for—*Continued.			
Secretary of state................	$186 73	....	....
State treasurer.	1 50	....	....
State superintendent	115 28	....	....
State library	70 54	....	....
State land office	25	....	....
Supt. public property.	114 76	....	....
State agricultural society........	97 63	....	....
State board of control..........	21 60	....	....
State historical society	29 40	....	....
John Hunner, on Plattville and Waupaca bonds....	3 50	....	....
John Hunner, on remittance, Wis. F. & M. bank................	10 00	....	....
		$774 25	....
	....		$2,568 61
PAPER.			
H. Niedecken Co., on contract.....	....	$15,467 49	....
STATIONERY.			
Badger Typewriter & Stationery Co.	$187 57	....	....
M. J. Cantwell................	275 00	....	....
Dunning & Sumner..............	1 50	....	....
Democrat Printing Co...	2 50	....	....
Des Forges & Co	17 75	....	....
Wm. Frankfurth Hardware Co.....	242 81	....	....
The Gugler Lithographing Co.....	133 40	....	....
J. B. Hoeger & Co.......	2,709 82	....	....
J. Krueger	108 00	....	....
J. Knauber Lithographing Co......	683 95	....	....
Julius Lando....	4 50	....	....
Madison Hardware Co.............	134 13	....	....
John Morris Co.................	1 20	....	....
Martin Madson & Co...	47 60	....	....
J. E. Moseley..	3 75	....	....
H. Niedecken Co	374 53	....	....
Wm. J. Park & Sons...	1 18	....	....
J. G. Rider....................	5 00	....	....
August Scheibel............	14 00	....	....
Wilmanns Bros....	35 00	....	....
Wis. Bank Note & Litho. Co	132 75	....	....
Franz Wollaeger................	103 00	....	....
		$5,218 94	....
GAS.			
Madison Gas Light & Coke Co......	....	$5,666 85	....
FUEL.			
Conklin & Son....................	$521 71	....	....
E. C. Hammersley..............	149 50	....	....
Philadelphia & Reading Coal & Iron Co....	4,475 64	....	....
		$5,146 85	....

"A."—General Fund Disbursements for 1893.

TREASURY AGENT.

Thomas Kennedy, percentage on peddlers' licenses...............	....	$3,808 04	....

COMPILING WAR RECORDS.

H. C. Allen	$1,380 00	....	....
Theo. F. Ballring..................	345 00	....	....
Lena Bresee....	210 00	....	....
F. W. Grumm............	460 00	....	....
O. S. Holum	345 00	....	....
Joe. H. Janda	1,380 00	....	....
Gustav A. Kuechle................	230 00	....	....
Agnes L. Morrissey................	770 00	....	....
Mary W. Priestly........	840 00	....	....
Louis Ungrodt...........	345 00	....	....
		$6,305 00	....

MILITIA.

Louis Auer & Sons, insurance on buildings at Camp Douglas	$50 00	....	.
Amory Riding School, service of horses at Milwaukee fire.........	22 00	....	....
Appleton Light Infantry, armory fund.......	300 00	....	....
Appleton Light Infantry, uniform fund....	275 00	....	....
Henry V. Allien & Co. mdse. W. N G.	623 00	....	....
Will Allds, subsistence, W. N. G....	62 22	....	....
David Adjer & Sons, clothing, W. N. G	755 25	....	....
D. H. Brown, pension clerk	1,380 00	....	....
M. U. Burns. pay W. N. G	7 00	....	....
E. S. borroughs, pay W. N. G......	6 67	....	....
Badger State Rifles, armory fund..	300 00	....	....
Badger St·te Rifles, uniform fund..	230 00	....	....
Beaver Dam Guards, armory fund..	300 00	....	....
Beaver Dam Guards. uniform fund.	275 00	....	....
Beloit City Guards, armory fund...	300 00	....	....
Beloit City Guards, uniform fuud..	240 00	....	....
L. W. Brown, labor W. N. G......	57 00	....	....
Chas. Baumbach Co., mdse W. N. G.	42 13	....	....
M. H. Ball. mdse W. N. G	26 00	....	....
R. G. Buglas, service on board of survey.....	8 44	....	....
J. Brusnam, mdse. W. N. G.......	30 00	....	....
J. H. D. Baker, mdse. W. N G.....	21 20	....	....
L. Buffmeier labor and mdse. W. N. G.	109 12	....	....
Wm. L. Buck, expenses inspecting W. N. G.................	505 10	....	....
James Babcock, labor on military reservation...................	26 00	....	....
C. L. Clark, military secretary salary	405 47	....	....
C., M. & St. Paul Ry. Co , transportation W. N. G.............	3,940 03	....	....

"A."—General Fund Disbursements for 1893.

C., M. & St. Paul Ry. Co., freight W. N. G.	$152 99		
C. & N. W. Ry. Co., freight W. N. G.	116 69		
C. & N. W. Ry. Co., transportation W. N. G.	3,113 49		
C., St. Paul, M. & O. Ry. Co., transportation W. N. G.	38 06		
Fred. P. Cook, pay W. N. G.	6 67		
John H. Clark, mdse. W. N. G.	11 05		
Custer Rifles, armory fund	300 00		
Custer Rifles, uniform fund.	285 00		
Chapman Guards, armory fund	300 00		
Chapman Guards, uniform fund	260 00		
Capt. P. H. Conly, pay w. N. G.	14 00		
Jos. B. Doe, adj. general, salary	2,027 39		
Jos. B. Doe, adj. general, expenses	410 00		
Jos. B. Doe, adj. general, books	90 00		
Jos. B. Doe, adj. general, publishing notice organization Co. M., 3rd Reg	7 75		
Dyer Saddlery Company, mdse. Q. M. G.	21 00		
Darlington Rifles, armory fund	300 00		
Darlington Rifles, uniform fund	280 00		
Drake Bros., mdse. Q. M. G.	1 62		
Eau Claire Light Guards, armory fund	300 00		
Eau Claire Light Guards, uniform fund	240 00		
Evergreen City Guards, armory fund	300 00		
Evergreen City Guards, uniform fund	265 00		
Harry W. Ellis, labor W. N. G	35 00		
Jacob M. Everly, 2nd Lieut. L. H. Squadron W. N. G.	27 12		
Otto H. Falk, Q. M. G. salary	631 74		
Otto H. Falk, Q. M. G. expenses	125 14		
First Light Battery, extra horse hire.	300 00		
First Light Battery, armory fund	300 00		
First Light Battery, uniform fund	260 00		
Fond du Lac Guards, armory fund.	300 00		
Fond du Lac Guards, uniform fund.	325 00		
Capt. H. S. Fuller, pay inter state rifle contest	24 24		
J. J. Foley, pay inter state rifle contest	6 67		
Wm. Frankfurth Hardware Co., mdse. Q. M. G	24 17		
Capt. W. J. Grant, pay and sub. L. H. Squadron W. N. G	588 18		
Capt. George Graham, pay interstate rifle contest	30 84		
Capt. Wm. A. Grimmer, pay interstate rifle contest	7 00		
James Gibson, pay inter-state rifle contest	7 00		

"A."—General Fund Disbursements for 1893.

J. G. Graham, pay inter-state rifle contest	$6 67	....
Capt. W. J. Grant, L. H. squadron expenses and transportation ded exercises at World's Fair	247 50	....
Guppy Guards, armory fund	300 00	....
Guppy Guards, uniform fund......	270 00	....
Griffin Rifles, armory fund.........	300 00	....
Griffin Rifles, uniform fund	245 00	....
Governor's Guards, La Crosse, armory fund ....:	300 00	....
Governor's Guards, La Crosse, uniform fund....	325 00	....
Governor's Guard, Madison, armory fund	300 00	....
Governor's Guards, Madison, uniform fund............	370 00	........·.... ....
John Greig. mdse. W. N. G	$5 25	....
Gray Graham, mdse. W. N. G	23 50	....
John Gallagher, labor W. N. G....	22 50	....
L. E. Gleason & Son, mdse. W. N. G....................	115 19	
J. H. Hardy, custodian rifle range..	720 00	....
J. H. Hardy, labor W. N G	7 35	....
Elmer Hamilton, pay inter-state rifle contest....................	7 66	....
W. H. Hammon, pay inter state rifle contest	7 00	....
Hudson City Guards, armory fund..	300 00	....
Hudson City Guards, uniform fund.	245 00	....
Hoard Rifles, armory fund.........	300 00	....
Hoard Rifles, uniform fund.......	270 00	....
F. Huels, repairing and mdse. Q. M. G....................	77 00	....
W. T. Hardy, labor W. N. G........	50 75	....
C. H. Hoton, mdse. W. N. G.........	41 07	....
John C. Henry, mdse. W. N. G.....	45 00	....
Hinrichs & Thompson, mdse. W. N. G.	17 04	....
Illinois Central Railway Co., transportation W. N G...............	1 11	....
O. R. Jackson, pay inter-state rifle contest....................	6 67	....
Janesville Light Infantry, armory fund............................	300 00	....
Janesville Light Infantry, uniform fund............................	230 00	....
S. E. Jones, firing salute Washington's birthday....................	10 00	....
D. R. Jones, mdse. Q. M. G.........	13 75	....
Joys Bros. & Co., mdse. W. N. G....	14 00	....
Capt. Geo. H. Joachin, pay and sub. Co. I, w. N. G. special duty.......	113 79	....
Capt. J B. Kerr, inspector W. N. G.	238 30	....
Robt. A. Kane, pay inter-state rifle contest.......................	6 67	....

"A."—General Fund Disbursements for 1893.

E. H. Kehr, pay inter-state rifle contest	$6 67		
Kosciusko Guards, armory fund	800 00		
Kosciusko Guards, uniform fund	250 00		
Krull & Volger, mdse. W. N. G	79 60		
Joseph Kalt, subsistence W. N. G., Milwaukee fire	23 10		
J. E. Lambert, pay inter-state rifle contest	6 67		
Light Horse Squadron, armory fund	800 00		
Light Horse Squadron, uniform fund	200 00		
Ludington Guards, armory fund	300 00		
Ludington Guards, uniform fund	250 00		
Lincoln Guards, armory fund	300 00		
Lincoln Guards, uniform fund	220 00		
The M. C. Lilly Co., mdse.. W.N.G.	133 50		
W. B. McPherson, asst. adjt. gen., salary	1,380 00		
W B. McPherson, engraving marksmen's buttons	4 00		
Della McCarl, labor, W. N. G	35 50		
Wm. J. McMann, labor, W N. G.	23 38		
William Mahoney, salary, asst. Q. M. G.	1,380 00		
William Mahoney, expenses for labor, freight and material	1,516 69		
Manitowoc Volunteers, armory fund	300 00		
Manitowoc Volunteers, uniform fund	265 00		
Marinette Guards, armory fund	300 00		
Marinette Guards, uniform fund	225 00		
Mauston Light Guards, armory fund	300 00		
Mauston Light Guards, unif'rm fund	270 00		
Monroe City Guards, armory fund	300 00		
Monroe City Guards. uniform fund.	315 00		
Madison Hardware Co., mdse., W. N. G	15 06		
James Morgan, mdse., W. N. G.	150 02		
John C. Ohnstad, pay inter state rifle contest	19 33		
Ole J Olson, pay inter state rifle contest	6 67		
Oconto Centennial Rifles, armory fund	300 00		
Oconto Centennial Rifles, uniform fund	325 00		
Oshkosh Rifles, armory fund	300 00		
Oshkosh Rifles. uniform fund	280 00		
Oshkosh Guards, armory fund	300 00		
Oshkosh Guards. uniform fund	270 00		
J. A. Older, labor, W. N. G.	9 86		
Chas. M. Parsons, pay inter-state rifle contest	6 67		
Pabst Guards, armory fund	300 00		
Pabst Guards. uniform fund	260 00		
F. F. Proudfit, paymaster general 1st Reg. W. N. G.	7,041 52		

"A."—General Fund Disbursements for 1893.

F. F. Proudfit, paymaster general 2nd Reg. W. N. G.	$9,882 08		
F. F. Proudfit, paymaster general 3rd Reg W. N. G.	10,230 17		
F. F. Proudfit, paymaster general 4th Reg. W. N. G.	5,964 90		
F. F Proudfit, paymaster general Light Horse Squadron W. N. G..	307 64		
F. F. Proudfit, paymaster general, expenses.	4 15		
F. F. Proudfit. paymaster general First Light Battery, W. N. G....	712 65		
W. J. Park & Sons, mdse. W. N. G.	24 00		
Pettybone mfg. Co., mdse. W. N. G.	155 73		
Capt. Thos. J. Rogers, pay inter-state rifle contest	7 00		
Racine Light Guards, armory fund.	300 00		
Racine Light Guards, uniform fund.	215 00		
Rankin Guards, armory fund	300 00		
Rankin Guards, uniform fund	235 00		
Ripon Rifles, armory fund	300 00		
Ripon Rifles, uniform fund	195 00		
Rusk Guards, armory fund	300 00		
Rusk Guards, uniform fund	335 00		
Gen. J. N. Reece, adj. gen. Ill. N. G., ⅓ share medals	16 66		
Ramsay & Lerdall. mdse. W. N. G..	6 00		
Capt Thos. J. Rodgers, services on pay roll 1st infantry	14 00		
First Lieut. John G. Salsman, pay Light Horse Squadron	28 93		
C. E. Schultz, pay inter-state rifle contest	6 67		
Frank A. Sullivan, pay inter state rifle contest	19 32		
August Scheibel, mdse. Q. M. G....	16 79		
K. F. Steul, freight and cartage Q. M. G.	106 00		
Sparta Rifles, armory fund	300 00		
Sparta Rifles, uniform fund	210 00		
Sheridan Guards, armory fund	300 00		
Sheridan Guards, uniform fund	210 00		
Sherman Guards, armory fund	300 00		
Sherman Guards, uniform fund	290 00		
John Singleton, mdse. W. N. G...	191 47		
Mrs. John Singleton, mdse. W. N. G.	273 00		
J. F. Stillman, mdse. W. N. G.	1 10		
Chas. Stickney, labor rifle range...	19 66		
H. Strelow, labor, Q. M. G.	7 50		
M. Thierbach & Co., mdse. W. N. G	38 75		
Chas. H. Tucker, pay inter state rifle contest	6 67		
Tomah Guards, armory fund	300 00		
Tomah Guards, uniform fund	240 00		
C. J. Van Etta, pay inter-state rifle contest	7 00		
Chas. R. Williams, asst Q M.G.. salary	225 50		
Chas. R. Williams, labor Q. M. G...	596 25		

"A."—General Fund Disbursements for 1893.

Chas. R. Williams. expense Q. M G.	$72 07		
Wisconsin Central Lines, transportation W. N. G.	4 74		
John R. Winkler, pay and subsistence W. N. G. encampment.	859 46		
Lt. Chas R. Williams, sub. and pay inter state rifle contest	153 32		
W. F. Winsor, pay inter state rifle contest	8 88		
Wausau Light Guards, armory fund	800 00		
Wausau Light Guards, uniform fund	810 00		
J. B Whiting, labor W. N. G.	26 52		
Gordon H. Winsor, inspecting W. N G.	252 98		
J. N. Washburn, blacksmithing	19 90		
Chas. Wehrman, labor Q. M. G.	8 50		
Capt. Oscar Zwietusch, pay inter-state rifle contest	27 18		
Capt. Oscar Zwietusch expenses, dedicatory exercises at World's Fair	21 78		
		$82,459 79	

WISCONSIN RIFLE RANGE.

L. Buffmeier, labor	$852 00		
L. W. Brown. labor	895 00		
J. H. Hardy, labor and mdse	19 63		
Dwight Hodges, labor and mdse	11 25		
W. T. Hardy, labor	81 50		
Robert L. Hanson, labor	26 38		
Henry Miner, labor	24 00		
John Singleton, labor and mdse.	369 74		
Reinhard Schroeder, labor	248 00		
George Wonderly, labor	169 50		
Wisconsin Telephone Co., telephone service	57 60		
		$2,204 59	

EXAMINERS OF STATE TEACHERS.

C. R. Barnes	$128 00		
R. H. Halsey	205 66		
A. J. Hutton	184 21		
		$517 87	

EXAMINERS FOR ADMISSION TO BAR.

Geo. G. Green	$133 30		
L. J. Rusk	215 10		
A. L. Sanborn	74 90		
Joshua Stark	105 38		
Moses M. Strong	256 52		
		$785 20	

"A."—General Fund Disbursements for 1893.

GOVERNOR'S CONTINGENT FUND.

Geo. W. Peck...................	$2,147 96	....	....
		$2,147 96	....

VETERINARY SURGEON.

Dr. F. J. Toussaint, salary..........	$2,000 00	....	....
Dr. F. J. Toussaint. expenses.......	2,594 01	....	....
Dr. F. J. Toussaint, experiments....	1,049 00	....	....
Dr. Geo. H. Bartoe, consultation with state veterinarian	20 00	....	....
Dr. P. H. Clute, consultation with state veterinarian..............	7 00	....	....
Dr. W. P. Freeman, consultation with state veterinarian......... ..	85 00	....	....
Dr. B. F. Holmes, consultation with state veterinarian..............	7 00	....	....
Dr. J. P. Lane, consultation with state veterinarian..	7 00	....	....
Dr. M. F. Leffingwell, consultation with state veterinarian...........	10 40	....	....
Dr. W. P. Morten, consultation with state veterinarian................	7 00	....	....
Dr. F. Wrigglesworth, consultation with state veterinarian..........	7 00	....	....
		$5,743 41	....

GLANDERED HORSES SLAUGHTERED

E. Ackerman...............	$33 33	....	....
Chas. Burgess.....................	26 66	... .	....
Buegel & Hellberg.................	33 33	....	....
F. J Curry.......................	10 00	....	....
Richard Dorgan...................	66 66	....	....
E. Dunham.......................	100 00	....	....
Wm. Diamond.....................	33 33	....	....
Thos. Deehame....................	33 33	....	....
Capt. E. J. Day...................	33 33	....	....
Julius Dohm............	100 00	....	....
Gill Ellis........................	33 33	....	....
T. Edwards	66 66	....	....
Harvey Gehring...................	33 53	....	....
Joe Germain	50 00	....	....
F. Hankwitz......................	33 33	....	....
Henry Herman	96 66	....	....
D. W. Howie.....................	33 33	....	....
O. P. Hanson..................	10 00	....	....
Kittell & Jacobs	33 33	... .	....
A. Oligney.....................:	100 00	....	....
John Larson	33 33	... .	....
Rolf Melling.....................	33 33	....	....
Madson & Anderson	33 33	....	....
H. F. Muzzy...	33 33	....	....
Wm. Ott.........................	66 66	....	....
Louis Oligney...	66 66	....	....
Henry Rhode.....................	33 33	....	....
A. S. Stiles......................	33 33	....	....
Chas. Seymer....................	33 33	....	....

6—Sec'y.

"A."—General Fund Disbursements for 1893.

H. Thorne.....................	$33 33	....	....
Warren Underhill................	66 66	....	....
Eb. Wright...........	66 66	....	....
Wm. Worthanoske...	33 33	... .	....
Jos. Waters	33 33	....	... .
Arthur Wilson..................	26 66	....	....
Sam Wright.............	33 33		
		$1,659 87	....

STATE FISH AND GAME WARDEN.

D. W. Fernandez, salary...	$1,450 00	....	....
D. W. Fernandez, expenses.........	580 12	....	....
D. W. Fernandez, contingent ex-			
penses.........................	354 47	....	....
		$2,384 59	....

ILLUSTRATIONS REPORT AGRICULT-
URAL EXPERIMENTAL STATION.

Binner Engraving Co., engraving			
plates and maps..................	$216 15	....	....
Hugh Boyd.......................	5 50	....	....
A. L. Hatch, illustrations	2 75	....	....
N. P. Jones. labor and material....	5 00	....	....
Milwaukee Lithographing & Engrav-			
ing Co., mdse........	135 00	....	... ...
F. Pecher, photographs	18 00	... .	....
W. L. Woodward, drafting.........	6 00		
		$388 40	....

EX-STATE TREASURERS' SUITS.

R. M. Bashford, attorney fees	$7,500 00	....	....
Wm Fehlandt, clerk circuit court,			
Dane county, fees.............	198 45	... .	....
Chas. W. Mead, sheriff Dane county,			
fees	549 84	... .	....
		$8,248 29	....

PUBLISHING AND ADVERTISING.

Democrat Printing Co.............	$14 00	....	....
The Milwaukee Journal Co.........	170 75	....	....
W. J. P. McFail...................	51 15	....	....
Madison Times.	53 20	....	....
Times Printing Co.................	363 70	... .	....
		$657 80	....

PUBLISHING GENERAL LAWS.

Henry Arnold, Chilton Demokrat...	$100 00	....	....
Axtell Bros, Pepin Star............	100 00	....	....
C. F. Augustin, Menasha Press......	100 00	....	....
H. C. Aushbaugh, Eau Claire Free			
Press.......................	100 00	....	... .
E. E. Atherton, Albany Vindicator.	100 00	....	....
C. J. Augustine, Glenwood Tribune.	100 00	....	....

"A."—General Fund Disbursements for 1893.

Ashland News Co	$100 00		
Allen & Weidner, Oshkosh Telegraph	100 00		
A. M. Anderson, Grantsburg Sentinel	100 00		
Abend Post Pub. Co., Milwaukee	200 00		
L. C. Bold, Shawano Wochenblatt	100 00		
Chas. A. Booth. Monroe Sentinel	100 00		
H. L. Brown, Darlington Journal	100 00		
W. H. Bennett. Edgerton Index	100 00		
E. N. Bowers, Bloomer Advance	100 00		
W. M. Barnum, New London Tribune	100 00		
L. G. Blaire, Boscobel Leader	100 00		
F. H. Brady, Wittenberg Leader and Clintonville Tribune	200 00		
James A. Barager, Cadotte Blade	100 00		
E. J. Browne, Elva Recorder	100 00		
F. C. Blied & Co., Madison Botschafter	100 00		
Badour & Noel, Marinette Argus	100 00		
Bolens & Krause, Pt. Washington Star	100 00		
D. Blumenfeld & Son, Watertown Weltbuerger	100 00		
C. H. Bissell, Montello Express	100 00		
J. B. Beach, Whitehall Times	100 00		
S. W. Brown. West Salem Journal	100 00		
M. H. Barnum, Wausau Torch of Liberty	100 00		
Badger & Tubbes, Elkhorn Blade and Palmyra Enterprise	200 00		
Abija Bresee, Montford Monitor	100 00		
Chas. F. Bone, Rice Lake Times	100 00		
Chas. F. Barnes, Rhinelander Vindicator	100 00		
Curry G. Bell, Bayfield Press	100 00		
P. H. Bolger, Waterloo Democrat	100 00		
E. R. Barager, Washburn Itemizer	100 00		
Banner Pub Co, Clinton Banner	100 00		
C. H. Browne & Co., La Crosse "La Crosse"	100 00		
M. G. Bohan, Port Washington Advertiser	100 00		
E. R. Beebe, Princeton Republic	100 00		
B. J. Bennett. Mineral Point Tribune	100 00		
Banner und Volksfreund, Milwaukee, Banner und Volksfreund	100 00		
Barnes Bros , Darlington Democrat and Register	100 00		
J. R. Bloom, Fond du Lac Journal	100 00		
Geo. D. Cline, Hudson True Republican	100 00		
D. M. Carter, Wonewoc Reporter	100 00		
Citizen Co., Catholic Citizen, Milwaukee	100 00		
Dan L. Camp, Mukwonago Chief	100 00		
Columbia Pub. Co., Milwaukee Columbia	100 00		

"A."—*General Fund Disbursements for 1893.*

Charles S. Crosse, Stoughton Hub..	$100 00	....	....
Adolph Candrian, La Crosse Nord-Stern..................	100 00	....	....
L. W. Chapman, Plainfield Sun....	100 00	....	....
R. R. Crowe, Wonewoc Local......	100 00	....	....
J. Lute Christie, Superior Times....	100 00	....	....
Crawford Bros., Iowa County Democrat	100 00	....	....
Joe M. Chapple, Ashland Weekly Press	100 00	....	... .
F. W. Coon, Edgerton Reporter....	100 00	....	....,.......
R. W. Cheever, Clinton Herald.....	100 00	....	....
J. C. Cedarburg, Superior Svenska Tribunen	100 00	....	....
A. P. Colby, Union Grove Enterprise	100 00	....	....
Frank A. Carr, Dodgeville Sun	100 00	....	....
Commonwealth Printing Co., Fond du Lac Commonwealth	100 00	....	....
Al. Creutz, Milwaukee Advertiser..	100 00	....	....
P. H. Carney, Waukesha Democrat.	100 00	....	....
Geo. F. Cooper, Black River Falls Banner............	100 00	....	....
Charlton & Hanford, Brodhead Independent....................	100 00	....	....
Call Pub. Co., Superior Call	100 00	....	....
Frank L. Clark, Augusta Times ...	100 00	....	....
Chippewa Valley Pub. Co., Chippewa Times	100 00	....	....
Jed W. Coon, Tomahawk Blade ...	100 00	...........·...	.. ..
Frank Cully, Kenosha Gazette......	100 00	....	....
E. D. Coe, Whitewater Register....	100 00	....	....
Decker, Hoppe & Dockery, Green Bay Advocate	100 00	...........·	....
Ernest A. Dunn, Merrill News	100 00	.......·...	....
C. H. Dunn, Hillsborough Sentry...	100 00	....	....
W. H. Dawley. Antigo Special	100 00	....	....
T. K. Dunn, Elroy Tribune	100 00	..........·.	....
R. W. Davis, Bangor Independent..	100 00	....	....
J. W. DeGroff, Marshfield Times...	100 00	....	....
L. E. Davis, Berlin Courant	100 00	....	....
Democrat Printing Co., Madison....	100 00	....	....
W. R. Devor, Burlington Free Press	100 00	....	....
Demokrat Printing Co , Sheboygan Demokrat..................	100 00	....	....
Democrat Publishing Co., Depere..	100 00	......· ...	....•.......
E. S. Doolittle, Elsworth Herald....	100 00	....	....
E. W. & A. G. Dankoeler, Milwaukee Saturday Star ... .,...	100 00	....	....
J. R. Decker, Columbus Republican.	100 00	....	....
Despatch Publishing Co., Waukesha Despatch..	100 00	....	
L. H. Doyle, Rio Reporter.......	100 00	....	....
F. A. Dean, Blanchardville Blade ..	100 00	....	....
P. V. Deuster Co., Milwaukee Telephone..........	100 00	....	....
Eagle Printing Co., Marinette Eagle	100 00	...........·.	....
C. C. Eaton, Columbus Democrat...	100 00	....	....

"A."—General Fund Disbursements for 1893.

P. O. Evenson, La Crosse Varden...	$100 00		
Excelsior Pub. Co., Milwaukee Excelsior..........................	100 00		
H. R. Erichson, Kewaunee county Banner and New Era.............	200 00		
Ellerson & Berrey, Wautoma Argus	100 00		
Otto Elander, Ashland Freiheit	100 00		
A. A. Emmel, Barneveld Register and Friend	100 00		
Thos. Everill, Verona Enquirer	100 00		
C. H. Ellsworth & Co., Ripon Commonwealth	100 00		
Frank A. Flower, Superior Leader..	100 00		
Freidenker Pub. Co., Freidenker and Turnzeitung...................	200 00		
Carl Fehlandt, Port Washington Zeitung.....................	100 00		
Arthur Frankenburg, West Bend Democrat and Beobachter........	200 00		
A. L. Fontaine, Grand Rapids Reporter	100 00		
H. W. Frick, Janesville Journal....	100 00		
M. G. Fallow, Oconomowoc Democrat	100 00		
C.M. Fairchild, Marinette North Star	100 00		
M. C. French, Eau Claire Forum....	100 00		
W. R. Finch, La Crosse Republican and Leader...................	100 00		
A. L. Falbe, Racine Correspondent.	100 00		
Forbes & Son, Westfield Union.....	100 00		
W. M. Fogo, Richland Center Republican and Observer...	100 00		
M. A. Frissell, Avery Free Press....	100 00		
Family Friend Pub Co., Janesville Republican Signal	100 00		
R. B. Frederick, Cross Plains Arrow	100 00		
John Foley, Cassville Index........	100 00		
Adolph Fisher, Kenosha Volksfreund.....	100 00		
John G. Foulds, Arcadia Leader....	100 00		
Flint & Weber, Menomonie News...	100 00		
C. W. Fraser, Menomonie Falls News..........................	100 00		
Mrs. Rosamund Follett, Green Bay Gazette.......................	100 00		
Jessie S. Field, Prescott Tribune....	100 00		
W. T. Gilds, Monroe Gazette.......	100 00		
Gowdy & Goodell, Hurley Miner ...	100 00		
Miles T. Gettings, Monroe Sun......	100 00		
Alletta D. Goodhue, Trempealeau Herald	100 00		
E. D. Glennon, Stevens Point Gazette	100 00		
Geo. W. Goldsmith, Boscobel Dial..	100 00		
R. H. Gile, Merrillan Leader........	100 00		
Geo. G. Gilkey, Eau Claire Gazette.	100 00		
Carl Gebhard, Madison Staatz Zeitung	100 00		

"A."—General Fund Disbursements for 1893.

German Printing Co., Menomonie Nord Stern	$100 00	
E. F. Ganz, Alma Journal	100 00	
Geo. G. Gaskell, Argryle Atlas	100 00	
F. B. Gregg, Superior Wave	100 00	
O. Gaffron, Plymouth Reporter	100 00	
Gegenwart Co., Appleton Gegenwart	100 00	
Arthur Gough, Catholic Sentinel	100 00	
Gorham Bros., Shawano Journal	100 00	
Ed Goebel, Antigo Herold	100 00	
Gazette Printing Co., Janesville Gazette	100 00	
F. H. Graves, Viroqua Leader	100 00	
W. L. Houser, Mondovi Herald	100 00	
Carl W. Honigmann, Merrill Anzeiger	100 00	
Alex. W. Horn, Cedarburg News	100 00	
Howe & Rothe, Fennimore Times Review	100 00	
A. L. Hutchinson, Weyauwega Chronicle	100 00	
Frank H. Hall, Kenosha Telegraph Courier	100 00	
H. H. Hartson, Greenwood Gleaner	100 00	
D. J. Hotchkiss, Fox Lake Representative	100 00	
F. B. Hand, Hurley Tribune	100 00	
C. M. Hutchinson, Necedah Republican	100 00	
W. A. Hume, Chilton Times	100 00	
Thos. Hughes, Beaver Dam Citizen	100 00	
E. P. Huntington, New Richmond Voice	100 00	
A. G. Hinckley, Tomah Herald Advertiser	100 00	
Halline & Hase, De Pere News	100 00	
Herald Pub. Co., Rhinelander Herald	100 00	
Edwin Hurlbut, Oconomowoc Free Press	100 00	
Hicks Printing Co., Oshkosh Northwestern	100 00	
J. E. Harris, Sturgeon Bay Democrat	100 00	
J. W. Hall, Oconto Lumberman	100 00	
W. A. Hidden, Sun Prairie Countryman	100 00	
C. W. Hooper, Minoqua Times	100 00	
Heg & Nethercut, Lake Geneva Herald	100 00	
Heyrman & Kuypers, De Pere Volk Stern	100 00	
A. S. Hearn, Dodgeville Chronicle	100 00	
Frank Heidt, Portage Rundshau	100 00	
W. H. Huntington, Durand Courier	100 00	
J. A Hoxie, Evansville Weekly Review	100 00	
Hume & Paulus, Marshfield News	100 00	
Chas. L. Harper, Lancaster Herald	100 00	

"A."—General Fund Disbursements for 1893.

C. L. Hart, Oconto Reporter........	$100 00	....	....
W. H. Holmes, Waupaca Republican..................	100 00	....	....
L. K. Howe, Sheboygan Herald....	100 00	....	....
J. D. Hurlbut, Prairie du Chien Union.................. ..	100 00	....	....
Hallenbach & Nye, Hortonville Weekly Review...	100 00	....	....
Hawley Bros., Baldwin Bulletin....	100 00	....	....
C. L. Hubbs, Lake Mills Leader....	100 00	....	....
H. D. Hanson, Oregon Observer....	100 00	....	....
Hooker, Bell & Hooker, Waupun Times..................	100 00	....	....
W. F. Hill, Reedsburg Free Press..	100 0v	... .	....
W. D. Hoard, Ft. Atkinson Dairyman and Jefferson Co. Union.....	200 00	....	....
W. W. Hall, Whitewater Gazette..	100 00	....	....
H. J. Heise, Wausau Wochenblatt..	100 00	....	....
Inland Ocean Co., Superior Inland Ocean..................	100 00	....	....
Cham Ingersoll, Beloit Free Press..	100 00	....	....
C. N. Johnson, Merrill Advocate....	100 00	....	....
Edward Jenson, Racine Falkets Avis	100 00	....	....
J. E. Jones, Portage Democrat and Kilbourn City Mirror Gazette.....	200 00	....	....
Fred Jonas, Racine Slavi...	100 00	....	....
Griff O. Jones, Augusta Eagle.....	100 00	....	....
Mrs. F. W. Johns, Mazomanie Sickle and Prairie du Sac News........	200 00	....	....
G. L. & J. E. Jones, Shell Lake Watchman	100 00	....	....
Journal Printing Co.,Racine Journal	100 00	....	....
Kelsey & Vasey, Menominee Herald	100 00	....	....
Michael Kruzka, Tygochur Polski, and Pazeglad Figgoderong......	200 00	....	....
H. M. Knowlton, Waterloo Journal.	100 00	....	....
J. F. Kartack, Baraboo News.......	100 00	....	....
John Kelly, Juneau Telephone.	100 00	....	....
C. C. Kuntz, Sauk City Pionier.....	100 00	....	....
D. W. Kutchin, Ontario Sentinel...	100 00	....	....
John C. Klinker, Menasha Anzeiger.	100 00	....	....
Robt. Kohli, Monroe Herold........	100 00	....	....
H. E. Kelley, Sparta Independent..	100 00	....	....
R. E. Kenyon, South Superior Sun .	100 00	....	....
L. H. Kimball, Neenah Twin City News..................	100 00	....	....
Kewaunee Bohemian Ptg. Co., Kewaunee Listy..................	100 00	....	....
John A Killeen, Kenosha Union. .	100 00	....	....
F. J. Kempter, Alma Mirror......i.	100 00	....	....
James Kerr & Sons, Ft. Howard Review..................	100 00	....	....
Lehman & Robinson, Green Bay Der Landsmann...	100 00	....	....
Chas. A. Leicht, New Lisbon Argus.	100 00	....	...
W. S. Luce, La Crosse Press........	100 00	....	....

"A."—General Fund Disbursements for 1893.

C. A. Libby & Sons, Evansville Enterprise and Tribune............	$200 00	....	....
Luehr & Brundage, Centralia Enterprise............, ...	100 00	....	....
J. M. LeCount & Sons, Hartford Press................, ...	100 00	....	....
L. A. Lange, Fond du Lac Reporter.	100 00	....	....
Frank Long, Sturgeon Bay Advocate......	100 00	....	....
T. J. Law, Shullsburg Pick and Gad	100 00	....	....
Z. Luazycki, Manitowoc Gosc	100 00	....	....
B. E. McCoy, Sparta Democrat.....	100 00	....	....
T. H. McElroy, Shullsburg Local...	100 00	....	....
L. C. McKenney, Plattville News ..	100 00	....	........, ..
G. D. McDowell, Soldiers Grove Transcript..........	100 00	....	....
McCullough Ptg. Co., Iola Herald. .	100 00	....	....
McGlachlin & Simons, Stevens Point Journal.............	100 00	....	....
McBride Bros , Sparta Herald......	100 00	....	.... ..
H. W. & C. H. McCourt, St. Croix Falls Standard....	100 00	....	....
W. J. P. McFail, Madison Times....	100 00	....	....
E. H. Merrill, Ripon Free Press	100 00	....	....
F. R Morris & Co., Milton Junction News......................	100 00	....	....
Millard Pub. Co., Antigo News Item	100 00	....	....
G. A. Markham, Independent Good Templar and News Wave........	200 00	....	....
J. W. Moore, Watertown Gazette ..	100 00	....	......."...
J. G. Monahan, Darlington Republican...................	10' 00	....	....
F. F Morgan, Cumberland Advocate	100 00	....	....
C. B. Moon, Eagle River Review....	100 00	....	.....:......
Paul F. Mueller, Fountaiu City Republikaner......	100 00	... .	....
Milwaukee Telegraph Pub. Co., Milwaukee Telegraph.	100 00	....	....
Franz Markus, Medford Walbote. ..	100 00	....	... .
Wm. D. Merrill, Prairie du Chien Courier......	100 00	....	....
Monger & Biorseth, Superior Citizen	100 00	....	....
Edward Malone, Waterford Post...	100 00	....	....
Walter Mayer, Deerfield Enterprise.	100 00	....	....
O. G. Munson, Viroqua Censor.....	100 00	....	....
E. H. Mosher, Wauwatosa Times...	200 00	....	....
Jacob Mueller, Mayville Pionier	100 00	....	....
George Meacham, Black River Falls Journal.....................	100 00	....	....
John L. Millard, Markesan News ...	100 00	....	....
Clay W. Metsker, Beloit News......	100 00	....	....
Mt. Horeb Ptg Co., Mt. Horeb Sun and Progress...................	200 00	....	....
Chas. E. Mears, Osceola Mills Press.	100 00	....	....
O. O. Melaas, Stoughton Norsman ..	100 00	....	....
H. A. Miner, Madison N. W. Mail...	100 00	....	....
Ernst Mussgang, Superior Zeitung.	100 00	....	....
H. W. Meyer, Appleton Volksfreund	100 00	....	....

"A."—General Fund Disbursements for 1893.

C. R. Morse, River Falls Journal....	$100 00	.. ..	....
Peter J. Mouat, Janesville Recorder	100 00	....	....
H. M. Marden, Kenosha Blade.....	100 00	....	....
Wm. J. New, Three Lakes Forest Leaves........................	100 00	....	....
Wm. L. Norris, Watertown Republican......................	100 00	....	....
Anton Novak, Milwaukee Democrat	100 00	....	....
Wm. F. Nash, Two Rivers Chronicle	100 00	....	....
John Nagle, Manitowoc Pilot.. ,...	100 00	....	....
A. K. Owen, Lake Geneva News....	100 00	....	....
J. A. Ogden, Antigo Republican....	100 00	....	....
Ole B. Olson, Eau Claire Reform ...	100 00	....	....
Oliver Bros., Waupun Leader.....	100 00	....	....
Edward Duthwait, Chippewa Herald	100 00	....	....
Park & Kenney, Elkhorn Independent	100 00	....	....
Edward Pollack, Lancaster Teller ..	200 00	....	....
W. R. Purdy, Spring Green Home News...........	100 00	....	....
A. W. Pott, Sheboygan Zeitung....	100 00	....	....
Walter W. Pollack, Milwaukee Record	100 00	....	....
M. S. Parker, Mauston Chronicle...	100 00	....	....
H. J. Pankow, Marshfield Demokrat	100 00	....	....
Powers & Briscoe, Baraboo Republic	100 00	....	....
S. W. Pierce, Friendship Press.	100 00	....	....
C. E. Parish, Stoughton Courier....	100 00	....	....
Post Pub. Co., Appleton Post.......	100 00	....	....
Byron J. Price, Hudson Star and Times	100 00	....	....
M D. Peavy, Dodgeville Eye and Star...	100 00	....	....
D. H. Richards, Richland Center Rustic....	100 00	....	....
Christ. Roemer, Appleton Wecker..	100 00	....	....
Ellis Rodgers, B. R. Falls Post......	100 00	....	....
Wm. Reber, Watertown Journal...	100 00	....	....
Register Pub. Co..............	100 00	....	....
Geo. A. Rodgers, Whitefish Bay Pioneer	100 00	....	....
C. F. Roessler, Jefferson Banner ...	100 00	....	....
Valentine Raeth, Milwaukee Vorwaerts and Wahrheit............	200 00	....	....
Carl Rabenstein, Neillsville Deutsch Amerikaner.....	100 00	....	....
C. E. Robinson, West Bend Pilot ...	100 00	....	....
Ryan Bros., Appleton Crescent.....	100 00	....	....
H. N. Ross, Sheboygan Times.......	100 00	....	....
Byron Ripley, Iron River Times....	100 00	....	....
Peter Richards, Lodi News.........	100 00	....	....
M. P. Rindlaub, Plattville Witness.	100 00	....	....
Rowland & Durkee, Phillips Bee...	100 00	....	....
F. C. Rumpf, Cambridge News.....	100 00	....	....
Aug. E Runge, Baraboo Democrat.	100 00	....	....
Rhinelander Printing Co., Rhinelander New North.	100 00	....	....
C. E. Raugh & Co., Kaukauna Times	100 00	....	....

"A."—General Fund Disbursements for 1893.

L. B. Ring, Neilsville Times........	$100 00	....	....
Douglas Ross, Ellsworth Eagle......	100 00	....	....
Jacob Rohr, Milwaukee World......	100 00	....	....
Mary A. Selbach, Portage Wecker..	100 00	....	....
W. J. Showers, Onalaska Record...	100 00	....:. .	....
Shafer Bros., Colby Phonograph....	100 00	....	....
J. A. Smith	100 00	...:	
Geo. E. Sacket, Fifield Advocate....	100 00	....	....
D. W. Stebbins, Ahnapee Record...	100 00	....	....
Martin C. Short, Brandon Times....	100 00	....	....
Henry Sanford, Manitowoc Tribune.	100 00	....	... .
B. F. Sherman & Son, Beaver Dam Argus	100 00	....	....
G. L. Schwartz, Poynette Press.....	100 00	....	....
J. F. Sprague & Son, Mauston Star.	100 00	....	....
Sturdevant, Ogden & Ware, Waupaca Post......................	100 00	....	....
C. G. Stacks, Berlin Journal.......	100 00	....	....
Harry L. Snow, Reeseville Review.	100 00	....	....
J. N. Stone, Neenah Times	100 00	....	....
J. Ed. Sawyer, Horicon Reporter...	100 00	....	....
E. J. Scott, Hayward Journal......	100 00	....	....
C. Swayze, Stevens Point Pinery....	100 00	....	....
L. B. Squire, Tomah Journal.......	100 00	....	....
H. A. Stone, Neenah Gazette.......	10·) 00	....	....
Standard Printing Co., DePere Echo.	200 00	....	....
Sauk City Pub. Co., Sauk City Presse	100 00	....	....
Signal Pub. Co., Menominie Signal.	100 00	....	....
P. O. Stromme, Superior Posten....	100 00	....	....
Mrs. R. A. Sharp, Oconto Enquirer.	100 00	....	....
Henry Spiering, Mayville News.....	100 00	....	....
J. J. Smith, Barron Republican.....	100 00	....	....
State Journal Ptg. Co., Madison State Journal	100 00	....	....
Schilling & Co., Milwaukee Advance, National Reformer, Racine Reformer, National Advance, Mil. Reformer, Racine Advance.......	600 00	....	....
Chas. S. Smith, Reedsburg Times...	100 00	....	....
P. H. Swift, Rice Lake Chronotype.	100 00	... .	....
Walter Speed, Chetek Alert... ...	100 00	....	....
H. T. Sharp, Delavan Enterprise....	100 00	....	....
Mrs. Carl Schmidt, Manitowoc Nordwesten	100 00	....	....
W. W. Stoddard, Prentice Calumet.	100 0·)	....	....
E. L Spence, Milton Telephone.....	100 00	....	....
M. T. Stokes, Sheboygan Journal ..	100 00	....	....
Wilson A Sprague, Brodhead Register	100 00	....	....
F. W. Sackett, Phillips Times......	100 00	....	....
Samuel Shaw, Crandon Forest Republican	100 00	....	....
John E. Thomas, Sheboygan Falls News........	100 00	....	....
Towell Bros., Milwaukee and Wisconsin Times......................	200 00	....	....
John Tenfen, Peck's Sun...........	100 00	....	....
E. B. Thayer, Wausau Pilot Review	100 00	....	....

"A."—*General Fund Disbursements for 1893.*

Times Pub. Co., Racine Utley's Weekly	$100 00	....	....
Telegram Printing Co., West Superior Telegram	100 00	....	....
J. H. Tifft, Neillsville Republican and Press	100 00	....	....
D. C. Talbot, Elroy Statesman	100 00	....	....
Times Co., Ashland News	100 00	....	....
Times Printing Co., Menomonie Times	100 00	....	....
Charles S. Taylor, Barron Shield	100 00	....	....
Ellis B. Usher, La Crosse Chronicle	100 00	....	....
C. S. Utter, Trempealeau Gazette	100 00	....	....
A. C. Van Meter, New Richmond Republican	100 00	....	....
H. L. Vandervort, Galesville Independent	100 00	....	....
A. C. Voshardt, Kewaunee Enterprise	100 00	....	....
Volksfreund Pub. Co., La Crosse Volksfreund	100 00	....	....
E. W. Viall & Co., Oshkosh Times	100 00	....	....
G. E. Vandercook, Spencer Tribune	100 00	....	....
R. M. Voll, Ashland Herald	100 00	....	....
B. E. Van Keuren, Oshkosh Signal	100 00	....	....
H. J. Van Vuren, Seymour Press	100 00	....	....
W. E. Williams, Kingston Spy	100 00	....	....
Wilbur G. Weess, Delavan Republican	100 00	....	....
Wm. Wagner, Thorp Courier	100 00	....	....
A. Wittman, Manitowoc Post	100 00	....	....
Woodle & Turner, Monroe Co. Journal	100 00	....	....
H. D. Wing. Kaukauna Sun	100 00	....	....
J. H. Waggoner, Portage State Register	100 00	....	....
O. O. Wiegand, Shawano Advocate	100 00	....	....
L. Woodward, Pardeeville Times	100 00	....	....
W. F. Weber, Fond du Lac Courier	100 00	....	....
Frank Wagner, Bloomington Record	100 00	....	....
Gertrude Wells, Viola Intelligencer	100 00	....	....
Jos. F. Wilson, Tomahawk, Tomahawk	100 00	....	....
Wandersleben Bros, Plymouth N. W. Post	100 00	....	....
A. C. Williams, Cambria News	100 00	....	....
Weiss & Auer, Eau Claire Herold	100 00	....	....
J. M Williams, Belleville Recorder	100 00	....	....
P. M. Wright, Omro Journal	100 00	....	....
Clarence J. Wells, Tomah Monitor	100 00	....	....
Ed. T. Wheelock, Medford Star and News	100 00	....	....
J. F. Willey, Janesville Wis. Tobacco Leaf	100 00	....	....
A. W. Young, Wausau Pionier	100 00	....	....
G. H. Yenowine, Yenowine's Mil. News	100 00	....	....
Fred T. Yates, Washburn News	100 00	....	....
Young Bros., Florence Mining News	100 00	....	....

"A."—General Fund Disbursements for 1893.

H. M Youmans, Waukesha Freeman	$100 00	....	... .
H.E. Zimmerman, Burlington Standard Democrat	100 00	....	....
Geo. Ziegans, Sharon Reporter	100 00	....	....
		$42,000 00	....

PUBLISHING PRIVATE AND LOCAL LAWS.

Ashland News Co	$30 60	....	....
W. K. Atkinson	6 60	....	....
A. M. Anderson	10 80	....	....
C. H. Bissell	3 00	....	....
Badour & Noel	6 00	....	....
W. F. Boland	15 60	....	....
Chas. F. Bone	7 80	....	....
Frank A. Carr	1 20	....	....
Call Publishing Co	9 60	....	....
Carlton & Hanford	2 40	....	....
Democrat Printing Co	1 80	....	....
Decker, Hoppe & Dockery	1 20	....	....
Ernest A. Dunn	8 40	....	....
C. C. Eaton	5 40	....	....
Ellerson & Berry	1 80	....	....
John G. Foulds	3 00	....	....
M. J. Fallow	2 40	....	....
Gowdy & Goodell	32 40	....	....
F. H. Graves	5 40	....	....
W. T. Giles	1 80	....	....
E. D. Glennon	1 80	....	....
Heg & Nethercut	6 00	....	....
J. E. Harris	9 00	....	....
J. R. Howe	1 80	....	....
Herold Pub. Co	28 20	....	....
W. A. Hume	17 40	....	....
W. H. Holmes	6 60	....	....
Alex. W. Horn	2 40	....	....
D. J. Hotchkiss	3 00	....	....
J. E. Jones	1 80	....	....
F. J. Kempter	2 40	....	....
L. A. Lange	9 60	....	....
Leuhr & Brundage	21 00	....	....
B. E. McCoy	5 40	....	....
W. J. P. McFail	16 20	....	....
E. H Merrill	3 00	....	....
Jas. W. Moore	1 80	....	....
Millard Pub. Co	4 80	....	....
C. B. Moon	15 00	....	....
Geo Meacham	1 80	....	....
Jno. L. Millard	1 80	....	....
Wm. J. New	5 40	....	....
John Nagle	12 60	....	....
S. W. Pierce	3 00	....	....
M. S. Parker	5 40	....	....
C. F. Roessler	1 80	....	....
Recorder Printing Co	4 20	....	....
Aug. E. Runge	1 80	....	....

"A."—General Fund Disbursements for 1893.

Ryan Bros	$13 20		
Mrs. R. A. Sharpe	9 60		
Stokes & Heyn	1 80		
Ed. L. Luckow	3 00		
B. F. Sherman & Son	1 80		
M. T. Stokes	7 20		
E. J. Scott	8 40		
Geo. E. Sackett	8 00		
E. B. Thayer	9 00		
Times Printing Co., Menomonie	2 40		
E. B. Usher	5 40		
E. W. Viall & Co	8 40		
Wm. Wagner	4 80		
O. O. Wiegand	18 60		
J. F. Wilson	1 80		
Ed. T. Wheelock	4 80		
Fred T. Yates	18 60		
H. E. Zimmerman	1 80		
Arthur Gough	8 00		
		$478 80	

PUBLISHING LAWS IN STATE PAPER.

Milwaukee Journal Company		$1,422 60	

PUBLISHING BANK REPORTS.

Ashland News Co	$3 60		
C. J. Augustin	1 20		
E. E. Atherton	4 80		
P. H Bolger	3 60		
C. H. Bissell	1 20		
Currie G. Bell	2 40		
Chas. F. Bone	2 40		
E. N. Bowers	2 40		
F. H. Brady	2 40		
W. G. Barry	1 20		
S. W. Brown	3 00		
J. B. Beach	2 40		
J. R. Bloom	1 20		
Abijah Bresee	2 40		
W. M. Barnum	2 40		
E. R. Beebe	2 40		
Frank A. Carr	13 80		
R. R. Crowe	1 20		
L. W. Chapman	2 40		
D. M. Carter	2 40		
Chippewa Valley Pub. Co	3 60		
Crawford Bros	13 80		
Geo. D. Cline	4 80		
Democrat Printing Co	2 40		
E. A. Dunn	3 00		
E. S. Doolittle	1 80		
T. K. Dunn & Son	3 60		
R. W. Davis	3 60		
C. H. Dunn	2 40		
F. A. Dean	3 15		
C. C. Eaton	4 80		

"A."—*General Fund Disbursements for 1898.*

John Foley	$2 40		
Arthur Frankenberg	2 40		
Frazier & Frazier	1 20		
John G. Foulds	1 20		
Wm. T. Giles	2 40		
Geo. W. Goldsmith	2 90		
C. L. Hubbs	2 40		
W. A. Hume	8 00		
F. W. Hill	1 80		
C. M. Hutchinson	1 20		
Howe & Rothe	2 40		
A. L. Hutchinson	1 20		
W. S. Hidden	6 00		
J. E. Harris	2 40		
H. D. Hanson	1 20		
Albert G. Hinckley	4 80		
Herald Publishing Co	2 40		
E. S. Holman	1 20		
J. E. Jones	4 80		
John A. Killeen	2 40		
John Kelly	2 40		
H. S Keeney	1 20		
Frank J. Kempter	2 70		
Chas. A. Leicht	2 40		
L. A. Lange	1 20		
Luehr & Brundage	2 40		
J. L. LeCount & Son	8 60		
B. E. McCoy	2 40		
Geo. D. McDowell	1 20		
C. W. Metsker	8 40		
F F. Morgan	2 40		
F. R. Morris	2 40		
Geo. Meacham	9 60		
Walter Mayer	1 20		
C. B. Moon	2 40		
Wm. F. Nash	2 40		
Mrs. M. S. Parker	2 40		
W. R. Purdy	2 40		
Frank L. Perrin	1 20		
Peter Richards	1 20		
Reporter Pub. Co	1 20		
H. T. Sharp	2 40		
Shafer Bros	2 40		
E. J. Scott	2 40		
Martin O. Short	2 40		
Geo. A. Smith	2 90		
Chas. S. Smith	1 20		
W. C. Thomas	2 40		
Times Pub. Co	1 20		
Times Printing Co. (Menomonie)	2 40		
E. B. Thayer	2 40		
Ellis B. Usher	8 60		
H. J. Van Vuren	2 40		
A. C. Voshardt	1 20		
E. T. Wheelock	1 20		
O. C. Williams	3 40		
Wm. Wagner	2 40		
Gertrude Wells	1 20		

A."—General Fund Disbursements for 1898.

Frank Wagner	$2 40		
J. F. Wilson	1 20		
Fred T. Yates	1 20		
Geo. Ziegans	4 40		
H. E. Zimmerman	2 40		
		$261 05	

ADVERTISING LANDS.

Advocate Printing Co..	$18 80		
Ashland News Co.	11 75		
A. M. Anderson	21 15		
C. H. Bissel	14 10		
Chas. F. Bone	18 80		
Abijah Bresee	17 00		
George D. Cline	9 40		
E. A. Dunn	18 80		
C. C. Eaton	13 60		
F. H. Graves	14 10		
Arthur Gough	10 80		
Herald Pub. Co.	9 40		
W. A. Hume	9 40		
E. H. Ives	11 75		
Luehr & Brundage	18 80		
B. E. McCoy	11 75		
H. W. McCourt	18 80		
James W. Moore	9 40		
Milwaukee Journal Co.	9 40		
Millard Bros.	21 15		
W. D. Merrill	9 40		
Wm. J. Neu	14 10		
Post Pub. Co.	9 40		
S. W. Pierce	14 10		
Pauly Bros.	11 75		
Register Pub. Co.	21 15		
R. A. Sharp	12 50		
P. O. Stromme	23 50		
C. Swayze	10 80		
B. F. Sherman & Son	9 40		
F. A. Smith	9 40		
E. B. Thayer	9 65		
Times Printing Co.	18 90		
Wells & Robbins	11 75		
		$473 95	

REAL ESTATE RETURNS.

Wm. Ahlhauser	$4 80		
Louis Auer	138 24		
Andrew A. Anderson	18 64		
E. M. Brendson	21 04		
Joseph Boschert	16 88		
R. S. Burbank	31 68		
A. S. Bostwick	15 72		
Jno. M. Baer	22 48		
J. M. Chapel	5 76		
Otto Christiansen	74 12		
G. E. Crocker	15 20		

"A."—General Fund Disbursements for 1893.

Jacob Delos...............	$17 60	
John H. Dooley............	20 00	
Henry Duffy....	65 00	
Fred L. Coughlin.................	7 76	
Halfor Erickson...............	575 28	
Niels Heggen.......	16 00	
G. J. Huhn......................	22 74	
H. Hanson	10 24	
W. H. Hardy.................	8 00	
Frank Hamlin	42 27	
W. C. Haberkorn.................	2 00	
W. H. Irish..............	10 80	
Huff Jones......................	12 24	
D. S. Johnson....................	12 80	
Edward Kluetz..................	20 08	
Hugo Koeuen	6 80	
Chas. Knutson.......	10 16	
O. J. Kerschensteiner............	28 00	
Julius Koehler....	5 12	
Edward C. Kretlow.	40 80	
J. A. Kettleson	4 00	
E. W. Lawrence................	18 80	
Frank McCormick....	6 64	
A. J Mallmann...	16 40	
M. Michaelson	11 52	
John F. Menting................	39 60	
George H. Miller................	30 00	
E. J. Mconey	6 08	
Simon Olson....................	6 80	
M G. O'Donnell	3 60	
Martin Oswald..............	17 04	
Andrew Oettinger................	15 60	
Mark L. Patterson...............	18 56	
Wm. E. Plummer............	2 80	
J. P. Rice	43 84	
L. C. Steinberg..................	14 80	
Thos. F. Scanlan.................	24 16	
Julius Stimm............	20 00	
August Siecker	4 64	
J. W. Stone....................	31 36	
J. D. Stuart	47 18	
J. A. Suhl	14 40	
W. J. Slater..................	8 96	
Andrew Schleis.......	7 00	
Mat Serve	16 88	
W. J. Thomas	11 60	
W. T. Taylor	3 84	
J. G. Teal.....	5 60	
C. L. Valentine	18 08	
R. G. Webb	5 92	
Austin White...	20 00	
Theo. Wolf....................	17 60	
W. E. Warren	12 00	
J. W. Wilson	56 60	
Wm. C. Wilson	23 94	
Wm. Zassenhaus....	15 20	
E. R. Zimmer..	17 44	
	$1,986 13	

"A."—General Fund Disbursements for 1893.

FREE HIGH SCHOOLS.

Avoca	$131 62		
Amherst	107 34		
Alma	234 00		
Appleton District No. 2	292 50		
Appleton District No. 3	292 50		
Ashland	292 50		
Augusta	292 50		
Almond	80 43		
Argyle	223 76		
Antigo	292 50		
Ahnapee	292 50		
Arcadia	257 40		
Brandon	234 00		
Bangor	219 37		
Brodhead	292 50		
Burlington	292 50		
Black Earth	292 50		
Bloomer	292 50		
Boscobel	292 50		
Baraboo	292 50		
Berlin	292 50		
Black River Falls	292 50		
Barron	286 28		
Bayfield	257 40		
Brillion	76 78		
Beaver Dam	292 50		
Bloomington	292 50		
Beloit	292 50		
Belleville	219 37		
Cadott	197 43		
Cambridge	190 12		
Cassville	248 62		
Colby	197 43		
Clinton	254 47		
Cuba City	197 43		
Centralia	292 50		
Chilton	292 50		
Chippewa Falls	292 50		
Columbus	292 50		
Cumberland	292 50		
Chetek	204 75		
Clintonville	226 98		
Durand	292 50		
Dodgeville	292 50		
De Pere	292 50		
Delavan	292 50		
Darlington	292 50		
Ellsworth	223 76		
Edgerton	292 50		
Evansville	292 50		
Elroy	292 50		
Elkhorn	292 50		
East Troy	292 50		
Eau Claire	292 50		
Fairchild	71 66		
Fennimore	263 28		

7—Sec'y.

"A."—General Fund Disbursements for 1893.

Fox Lake	$292 50		
Fort Atkinson	292 50		
Fond du Lac	292 50		
Fort Howard	292 50		
Florence	292 50		
Fremont	157 95		
Friendship	157 95		
Grand Rapids	292 50		
Green Bay	292 50		
Glenbeulah	204 75		
Humbird	184 27		
Hazel Green	210 60		
Highland	197 43		
Hillsborough	197 43		
Horicon	292 50		
Hudson	292 50		
Hartford	292 50		
Jefferson	292 50		
Janesville	292 50		
Juneau	292 50		
Kenosha	292 50		
Kewaunee	292 50		
Kiel	292 50		
Kaukauna	292 50		
Linden	157 95		
Lancaster	292 50		
Lake Mills	292 50		
Lone Rock	105 30		
Lodi	292 50		
Lake Geneva	292 50		
Mount Hope	140 40		
Muscoda	263 28		
Montello	175 50		
Montford	175 50		
Mondovi	263 28		
Merrillan	210 60		
Milton Junction	266 17		
Monroe	292 50		
Mineral Point	292 50		
Mazomanie	292 50		
Medford	292 50		
Mauston	292 50		
Marshfield	292 50		
Marinette	292 50		
Manawa	292 50		
Menasha	292 50		
Merrill	292 50		
Mayville	292 50		
Madison	292 50		
Middleton	146 25		
Marshall	500 00		
New London	263 28		
New Richmond	292 50		
Necedah	292 50		
Neillsville	292 50		
New Lisbon	292 50		
Neenah	292 50		
Oakfield	175 50		

"A."—General Fund Disbursements for 1893.

Oakwood	$234 00		
Omro	292 50		
Oconomowoc	292 50		
Onalaska	292 50		
Oregon	292 50		
Oconto	292 50		
Phillips	117 00		
Potosi	289 57		
Pepin	197 43		
Peshtigo	286 65		
Plainfield	197 43		
Prescott	292 50		
Prairie du Sac	292 50		
Poynette	292 50		
Port Washington	292 50		
Portage	292 50		
Plymouth	292 50		
Pewaukee	292 50		
Prairie du Chien	292 50		
Platteville	292 50		
River Falls	292 50		
Ripon	292 50		
Rice Lake	292 50		
Racine	292 50		
Rhinelander	292 50		
Reedsburg	292 50		
Richland Centre	292 50		
St. Martins	76 05		
Stockbridge	131 62		
Seymour	197 43		
South Milwaukee	187 20		
Shell Lake	277 87		
Sharon	292 50		
Sauk City	292 50		
Stoughton	292 50		
Sparta	292 50		
Spring Green	292 50		
Sun Prairie	292 50		
Sheboygan	292 50		
Sheboygan Falls	292 50		
Shullsburg	292 50		
Sturgeon Bay	292 50		
Shawano	292 50		
Stevens Point	292 50		
Sextonville	204 75		
Tomah	292 50		
Two Rivers	292 50		
Unity	197 43		
Viroqua	292 50		
Wonewoc	258 86		
Wilton	157 95		
Weyauwega	244 82		
Westfield	223 76		
Waldo	171 11		
West Salem	292 50		
Whitewater	292 50		
Washburn	292 50		
Waterloo	292 50		

"A."—General Fund Disbursements for 1893.

Watertown	$292 50	
West Bend	292 50	
Waukesha	292 50	
Waupun (Fond du Lac)	292 50	
Waupun (Dodge)	292 50	
Wausau	292 50	
Wauwatosa	292 50	
West De Pere	292 50	
Walworth	157 95	
Waupaca	292 50	
Total		$47,623 45

Presidential Electors.

Gustav Wollaeger	$22 50	
Robt. J. MacBride	83 10	
Andrew Jensen	7 50	
Michael Johnson	7 90	
John Montgomery Smith	27 50	
John Black	22 50	
Henry B. Schwin	28 50	
Ferdinand T. Yahr	89 50	
James J. Hogan	25 50	
John Wattawa	51 70	
Lewis S. Bailey	54 50	
William F. Cirkel	49 90	
		$370 60

For Maintaining Chronic Insane in County Hospitals.

Brown county	$5,647 29	
Brown county for Door county	175 71	
Brown county for Kewaunee county	1,345 47	
Brown county for Marinette county	835 08	
Brown county for Oconto county	2,060 96	
		$10,064 51
Columbia county	$3,753 21	
Columbia county for Adams county	151 65	
Columbia county for Jackson county	169 70	
Columbia county for Marathon county	165 85	
Columbia county for Marquette county	620 67	
Columbia county for Portage county	871 84	
Columbia county for Waushara county	601 01	
Columbia county for state at large	3,059 15	
		$8,892 58
Dane county	$7,401 01	
Dane county for Pierce county	502 48	
		$7,903 49
Dodge county	$5,581 71	
Dodge county for Oconto county	901 06	
Dodge county for Shawano county	336 16	

"A."—General Fund Disbursements for 1893.

Dodge county for Washington county......................	$3,966 51	....	....
		$10,785 44	
Dunn county	$2,018 78	....	....
Dunn county for Barron county...	78 89	....	....
Dunn county for Chippewa county.	744 19	....	....
Dunn county for Douglas county...	293 84	....	....
Dunn county for Eau Claire county.	332 80	....	....
Dunn county for Pepin county.....	39 85	....	....
Dunn county for St. Croix county..	1,586 23	....	....
Dunn county for Taylor county.....	527 21	....	....
Dunn county for state at large	1,203 64	....	....
		$6,823 93	
Fond du Lac county....	$6,078 43	....	....
Fond du Lac county for Green Lake county ...·..........	2,002 10	....	....
Fond du Lac county for Marquette county....	1,219 12	.......·....	....
Fond du Lac county for Portage county...........	882 70	....	... ...
Fond du Lac county for Waupaca county.........................	308 99	....	....
		$10,436 34	
Grant county	$4,689 43	....	....
Grant county for Barron county....	340 75	....	....
Grant county for Crawford county..	3,251 27	....	....
Grant county for La Fayette county.	170 51	....	....
Grant county for Richland county..	1,992 21	....	....
		$10,444 17	
Green county......	$4,172 59	....	....
Green county for Buffalo county ...	502 28	....	....
Green county for Eau Claire county	2,204 58	....·.......	....
Green county for Jackson county...	1,004 56	....	....
Green county for La Fayette county.	3,695 51	... .	....
Green county for Polk county......	1,115 02	....	....
		$12,694 54	
Iowa county...	$3,519 28	....	....
Iowa county for Jackson county....	521 88	....	....
Iowa county for Pierce county.	499 23	....	....
Iowa county for Polk county... ...	2,258 76	....	....
Iowa county for Waukesha county.	5,000 83	....	....
		$11,799 98	
Jefferson county	$5,819 00	....	....
Jefferson county for Burnett county	1,210 34	....	....
Jefferson county for Eau Claire county........	169 93	....	....
Jefferson county for Juneau county	4,829 58	....	....
		$11,528 85	
La Crosse county	$4.035 64	....	....
La Crosse county for Barron county	290 14	....	....
La Crosse county for Buffalo county	1,890 21	....	....

"A."—General Fund Disbursements for 1893.

La Crosse county for Clark county..	$1,297 04		
La Crosse county for Dunn county..	1,585 24		
La Crosse county for Jackson county	814 95		
La Crosse county for St. Croix county.....	535 58		
La Crosse county for Trempealeau county..................·........	518 94		
La Crosse county, state at large....	1,237 38		
		$12,205 12	
Manitowoc county	$4,585 28		
Manitowoc county for Marathon county.........................	1,825 03		
Manitowoc county for Ozaukee county.	3,158 55		
Manitowoc county, state at large...	1,140 48		
		$10,709 34	
Milwaukee county.....................		$48,172 85	
Outagamie county..................	$3,792 21		
Outagamie county for Calumet county..................	2,150 48		
Outagamie county for Door county.	1,484 35		
Outagamie county for Kewaunee county.	999 05		
Outagamie county for Langlade county....	173 21		
Outagamie county for Oconto county.....	1,060 07		
Outagamie county for Shawano county............	337 97		
Outagamie county for Waupaca county......................	2,503 36		
		$12,500 70	
Racine county......	$5,003 56		
Racine county for Eau Claire county..............	2,076 15		
Racine county for Kenosha county.	3,753 96		
		$10,833 67	
Rock county.......................	$6,018 21		
		$6,018 21	
Sauk county........................	$3,082 50		
Sauk county for Trempealeau county......................	1,435 37		
		$4,517 87	
Sheboygan county.................	$6,885 71		
Sheboygan county for Calumet county...	1,017 14		
Sheboygan county for Chippewa county....	676 92		
Sheboygan county for Washington county......................	168 10		
		$8,247 87	

"A."—General Fund Disbursements for 1893.

Vernon county......................	$2,893 07	....	....
Vernon county for Chippewa county	2,467 99	....	....
Vernon county for Crawford county	419 43	....	....
Vernon county for Monroe county..	1,974 17	... .	....
Vernon county for Portage county..	340 97	....	....
Vernon county for Richland county..	546 90	....	....
Vernon county for Trempealeau county...	1,082 49	....	....
Vernon county for Wood county...	165 94	....	....
Vernon county for state at large....	4,494 53	....	....
		$14,335 49	....
Walworth county................ ..	$4,215 64	....	....
Walworth county for Chippewa county	1,455 19	....	....
Walworth county for Pepin county.	511 73	....	....
Walworth county for Richland county	1,008 38	....	....
Walworth county for St. Croix county	325 43	....	....
Walworth county for Waukesha county	1,914 24	....	....
		$9,430 56	....
Winnebago county............	$4,871 99	....	....
Winnebago county for Portage county	207 53	....	....
		$5,079 52	....
A. Forbes, for transporting state patients.....................	$145 00	....	....
Trustees Columbia county insane asylum......	13 42	....	....
Trustees Dodge county insane asylum............	48 32	....	....
Treasurer Oconto county, refunded for maintaining George Pinkham et al. in northern hospital for insane......................	471 38	....	....
Superintendent of Columbia county asylum......	20 42	....	....
Superintendent of La Crosse county asylum......................	29 90	....	....
Superintendent of Racine county asylum......................	79 26	....	....
Superintendent of Dodge county asylum.........................	6 50	....	....
		$814 15	....
Total.......	....	....	$244,239 18

DEAF MUTE INSTRUCTION IN CITIES AND VILLAGES.

Treasurer City of La Crosse........	....	$5,236 10	....
BOUNTY ON WILD ANIMALS.......	....	12,778 00	....

"A."—General Fund Disbursements for 1893.

CIRCUIT COURT REPORTERS.

F. S. Bradford, deficiency in salary, 10th circuit......	$1,150 00	....	... .
H. A. Bush, deficiency in salary, 4th circuit	450 00	....	....
Joseph Cover, deficiency in salary, 15th circuit....	590 00	....	....
Chas. A. Cross, deficiency in salary, 8th circuit.......	1,170 00	........_ ...	....
Chas. W. Fiske. deficiency in salary, 17th circuit.................	165 00	............,	....
F. C. Grant, deficiency in salary, 9th circuit	640 00	.... •	....
Alfred Harrison, deficiency in salary, 6th circuit	870 00	....	....
George Hart, deficiency in salary, 16th circuit	.440 00	....	....
Albert Kavelage, deficiency in salary, 12th circuit	140 00	....	....
W. C. Kimball, deficiency in salary, 3rd circuit....	590 00	....	....
Chas. Orton, deficiency in salary, 5th circuit	520 00	....	....
James T. Parker, deficiency in salary, 14th circuit	440 00	....	....
J. H. Sawyer, deficiency in salary, 13th circuit....	750 00	....	....
F W. Spencer, deficiency in salary, 7th circuit.......	927 50	....	... .
Chas. H. Welch, deficiency in salary, 1st circuit.............	950 00	....	....
T. H. Wolford, deficiency in salary, 11th circuit...................	320 00	....	....
Total.....................	....	$10,112 50	....

COUNTY AGRICULTURAL SOCIETIES— STATE AID.

Arcadia Agricultural and Driving Association	$385 50	....	....
Adams County Agricultural Society	200 00	....	....
Baraboo Valley Agricultural Society	339 30	....	....
Barron County Agricultural Society	276 48	....	....
Boscobel Agricultural and Driving Park Association................	384 90	....	....
Brown County Agricultural and Mechanics Association.....	492 72	....	....
Brown County Fair and Park Association.......................	843 54	....	....
Buffalo County Agricultural Society	470 94		
Blake's Prairie Agricultural Society	391 90	....	....
Burnett County Agricultural Society.......	200 00	....	... .
Calumet County Agricultural Society	330 00	....	....
Clark County Agricultural Society..	391 06	....	....

"A."—General Fund Disbursements for 1893.

Crawford County Agricultural Society	$200 00		
Cumberland Agricultural and Driving Park Association	330 60		
Central Wisconsin Agricultural, Mechanic and Scientific Association.	808 60		
Columbia County Agricultural Society	339 45		
Dodge County Fair Association	884 50		
Door County Agricultural Society..	285 46		
Dunn County Agricultural Society..	461 08		
Dane County Agricultural Society..	1,200 00		
Eastern Monroe County Agricultural Society	325 18		
Green County Agricultural Society.	737 90		
Grant County Agricultural Society.	513 30		
Industrial Association of Manitowoc County.	733 10		
Iowa County Agricultural Society ..	651 30		
Jackson County Agricultural Society	563 96		
Jefferson County and Rock River Valley Agricultural Society	900 96		
Juneau County Agricultural Society	367 76		
Kewaunee County Agricultural Society	200 00		
Lake Superior Agricultural, Industrial and Fine Art Society	181 40		
La Fayette County Agricultural Society	625 40		
Langlade County Agricultural Society	353 00		
Little Baraboo Valley Agricultural Society	341 04		
Lodi Union Agricultural Society....	353 30		
La Crosse Inter State Fair Association	1,200 00		
La Crosse Agricultural Society	496 20		
Marathon County Agricultural Society	200 00		
Marquette County Agricultural Society..	352 30		
Monroe County Agricultural Society	261 90		
Northwestern Agricultural and Mechanical Society	254 00		
Outagamie County Agricultural Society	351 20		
Ozaukee County Agricultural Society	444 32		
Pepin County Agricultural Society	328 06		
Pierce County Central Fair Agricultural Society	265 90		
Polk County Agricultural Society...	406 50		
Portage County Agricultural Society	200 00		
Price County Agricultural Society	200 00		

"A."—General Fund Disbursements for 1893.

Richland County Agricultural Society....	$590 16	....	....
Rock County Agricultural Society..	732 90	....	....
Southwestern Wisconsin Industrial Association....	803 10	....	....
Shawano County Agricultural Society......	346 92	....	....
Sheboygan Exposition and Driving Park Association	588 00	....	....
Seymour Fair and Driving Park Association	353 45	....	....
St. Croix County Agricultural Society.......	438 60	....	....
Sauk County Agricultural Society..	675 40	....	....
Trempealeau County Agricultural Society....................	444 60	.. . .	....
Trempealeau County Industrial, Agricultural and Driving Park Association.	415 00	....	....
Taylor County Agricultural Society	201 00	....	....
Vernon County Agricultural Society	626 46	....	....
Washington County Agricultural Society....................	386 90	....	....
Wood County Agricultural and Mechanical Association..	377 72	....	....
Waupaca County Agricultural Society....	362 00	....	....
Waukesha County Agricultural Society......	787 08	....	....
Walworth County Agricultural Society.	1,200 00	....	....
Waushara County Agricultural Society........................	350 60	....	....
Wisconsin Central Stock Growers' Industrial Association............	495 01	... .	....
Total.......	....	$31,203 91	....

SPECIAL APPROPRIATIONS.

State Agricultural Society, ten per cent. premium paid under chapter 423, Laws of 1889....	1,406 80	....	....
State Agricultural Society, chapter 194, Laws of 1885	4,000 00	....	....
Callaghan & Co., Annotated Statutes, chapter 53, Laws of 1893 ...	324 00	....	....
Callaghan & Co., Annotated Statutes, chapter 299, Laws of 1893..	36 00	....	....
Wisconsin Digest and Reports, chapter 70, Laws of 1893...	310 00	....	....
Wisconsin State Firemen's Association, chapter 58, Laws of 1893 ...	500 00	... .	....
Wisconsin State Horticultural Society, chapter 117, Laws of 1893....	1,250 00	....	....
World's fair commission, chapter 433, Laws of 1891................	15,000 00	....	....

"A."—General Fund Disbursements for 1893.

World's fair commission, chapter 140, Laws of 1893	$84,500 00		
Louis Kirch, injury at school for deaf, chapter 158, Laws of 1893	2,000 00		
Wisconsin industrial school for girls, chapter 159, Laws of 1893	5,000 00		
Fifth normal school, chapter 364, Laws of 1885	10,000 00		
Wisconsin fish commission car, chapter 186, Laws of 1893	5,000 00		
Mary O'Laughlin, capitol disaster, chapter 239, Laws of 1893	700 00		
Wisconsin Dairymen's Association, chapter 240, Laws of 1893	4,000 00		
Wisconsin Veterans' Home, chapter 293, Laws of 1891	2,500 00		
Wisconsin Veterans' Home, chapter 248, Laws of 1893	10,000 00		
State University for Washburn Observatory, chapter 418, Laws of 1887	3,000 00		
Purchase Camp Randall, chapter 288, Laws of 1893	25,000 00		
Wisconsin Cranberry Growers' Association, chapter 263, Laws of 1893	250 00		
J. E. Lounsberry, chapter 297, Laws of 1893	91 89		
O. E. Wells, codifying school laws, chapter 178, Laws of 1893	4,285 71		
Warden's residence at state prison, chapter 152, Laws of 1893	4,000 00		
Finishing shop at school for blind, chapter 152, Laws of 1893	2,500 00		
Heating apparatus at school for blind, chapter 152, Laws of 1893	8,000 00		
Water supply at school for deaf, chapter 152, Laws of 1893	1,000 00		
Stone school house at industrial school for boys, chapter 152, Laws of 1893	6,500 00		
Agricultural institutes, chapter 62, Laws of 1887	6,000 00		
H. N. Moulton, shelving historical society, chapter 396, Laws of 1887	288 59		
Treasurer board of normal school regents, chapter 7, Laws of 1885	1,477 99		
Total		$208,920 98	

MISCELLANEOUS.

H. E. Driggs, sidenoting Laws of 1893	$200 00		
Edwin E. Bryant, compiling Laws of 1893	375 00		
Cuddy and Fleming, compiling Assessment Laws of 1893	100 00		

"A."—General Fund Disbursements for 1893.

T. J. Cunningham, refunded fees for articles of incorporation	$20 00	....	....
T. J. Cunningham, national library fees, Wis supreme court reports	1 05	....	....
T. J. Cunningham, filing title page, Wis. supreme court	2 00	....	....
M. H. Eaton, attorney in Wisconsin vs. U. S., Wis. & Fox River Imp. Co....	450 00	....	....
Gugler Lithograph Co., printing certificates of incorporation.	22 50	....	....
J. M. Glenn, annual report of national conference of charities and corrections.....................	180 00	....	....
John Hunner. fees for recording mortgage Wisconsin agricultural society....................	1 00	....	....
John Hunner, fees on protested drafts	11 36	....	....
August Kieckhefer, recording as signment of mortgage...........	50	....	....
H. A. Kinney, fees as witness, State vs. Insurance Cases.............	8 04	....	....
H. C. Mumbrue, services to commissioners of public printing.	50 00	....	....
Milwaukee Lithographing and En graving Co. railroad maps	3,867 50	....	....
Thomas McBean, compiling and indexing Game Laws of 1893	25 00	....	....
C. H. Phillips, serving notice of special election, Milwaukee..	5 38		
C. K. Pier, secretary soldiers' orph ans' home...................	23 00	....	....
Frank Craney, refunded patent fees	50	....	....
H. W. Reed, refunded corporation fees.............................	10 00	....	....
Fred Sperling, freight for board of control	1 02	....	....
A. F. Warden, serving notice of special election, Kenosha...........	8 38	....	....
Wisconsin veterans' home, maintaining inmates	31,579 73	....	....
Loan to state agricultural society, chapter 184, Laws of 1893........	30,000 00	....	....
Goosum Bush, refunded penalty and advertising	5 04	....	....
Geo. Baldwin, refunded penalty and advertising	7 49	....	... .-..
Geo. B. Burrows, refunded penalty and advertising................	6 95	....	....
E. P. Sherry, refunded penalty and advertising......................	2 99	....	....
Dictionaries for state superintendent	2,417 50		
		$69,383 63	....
Total disbursements, general fund.............................	....	....	$1,786,501 55

"A"—School Fund Receipts for 1893.

SCHOOL FUND.

RECEIPTS.		
Sales of lands	$4,288 00	....
Due on certificates of sales	15,025 46	....
Loans	39,835 86	....
Penalties	10 34	....
Fines	16,606 80	....
Escheat estate of Anna Riley, per J. W. Sales, judge probate, Rock Co.	195 72	....
United States 5 per cent. sales of public lands	2,656 37	....
Milwaukee city bonds	18,000 00	....
Marathon county court house bonds	8,000 00	....
Marathon county court house bonds, premium	424 56	....
Oconomowoc city hall bonds	2,000 00	....
Ripon city bonds	1,500 00	....
Superior city bonds, premium	470 62	....
Superior city fire bonds, premium	590 77	....
Loan to Barron county	2,000 00	....
Loan to Brown county	4,350 00	....
Loan to Jackson county	2,000 00	....
Loan to Lincoln county	4,198 50	....
Loan to Oneida county	4,573 91	....
Loan to Price county	4,000 00	....
Loan to town of Ashland	1,075 50	....
Loan to town of Apple River	120 00	....
Loan to town of Arcadia	1,666 66	....
Loan to town of Arena	100 00	....
Loan to town of Arthur	600 00	....
Loan to town of Auburndale	220 00	....
Loan to town of Chelsea	1,200 00	....
Loan to town of Crandon	200 00	....
Loan to town of Clinton	200 00	....
Loan to town of Cleveland	96 48	....
Loan to town of Day	350 00	....
Loan to town of Eau Pleine	100 00	....
Loan to town of Gillett	100 00	....
Loan to town of Hixon	660 00	....
Loan to town of Millston	666 67	....
Loan to town of Mineral Point	1,000 00	....
Loan to town of Maine	250 00	....
Loan to town of Mosinee	350 00	....
Loan to town of Moscow	757 00	....
Loan to town of Pleasant Valley	766 48	....
Loan to town of Richfield	275 00	....
Loan to town of Russel	500 00	....
Loan to town of Rolling	100 00	....
Loan to town of St Croix Falls	250 00	....
Loan to town of Waldwick	850 00	....
Loan to town of Washburn	750 00	....
Loan to town of Weston	170 00	....

"A."—School Fund Disbursements for 1893.

Loan to town of Wood............................	$1,000 00	....
Loan to village of Bloomer........	200 00	....
Loan to board of education, city of Madison ...	5,000 00	....
Loan to city of Berlin...	2,000 00	....
Loan to city of Merrill. ...	1,180 00	....
Loan to city of New London....................	2,000 00	....
Loan to city of Rice Lake....................	300 00	....
Loan to city of Wausau.....	2,000 00	... .
Total...	....	$157,779 65

DISBURSEMENTS.

School District Loans:

School district No. 3, Albion, Jackson county..	$369 50	....
School district No. 3, Animo, Shawano county.	300 00	....
Joint district No. 1, Almond and Oasis, Plain field and Pine Grove, Waushara county.....	700 00	....
School district No 4, Armenia, Juneau county	424 00	....
School district No. 2, Apple River, Polk county	350 00	... .
School district No. 2, city of Appleton, Winnebago county........	25,000 00	....
Joint district No. 5, Brighton and Unity, Marathon and Clark counties	250 00	....
Brule school directors, Douglas county	500 00	....
School district No. 5, Big Bend, Chippewa county.	400 00	....
School district No. 5, Cleveland, Marathon county	480 00	....
Joint district No. 2, town and village of Clinton, Rock county...........................	8,000 00	....
Eagle River school director, Vilas county.. ...	7,500 00	....
School district No. 2, Fairbanks, Shawano county..... ..	4,000 00	....
Joint district No. 1, Grover and Molitor, Taylor county.....	400 00	....
School district No. 5, Hutchins, Shawano county....	380 00	... .
School district No. 4, Harrison, Waupaca county	350 00	.. ..
School district No. 3, Harrison, Lincoln county	383 00	. ...
Joint district No. 1, Jefferson and Viroqua, Vernon county........................	400 00	....
School district No. 7, Little River, Oconto county...............................	400 00	....
School district No. 11, Madison, Dane county..	2,300 00	....
School district No. 13, Mosinee, Marathon county.......	250 00	....
School district No. 6, Maple Valley, Oconto county........	1,000 00	....
School district No. 3, Mattison, Waupaca county....................................	200 00	... .
School district No. 3, Mayville, Clark county.	300 00	... .
School district No. 5, Omro, Winnebago county	2,000 00	....
School district No. 5, Pleasant Valley, Eau Claire county.....	400 00	....

A."—School Fund Disbursements for 1893.

School district No. 5, Pine Valley, Clark county	$500 00	....
Pelican school directors, Oneida county.......	3,500 00	... .
Joint district No. 8, Royalton, Mukwa and Weyauwega, Waupaca county	180 00	....
Joint district No. 8, Sterling and Jefferson, Vernon county...	325 00	....
Joint district No. 2, Springfield and Cady, St. Croix county.............	500 00	....
Joint district No. 8, Stanton and Tiffany, Dunn county.......	450 00	....
School district No. 5, Siegel. Chippewa county	438 00	....
School district No. 5, Sherman, Dunn county..	600 00	....
School district No. 1, Turtle Lake, Barron county..................................	425 00	....
School district No. 8. Medford, Taylor county.	250 00	....
Veazie directors, Washburn county...........	650 00	....
School district No. 7, Wittenberg, Shawano county......	350 00	....
Washburn school directors, Bayfield county ...	25,000 00	....
Joint district No. 10, Woodland and Westford, Sauk and Richland counties	250 00	....
Total, school district loans................. ...	....	$90,454 50
Loan to city of Green Bay....	... .	35,000 00
Loan to city of Neenah	... .	3,000 00
Loan to Winnebago county........	....	4,000 00
Oshkosh city sewer bonds purchased............	....	21,800 00
Total disbursements................	....	$154,254 50

SCHOOL FUND INCOME.

RECEIPTS.		
Interest on land certificates and loans...........	$21,202 90	....
Interest on certificates of indebtedness	109,801 18	....
Mill tax....	653,057 00	....
Interest on school fund in banks................	3,656 01	....
Interest on Ashland county bonds..............	1,000 00	....
Interest on Ashland city bonds	1,250 00	....
Interest on Chilton town bonds	842 00	....
Interest on Chippewa Falls city bonds	1,000 00	....
Interest on Eau Claire water bonds.............	1,850 00	....
Interest on Elroy water bonds	285 75	....
Interest on Chilton city bonds	788 00	....
Interest on village of Elkhorn bonds............	500 00	....
Interest on Fond du Lac bonds.........	1,500 00	....
Interest on Milwaukee city bonds	18,240 00	....
Interest on Madison city bonds...	3,000 00	....
Interest on Marathon county court house bonds..	1,575 44	....
Interest on Mineral Point city bonds............	800 00	....
Interest on Oconomowoc city bonds.............	240 00	....
Interest on Oshkosh city bonds	788 50	....
Interest on Stoughton city bonds................	1,500 00	....
Interest on Superior city bonds	13,938 61	....
Interest on Ripon city bonds	875 00	....
Interest on Wausau city bonds	750 00	....
Interest on loan to town of Ashland. Ashland Co.	240 92	....
Interest on loan to town of Arcadia, Trempealeau Co...	816 66	....
Interest on loan to town of Arena, Iowa Co......	85 00	....
Interest on loan to town of Arthur, Chippewa Co.	60 00	....
Interest on loan to town of Clinton, Barron Co..	86 00	....
Interest on loan to town of Crandon, Forest Co..	70 00	....
Interest on loan to town of Cleveland, Marathon Co......	6 75	....
Interest on loan to town of Chelsea, Taylor Co...	18 00	....
Interest on loan to town of Day, Marathon Co...	49 00	....
Interest on loan to town of Gillett, Oconto Co...	10 00	....
Interest on loan to city of Green Bay...........	1,058 75	....
Interest on loan to town of Hixon, Clark Co.....	46 20	....
Interest on loan to town of Maine, Outagamie Co.	138 00	....
Interest on loan to town of Millston, Jackson Co.	100 00	....
Interest on loan to town of Mineral Point, Iowa Co....................	140 00	....
Interest on loan to town of Moscow, Iowa Co ...	817 94	....
Interest on loan to town of Mosinee, Marathon Co...	42 00	....
Interest on loan to town of Pleasant Valley, Eau Claire Co....	114 98	....
Interest on loan to town of Richfield, Wood Co..	96 25	....

"A."—School Fund Income Disbursements for 1893.

Interest on loan to town of Rolling, Langlade Co.	$21 00	....
Interest on loan to town of Russell, Lincoln Co .	240 00	....
Interest on loan to town of St. Croix Falls, Polk Co.	70 00	....
Interest on loan to town of Waldwick, Iowa Co.	654 50	....
Interest on loan to town of Washburn, Bayfield Co.	21 88	....
Interest on loan to town of Weston, Clark Co ...	11 90	....
Interest on loan to town of Wood, Wood Co....	280 00	....
Interest on loan to Barron Co..................	840 00	....
Interest on loan to Brown Co..............	3,132 00	....
Interest on loan to Jackson Co..................	700 00	....
Interest on loan to Lincoln Co................. .	293 90	....
Interest on loan to Oneida Co..	210 00	....
Interest on loan to Price Co.....................	1,680 00	....
Interest on loan to Winnebago Co..........	76 50	....
Interest on loan to city of Berlin	400 00	....
Interest on loan to city of Merrill..............	82 60	....
Interest on loan to city of Neenah . .;..........	111 25	....
Interest on loan to city of New London.........	930 00	....
Interest on loan to city of Rice Lake...........	126 00	....
Interest on loan to city of Wausau	280 00	....
Transfer to normal school fund income, interest received on normal fund loan...........	2,062 50	....
Interest on loan to village of Bloomer	12 00	....
Interest on loan to board of education, city of Madison......	1,000 00	....
Total receipts	....	$852,512 87

DISBURSEMENTS.

Apportionment to Counties.

Adams......... ....;............	$3,551 90	....
Ashland.......... .....;................	6,927 11	....
Barron...	8,854 34	....
Bayfield.....................................	2,571 18	....
Brown	21,389 74	....
Buffalo.....................................	8,224 85	....
Burnett.....................;................	2,548 25	....
Calumet.................................. .. .	9,059 87	....
Chippewa...................................	18,158 14	....
Clark	9,646 69	....
Columbia.	13,087 98	....
Crawford	8,409 66	....
Dane.	27,355 01	....
Dodge......	21,543 58	....
Door.......................................	8,885 86	....
Douglas	6,843 46	....
Dunn...	11,505 61	....
Eau Claire ...;	14,442 38	....
Florence	1,080 54	....
Fond du Lac................................	21,222 46	....
Forest......................	288 68	....
Grant	17,777 11	....
Green	10,345 47	....
Green Lake..........	7,289 78	....

"A."—School Fund Income Disbursements for 1893.

Apportionment to Counties—Continued.

Iowa	$10,654 89	....
Jackson	8,116 93	....
Jefferson	16,167 76	....
Juneau	8,290 94	....
Kenosha	6,856 95	....
Kewaunee	9,351 26	....
La Crosse	18,334 25	....
La Fayette	9,495 60	....
Langlade	4,364 01	....
Lincoln	5,938 29	....
Manitowoc	20,263 83	....
Marathon	17,071 58	....
Marinette	9,847 70	....
Marquette	5,391 95	....
Milwaukee	120,373 96	....
Monroe	11,867 15	....
Oconto	8,593 13	....
Oneida	2,394 47	....
Outagamie	20,279 50	....
Ozaukee	8,172 28	....
Pepin	3,526 28	....
Pierce	10,323 88	....
Polk	7,068 76	....
Portage	12,947 69	....
Price	2,407 96	....
Racine	18,408 05	....
Richland	9,305 39	....
Rock	19,699 43	....
St. Croix	11,680 96	....
Sauk	15,249 09	....
Sawyer	720 36	....
Shawano	10,674 62	....
Sheboygan	22,213 98	....
Taylor	3,638 25	....
Trempealeau	10,048 69	....
Vernon	13,177 02	....
Walworth	10,538 38	....
Washington	11,818 58	....
Waukesha	14,064 66	....
Waupaca	13,554 74	....
Waushara	6,964 87	....
Winnebago	24,601 71	....
Wood	10,033 85	....
Total apportionment to counties	839,996 17	....
Refunded	176 65	....
Accrued interest on Oshkosh city bonds	653 25	....
Grand total	....	$840,826 07

"A."—University Fund Income for 1893.

UNIVERSITY FUND.

RECEIPTS.		
Sales of land	$59 70	....
Dues on certificates of sales.	1,613 00	....
Loans	266 58	....
Tomahawk city bonds	1,500 00	....
Loan to Dunn Co	2,000 00	....
Loan to Shawano Co	1,500 00	....
Total receipts	....	$6,939 28
DISBURSEMENTS.		
Loan to Winnebago Co	$8,000 00	$8,000 00

UNIVERSITY FUND INCOME.

RECEIPTS.		
Interest on land certificates and loans	$895 85	....
Interest on certificates of indebtedness	7,758 90	....
From $\frac{1}{10}$ mill tax	146,987 82	....
Interest on university fund deposited in banks	1,661 52	....
United States treasurer, appropriation for experimental station	15,000 00	....
Secretary board of regents for students' fees etc.	41,558 67	....
Interest on M. M. Jackson bequest	154 74	....
Interest on Eau Claire county bonds	500 00	....
United States treasurer, appropriation for agricultural and mechanical arts	19,000 00	....
Interest on Manitowoc county bonds	1,200 00	....
Interest on Stoughton city bonds	150 00	....
Interest on Tomahawk city bonds	620 00	....
Interest on Vernon county asylum bonds	1,000 00	....
Interest on Waupaca county bonds	560 00	....
Interest on Platteville city hall bonds	240 00	....
Interest on loan to city of Menomonie	200 00	....
Interest on loan to Shawano Co	785 00	....
Interest on loan to Winnebago Co	153 00	....
Total receipts	....	$238,325 50
DISBURSEMENTS.		
Treasurer of state university	$238,319 84	....
Refunded for over-payment	5 66	....
Total disbursements	....	$238,325 50

"A."—Agricultural College Fund for 1893.

AGRICULTURAL COLLEGE FUND.

RECEIPTS.		
Sales of land..	$62 47	....
Dues on certificates of sales.......................	5,329 00	....
Eau Claire county bonds, part premium paid	44 46	....
Grand Rapids bridge bonds.......................	1,000 00	... .
New Richmond city bonds....	500 00	....
Platteville city bonds........................... ..	2,500 00	....
Loan to town of Hancock, Waushara Co........	1,000 00	....
Loan to city of Merrill, Lincoln Co..............	1,000 00	....
Manitowoc county bonds.........................	9,000 00	... .
Total receipts.....	....	$20,435 93
DISBURSEMENTS.		
Purchase of Eau Claire bonds....................	$15,000 00	....
Premium on Eau Claire bonds..........	817 50	....
Refunded Geo. Baldwin	2 59	....
Refunded Geo. B. Burrows.......................	5 11	....
Refunded E. P. Solberg	2 59	....
Loan to to Manitowoc Co........................	9,000 00	....
Loan to Winnebago Co...........................	4,000 00	....
Total disbursements...........................	....	$28,827 79

"A."—Agricultural College Fund Income for 1893.

AGRICULTURAL COLLEGE FUND INCOME.

RECEIPTS.		
Interest on land certificates and loans...........	$4,606 39	....
Interest on certificates of indebtedness.........	4,285 89	....
Interest on Eau Claire county bonds....	1,080 54	....
Interest on Black River Falls bridge bonds.......	1,000 00	....
Interest on Grand Rapids bridge bonds..........	350 00	....
Interest on Milwaukee water bonds.............	1,500 00	....
Interest on Madison city bonds.................	125 00	....
Interest on Manitowoc county bonds....	2,480 00	....
Interest on Neenah city bonds	150 00	....
Interest on Platteville city bonds.	365 00	....
Interest on Tomahawk city bonds..............	330 00	....
Interest on New Richmond city bonds..........	125 00	....
Interest on loan to Manitowoc Co......	202 50	....
Interest on loan to Winnebago Co....	76 50	....
Interest on loan to town of Hancock, Waushara Co....................................	200 00	....
Interest on loan to city of Merrill, Lincoln Co...	420 00	....
Interest on agricultural college fund deposited in banks.....................................	143 28	....
Total receipts........	....	$17,890 10
DISBURSEMENTS.		
Treasurer state university.......................	$17,171 48	....
Refunded over payments	29 72	....
Accrued interest on Eau Claire county bonds....	188 90	....
Total disbursements.....	....	$17,890 10

"A."—Normal School Fund for 1893.

NORMAL SCHOOL FUND.

RECEIPTS.		
Sales of land..	$22,006 53	....
Dues on certificates of sales................	1,302 00	....
Loans...	1,569 50	....
Ashland city bonds................	5,000 00	....
Ashland city bonds premium.....................	28 70	....
Edgerton school bonds	1,000 00	....
Eau Claire bridge bonds premium	35 44	....
Centralia bridge bonds........................	1,000 00	....
Columbus city school bonds......	1,000 00	....
Menasha city bonds	1,000 00	....
Milwaukee city bonds.........................	43,000 00	....
Menasha city hall bonds................... ...	5,000 00	....
Neenah city bonds......	2,000 00	....
Oshkosh city hall bonds......................	3,000 00	....
Oshkosh bridge bonds...................	7,000 00	....
Richland Center city water bonds.......	1,000 00	....
Taylor county bonds	1,000 00	....
Vernon county asylum bonds...................	4,000 00	....
Waushara county bonds........................	1,000 00	....
School district No. 5 Viroqua bonds............ .	100 00	....
Loan to Brown county.	2,500 00	....
Loan to Florence county.....................	3,000 00	....
Loan to city of Chippewa Falls.................	3,000 00	....
Loan to city of Menasha.....................	1,500 00	....
Loan to city of Phillips	666 67	....
Loan to city of Waupaca......................	1,000 00	....
Loan to village of Osceola, Polk county........	200 00	....
Loan to town of Grover, Taylor county........	900 00	....
Loan to town of Waupaca, Waupaca county....	1,000 00	....
Loan to town of Worcester, Price county.......	500 00	....
Indemnity fund transfer....	7,659 44	....
Total receipts.........................	....	$122,968 28
DISBURSEMENTS.		
Eau Claire city bonds...........................	$10,000 00	....
Eau Claire city bonds premium.......	547 00	....
Ashland city bonds..............................	22,000 00	....
Chippewa Falls city bonds......................	5,000 00	....
Eau Claire light guard armory bonds...........	10,000 00	....
Premium on Ashland city bonds................	1,096 50	....
District No 8 Plymouth school bonds............	12,000 00	....
Madison city bonds.............................	25,000 00	....
Loan to Winnebago county....................	44,000 00	....
Total disbursements....................... .	....	$129,643 50

"A."—Normal School Fund Income Receipts for 1893.

NORMAL SCHOOL FUND INCOME.

RECEIPTS.		
Interest on land certificates and loans............	$1,529 90	....
Interest on certificates of indebtedness	36,046 95	....
Interest on Ashland county bonds...............	2,250 00	....
Interest on Ashland city bonds	646 30	....
Interest on Beaver Dam city bonds.............	480 00	....
Interest on Centralia city bonds...........	195 00	....
Interest on Columbus city bonds	950 00	....
Interest on Chippewa Falls city bonds...	1,625 00	....
Interest on Eau Claire city bonds	232 20	....
Interest on Eau Claire bridge bonds	232 36	....
Interest on Edgerton city bonds	800 00	....
Interest on Glenwood town bonds....	600 00	....
Interest on Hudson city bonds	1,980 00	....
Interest on Kenosha city bonds.	5,000 00	....
Interest on La Crosse city bonds...............	500 00	....
Interest on Madison city bonds	4,500 00	....
Interest on Manitowoc county bonds	2,800 00	....
Interest on Milwaukee city bonds...............	11,120 00	....
Interest on Menasha city bonds	662 50	....
Interest on Durand city bonds	150 00	....
Interest on Neenah school bonds	225 00	....
Interest on Neenah city hall bonds...	250 00	....
Interest on Milwaukee water bonds	7,700 00	....
Interest on Oshkosh city hall bonds............ .	2,681 25	....
Interest on Oshkosh bridge bonds	2,702 50	....
Interest on Portage county bonds	960 00	....
Interest on Plymouth district No. 8 school bonds.	300 00	....
Interest on Taylor county bonds	100 00	....
Interest on Vernon county bonds....	200 00	....
Interest on Viroqua district No. 5, bonds........	294 00	....
Interest on Richland Center water bonds........	350 00	....
Interest on Viroqua village bonds..............	140 00	....
Interest on Waushara county bonds.............	300 00	....
Interest on Waupaca city bonds.............	187 50	....
Interest on loan to Brown county	1,400 00	....
Interest on loan to Dunn county................	2,925 00	....
Interest on loan to Florence county...	450 00	....
Interest on loan to Jackson county	900 00	....
Interest on loan to Lincoln county.............	118 35	....
Interest on loan to Manitowoc county..........	580 00	....
Interest on loan to Winnebago county..........	841 50	....
Interest on loan to Oneida county..............	137 89	....
Interest on loan to city of Chippewa Falls.......	540 00	....
Interest on loan to city of Menasha.	300 00	....
Interest on loan to city of Phillips	466 66	....
Interest on loan to city of Waupaca	625 00	....
Interest on loan to town of Grover, Taylor Co...	135 00	....
Interest on loan to Light Horse Squadron.......	1,000 00	....
Interest on loan to city of Mineral Point........	400 00	....

"A."—Normal School Fund Income Disbursements for 1893.

Interest on loan to town of Waupaca, Waupaca Co...	$150 00	....
Interest on loan to town of Worcester, Price Co.	105 00	....
Interest on loan to village of Osceola....	56 00	....
Interest on normal school funds deposited in banks..	1,624 49	....
General fund for fifth normal school......	10,000 00	....
Drainage fund under chapter 185. Laws 1893 ..	70,939 02	....
F. P. Ainsworth, regent River Falls normal, tuition, etc...	3,223 56	....
D. J. Gardner, regent Platteville normal, tuition, etc	2,093 40	....
B. Goldsmith, regent Milwaukee normal, tuition, etc...	1,578 39	....
J. W. Hume, regent Oshkosh normal, tuition, etc	4,820 78	....
E. M. Johnson, regent Whitewater normal, tuition, etc...	2,650 16	....
Portage county donation for new normal school at Stevens Point	30,000 00	....
Stevens Point donation for new normal school at Stevens Point	20,000 00	....
City of Superior's donation for new normal school at West Superior.....................	65,000 00	....
Refunds.		
Library bureau	50	....
B. B. Park....................................	14 14	....
Drainage fund on certificate No. 250 Marquette county...................................	8 15	....
Smead Warming & Ventilating Co...........	10 24	....
Secretary board of regents........	5 00	....
Secretary board of regents witness fees........	1 40	....
Total receipts.................	....	$311,780 09

DISBURSEMENTS.

Treasurer board of regents normal schools.......	$308,854 88	....
Refunded for overpayment...	41 47	....
Accrued interest Eau Claire city bonds..........	149 32	....
Accrued interest Chippewa Falls bonds..........	60 42	....
Premium on Chippewa Falls bonds.............	199 50	....
Accrued interest Ashland city bonds	212 59	....
Accrued interest district No. 8, Plymouth school bonds..	200 00	....
Transfer to school fund income........	2,062 50	....
Total disbursements........................	.. ..	$311,780 09

"A."—Drainage Fund Receipts and Disbursements for 1893.

DRAINAGE FUND.

RECEIPTS.		
Interest on land certificates.	$145 34	....
Sales of land	22,306 24	....
Dues on certificates of sales....................	108 00	....
General fund transfer, one-half indemnity fund.	7,659 43	....
Total receipts...........................	....	$30,219 01

DISBURSEMENTS TO COUNTIES.		
Adams county.............................	$74 62	....
Ashland county................................	909 01	....
Barron county................................	166 31	....
Bayfield county	564 91	....
Brown county	31 47	....
Buffalo county..........	142 28	....
Burnett county	871 66	....
Calumet county	7 76	....
Chippewa county	690 24	....
Clark county	55 94	....
Columbia county....	153 53	....
Crawford county................................	460 21	....
Dane county....................................	127 10	....
Dodge county....................	98 25	....
Door county...........	49 55	....
Douglas county.......	404 14	....
Dunn county....................	268 56	....
Eau Claire county..........................	59 18	....
Florence county.........	$1,415 81	....
Fond du Lac county...........................	33 22	....
Forest county.......	612 06	....
Grant county...	25 63	....
Green county................................	15 73	....
Green Lake county......................:.....	109 45	....
Jackson county..........................	165 92	....
Jefferson county....	105 93	....
Juneau county.......	303 36	....
Kenosha county.	3 50	....
Kewaunee county.............................	165 53	....
La Crosse county.............................	514 84	....
Langlade county..........................	1,522 80	....
Lincoln county ....'	2,055 31	....
Manitowoc county........	578 26	....
Marathon county.............................	73 40	....
Marinette county.......................	1,234 11	....
Marquette county...............................	157 87	....
Monroe county.................................	128 40	....
Oconto county.......	530 45	....

"A."—Drainage Fund Disbursements for 1893.

Oneida county	$1,573 91	....
Outagamie county............................	71 06	....
Pepin county................................	77 58	....
Polk county.......	255 74	.. ..
Portage county...........	543 72	....
Price county...	653 60	....
Racine county...............................	1 75	....
Richland county.............................	55 12	....
Rock county.............................	33 05	....
Sauk county.................................	82 12	....
Sawyer county...........	567 55	....
Shawano county.............................	294 28	....
Sheboygan county........................... ..	15 73	....
Taylor county...............................	590 00	....
Trempealeau county.........................	41 85	....
Vernon county..............................	67 05	....
Walworth county...........................	57 46	....
Washburn county............................	327 89	....
Washington county..........................	29 75	....
Waukesha county............................ ..	170 00	... .
Waupaca county.............................	298 02	....
Waushara county............................	203 05	....
Winnebago county..................	148 47	....
Wood county...	95 63	....
Refunded normal school fund, land certificate No. 2,050...................	3 15	....
Transfer normal school fund income, chapter 185, Laws 1893....	70,939 02	....
Chas. Franz, commission on trespass on state lands...	24 79	....
Total disbursements...............	....	$92,102 64

"A."--Delinquent Tax Fund Receipts and Disbursements for 1893.

DELINQUENT TAX FUND.

RECEIPTS.		
Taxes on state lands	$5,914 02	....
Total receipts................................	....	$5,914 02
DISBURSEMENTS.		
Apportionment to Counties—		
Adams.....................................	$32 82	....
Ashland...................................	96 86	....
Barron....................................	27 82	....
Bayfield..................................	215 27	....
Brown.....................................	18 75	....
Buffalo...................................	34 08	....
Burnett...................................	101 38	....
Chippewa..................................	55 76	....
Clark.....................................	32 04	....
Columbia..................................	62 71	....
Crawford..................................	59 82	....
Door......................................	34 26	....
Douglas...................................	187 81	....
Dunn......................................	104 04	....
Eau Claire................................	212 24	....
Florence..................................	5 90	....
Forest....................................	103 41	....
Grant.....................................	10 14	....
Green Lake................................	13 57	....
Jackson...................................	32 04	....
Jefferson.................................	14 98	....
Juneau....................................	78 54	....
Kewaunee..................................	52 07	....
La Crosse.................................	2 67	....
La Fayette................................	5 91	....
Langlade..................................	132 21	....
Lincoln...................................	478 91	....
Manitowoc.................................	4 88	....
Marathon..................................	135 06	....
Marinette.................................	246 71	....
Marquette.................................	20 44	....
Monroe....................................	41 37	....
Oconto....................................	405 29	....
Oneida....................................	21 57	....

"A."—Delinquent Tax Fund Disbursements for 1893.

*Apportionment to Counties—*Continued.

Outagamie	$48 86	... .
Pepin	9 01	....
Pierce	28 26	....
Polk	220 22	....
Portage	67 46	....
Richland	33 86	....
Rock	2 89	....
St. Croix	123 17	....
Sauk	24 01	....
Sawyer	24 84	....
Shawano	329 68	....
Taylor	1,588 95	....
Trempealeau	38 60	....
Vernon	59 28	... .
Washburn	54 96	....
Waukesha	8 05	....
Waupaca	24 92	....
Waushara	54 22	....
Wood	136 34	....
Refunded.		
Geo. B. Burrows	$6 18	....
Chas. Schriber	6 87	....
Total disbursements	....	$6,020 46

"A."—Deposit Fund for 1893.

DEPOSIT FUND.

RECEIPTS.		
Balance deposited............	$867 06	....
Total receipts	....	$867 06
DISBURSEMENTS.		
August W. Gratz, surplus....	$224 08	....
James McCrossen, surplus......................	110 97	....
Henry Sherry, surplus....	20 91	....
Geo. B. Burrows, surplus.......................	64 86	....
P. Berg, surplus..............................	292 60	....
Ph. Berg, surplus	29 01	....
E. P. Sherry, surplus	12 42	....
Total disbursements.................	....	$754 80

"A."—Redemption and Swamp Land Funds for 1893.

REDEMPTION FUND.

RECEIPTS.		
Advertising interest, penalties and fees...... ...	$29 50	....
Total receipts............,....................	....	$29 50

MANITOWOC AND CALUMET SWAMP LAND FUND.

RECEIPTS.		
Calumet county................................	$7 76	....
Manitowoc county...	578 26	....
Total receipts.................................	....	$586 02

"A."—Indemnity Funds for 1893.

COLUMBIA AND SAUK COUNTY INDEMNITY FUND.

RECEIPTS.		
Columbia county	$98 28	
Sauk county	82 12	
Total receipts.		$180 40

INDEMNITY FUND.

RECEIPTS.		
Sales of land	$15,318 87	
Total receipts		$15,318 87
DISBURSEMENTS.		
Transfer to normal school fund	$7,659 44	
Transfer to drainage fund	7,659 43	
Total Disbursements		$15,318 87

"A."—Ex-State Treasurers' Judgment Fund for 1893.

EX-STATE TREASURERS' JUDGMENT FUND.

RECEIPTS.		
H. B. Harshaw, by clerk of circuit court Dane Co..	$72,407 51	....
E. C. McFetridge, by clerk of circuit court Dane Co...........	104,905 03	... .
Total receipts...........................	....	$177,312 54

APPENDIX "A."

DETAILED STATEMENT

OF THE

Receipts and Disbursements of the Several Funds

FOR THE

Fiscal Year Ending September 30, 1894.

GENERAL FUND RECEIPTS, 1894.

Counties.	Suit Tax.	Revenues.	
Adams	$4 00	$854 82	....
Ashland	199 00	2,677 06	....
Barron	36 00	2,641 88	....
Bayfield	187 00	1,155 74	....
Brown	81 00	4,235 49	....
Buffalo	12 00	3,083 81	....
Burnett	33 00	1,319 84	....
Calumet	41 00	3,159 88	.. ..
Chippewa	113 00	5,869 67	....
Clark	77 00	2,588 84	....
Columbia	41 00	2,387 60	....
Crawford	30 00	3,714 39	....
Dane	244 00	7,944 17	....
Dodge	43 00	4,433 21	... .
Door	56 00	2,193 22	....
Douglas	1,097 00	3,933 88	....
Dunn	57 00	1,870 15	....
Eau Claire	216 00	5,818 65	....
Florence	12 00	474 07	....
Fond du Lac	75 00	8,705 9?	....
Forest	15 00	246 17	....
Grant	114 00	3,785 86	....
Green	85 00	2,576 23	....

9—Sec'y.

"A."—General Fund Receipts for 1894.

Counties.	Suit Tax.	Revenues.	
Green Lake	$29 00	$2,767 45	
Iowa	55 00	1,797 02	
Iron	53 00	237 89	
Jackson	68 00	3,263 01	
Jefferson	32 00	3,536 49	
Juneau	44 00	4,703 26	
Kenosha	36 00	4,012 61	
Kewaunee	84 00	2,766 57	
La Crosse	189 00	3,705 97	
La Fayette	33 00	5,104 95	
Langlade	64 00	1,023 19	
Lincoln	92 00	1,581 16	
Manitowoc	72 00	3,223 48	
Marathon	185 00	4,246 87	
Marinette	101 00	3,484 22	
Marquette	10 00	2,066 07	
Milwaukee	1,852 00	12,131 51	
Monroe	69 00	3,886 19	
Oconto	38 00	4,216 06	
Oneida	52 00	568 02	
Outagamie	101 00	2,954 48	
Ozaukee	22 00	3,436 98	
Pepin	19 00	1,111 27	
Pierce	63 00	3,421 46	
Polk	37 00	3,480 85	
Portage	37 00	3,150 12	
Price	59 00	1,249 46	
Racine	103 00	2,642 88	
Richland	79 00	3,595 33	
Rock	238 00	5,575 08	
St. Croix	167 00	3,902 30	
Sauk	76 00	2,230 71	
Sawyer	2 00	694 05	
Shawano	78 00	1,593 33	
Sheboygan	85 00	4,238 87	
Taylor	75 00	1,089 21	
Trempealeau	40 00	4,614 27	
Vernon	52 00	2,490 86	
Vilas	16 00	146 04	
Walworth	84 00	3,196 82	
Washburn tax. { 1892 / 1893	53 00	1,181 07	
Washington	36 00	4,617 50	
Waukesha	160 00	3,032 40	
Waupaca	60 00	4,631 22	
Waushara	14 00	1,585 78	
Winnebago	111 00	6,155 67	
Wood	65 00	1,963 90	
Washburn, penalty for non-payment state tax 1892		61 93	
Total for fiscal year, Sept. 30, 1894	$7,903 00	$221,484 39	
Grand total			$229,887 39

'A."—General Fund Receipts for 1894.

RAILROAD COMPANIES—LICENSE
TAX.

Ahnapee & Western R'y Co........	$140 00	....	....
Abbotsford & North Eastern R. R. Co...............	75 80	....	....
Chicago, Burlington & Northern R'y Co	58,872 14	....	....
Chicago, St. Paul, Minneapolis & Omaha R'y Co	136,464 10	. ...	....
Chicago, Milwaukee & St. Paul R'y Co.............	584,716 27	....	....
Chicago, Milwaukee & St. Paul R'y Co., interest on deferred payments	827 27	....	....
Chicago, Milwaukee & St. Paul R'y Co., interest on deferred payments	848 20	....	....
Chicago, Fairchild & Eau Claire R'y Co	50 00	....	.........,
Chippewa River & Menomonie R'y Co..............................	133 05	... .	......., ..
Chicago & Northwestern R'y Co...	405,038 12	....	....
Drummond & South Western R'y Co	50 00	....	....
Duluth Short Line R'y Co..........	696 04	....	....
Duluth, South Shore & Atlantic R'y Co....	1,781 64	....	....
Duluth & Winnepeg R'y Co........	57 50	....	...
Eastern Railway Company of Minnesota	12,239 27	....	....
Green Bay, Winona & St. Paul R'y Co....	3,248 38	....	....
Goodyear & Neillsville R'y Co	75 00	....	....
Kewaunee, Green Bay & Western R'y Co...........................	486 25	....	....
Kickapoo Valley & Northern R'y Co	170 00	....	....
Lake Superior Terminal Transfer R'y Co...........................	72 50	....	....
Milwaukee, Wauwatosa Motor R'y Co............................	97 47	....	....
Milwaukee & Superior R'y Co	217 89	....	....
Menomonie R'y Co	32 00	....	....
Milwaukee, Chicago & Bay View R'y Co............................	1,704 20	....	....
Minneapolis, St. Paul & Sault Ste. Marie R'y Co...................	66,134 89	....	....
Minnesota & Wisconsin R'y Co.	180 00	....	...., ...
Northern Pacific R'y Co...........	16,787 28	....	....
Oshkosh Transportation Co........	49 56	... .	....
Prairie du Chien & McGregor R'y Co...............	1,101 70	....	....
' Saint Cloud, Grantsburg & Ashland R'y Co.................	331 44	... .	....
Winona Bridge R'y Co..............	233 40	....	....
West Range R'y Co...	5 00	....	... .
Wisconsin & Chippewa R'y Co.	30 00	....	....
Wisconsin Central Lines............	144,255 51	....	....
Wisconsin Central Lines, interest on deferred payments...............	1,015 24	....	....

"A."—General Fund Receipts for 1894.

Chicago, Madison & Northern, by Illinois Central.................	$456 55	....	....
Port Edwards, Centralia & Northern.	150 00	....	....
Total.................	....	$1,438,758 66	....
PALACE CAR COMPANIES — LICENSE TAX.			
Pullman Palace Car Co.............	$490 35	....	....
Wagner Palace Car Co.............	733 04	....	....
Total..........	.;..........	$1,223 39	....
TELEGRAPH COMPANIES — LICENSE TAX.			
Western Union Telegraph Co.......	$9,560 90	....	....
Grant County Telegraph Co	8 91	....	....
Chicago & Milwaukee Telegraph Co.	66 00	....	....
Chicago, Milwaukee & Lake Shore Telegraph Co.....	232 00	....	....
Postal Telegraph Co................	67 90	....	....
Total	....	$9,935 71	....
FIRE INSURANCE COMPANIES — LICENSE TAX.			
Atlas Assurance Co., London, Eng.	$433 79	... .	....
American Central Fire Ins. Co., St. Louis, Mo.	455 58	....	....
American Fire Insurance Co., Newark, N. J.	335 62	....	....
Ætna Fire Ins. Co., Hartford, Conn.	2,148 57	....	....
Allemania Fire Ins. Co , Pittsburg, Pa.	176 11	....	....
American Fire Ins Co., Philadelphia, Pa.....	1,762 76	....	....
American Fire Ins. Co., New York, N. Y............	833 48	....	....
Agricultural Fire Ins. Co., Watertown, N. Y.....................	248 92	....	....
Albany Fire Ins. Co , Albany, N. Y.	120 48	....	....
American Fire Ins. Co., Boston, Mass	194 07	....	....
Buffalo German Fire Ins. Co., Buffalo, N. Y.	427 18	....	....
British American Assurance Co., Toronto, Can	1,036 15	....	....
British Foreign Marine Ins. Co., London, Eng.............	315 33	....	....
Broadway Fire Ins. Co., New York, N. Y.................	90 04	....	....
Boylston Fire Ins. Co., Boston, Mass.	358 04	....	....
Commerce Fire Ins. Co., Albany, N. Y........................	67 88	... .	....

"A."—General Fund Receipts for 1894.

Commonwealth Fire Ins. Co., New York, N. Y.	$212 29		
Connecticut Fire Ins. Co., Hartford, Conn	1,003 95		
Concordia Fire Ins. Co., Milwaukee, Wis	1,282 08		
Citizens' Fire Ins. Co., New York City, N. Y	347 06		
Continental Fire Ins Co., New York City, N. Y	951 65		
Caledonia Fire Ins. Co., Edinburgh, Scotland	708 67		
Commercial Union Ins. Co., London, Eng	1,963 00		
Detroit Fire & Marine Ins. Co., Detroit, Mich	408 52		
Delaware Fire Ins. Co., Philadelphia, Pa	309 06		
Dwelling House Ins. Co., Boston, Mass	205 76		
Equitable Fire & Marine Ins. Co., Providence, R. I	168 58		
Fire Association, Philadelphia, Pa.	1,976 39		
Fireman's Fund Ins. Co., San Francisco, Cal	815 74		
Fire Ins. Co., County of Philadelphia, Philadelphia, Pa	3 16		
Farmers' Ins. Co., York, Pa	309 02		
Firemen's Ins. Co., Newark; N. J	177 16		
Franklin Fire Ins. Co., Philadelphia, Pa	274 52		
Greenwich Fire Ins. Co., New York, N. Y	396 88		
Granite State Fire Ins. Co., Portsmouth, N. H	812 37		
German Fire Ins. Co., Freeport, Ill.	2,099 73		
Guardian Life & Fire Ins. Co., London, Eng	876 48		
Germantown Farmers' Mutual Ins. Co., Rockfield, Wis	874 47		
Girard Fire & Marine Ins. Co., Philadelphia, Pa	316 17		
German Fire Ins. Co., Peoria, Ill	201 89		
Grand Rapids Fire Ins. Co., Grand Rapids, Mich	368 70		
German American Ins. Co., New York, N. Y.	1,895 09		
Germania Fire Ins. Co., New York, N. Y.	653 03		
German Fire Ins. Co.. Pittsburg, Pa.	159 21		
Glen Falls Fire Ins. Co., Glen Falls, N. Y.	287 10		
Hartford Fire Ins. Co., Hartford, Conn	2,580 33		
Home Fire Ins. Co., New York, N. Y	2,824 48		
Hanover Fire Ins. Co., New York, N. Y.	694 12		

"A."—General Fund Receipts for 1894.

Hartford Steam Boiler Inspection Co..........................	$613 62	....
Herman Farmers' Mutual Ins. Co., Herman. Wis....	203 44	....
Hamburg-Bremen Fire Ins. Co., Hamburg, Germany	780 82	....
Lion Fire Ins. Co., London, Eng ...	337 44	....
Liverpool, London & Globe Ins. Co., Liverpool, Eng	2,323 67	....
London and Lancashire Ins. Co., Liverpool Eng.............	1,457 14	....
London Assurance Corporation, London, Eng	917 44	....
Lancashire Fire Ins. Co., Manchester, Eng	1,396 70	....
Mannheim Fire Ins. Co., Mannheim, Germany	23 27	....
Manchester Fire Assurance Co., Manchester, Eng.................	1,451 75	....
Manufacturers' & Merchants' Fire Ins. Co., Pittsburg, Pa...........	160 80	....
Millers' & Manufacturers' Fire Ins. Co., Minneapolis, Minn...	300 38	....
Millers' National Ins. Co., Chicago, Ill	199 43	....
Milwaukee Mechanics' Ins. Co., Milwaukee, Wis	3,137 73	....
Manufacturers' & Merchants' Mutual Ins. Co., Rockford, Ill	255 88	....
Mechanics' Fire Ins. Co., Philadelphia, Pa	235 64	....
Marine Fire Ins. Co., London, Eng..	5 81	....
Merchants' Fire Ins. Co., Newark, N J	443 61	....
Mercantile Fire & Marine Ins. Co., Boston, Mass	180 42	....
Mutual Fire Ins. Co.. New York, N. Y.	956 30	....
Michigan Fire & Marine Ins. Co., Detroit, Mich	694 60	....
Merchants' Fire Ins Co., Providence, R. I.......	168 58	....
Manufacturers' & Builders' Fire Ins. Co , New York, N. Y.	85 02	....
Northern Assurance Co., London, Eng	769 10	....
New York Bowery Ins. Co., New York, N. Y..............	54 17	....
National Fire Ins. Co., Hartford, Conn	1,092 13	....
North British & Mercantile Ins Co., London, Eng..............	2,077 89	....
Newark Fire Ins. Co., Newark, N. J....	150 15	....
New Hampshire Fire Ins. Co., Manchester, N. H...	516 75	....
Northwestern National Ins. Co., Milwaukee, Wis.................	1,174 79	....

"A."—General Fund, Receipts for 1894.

Norwich Union Society, Norwich, Eng...............................	$753 89	....	....
Niagara Fire Ins. Co., New York, N. Y............................	1,168 44	....	....
Orient Fire Ins. Co., Hartford, Conn.	927 98	....	....
Oakland Home Fire Ins. Co., Oakland, Cal......................	1,233 65	....	....
Phoenix Fire Ins. Co., Brooklyn, N. Y...........................	3,858 43	....	....
Pacific Fire Ins. Co., New York, N. Y...........................	200 08	....	....
Pennsylvania Fire Ins. Co., Philadelphia, Pa.....................	1,252 60	....	....
Prussian National Fire Ins. Co,, Stettin, Germany.................	483 17	....	....
Queen Ins. Co of America, New York, N. Y......................	1,466 90	....	....
Royal Ins. Co. of Liverpool, England	1,760 06	....	....
Reliance Marine Ins. Co., Liverpool, Eng	4 28	....	....
Rochester German Ins. Co., Rochester, N. Y......................	503 38	....	....
Reading Fire Ins. Co., Reading, Pa.	131 60	....	....
Reliance Fire Ins. Co., Philadelphia, Pa........................	77 92	....	....
Rutger Fire Ins. Co., New York, N. Y...........................	89 13	....	....
Rockford Fire Ins. Co., Rockford, Ill.	1,345 77	....	....
Spring Garden Ins. Co., Philadelphia, Pa........................	193 83	....	....
St. Paul Fire & Marine Ins. Co., St. Paul, Minn	828 28	....	....
Security Fire Ins. Co., New Haven, Conn........................	480 33	....	....
Scottish Union & National Ins. Co., Edinburgh, Scotland............	917 13	....	....
Standard Marine Ins. Co., Liverpool, Eng.....	376 12	....	....
Springfield Fire & Marine Ins. Co., Springfield, Mass...............	1,236 65	....	....
Sun Fire Ins. Co., London, Eng....	1,796 99	....	....
Transatlantic Fire Ins. Co., Hamburg, Ger......................	292 63	....	....
Teutonia Fire Ins. Co., Philadelphia, Pa........................	1 56	....	....
Traders' Ins. Co., Chicago, Ill	1,125 70	....	....
Union Marine Ins. Co., Liverpool, Eng..........................	316 54	....	....
United States Fire Ins. Co., New York, N. Y.....................	167 88	....	....
United Fireman's Ins. Co., Philadelphia, Pa......................	142 79	....	....
Union Fire Ins. Co., Philadelphia, Pa...........................	220 98	....	....
Union Assurance Society, London, Eng	221 36	....	....
Westchester Fire Ins. Co., New York, N. Y......................	870 86	....	....

"A."—General Fund Receipts for 1894.

Western Assurance Co.; Toronto, Can	$3,002 50	....	....
Williamsburg City Fire Ins. Co., New York, N. Y....................	257 97	....	....
Capitol Fire Ins. Co., Concord, N. H.	360 88	....	....
General Marine Fire Ins. Co., Dresden, Ger....	45 85	....	....
Imperial Fire Ins. Co., London, Eng.	622 28	....	....
Ins. Co. State of Pennsylvania, Philadelphia, Pa.	297 01	....	....
Ins. Co. of North America, Philadelphia, Pa	2,413 60	....	....
Minnesota Fire Ins. Co., Minneapolis, Minn....................	304 45	....	....
Providence-Washington Fire Ins Co	700 74	....	....
Columbia Fire Ins. Co., Louisville, Ky.	387 00	....	....
Phoenix Fire Ins. Co., Hartford, Conn	1,495 00	....	
Palitin Insurance Co., Manchester, England	580 89	....	....
Total......................	....	$90,689 21	....

LIFE INSURANCE COMPANIES — LICENSE TAX.

Ætna Life Ins. Co., Hartford, Conn.	$300 00	....	....
Bankers' Life Association, St. Paul, Minn	300 00	....	....
Connecticut Life Ins. Co., Hartford, Conn	300 00	....	....
Equitable Life Association, New York, N. Y	300 00	....	....
Germania Life Ins. Co., New York, N. Y	300 00	....	....
Home Life Ins. Co., New York, N. Y.	300 00	....	....
Hartford Life Annuity Co., Hartford, Conn....	300 00	....	....
Life Insurance Clearing Co., St. Paul Minn....................	300 00	... .	... .
Mutual Reserve Life Association, New York, N. Y.................	300 00	....	....
Metropolitan Life Ins. Co., New York, N. Y.	300 00	....	....
Michigan Mutual Life Ins. Co., Detriot, Mich	300 00	....	....
Mutual Life Ins. Co., New York City	300 00	....	....
Mutual Benefit Life Ins. Co., Newark, N. J...............	300 00	....	....
Massachusetts Mutual Life Ins. Co., Springfield, Mass..............	300 00	....	....
Manhattan Life Ins. Co., New York, N. Y....................	300 00	....	....
Northwestern Mutual Life Ins. Co., Milwaukee, Wis	24,274 05	....	....

"A."—General Fund Receipts for 1894.

New England Mutual Life Ins. Co., Boston, Mass	$300 00		
New York Life Ins. Co., New York, N. Y.	300 00		
National Life Ins. Co., Montpelier, Vt.	763 14		
Pennsylvania Mutual Life Ins. Co., Philadelphia, Pa	906 85		
Phoenix Mutual Life Insurance Co. Hartford, Conn.	300 00		
Provident Savings Life Ins. Co., New York City	300 00		
Prudential Life Ins. Co., Newark, N. J.	300 00		
Travelers' Ins. Co., Hartford, Conn..	300 00		
Union Central Life Ins. Co., Cincinnati, O.	300 00		
United States Life Ins. Co, New York, N. Y.	300 00		
Washington Life Ins. Co., New York, N. Y.	300 00		
Iowa Life Ins. Co.	300 00		
Union Mutual Life, Portland, Maine	300 00		
Total		$33,744 04	
ACCIDENT INSURANCE COMPANIES— LICENSE TAX.			
American Surety Co., New York, N. Y	$236 72		
American Employers' Liability Co., Jersey City, N. J.	164 68		
American Mutual Accident Ins. Co., Oshkosh, Wis.	503 64		
Casualty & Fidelity Co., New York, N. Y.	1,566 84		
Employers' Liability Assurance Corporation. London, Eng.	505 82		
Guaranty Ins. Co. of North America, Montreal, Can	18 15		
Lloyds' Plate Glass Ins. Co., New York, N. Y.	147 38		
Masonic Fraternal Accident Ass'n, Westfield, Mass	90 82		
Metropolitan Accident Association, Chicago, Ill.	161 90		
Metropolitan Plate Glass Co., New York, N. Y.	25 05		
New York Plate Glass Ins. Co., New York, N. Y.	85 75		
New England Mutual Accident Ass'n, Boston, Mass	77 16		
National Accident Society, New York, N. Y.	2 10		
Preferred Masonic Mutual Accident Ass'n, Detroit, Mich	22 59		
Preferred Mutual Accident Ass'n, New York, N. Y.	102 62		

"A."—General Fund Receipts for 1894.

Railway Officials' & Employes' Accident Ass'n, Indianapolis, Ind ...	$150 34	....	...
Standard Life & Accident Ins. Co., Detroit, Mich....	1,142 04	....	....
United States Mutual Accident Ass'n, New York, N. Y	218 00	....	...
Union Casualty Surety Co., St. Louis, Mo	12 63	....	...
Interstate Casulty Co., New York City.......	4 06	....	... .
Star Accident Ins. Co., Chicago, Ill.	82 26	....	...
North American Accident Ass'n, Chicago, Ill	28 48	....	...
Travelers' Preferred Accident Ass'n.	145 77	... .	....
Total...........................	....	$5,497 80	....
TELEPHONE COMPANIES — LICENSE TAX.			
Duluth Telephone Co	$384 28	....	....
Wisconsin Telephone Co	9,332 01	... .	....
Total....................... .	....	$9,716 29	....
SAVINGS, LOANS & TRUST COMPANIES—LICENSE TAX.			
Saving, Loan & Trust Co., Madison, Wis............................	$460 68	....	....
Wisconsin Trust Co., Milwaukee, Wis...........................	674 25	....	....
Milwaukee Trust Co., Milwaukee, Wis........	300 00	....	... ...
Northern Trust Co., West Superior, Wis................	467 91	....	....
Total...................... ..	....	$1,902 84	....
LOG DRIVING & BOOMING COMPANIES—LICENSE TAX.			
Black River Imp'nt Co., La CrosseWis.	$35 70	....	....
James Bardon for Amer. River Douglas Co.	5 74	....	....
East Fork Imp'nt Co., La Crosse, Wis	165 95	....	....
Hay Creek Imp'nt & Log Driving Co., La Crosse, Wis.....	36 78	....	....
Knapp, Stout & Co., Company, Menomonie, Wis	22 22	....	... .
Merrill Boom Co., Merrill, Wis.....	761 71	....	....
Nina Desert Imp'nt Co., Rhinelander, Wis...	27 74	....	....
Nemadji Boom Co., Superior.......	236 55	....	....

"A."—General Fund Receipts for 1894.

Pelican Boom Co., Rhinelander, Wis.	$82 58		
Pioneer Imp'nt Co., Rhinelander, Wis.	22 00		
Wausau Boom Co., Wausau, Wis...	56 54		
Buckalaba Imp'nt Co.	3 00		
Fish Creek Boom & Log Driving Co., Ashland	122 60		
Total		$1,579 11	

SUNDRY SOURCES.

Secretary of state, office fees	$6,372 57		
Secretary of state, notary fees	2,771 00		
Land commissioners' fees	917 50		
Insurance commissioner's fees	20,669 00		
Geo. W. Peck, governor, commissioner of deed fees	250 00		
Superintendent of public propt., sale of books & mdse.	354 11		
State superintendent, sale of books.	270 21		
Income penalty	810 27		
U. S. by Geo. W. Peck, Gov., care of inmates Wis. Vet. Home	12,662 21		

Refunds.

F. F. Proudfit, paymaster gen., W. N. G. excess warrant No. 6544	10 00		
Barny Corcoran on warrant No. 5709	11 06		
F. A. Hutchins, overpayment library clerk	5 93		
Hon. Chas. Jonas, refund salary, lieutenant governor	46 20		
Treas. World's Fair Comm. from Milwaukee Museum	411 85		
Goodyear Rubber Company	10 00		
Total		$45,571 91	

HAWKERS AND PEDDLERS.

Licenses	$12,841 95	$12,841 95	

FINES FOR VIOLATION OF GAME LAWS.

Benedict Lange, fine violating game laws	$8 34		
Municipal judge Dane Co., for fines violating game laws	25 00		
V. E. Brewer	20 83		
G. C. Prentice	16 67		
J. S. Thompson, J. P.	5 00		
Chas. Krous, J. P.	8 33		
A. R. Livingstone, deputy G. W.	2 00		

"A."—General Fund Receipts for 1894.

A. L. Lord, deputy G. W..........	$4 00	....	....
Treas. Outagamie Co............	5 00	....	....
Treas. Bayfield Co.................	16 67	....	....
Treas. Chippewa Co..............	12 50	....	....
Treas. Shawano Co	2 25	....	....
Treas. Forest Co	12 50	....	....
D. S. Markie, deputy G. W...	6 66	....	....
Total......................	....	$145 75	....
MISCELLANEOUS.			
Interest on general fund deposited in banks.................	$14,178 18	....	....
Board of education, city of Madison, interest on gen'l fund loan......	186 78	....	....
Q. M. general, Ins., loss on clothing, W. N. G..	136 00	....	....
Marathon county land sales	27 15	....	....
Alfred James, certificates..	2 25	....	....
North Western Mutual Life Ins. Co., certificates.....	10 00	....	....
John M. Olin, certificates... ·	1 25	....	....
Semi-annual bank statements, pub. of..	656 00	....	....
Nat. Benefit & Casualty Co., certificate.....	1 00	....	....
Ex-state treasurers judgment, fund transfer.........................	327,902 55	....	....
Edward Brook, certificates.	1 62	....	....
St. Croix & Lake Superior Railroad trespass, fund transfer...........	2,067 46	$345,170 19	....
Total general fund receipts.....	....	....	$2,226,164 24

"A."—General Fund Disbursements for 1894.

GENERAL FUND DISBURSEMENTS FOR 1894.

FOR SALARIES AND EXPENSES.			
Governor's Office—			
Geo. W. Peck, governor, salary..	$4,583 00	....	... .
C. L. Clark, priv. sec , salary	133 00	... .	....
Geo. P. Mathes, priv. sec., salary.	1,467 00	....	....
		$6,183 00	
Secretary of State's Office—			
T. J. Cunningham, secretary of state, salary....	$5,000 00	... .	....
T. B. Leonard, assistant secretary of state, salary..............	2,000 00	....	....
		$7,000 00	....
Treasurer's Office—			
John Hunner, treasurer. salary...	$5,000 00	....	.. ..
F. F. Proudfit, assistant treasurer, salary......................	2,000 00	....	....
		$7,000 00	....
Attorney General's Office—			....
J. L O'Connor, atty. gen., salary.	$3,500 00	....	
J. M. Clancy, asst. atty. gen., salary...	2,000 00	... ...	....
		$5,500 00	
State Superintendent's Office—			
O. E. Wells. state supt., salary...	$1,200 00	....	....
O. E. Wells, state supt., expenses.	427 26	....	....
C. A. Hutchins, asst. state. supt., salary	1,800 00	....	....
C. H. Sylvester, high school inspr., salary	1,380 74	....	....
C. H. Sylvester, high school inspr., expenses	585 69	....	....
Des Forges & Co., books for state supt	57 10	....	....
Henry Holt & Co., books for state supt	3 27	....	....
J. A. Sheridan, high school inspr.	450 00	... .	....
D. Appleton & Co., books, state supt...........	6 00	... ...	....
		$5,910 06	....

"A."—General Fund Disbursements for 1894.

Railroad Commissioner's Office—

Thomas Thompson, comm., salary	$2,750 00	....	....
Thomas Thompson, comm., expenses	328 00	....	....
J. B. Webb, deputy comm., salary	1,749 96	....	....
J. B. Webb, deputy comm., expenses	72 00	....	....
		$1,894 96	....

Insurance Commissioner's Office—

W. M. Root, commissioner, salary	$3,250 00	....	....
W. M. Root, commissioner, expenses	97 54	....	....
Ned M. Root, deputy commissioner, salary	1,500 00	....	....
		$4,847 54	....

Supt. Public Property's Office—

E. V. Briesen, supt., salary	$2,000 00	....	....
		$2,000 00	....

Supreme Court—

Wm. P. Lyon, chief justice	$1,250 00	....	....
H. S. Orton, associate and chief justice	5,000 00	....	....
J. B. Cassoday, associate justice	5,000 00	....	....
J. B. Winslow, associate justice	5,000 00	....	....
S. U. Pinney, associate justice	5,000 00	....	....
A. W. Newman, associate justice	3,750 00	....	....
Clarance Kellogg, clerk, per diem	450 00	....	....
Clarance Kellogg, clerk, fees	183 25	....	....
F. K. Conover, reporter	2,750 00	....	....
C. H. Beyler, crier	176 00	....	....
C. H. Beyler, copyist	900 00	....	....
J. Fleigler, Jr., proofreader	300 00	....	....
Chas. E. Whelan, proofreader	900 00	....	....
W. T. Wolf, messenger	278 23	....	....
Oscar H. Ecke, messenger	621 77	....	. ...
Frank D. Reed, copyist	900 00	....	....
Frederick A. Foster, copyist	900 00	....	....
Leo A. Williams, copyist	825 00	....	....
Jno. T. Jones, copyist	67 50	....	....
		$34,251 75	....

Circuit Courts—

F. M. Fish, judge, 1st circuit	$4,000 00	....	....
D. H Johnson, judge, 2nd circuit	4,000 00	....	....
Geo. W. Burnell, judge, 3rd circuit	4,000 00	....	....
Norman S. Gilson, judge, 4th circuit	4,000 00	....	....
Geo. C. Clementson, judge, 5th circuit	4,000 00	....	....
J. M. Morrow, judge, 6th circuit	2,666 65	....	....
Chas. M. Webb, judge, 7th circuit	4,000 00	....	....
Egbert B. Bundy, judge, 8th circuit	4,000 00	....	....

"A."—General Fund Disbursements for 1894.

*Circuit Courts—*Continued.			
R. G. Siebecker, judge, 9th circuit	$4,000 00	....	....
Jno. Goodland, judge, 10th circuit	4,000 00	... .	....
R. D. Marshall, judge, 11th circuit	4,000 00	....	....
Jno. R. Bennett, judge, 12th circuit	4,000 00	....	....
A. Scott Sloan, judge, 13th circuit	4,000 00	....	....
Samuel D. Hastings, judge, 14th circuit	4,000 00	....	....
J. K. Parish, judge, 15th circuit .	4,000 00	....	....
Chas. V. Bardeen, judge, 16th circuit	4,000 00	... .	....
W. F. Bailey, judge, 17th circuit..	4,000 00	....	....
O. B. Wyman, judge, 6th circuit..	1,289 55	....	....
		$67,956 20	....
State Historical Society—			
R. G. Thwaites, cor. sec'y	$1,833 00	....	....
I. S. Bradley, librarian	1,466 00	....	....
Minnie Oakley, asst. librarian	1,200 00	....	....
Treasurer apropriation	5,000 00	....	....
		$9,499 00	....
State Library—			
J. R. Berryman, librarian	$2,000 00	....	....
Banks & Bros	74 50	....	....
Boston Book Co	467 85	....	....
Beauchemin & Fils...............	24 96	....	....
Callahan & Co	527 60	....	....
Carswell Co., Ltd	61 46	....	....
College Pub. Co	2 00	....	....
Chicago Legal News	2 20	....	....
T. H. Flood & Co	28 00	....	....
T. J W. Johnson.................	9 00	....	... .
Kay & Bros.....................	15 00	....	....
Harvard Law Review	2 50	....	....
Lawyers Co operative Pub. Co....	40 00	....	....
Law Journal Publishing Co.......	2 00	....	....
Medico-Legal Journal	6 00	....	....
Rosell & Hutchinson.............	23 50	....	....
F. H. Thomas Law Book Co......	6 25	.. ..	....
Edward Thompson Co............	54 00	....	....
United States Corporation Bureau	5 00	....	....
W. st. Publishing Co.............	235 85	....	....
North American Review..........	5 00	....	....
Northwestern Law Review........	3 00	....	....
Strumpf & Steuer.......	1 00	....	....
Frank Shepard..................	40 00	....	... ..
Stephens & Haynes......	96 35	....	....
Yale Law Review........	2 00	....	....
Review Pub. Co.................	10 00	....	....
University Caw Review..	2 00	....	....

"A."—General Fund Disbursements for 1894.

State Library—Continued.

Marshall & Bruce Co............	$13 50	....	....
Weekly Law Bulletin and Ohio Law Journal...................	5 00	....	....
Frank P. Dufresen.... ... ;......	2 00	....	....
The Banking Law Journal Co ...	3 00		
		$3,770 53	....

Board of Control—

J. E. Jones, salary and expenses..	$2,736 57	....	....
Clarence Snyder, salary and expenses...................	2,725 61	....	....
J. L. Cleary, salary and expenses.	2,490 52	....	....
C. D. Parker, salary and expenses	2,490 77	....	....
W. H. Graebner, sal. and expenses	2,721 35	....	....
J. W. Oliver, salary and expenses.	2,429 23	....	....
D. S. Comly, secretary, salary	1,834 00	....	....
C. B. Goodwin, assistant secretary, salary................	1,150 00	....	....
		$18,578 05	
			$177 591 08

PERMANENT APPROPRIATIONS.

Bureau of Labor Statistics—

Jerre Dobbs, com., salary.	$2,000 00	....	....
Jerre Dobbs, com., expenses	1,000 00	....	....
F. M. Dye·, dep. com., salary.....	1,500 00	....	....
John W. Zwaska, factory inspector, salary...............	1,200 00	....	....
John W. Zwaska, factory inspector, office rent........	146 83	....	....
J. L. Van Etten, asst. factory inspector, salary...............	1,000 00	....	....
J. L. Van Etten, asst. factory inspector, expenses.......	402 14		
		$7,248 47	....

State Board of Health—

J. T. Reeve, secretary, expenses of board..................	$4,469 56	....	....
U. O. B. Wingate, secretary, expenses of board.................	1,199 24		
		$5,668 80	....

Fish Culture—

Treasurer of fish commission, appropriation	$13,000 00		
		$13,000 00	....

Dairy and Food Commissioner--

D. L. Harkness, com., sala·y.....	$1,664 00	....	....
D. L. Harkness, com., expenses...	362 03	....	....
Geo. S. Cox, dep'y com., salary...	1,650 00	....	....
Geo. S. Cox, dep'y com., expenses	373 95	....	....
Walter A. West, salary..........	1,650 00	....	....
Walter A West, expenses........	521 15	....	....
M. J. Cantwell, mdse.............	53 00	....	....
Wm. Owen, plumbing............	3 15	....	....

"A."—General Fund Disbursements for 1894.

Dairy and Food Commissioner—
Continued.

Wm. J. Park & Sons, mdse.......	$11 20		
Dexter Curtis, mdse..............	7 00		
A. P. Davis. mdse	8 00		
Thos. Luschinger, com., salary...	624 00		
Thos Luschinger, com., expenses.	83 05		
Jno. H. Clark, mdse..	12 65		
Madison Gas Co., gas.	2 10		
Cornish Green & Curtiss, mdse...	14 40		
Chas. Todd, services, clerk... ...	6 64		
		$7,046 32	

Dairy and Food Commissioner—
Laboratory—

Geo. S. Cox, expenses............	$333 16		
Edwin Sumner, mdse..............	12 80		
Jno. H. Clark, mdse..............	78 21		
Wm F. Vilas, rent...............	500 00		
Einer & Amund, mdse...........	1 50		
		$925 67	

Land Protection—

J A. Kennedy....................	$186 00		
J. O. Chandler...................	335 41		
James Whelan...	184 78		
J. C. Daley, per diem and expenses	2,153 55		
Jno. J. Thornton, per diem and expenses......................	35 00		
Martin Page, per diem and expenses........................	1,721 01		
Hugh Gough, per diem and expenses..	360 00		
A. N. Dickey, per diem and expenses	646 12		
Geo. H. Jalley, per diem and expenses.. ... ./.....	376 62		
Richard Dooher..........	100 00		
W. H. Cannon, expenses.........	50 40		
		$6,148 89	

Teachers' Institutes—

J. C. Freeman....................	$378 20		
M. R. Winslow.........	25 00		
J. W Stearns..	346 80		
A. J. Hutton....................	91 60		
L D. Harvey	120 00		
R. W Halsey....................	119 62		
T. B Pray..........	150 32		
Albert Salisbury.............	80 00		
		$1,311 54	
			$41,349 69

LEGISLATIVE EXPENSES.

Salary lieutenant governor.........		$500 00	

Blue Book—

Geo Levis.		100 00	

"A."—General Fund Disbursements for 1894.

Legislative Printing—			
Democrat Printing Co.............	....	$105 21	....
Total legislative expenses.....	....	....	$705 21
CHARITABLE AND PENAL INSTITU-TIONS.			
State Hospital for Insane, expenses.	$94,403 65	....	....
Northern Hospital for Insane, expenses..........................	121,686 52	....	....
Wisconsin School for Deaf, expenses	39,938 43	....	....
Wisconsin School for Blind, expenses..........................	25,523 45	....	....
Industrial School for Boys, expenses	54,458 97	....	....
State Prison, expenses..............	28,829 34	....	....
State Public School, expenses.......	37,538 12	....	....
Total.......	....	....	$402,378 48
CLERK HIRE.			
Governor's Office—			
Werner Pressentin, executive clerk	$1,500 00	$1,500 00	....
Secretary's Office—			
F. W. Grumm, chief clerk	1,800 00	....	....
Geo. W. Levis, bookkeeper.......	2,000 00	....	....
C. H. Phillips, assistant bookkeeper.......	1,500 00	....	....
A. F. Warden, printing clerk.....	1,800 00	....	....
A. N. Altenhofen, filing clerk....	1,500 00	....	....
Julius Bruess, draughtsman.....	1,150 00	....	....
Nellie Leonard, warrant clerk....	1,380 00	....	....
Isabella Schneider, recording clerk	1,380 00	....	....
Henry Lebeis, general clerk.....	600 00	....	....
Geo. W. Brower, general clerk...	1,200 00	....	....
John J. Thornton, general clerk..	1,200 00	....	....
Thomas McBean, general clerk...	1,200 00	....	....
John H. Kernan, general clerk...	1,200 00	....	....
H. J. Lohmar, general clerk	830 00	....	....
Paul O. Husting, general clerk....	1,125 00	....	....
Christina McDougall, stenographer	630 00	....	....
Evalena Bresse, stenographer. ..	140 00	....	....
Frank Dunnegan, mailing clerk..	675 00	....	....
		$21,310 00	....
Treasury Department—			
P. M. McMahon, bookkeeper	$2,149 98	....	....
L. B. Murphy, corresponding clerk	1,800 00	....	....
G. L. Blum, entry clerk..........	1,800 00	....	....
F. W. Bartz, mailing clerk.......	1,850 00	....	....
Rob't Henry, messenger..........	1,100 00	....	....
W. H. G. Mueller, janitor.......	730 00	....	....
Earl E. Hunner, watchman......	730 00	....	....
		$10,159 98	....

"A."—General Fund Disbursements for 1894.

Land Office—

W. H. Cannon, chief clerk.......	$1,800 00		
W. H. Cannon, clerk land coms..	199 92		
O. R. Skarr, asst chief clerk.....	1,699 92		
L. A. Brace, bookkeeper.........	1,698 26		
C. J. M. Malek, patent clerk.....	1,699 92		
W. F. Dockery, entry clerk......	1,560 00		
G. J. Reinsch, clerk..............	1,380 00		
John Byrne, clerk................	1,380 00		
Robt. Lamp, clerk...............	1,200 00		
Stella Keenan, stenographer......	775 00		
H. Schildhauer, bookkeeper......	9 18		
		$13,402 15	

State Superintendent's Office—

Jas. A. Sheridan, chief clerk....	$1,125 00		
F. A. Hutchins, library clerk.....	1,200 00		
F. A. Hutchins, library clerk expenses........................	213 65		
Anna J. Lum, stenographer......	999 96		
J. W. Stewart, chief clerk........	375 00		
Ina Johnson, clerk..............	40 00		
		$3,953 61	

Superintendent of Public Property's Office—

W. B. Vance....................	$1,520 24		
		$1,520 24	

Bureau of Labor Statistics—

Max A. Blumenfeld.............	$1,200 00		
		$1,200 00	

Total.....			$53,046 28

LABOR ABOUT CAPITOL.

Engineers and Firemen—

Jno. Doyle, engineer.............	$1,200 00		
Jno. Butler, asst. engineer	1,095 00		
Jno. Delaney, fireman	821 25		
Jno. Davenport, fireman..........	821 25		
Wm. J. Flock, asst. engineer.....	924 00		
Wm. Ledwith, fireman..........	821 25		
		$5,682 75	

Painters—

Chas. Dengler....................	$960 00		
Wm. J. Schleicher...	840 00		
		$1,800 00	

Janitors and Messengers—

C E. Alford, supreme court......	$730 00		
H. W. Bolte, bureau of labor statistics........	730 00		
Thos. Curley, board of control....	730 00		
Henry Cummings, treasury agent	730 00		
Oscar Dorschell, land office.......	730 00		
Chas. Ermatinger, art gallery...	670 00		

"A."—General Fund Disbursements for 1894.

Janitors and Messengers — Continued.			
Frank Erlich. supt. public property....	$730 00	....	.....
Chas. Fauerbach, ins. com. dept..	730 00	....	....
James Glennon, adj gen's office..	730 00	....	....
Frank Hubbard, water closet attendant	730 00	....	.....
Ida Herfurth, att'y gen's office...	900 00	....	... .
L. W. Joachim, insurance comm. office........................	960 00	....	....
Henry Lebeis, sec'y of state's office........,...............	600 00	....	....
Henry L. Leuders, supt. public property....	1,080 00	....	....
R. J. McCarl, qm. gen'ls office....	730 00	....	... .
Joseph Malec, historical rooms....	730 00	....	....
Thomas Mills....	730 00	....	....
Peter Nelton, railroad comm. office.......................	730 00	....	... ...
Louis Preuss, agricultural rooms..	730 00	....	....
Oscar Schubert, executive office..	730 00	....	... .
Mich'l Tighe, board of control ...	780 00	....	....
Chas. Todd, dairy and food comm. office..	730 00	....	....
S. H. Tuttle, art gallery..........	790 00	....	....
Will Wells, state supt. office......	804 00	....	....
Aug. Wandry, sec'y of state's office.................	730 00	....	....
		$18,944 00	
Police—			
Christ Graesen..........	$730 00	....	....
J. H. Holcomb............	730 00	....	....
A. R. Jones	730 00	....	....
Thos. Kingston.......	730 00	....	....
Chas. Stevens........	730 00	....	....
James Whitty....................	730 00	....	....
		$4,380 00	
Night Watchmen—			
W. H. Hammersley	$730 00	....	....
Iver Jensen.................	670 00	....	....
		$1,400 00	
Laborers—			
Christ Amoth....................	$660 00	....	....
H. R Brewer....................	660 00	....	....
Fred Buergin....................	660 00	....	....
Mrs Bradley.....................	151 85	....	....
Felix Dushek	660 00	....	....
Mrs. Erbe	133 35	....	....
Wm. Godenschwager........	730 00	....	....
Mrs Kelley	187 90	....	....
Jno. Lawlus.....................	660 00	....	....
Mary Lucas	365 00	....	....
Fritz Meibaum	660 00	....	....
Dan'l McCloskey.................	660 00	....	....

"A."— General Fund Disbursements for 1894.

Laborers—Continued.

Bridget McKenna	$365 00		
Jno. O'Neil	730 00		
Aug. Pengsdorf	660 00		
Andrew J. Smith	660 00		
Mrs. Starkweather	365 00		
Anna Stemple	365 00		
Ole Togstad	660 00		
Frank Vollander	660 00		
James A. Patton, foreman	900 00		
Miss Starkweather	1 00		
		$11,504 10	

Miscellaneous—

C. F. Crane, bookroom attdt	$900 00		
Peter Hyland, elevator attdt	730 00		
M. C. Foley, steam and gas fitter	821 25		
Chas. MoSorley, store keeper	730 00		
		$3,181 25	

Carpenters—

H. N. Moulton, state carpenter	$1,080 00		
Jacob Schwehm, asst. carpenter	900 00		
		$1,980 00	
			$48,872 10

TRANSIENT LABORERS.

M. Amonson	$297 97		
Wm. Boorman	157 50		
J. Barry	660 00		
J. Bush	7 47		
M. Brophy	13 78		
Mrs. A. Beinewiss	13 50		
W. Behrend	3 60		
J. Brannan	47 67		
C. Byrnes	1 77		
A. Beeneweis	1 96		
C. Behm	5 32		
C. Behrend	5 89		
M. Connell	10 23		
J. F. Conlin	254 25		
T. Casey	237 27		
Barney Corcoran	16 66		
P. Carey	10 70		
P. Connors	6 49		
T. Cavanaugh	19 25		
J. Cremmens	4 72		
J. Daley	199 03		
M. Derenzo	16 09		
D. Dyer	11 82		
Jno. E. Doyle	147 38		
P. Dolan	189 60		
M. Fury	1 96		
Jno. Fay	283 40		
M. Feeney	3 53		
F. Fowler	10 77		
T. Fox	5 89		

"A."—*General Fund Disbursements for 1894.*

G. Faber	$3 98		
A. Gannan	13 11		
M. Gary	316 87		
G. Barckhan	93 00		
G. J. Ellestad	112 36		
J. Hoffman	835 00		
S. Hanson	588 61		
W. Haley	47 67		
N. Heins	562 36		
T. Harrington	191 87		
J. Heiser	3 73		
J. Haley	3 98		
F. Hildebrandt	5 80		
A. Henry	1 96		
Mrs. Kelley	107 50		
Wm. Lamp	362 25		
T. Lally	56 66		
John Link	366 75		
Jos. Link	20 18		
M. Lawless	5 70		
P. Lochner	7 66		
M. Lavin	1 96		
P. McGowan	21 98		
J. McGowan	8 37		
H. Mueller	362 25		
S. Morrill	115 80		
A. Meyer	20 18		
F. N. Moulton	576 25		
T. Murphy	2 95		
P. Moran	1 96		
M. Matzka	1 96		
T. Moran	1 96		
V. Newman	558 81		
Jno. O'Neil	9 05		
J. Purcell	101 56		
W. Parsons	17 43		
E. Post	3 93		
T. Quinlan	1 96		
M. Reynolds	14 76		
J. Reynolds	1 77		
J. Replinger	362 25		
G. V. Roesch	286 95		
Will Ring	518 25		
L. Roman	14 31		
C. Roman	16 09		
T. Rammelfinger	1 96		
F. Repke	7 83		
Ed. Reynolds	89		
G. Reynolds	7 48		
H. Rimsnider	254 25		
H. Schott	283 40		
A. Sullivan	8 87		
Jno. Sullivan	21 98		
Henry Sanger	87 75		
J. Staar	5 82		
Jas. Sullivan	7 48		
D. Shea	5 70		
H. Seymour	2 95		

"A."—General Fund Disbursements for 1894.

Wm. Seymour	$1 33		
Herman Schwehm	66 38		
J. E Utter	13 83		
J. Wergin	562 86		
G. Wagner	98		
Ed. Warner	267 75		
Mrs. Zimmermann	122 75		
D. Traner	189 60		
			$11,289 87

INCIDENTAL EXPENSES.

Julius Andrae, mdse	$1 50		
Angell & Hastreiter, city directory	36 00		
Eugen Armstein, mdse	10 00		
Francis Bresee, mdse	10 00		
J. H. D. Baker & Co., mdse	15 88		
M Brahany, cartage	7 80		
Bishoff Bros., plastering	98 67		
G. Backhan, labor	54 00		
Bross & Quinn, labor	21 50		
Peter Behrend, sprinkling street	75 00		
Chas. Baumbach Co., mdse	867 61		
Badger Typewriter & Stationery Co., mdse	49 75		
Blind & Huegel, mdse	14 80		
H. Bolte & Sons, mdse	3 96		
Blied Bros., mdse	68 25		
M. H. Ball, mdse	9 44		
Brahany & Hilbert, blacksmithing	2 00		
Maurice Coughlin, mdse	45 00		
Cnare & Coyne, mdse	40 40		
C., M. & St. Paul Railway Co., freight	92 46		
Conklin & Son, mdse	514 88		
Christophers & Co., mdse	35 50		
C. & N. W. Railway Co., freight	39 75		
Chicago Paper Co., mdse	144 85		
T. A. Chapman, mdse	10 50		
D. F. Conlin, cartage	4 40		
M. J. Cantwell, mdse	9 75		
Jas. Conlin, drayage	2 00		
Jerome Clark, mdse	208 48		
Clark's Drug Store, mdse	34 75		
Clement Williams & Co., mdse	64 45		
Consolidated Time Lock Co., repairing vault	35 00		
Vincent Conahan, cartage	1 50		
Jno. E. Doyle, labor	49 50		
Jerre Dobbs, mdse	19 50		
Theo. Dresden, mdse	7 00		
T. Davenport, mdse	2 25		
Des Forges & Co., mdse	3 00		
Dorn Spence, mdse	23 50		
A. L. Dean & Co., labor on treasury vault	21 04		

"A."—General Fund Disbursements for 1894.

Four Lakes Light and Power Co., light for park........	$672 00	....	....
J. K. Fagin, mdse	25 09	....	....
Wm. Frankfurth Hardware Co., mdse	244 86	....	....
Jno Farwell & Co., mdse....... ..	5 02	....	....
C. F. Ford, mdse	17 95	....	....
A. H. Gardner, mdse................	104 15	....	....
H. E. Goodrich, mdse...	2 25	....	....
Jno. Greig, mdse	3 75	....	....
Henry Gugler Co., mdse	84 00	....	....
H. Gerling, mdse. and cartage.....	5 50	....	....
Goldsmith & Co., mdse....	1,212 58	....	....
Gimbel Bros., mdse.	242 50	....	... .
Joseph Hussey, mdse and plumbing	888 35	....	....
J. B. Hoeger & Sons, mdse......	250 15	....	...-........
Fred Huels, labor repairing	19 27	....	....
J. W. Harrington, sprinkling streets	85 00	....	....
Jno. D. Hayes, mdse..............	8 90	....	....
T. S. Henderson, mdse.............	3 00	....	....
Joseph Hussey, mdse..........	892 69	....	....
Theodore Hoeveler, mdse	79 50	....	... .
Hinricks & Thompson, mdse......	59 58	....	....
Hoffman, Keefe Office File Co., vault .fixtures	2,154 00	....	....
Hecht & Zummach, mdse.........	94 17	....	....
J. J Higgins, mdse...........	11 25	....	....
Hale Elevator Co., mdse	6 73	....	....
Ill. Cen. Railroad Co., freight.......	17 70	....	....
H. Ireland, cartage.......	3 50	....	... .
Joice Bros. & Co., mdse............	195 00	....	....
Krehl & Beck, mdse	48 90	....	....
H. Kasabian, mdse............. ...	53 00	....	....
Geo. Kraft, mdse. and plumbing...	209 43	....	....
Keeley, Neckerman & Kessenich, mdse............................	49 09	....	....
A. Klien, mdse	4 60	....	....
Keeley, Neckerman & Kessenich, mdse...........................	17 00	....	....
Wm. Kinney, mdse................	2 10	... .	....
Peter Lahm, cartage..............	77 77	....	....
Julius Lando, mdse.	2 25	....	....
James Ledwith, mdse	18 55	....	....
Lueders & Krause, mdse..........	40 32	....	....
Madison Hardware Co., mdse.......	42 35	....	....
H. N. Moulton, mdse	53 46	....	....
Manville Covering Co	162 54	....	....
Milwaukee Litho. & Engr. Co......	165 00	....	....
Henry Mann, assignee, mdse	396 05	....	....
Milwaukee Journal Co., list ins. comr	5 00	....	....
T. C. McCarty, mdse	18 00	....	....
Madison Water Works, rent ex. res.	42 32	....	....
George McArthur, mdse..........	3 50	....	....
Chas. McSorley, repairing.........	14 65	....	....
H. B. McGowan, mdse	15 03	....	....
Patrick McKenna, mdse...........	2 00	....	....

"A."—General Fund Disbursements for 1894.

T. B. Nelson, mdse....	$1 44	
T. A. Nelson, mdse.................	2 98	
M. L Nelson, mdse.	57 00	
H. Niedecken Co., mdse	232 85	
Chas. H. Naffs, mdse...............	328 43	
New York Store, mdse.............	23 65	
Northwestern Furniture Co., mdse..	15 00	
R. B. Ogilvie & Co., mdse..........	66 76	
Olson & Jacobson, mdse............	226 77	
Wm. Owen, mdse.................	4 44	
Olson & Jacobson, mdse............	26 60	
Peter Pauley, cartage	50	
Wm. J. Park & Son, mdse..........	5 78	
C. Pressentine, Sr., repairing.......	6 00	
E. S. Reynolds, cartage.............	273 52	
Rundle & Spence Mfg. Co., mdse....	122 73	
Phil. Ryan, plastering.............	22 45	
A. E. Thoreson, mdse..............	1 50	
Wm. Sigelkow, mdse	3 50	
Chas. Schmidt, mdse..............	15 20	
Aug. Schibel, mdse........	538 36	
Ernest Sommers, labor............	8 00	
A. Scott, cartage	1 00	
Sommers Bros., mdse..............	22 00	
J. A. Swenson. mdse..............	90 24	
Schlimgen & Son, mdse............	23 80	
Aug. Schmidt & Co., mdse..........	4 65	
K. F. Steul, mdse.................	13 86	
Spence & Foley, mdse....	80 85	
C. R. Stein & Co., mdse	355 96	
Schwab, Stamp & Seal Co., mdse...	9 56	
Fred Sperling, cartage........	1 50	
W. W. Swinyer, mdse	22 85	
Jay H. Snell, mdse.	14 63	
A. Sperling, mdse	3 50	
Silbernagle & Dean, mdse..........	40 12	
Stark Bros. & Co., mdse...........	19 38	
Sumner & Morris, mdse	23 60	
Smith Premier Typ'writing Co., mdse	95 00	
J. A. Swenson, mdse	11 00	
C. M. Telfor, mdse.................	3 00	
Wm. Theiss, mdse.................	19 00	
John H. Stark & Co., mdse........ .	106 03	
Teckemeyer & Kurz, mdse.........	29 50	
Vaughn & Cosgrove, mdse.........	15 45	
D. VanNostrand Co., mdse..........	6 00	
J. G. Wagner, mdse...............	6 00	
Wyckoff, Seaman & Benedict, mdse	244 20	
Wisconsin Telephone Co., rent	298 15	
West Pub. Co., mdse..............	11 00	
Emanuel Weil & Co., mdse........	40 30	
West Pub. Co., mdse....	22 50	$14,701 26

"A."—General Fund Disbursements for 1894.

DEMOCRAT PRINTING CO., PRINTING.

Blanks for—

Governor.......................	$32 46		
Secretary of state............	1,203 29		
State treasurer.....	132 55		
Attorney general, blanks and briefs	190 76		
State superintendent..............	546 48		
Railroad commissioner...........	33 54		
Insurance commissioner..........	106 41		
Supreme court....................	78 93		
State library....................	495 44		
State historical society............	1,533 04		
State land office	154 44		
Quartermaster general...........	164 21		
Adjutant general	210 02		
Superintendent of public property	14 80		
Treasury agent	47 01		
State board of control	206 77		
Bureau of labor statistics	40 21		
State prison	44 76		
State fish and game warden......	3 48		
State agricultural society....	2 00		
State board of examiners adm. to bar........................ .	4 96		

Reports, laws and proceedings—

Academy arts and sciences, Wis..	$1,061 04		
Agricultural experimental station	5,150 36		
State agricultural society........	1,824 23		
State horticultural society........	1,392 00		
Insurance commissioner, annual statement....................	379 49		
Fish and game laws, 1,000 copies.	48 32		
Manuals for free high schools ...	503 84		
Governor's message and documents, 700 copies	234 52		
State constitution, 500 copies	34 57		
Corporation laws...	96 99		
Assessment laws.................	104 62		
Insurance laws	74 08		
Milwaukee election laws........	391 33		
General election laws	885 77		
Election registers and laws.......	1,408 29		
Bank reports	575 95		
Wisconsin dairymen's association.	712 26		
State historical society...........	192 02		
Washburn observatory, vol 8.....	894 20		
Annual proceedings charities, corrections	268 26		
Proceedings annual convention W. N G., rules and regulations....	479 69		
Book list state supt	224 38		
Laws for board of control	149 31		$22,332 48

"A."—General Fund Disbursements for 1894.

POSTAGE.

Madison Post Office, stamps for—

Governor...	$207 50		
Secretary of state	773 50		
State treasurer	510 20		
Land department	235 00		
State superintendent	552 26		
Superintendent public property...	44 00		
Attorney general	79 50		
Railroad commissioner	67 10		
Insurance commissioner	178 05		
Adjutant general	256 00		
Quartermaster general	136 00		
Supreme court	263 50		
State board of control	294 00		
State librarian	20 00		
State historical society	415 00		
Treasury agent	48 20		
State agricultural society	332 00		
Bureau of labor statistics.....	263 50		
State fish and game warden	18 20		
Dairy and food commissioner	131 00		
Drawer rent for the several depts.	152 00		
		$4,975 51	

WESTERN UNION TELEGRAPH CO.

Telegrams for—

Adjutant general	$4 30		
Attorney general	60 20		
Bureau of labor statistics	75		
Dairy and food commissioner....	13 35		
Executive office	85 51		
Insurance commissioner	56 10		
Quartermaster general	31 75		
Railroad commissioner	8 65		
Secretary of state	51 95		
State board of control	17 80		
State land department	2 95		
State superintendent	13 20		
State treasurer	8 80		
State treasury agent	1 85		
State fish and game warden	3 50		
		$360 16	

WISCONSIN TELEPHONE CO.

Messages for—

Attorney general	$4 60		
Executive office	57 20		
Secretary of state	6 05		
State treasurer	50		
State board of control	13 60		
Insurance commissioner	3 00		
Treasury agent	20		
Railroad commissioner	90		
State superintendent	40		
		$86 45	
Total			$5,422 12

"A."—General Fund Disbursements for 1894.

EXPRESSAGE.

American Express Co. — Expressage for—

Attorney general	$3 10	....	....
Adjutant general	9 82	....	....
Academy of sciences, arts and letters	35 18	....	....
Bureau of labor statistics	8 68	....	....
Dairy and food commissioner.....	59 17	....	....
Executive office......	2 68	....	....
Insurance commissioner..........	6 88	....	....
Quartermaster general............	201 99	... .	....
Secretary of state..:..............	267 70	....	....
State treasurer	6 90	....	....
State superintendent.	96 21	....	....
State librarian	18 87	....	....
State land office...........	1 55	....	....
Supt. of public property	446 73	....	....
State agricultural society.........	280 77	....	....
State board of control...........	18 49	....	....
Railroad commissioner...........	16 28	....	....
		$1,480 45	....

Adams and United States Express Cos — Expressage for—

Attorney general........	$1 45	....	....
Adjutant general	22 36	....	....
Academy of sciences, arts and letters	56 32	....	.......'...
Bureau of labor statistics.........	1 20	....	....
Dairy and food commissioner.....	40 15	....	....
Executive office	1 55	....	....
Quartermaster general	52 88	....	....
Secretary of state	140 08	....	....
State treasurer	40 90	... .	....
State superintendent..............	62 16	... .	... ...
State library	82 25	....	.....*.....
State land office.................	1 20	....	....
Supt. of public property	255 10	... .	....
State agricultural society.........	133 82	....	....
State board of control	14 58	....	... .
Railroad commissioner...........	1 28	....	....
State historical society	8 45	... .	....
Insurance commissioner	1 54	....;.......	....
		$917 12	....
			$2,347 57

PAPER.

H. Niedecken & Co.................	$13,737 30	....	....
		....	$13,737 30

STATIONERY.

Badger Typewriter & Stationery Co.	$237 70	....	....
Des Forges & Co....................	85 60	....	....
H. Neidecken & Co.................	66 93	....	....

"A."—General Fund Disbursements for 1894.

J. B. Hoeger & Son	$1,688 81	
Wm. Frankfurth Hardware Co	157 75	
J. Kneuber Lithograph Co	167 60	
Julius Lindo	8 25	
Wisconsin Bank Note and Lithograph Co	22 90	
L. E. Waterman	42 00	
		$2,472 54

GAS.

Madison Gas Light and Coke Co	$3,849 99	
		$3,849 99

FUEL.

J. Conklin & Son	$6,313 91	
Christ Capaul	48 33	
E. C. Hammersley	64 00	
		$6,426 24

TREASURY AGENT.

Thomas Kennedy, percentage on peddler license	$2,972 72	
		$2,972 72

EX STATE TREASURY SUITS.

T. R. Frentz, witness, State vs. Harshaw	$15 06	
H. D. Goodwin, witness, State vs. Harshaw	10 00	
		$25 06

COMPILING WAR RECORDS.

H. C. Allen	$1,380 00	
Jos. H. Janda	1,380 00	
Agnes L. Morrissey	910 00	
Mary W. Priestley	840 00	
		$4,510 00

MILITIA.

Louis Auer, salary, Q. M. G	$441 77	
Louis Auer, expenses Q. M. G	77 89	
Antes & Young, mdse	15 00	
Wm. Alds, labor	23 75	
David Adler & Sons, clothing	16,772 44	
A. Bluel, labor	100 00	
Brigham & Co, mdse	109 61	
G. M. Barrett, mdse	152 28	
D. H. Brown, pension clerk	1,380 00	
W. L. Buck, expenses, insp. W. N. G	497 20	
L. Buffmire, labor and mdse. on rifle range	171 38	
Geo. Brumder, labor	1 25	
J. L. Byer, labor	11 25	

"A."—General Fund Disbursements for 1894.

P. H. Conley, services................	$3 00	....	....
Frank Cornelius	20 00	....	....
Co. A, 1st reg., uniform fund	270 00	....	....
Co. A, 1st reg., armory fund	300 00	....	....
Co. L, 2d reg., uniform fund... ...	185 00	....	....
Co. L, 2d reg., armory fund	300 00	....	....
Clarance L. Clark, military secy....	33 00	....	....
C., M. & St. P. Ry. Co., trans. stk., L.H S......	60 00	... .	
C., M. & St. P. Ry. Co., trans. W. N. G	1,043 06	....	....
C., M. & St. P. Ry. Co., freight, W. N. G........	163 91	....	... .
C. & N. W. Ry. Co., trans. W. N. G.	1,082 89	....	... .
C. & N. W. Ry. Co., freight Q. M. G.	48 41	....	... .
C., St. P., M. & O. Ry. Co., trans. W. N. G.	1,171 79	....	....
Co. B, 1st reg., uniform fund	265 00	....	....
Co. B, 1st reg., armory fund	300 00	....	....
Co. C. 1st reg., uniform fund	275 00	....	....
Co. C, 1st reg., armory fund	300 00	....	....
Co. E, 1st reg., uniform fund	275 00	....	....
Co. E, 1st reg., armory fund	300 00	....	....
Co. F, 1st reg., uniform fund......	230 00	....	....
Co. F, 1st reg., armory fund	400 00	....	....
Co. H, 1st reg., uniform fund......	270 00	....	....
Co. H, 1st reg., armory fund... ...	300 00	....	....
Co. I, 1st reg., uniform fund	280 00	....	....
Co. I. 1st reg., armory fund	300 0	....	....
Co. K, 1st reg., uniform fund	260 00	....	....
Co. K, 1st reg., armory fund......	300 00	....	....
Co B, 2d reg., uniform fund.......	260 00	....	....
Co B, 2d reg., armory fund.......	400 00	....	....
Co. C, 2d reg., uniform fund.......	265 00	....	....
Co. C, 2d reg., armory fund	300 00	....	....
Co. D, 2d reg., uniform fund.......	200 00	....	....
Co. D, 2d reg., armory fund.......	300 00	....	....
Co. E, 2d reg., uniform fund......	295 00	....	....
Co. E, 2d reg., armory fund.......	300 00	....	....
Co. F, 2d reg., uniform fund	250 00	....	....
Co. F, 2d reg., armory fund.......	400 00	....	....
Co. G, 2d reg., uniform fund......	275 00	....	....
Co. G, 2d reg , armory fund	300 00	....	....
Co. H, 2d reg., uniform fund.....	250 00	....	....
Co. H, 2d reg., armory fund... ...	300 00	....	....
Co. I, 2d reg., uniform fund.......	320 00	....	....
Co. I, 2d reg., armory fund.......	300 00	....	....
Co. K, 2d reg., uniform fund	305 00	....	....
Co. K, 2d reg., armory fund.......	300 00	....	....
Co. M, 2d reg., uniform fund	325 00	....	....
Co. M, 2d reg., armory fund.......	300 00	....	....
Co. A, 3d reg., uniform fund......	290 00	....	....
Co. A, 3d reg., armory fund.......	300 00	....	....
Co. B, 3d reg., uniform fund......	315 00	....	....
Co. B, 3d reg., armory fund.......	400 00	....\.......	....
Co. C, 3d reg., uniform fund......	300 00	....	....
Co. C, 3d reg., armory fund......	300 00	... .	....

"A."—General Fund Disbursements for 1894.

Co. D, 3d reg., uniform fund.......	$240 00	....	....
Co. D, 3d reg., armory fund.......	300 00	....	....
Co. E, 3d reg., uniform fund......	290 00	....	....
Co. E, 3d reg., armory fund.......	300 00	....	....
Co. F, 3d reg., uniform fund......	245 00	....	....
Co. F, 3d reg., armory fund.......	300 00	....	....
Co. G, 3d reg., uniform fund......	270 00	....	....
Co. G, 3d reg., armory fund......	300 00	....	....
Co. H, 3d reg., uniform fund......	265 00	....	....
Co. H, 3d reg., armory fund.......	300 00	....	....
Co. I, 3d reg., uniform fund.......	260 00	....	....
Co. I, 3d reg., armory fund	300 00	.. ..	....
Co. K, 3d reg., uniform fund......	240 00	....	....
Co. K, 3d reg., armory fund......	300 00	....	....
Co. L, 3d reg., uniform fund......	240 00	....	....
Co. L, 3d reg., armory fund.......	300 00	....	.
Co. M, 3d reg , uniform fund......	295 00	....	....
Co. M, 3d reg., armory fund......	400 00	....	....
Co. A, 4th reg., uniform fund. ...	280 00	....	....
Co. A, 4th reg., armory fund	500 00	....	....
Co. B, 4th reg., uniform fund.....	325 00	....	....
Co. B, 4th reg., armory fund......	500 00	....	....
Co. C, 4th reg., uniform fund.....	285 00	....	....
Co. C, 4th reg., armory fund	500 00	....	....
Co. D, 4th reg., uniform fund	245 00	....	....
Co. D, 4th reg., armory fund......	500 00	....	....
Co. E, 4th reg., uniform fund......	240 00	....	....
Co. E, 4th reg , armory fund......	500 00	....	....
Co. F, 4th reg , uniform fund......	255 00	....	....
Co. F, 4th reg., armory fund......	500 00	....	....
Co G, 4th reg., uniform fund......	260 00	....	....
Co. G, 4th reg., armory fund	500 00	....	....
Co. H, 4th reg., uniform fund......	210 00	....	....
Co. H, 4th reg., armory fund......	500 00	....	....
Joseph B. Doe, salary, adjt. gen....	416 50	....	....
Joseph B. Doe, expenses, adjt. gen..	79 20	... .	....
Delorme & Quentin, mdse........	60 00	....	....
Edwards & Co., mdse..............	3 10	....	....
H. W. Ellis, mdse...	261 85	....	....
First Light Battery, uniform fund..	275 00	....	....
First Light Battery, armory fund...	800 00	....	....
First ight Battery, special duty in 1894.............................	300 00	....	....
Otto H. Falk, salary adjt. gen......	1,416 57	....	....
Otto H. Falk, expenses adjt. gen...	201 71	....	....
Otto H. Falk, salary Q. M. gen.....	104 12	....	....
Wm. Frankfurth Hardware Co., mdse.............................	18 05	....	....
Abraham Cambier, maps rifle range	25 00	....	....
Col. A. F. Caldwell, expenses reg. headquarters....................	100 00	....	....
James H. Cleary, expenses burial of Geo. Cleary......................	75 .00	....	....
M. Finnecian, mdse................	129 56	....	....
E. E. Gatchell, mdse..............	8 50	....	....
J. G. Graham, labor	1 80	....	....
Globe Light & Heat Co., mdse......	199 75	....	....
Jno. Singleton, mdse...............	540 54	....	....

"A."—*General Fund Disbursements for 1894.*

H. Scheftels & Sons, mdse	$8 00	....	....
Col G. H. Winsor, inspector small arms practice..................	299 41	....	....
Westlake, De La Hunt & Smith Co., mdse	2 25	....	....
Leo Wilkinson, labor...............	55 50	....	....
Andrew Wilson, labor..............	5 00	....	....
J. H. Hardy, freight	5 08	....	....
J. H. Hardy, custodian rifle range..	660 00	....	....
Fred Hucks, mdse............	22 00	....	....
C. H. Horton, mdse	76 50	....	....
W. T. Hanly, labor at R. R.........	2 50	....	....
Hough & Hamlett mdse............	5 50	....	....
W. T. Hardy, labor	43 25	....	....
A. H. Hollister, mdse..............	3 50	....	....
J. C. Hodges, labor	46 50	....	....
Reuben Hodges, labor.............	18 75	....	....
Illinois Central Ry. Co., trans. W. N. G	2 20	....	....
Kipp Bros., mdse	40 84	....	....
Geo. H. Joachim, service at Racine.	28 45	....	....
Jno. J. Lynch, service at Racine....	11 84	....	....
Thos. Ryan, labor	44 62	....	....
Horace M. Seaman, services at Racine	18 08	....	....
Ed J. Slupecke, service at Racine..	16 44	....	....
C. Preusser Jewelry Co, mdse.	100 00	....	....
Light Horse Squadron, armory fund	800 00	....	....
Light Horse Squadron, uniform fund	320 00	....	....
Light Horse Squadron, expenses 1893	300 00	....	....
Jno. Larson & Co., mdse..........	8 00	....	....
Dennis Nash, labor	47 25	....	....
M. J. McLaughlin, mdse...........	7 50	....	....
Chas. McPherson, labor	60 00	....	....
W. B. McPherson, asst. adj. gen'l salary	1,380 00	....	....
W. B. McPherson, asst. adj. gen'l expenses	7 00	....	....
Della McCarl, labor..............	16 00	....	....
Madison Hdw. Co., mdse..........	21 27	....	....
Capt. M. F. Moore, expenses.......	100 00	....	....
Geo. P. Mathes, mil. sec'y, salary ...	367 00	....	....
Wm. Mahoney, asst. Q. M., salary..	1,380 00	....	....
Wm. Mahoney, asst. Q. M., expenses	286 56	....	....
Wm. Mahoney, asst. Q. M, disbursements for labor and mdse...... ..	369 90	....	....
Mil., L. S. & W. trans., W. N. G.	223 36	....	....
H. F. Miner, labor.................	64 50	....	....
Anton Metzger, labor.............	41 65	....	....
Manitowoc Savings Bank overdraft Co. A, 2d Reg., armory fund. ...	37 10	....	....
Dr. D. T. Nicoll, surgeon W. N. G...	15 00	....	....
Non-commissioned Staff Band 1st reg., W. N. G..................	100 00	....	....
Non commissioned Staff Band, 2d reg., W. N. G..................	145 00	....	....

"A."—General Fund Disbursements for 1894.

Non-commissioned Staff Band, 3d reg., W. N. G.	$110 00		
Non-commissioned Staff Band, 4th reg., W. N. G.	115 00		
Milwaukee Buggy Co , mdse.	45 00		
Milwaukee Paste Co.. mdse.	8 25		
James Morgan & Co., mdse.	16 01		
Julius Nemetz, mdse.	115 44		
F. F. Proudfit, paymaster gen'l, W. N G., sub. and exp. rifle team	969 68		
Pettibone Mfg. Co., mdse. W. N. G.	2,016 17		
J. F. Peterson, mdse.	55 00		
J Purcell, mdse.	15 00		
F. F. Proudfit, paymaster gen'l, sub. and exp. 1st reg. W. N. G.	7,711 55		
F. F. Proudfit, paymaster gen'l, sub. and exp., 2d reg., W. N. G	16,830 61		
F. F. Proudfit, paymaster gen'l, sub. and exp., 3d reg., W. N. G	10,974 76		
F. F. Proudfit, paymaster gen'l sub. and exp., 4th reg., W. N. G.	6,146 29		
F. F. Proudfit, paymaster gen'l, sub. and exp., 1st cavalry	492 64		
F. F. Proudfit, paymaster gen'l sub. and exp., 1st light artillery	826 30		
F. F. Proudfit. paymaster gen'l, sub. and exp., rifle competition	1,209 12		
F. F. Proudfit, paymaster gen'l, sub. and exp.	9 80		
Mrs. Jno. Singleton, mdse., W. N. G.	40 00		
K. F. Steul, cartage, W. N. G.	57 16		
Cash L. Stickney	14 90		
Louis Singlaub, rent Co. A, 2d reg., W. N. G.	50 00		
Jno. H. Stark & Co., mdse.	8 20		
Capt. Henry Schweitzer, mdse.	31 89		
Aug. Scheibel, mdse.	8 40		
F. J. Pfannerstill, labor.	278 10		
Charles Truax, Green & Co., mdse., W N. G.	$70 00		
Jno. Topp & Bros. Co., mdse.	10 39		
W. H. Patton, expenses	100 00		
Parker Pen Co., mdse.	5 00		
Chas. R. Williams, asst. Q. M. G., salary	975 00		
Chas. R. Williams, asst. Q. M. G., expenses	224 25		
Capt. Jos. B. Whiting, instructor, W. N. G.	15 68		
Wisconsin Central Lines, transp., W. N G	10 66		
Western Union Tel. Co , messages, Q. M. G.	92 68		
Wisconsin Telephone Co., messages. Q. M. G.	52 40		
J M. Washburn, labor	1 50		
Herbert A. Wood, labor	69 00		

"A."—General Fund Disbursements for 1894.

M. E. Williams, labor	$15 00		
Chas. Wehrman, mdse	40 50		
		$103,896 22	
MILITIA (Eau Claire Strike).			
Capt. J. M. Ballard, Co. E	$346 26		
Lieut. Sam'l F. Crabbe	12 66		
Lieut. Thos. P. Cochrane	13 56		
Lieut. Chas. J. McDowell	13 56		
Capt. Louis O. Haugen	340 26		
Capt. C. F. King	15 89		
Lieut. Otto H. Kilzman	13 56		
Capt. Edw. G. Grannis	19 23		
Lieut. Anton Mangwnson	12 66		
Capt. Geo. J. Nash	298 26		
Lieut Hiram E. Nye	12 66		
Col. M. T. Moore	82 56		
Lt. Jno. C. Ohnstad	13 56		
Capt Christ. Schlosser	304 26		
Lieut. Peter Schlosser	12 66		
Capt. Orlando Halloway	26 32		
Major J. E. Kirchies	35 60		
		$1,573 52	
Total			$105,469 74
WISCONSIN RIFE RANGE.			
Louis Auer & Son, ins. on bldgs, etc	$75 00		
Albert Albertson, labor	186 75		
Dwight Hodge, labor	350 00		
C. H. Hoten, mdse	12 03		
Gleason & Son, mdse	4 80		
Dennis Nash, labor	180 00		
Jno. Singleton, mdse	12 78		
Wm. Mahoney, labor	100 00		
W. T. Hardy, labor	6 00		
H. F. Miner, labor	15 75		
F. J. Pfaunerstill, building under contract	3,000 00		
		$3,942 61	
UNIVERSITY SUMMER SCHOOL.			
C. R. Barnes	$200 00		
W. W. Daniels	200 00		
B. W. Snow	200 00		
Chas. L. Schlichter	200 00		
F. J. Turner	200 00		
		$1,000 00	
EXAMINERS FOR ADMISSION TO BAR.			
George G. Green, per diem and exp.	$47 20		
L. J. Rusk, per diem and exp.	187 85		
Moses M. Strong, per diem and exp.	160 86		

"A."—General Fund Disbursements for 1894.

Joshua Stark, per diem and exp....	$81 63		
A. L. Sanborn, per diem and exp...	100 80		
		$577 84	
GOVERNOR'S CONTINGENT FUND.			
Geo. W. Peck......................	$572 69		
		$572 69	
VETERINARY SURGEON.			
Dr. F. J. Toussaint, sal. state vet...	$1,833,00		
Dr. F. J. Toussaint, expenses	2,828 56		
Dr. F. A. Norton, consultation, V. S.	7 45		
Dr. J.W. Wicker, consultation, V. S	21 00		
Dr. W. P. Freeman, consultation, V. S.	7 00		
		$4,697 01	
GLANDERED HORSES SLAUGHTERED.			
Wm. J. Miller...............	$100 00		
Carl Sellen.......	33 33		
J. P. Hayes..........	10 00		
Michael Massort.......	33 33		
Sam Wright...............	130 00		
Josiah Philips....................	33 33		
Archibel Allen....................	60 00		
Peter Clos......................	33 33		
Hans Larsen..	66 66		
F. J. Neubauer....................	33 33		
Edward Ryan..........	66 66		
Henry Speiring....................	33 33		
Anton Berkilen....................	33 33		
Christ Wilhelmson................	33 33		
Frank Bordoin......	33 33		
Mrs. Geo. Booth....	33 33		
G. Eggert..........................	66 66		
Louis Forthune.................. ..	17 77		
Albert Gott	100 00		
Mike Kappell......................	33 33		
Richard Phalen....................	66 66		
		$1,051 04	
STATE TEACHERS EXAMINERS.			
C. R. Barnes......................	$130 00		
A. J. Hutton.....................	98 19		
R. H. Halsey.................	107 18		
		$335 87	
STATE FISH AND GAME WARDEN CONTINGENT FUND.			
George Ayers......................	$5 00		
Chas R. Brainard.................	40 00		
Wm. B. Cheesman.................	18 70		
A. A. Cornell..... , ...	14 50		

"A."—General Fund Disbursements for 1894.

Louis Frank...	$287 00	....	....
D. W. Fernandez	225 08	....	....
H. C. Fuller	5 50	....	....
Hiram Fowler.....................	6 00	....	....
C. H Grubner....................	35 00	....	....
G. B Groy	99 60	....	....
George W. Hill	20 00	....	....
F. S. Husbrook....................	16 00	....	....
A. Hippmeyer.........	20 0U	....	....
C. E. Fero	15 00	....	....
Carl Johnson.....	20 00	....	....
Robert W. Johnson................	12 00	....	....
Otto Jorgenson.	12 00	....	....
Albert L Lord.....................	10 00	....	....
A R. Livingston.	9 50	....	....
Geo. S. Lawrence.................	55 00	....	....
D. S. Mackie	3u 88	....	....
John A. Mayers....................	45 00	....	....
Wm. J New.	10 86	....	....
H. F. Smith.	15 00	....	....
Antone Smith.....................	12 00	....	....
H. J Sharp	9 20	....	....
Charles Todd.	50 00	....	....
Fran S. Tibbitts........	10 00	....	....
		$1,103 82	....

STATE FISH AND GAME WARDEN.

D. W. Fernandez, warden, salary...	$1,800 00	....	....
D. W. Fernandez, warden, expenses	438 67	....	....
		$2,238 67	....

ILLUSTRATIONS FOR REPORT OF AGRICULTURAL EXPERIMENTAL STATION.

Binner Engraving Co., merchandise	$106 10	....	....
Hanson Bros., merchandise	4 45	....	....
Edward P. Carlton, draughting ...	1 58	....	....
Gugler Lith. Co., merchandise.....	76 95	....	....
		$189 08	....

CHICKAMAUGA VISITING COMMITTEE.

W. A. Collins	$87 50	....	....
Wm. W. Watkins....	76 00	....	....
J. H. Woodnorth..................	110 00	....	....
		$273 50	....

PUBLISHING AND ADVERTISING.

Milwaukee Journal Co	$350 85	....	....
State Journal Printing Co...........	35 20	....	....
Chicago Herald	165 00	....	....
Chicago Times	137 50	....	....
Madison Democrat	260 30	....	....
P. V. Deuster	17 00	....	....
J. N. Stone....	10 80	....	....

"A."—General Fund Disbursements for 1894.

Superior Leader....................	$10 80	....	....
Ellis B. Usher............	10 80	....	....
L. A. Lange........................	94 80	....	....
John Nagle	51 80	....	. ...
Ellis B. Usher	44 60	....	....
Ryan Bros	54 00	....	....
Sommers & Reynolds..............	54 40		
		$1,297 85	....
PUBLISHING GENERAL LAWS.			
W. K. Atkinson, Eau Claire Leader.	$100 00	....	....
		$100 00	....
PUBLISHING LAWS IN STATE PAPER.			
Milwaukee Journal Co............	$38 40	....	....
		$38 40	....
PUBLISHING BANK REPORTS.			
C. J. Augustin......................	$1 80	....	....
E. E. Atherton	4 80	....	....
Ashland News.................. ...	4 80	....	....
E. J. Brown.......................	2 40	....	... .
E. H. Brooks	1 20	....	....
Henry W. Bolens	1 20	....	....
P. H. Bolger.......................	1 20	....	... .
C. J. Bell	2 40	....	....
Chas. F. Bone....................	2 40	....	....
Barth Brothers	2 40	....	....
J. B. Reach.......................	2 40	....	....
E. H. Bowers	2 40	....	....
F. H. Brady.......................	2 40	....	....
S. W. Brown.......................	6 60	....	....
C. H. Bissell	2 40	....	....
Wm. M. Barnum	2 40	... .	....
Crawford Bros....................	13 20	....	....
D. M. Carter.....................	4 80	....	... .
Cole Bros	1 20	....	....
George D. Cline..................	4 80	....	....
L. W. Chapman...................	2 40	....	....
Frank L. Clark....................	2 40	....	....
R. W. Davis.......................	3 00	....	....
E. D. Doolittle...................	6 00	....	....
I. S. Dunn........................	2 40	....	....
F. A. Dean	1 34	....	....
Thos. Dovery	1 20	....	....
Democrat Printing Co	3 00	....	....
C. H. Dunn	2 40	....	....
Elroy Tribune	2 40	....	....
H. A. Flagg.......................	1 20	....	....
Frazier & Frazier.......	4 20	....	....
John Foley	1 80	....	....
Arthur Frankenberg....	2 40	....	....
E. F. Gans.......................	1 20	....	....
W. T. Giles...	4 80	... .	....
E. S. Holmor	3 00	....	....

"A."—General Fund Disbursements for 1894.

W. A. Hume	$3 60		
Walter S. Hidden	6 00		
Herald Pub. Co	1 20		
Albert G. Hinkley	2 40		
J. E. Harris	2 40		
Grant D. Harrington	2 40		
Alex W. Horn	2 40		
J. A. Hilleen	1 20		
Howie E. Rothe	2 40		
J. E. Jones	1 20		
W. B. Krause	2 40		
John A. Killeen	1 20		
H. S. Keeney	1 20		
John Kelley	1 20		
L. A. Long	3 60		
Chas. A. Leicht	1 20		
Lueher & Brundage	2 40		
J. M. Le Count	3 60		
George Meacham	11 40		
C. W. Metzker	5 40		
Walter Mayer	2 40		
F. K Morris	1 20		
F. F. Morgan	2 40		
O. B. Moon	2 40		
News Pub. Co	1 20		
Wm. F. Nash	3 00		
Wm. R. Purdy	2 40		
Mrs. S. M. Parker	2 40		
M. D. Peary	6 60		
J. F. Sweeter	2 40		
E. J. Scott	1 20		
Chas. G. Smith	3 60		
Mrs. M. C. Short	1 20		
D. W. Stebbins	2 40		
E. B. Thayer	2 40		
W. C. Thomas	2 40		
Tomahawk Pub. Co	1 80		
Portage Democrat	1 20		
A. G. Paulson	1 20		
G. L. Swartz	1 20		
Times Printing Co., Menomonie	4 80		
H. J. Van Vuren	2 40		
William Wagner	2 40		
Frank Wagner	1 20		
H. E. Zimmermann	2 40		
George Ziegans	2 40		
Sturdevant, Ogden & Ware	3 60		
W. A. Sanborn	1 20		
Sommers & Reynolds	1 80		
Ellis B. Usher	1 80		
F. H. Voshardt	1 20		
J. F. Wilson	1 80		
Fred T. Yates	1 80		
Ida J. Yorty	1 20		
	$246 14		

"A."—General Fund Disbursements for 1894.

ADVERTISING LANDS.

Advocate Printing Co.	$28 50		
Harry Arnold	9 40		
A. W. Anderson	11 75		
Democrat Printing Co.	9 40		
W. G. Barry	11 75		
George D. Cline.	11 75		
L. W. Chapman	11 75		
Call Publishing Co.	28 50		
W. H. Dawley	16 45		
Ernest A. Dunn	16 45		
C. C. Eaton	13 60		
John G. Foulds	11 75		
M. A. Frissell	21 15		
Jesse S. Field	11 75		
E. D. Glennon	11 75		
F H. Graves	11 75		
Herald Pub. Co., Rhinelander	9 40		
F. J. Kemmster	11 75		
Chas. A. Leicht	9 40		
Lueher & Brundage	18 80		
George Meacham	14 10		
Wm. J. Neu	16 45		
John Nagle	11 75		
S. W. Pierce	9 40		
Ryan Bros	11 75		
E. J. Scott	11 75		
Mrs. Rose A. Sharp	21 15		
E. B. Thayer	9 40		
Times Printing Co., Menomonie	14 10		
Rudolph Voll	11 75		
Ed. T. Wheelock	14 10		
H. E. Zimmerman	13 60		
		$441 10	

REAL ESTATE RETURNS.

Wm. Althauser	$3 68		
A. A. Anderson	9 68		
N. G. Blakeslee	9 76		
W. G. Bingman	10 32		
John N. Baer	15 52		
J. W. Brown	12 32		
Lewis Beitler	15 92		
Jos. Boschert	18 40		
Lewis Butler	8 00		
James M. Clapel	6 72		
S. S. Chandler, Jr	10 64		
Charles Donahue	40 48		
Henry Duffy	34 88		
F. J. Deckert	3 52		
John H Dooley	16 88		
Jacob Delros	15 44		
Fred L. Englin	12 00		
Halford Erickson	608 00		
F. B. Gould	10 40		
C. A. Haertel	8 26		
W. C. Habercorn	2 24		

"A."—General Fund Disbursements for 1894.

Neils Heggen	$12 48		
J. C. Hoffman	14 40		
Halbert Hansen	13 86		
G. J. Huhn	87 12		
Frank Hamlin	52 32		
W. H. Irish	14 56		
John W. Jones	58 40		
August Kreutz	5 60		
W. A. Kent	12 48		
August Kieckhefer	102 12		
Charles Knuston	11 60		
Hugo Koenen	5 76		
Edward Klentz	16 72		
Edward C. Kretlow	43 92		
E. Lawrence	12 08		
Julius Linstedt	19 76		
Frank McCormick	5 04		
E. J. Mooney	4 88		
F. X. Morrow	11 86		
Anton J. Mahlman	15 44		
M. Michaelson	12 96		
John H. Menting	29 60		
James L. Moran	20 88		
George H. Miller	17 84		
T. J. Madigan	14 88		
M. G. O'Donnell	4 00		
O. R. Olson	7 84		
Henry C. O'Connor	27 04		
Andrew Oettinger	10 48		
Wm. Prideaux	12 96		
A. F. Peterson	7 28		
T. R. Philips	6 16		
Chas. E. Paeske	1 04		
Frank M. Roberts	6 56		
O. F. Stoppenbach	21 76		
W. J. Slater	11 20		
Andrew Schleis	5 04		
J. C Southmayd	15 92		
C A. Shaver	63 52		
J. D. Stewart	29 84		
Christopher Senol	28 96		
Harvey M. Sowle	29 12		
John Shipping	26 48		
Thomas F. Scanlon	14 80		
W. T. Taylor	4 16		
C. L. Valentine	15 28		
R. G. Webb	7 20		
W. E. Warren	12 40		
Austin White	18 82		
William Zassenhaus	16 04		
		$1,842 02	

STATISTICS OF CRIME.

Clerks of courts for reporting criminal statistics	$29 60		
		$29 60	

"A." — General Fund Disbursements for 1894.

FREE HIGH SCHOOLS.

Alma	$254 25		
Amherst	183 62		
Argyle	226 00		
Augusta	282 50		
Appleton	282 50		
Appleton, 3d dist	282 50		
Ahnapee	282 50		
Almond	69 91		
Antigo	282 50		
Arcadia	282 50		
Ashland	282 50		
Avoca	152 55		
Barron	279 67		
Bangor	226 00		
Brandon	226 00		
Brillion	226 00		
Baraboo	282 50		
Bayfield	282 50		
Beloit	282 50		
Berlin	282 50		
Black Earth	282 50		
Black River Falls	282 50		
Bloomer	282 50		
Bloomington	282 50		
Boscobel	282 50		
Brodhead	282 50		
Burlington	282 50		
Beaver Dam	282 50		
Belleville	240 12		
Cambridge	204 81		
Chetek	197 75		
Clintonville	190 68		
Cassville	282 50		
Centralia	282 50		
Chilton	282 50		
Clinton	282 50		
Cuba City	229 30		
Columbus	282 50		
Cadott	190 68		
Cumberland	282 50		
Chippewa Falls	282 50		
Colby	190 68		
Darlington	282 50		
Delavan	282 50		
Dodgeville	282 50		
Durand	282 50		
De Pere	282 50		
East Troy	282 50		
Edgerton	282 50		
Elkhorn	282 50		
Elroy	282 50		
Evansville	282 50		
Eau Claire	282 50		
Ellsworth	203 40		
Fennimore	247 18		

"A."—General Fund Disbursements for 1894.

Fremont	$113 00		
Friendship	152 55		
Florence	282 50		
Fond du Lac	282 50		
Fort Atkinson	282 50		
Fort Howard	282 50		
Fox Lake	282 50		
Fairchild	282 50		
Glenbeulah	190 68		
Grand Rapids	282 50		
Green Bay	282 50		
Hazel Green	197 75		
Highland	190 68		
Hillsborough	190 68		
Humbird	190 68		
Hartford	282 50		
Horicon	282 50		
Hurley	282 50		
Hudson	282 50		
Hayward	282 50		
Janesville	282 50		
Jefferson	282 50		
Juneau	282 50		
Kiel	254 25		
Kaukauna	282 50		
Kenosha	282 50		
Kewaunee	282 50		
Linden	177 97		
Lone Rock	165 26		
Lake Mills	282 50		
Lancaster	282 50		
Lodi	282 50		
Lake Geneva	282 50		
Middleton	188 62		
Madison	282 50		
Merrillan	208 40		
Milton Junction	197 75		
Montello	169 50		
Montford	192 10		
Mt. Hope	152 55		
Muscoda	190 68		
Manawa	292 50		
Marshfield	282 50		
Mauston	282 50		
Mayville	282 50		
Mazomanie	282 50		
Medford	282 50		
Menasha	282 50		
Mineral Point	282 50		
Monroe	282 50		
Mondovi	190 68		
Marshall	498 60		
Marinette	282 50		
Merrill	282 50		
Neenah	282 50		
Necedah	282 50		
Neillsville	282 50		
New London	282 50		

"A."—General Fund Disbursements for 1894.

New Richmond	$282 50		
New Lisbon	282 50		
Oregon	282 50		
Oakfield	177 97		
Oak Wood	211 87		
Omro	264 42		
Oconomowoc	282 50		
Onalaska	282 50		
Oconto	282 50		
Pepin	198 88		
Pewaukee	254 25		
Plainfield	190 68		
Port Washington	240 12		
Potosi	279 67		
Peshtigo	282 50		
Phillips	282 50		
Platteville	282 50		
Plymouth	282 50		
Portage	282 50		
Poynette	282 50		
Prairie du Chien	282 50		
Prairie du Sac	282 50		
Prescott	282 50		
Rhinelander	282 50		
Racine	282 50		
Rice Lake	282 50		
Richland Center	282 50		
Ripon	282 50		
River Falls	282 50		
Reedsburg	282 50		
St. Martins	73 45		
Seymour	190 68		
Shell Lake	268 37		
South Milwaukee	203 40		
Stockbridge	127 12		
Sauk City	282 50		
Sharon	282 50		
Sheboygan Falls	282 50		
Sextonville	197 75		
Shawano	282 50		
Sturgeon Bay	282 50		
Sheboygan	282 50		
Stevens Point	282 50		
Shullsburg	282 50		
Sparta	282 50		
Spring Green	282 50		
Stoughton	282 50		
Sun Prairie	282 50		
Tomah	282 50		
Two Rivers	282 50		
Unity	190 68		
Viroqua	282 50		
Waldo	177 97		
Walworth	152 55		
Westfield	203 40		
West Salem	226 00		
Weyauwega	244 08		
Wilton	183 62		

"A."—General Fund Disbursements for 1894.

Washburn	$282 50		
Waterloo	282 50		
Watertown	282 50		
Waupaca	282 50		
Waukesha	282 50		
Waupun, Fond du Lac Co	282 50		
Waupun, Dodge Co	282 50		
Wausau	282 50		
Wauwatosa	282 50		
West Depere	282 50		
Wonewoc	282 50		
Whitewater	282 50		
West Bend	282 50		
Total		$47,402 91	

MAINTAINING CHRONIC INSANE.

Brown county	$6,094 43		
Brown county for Door	179 92		
Brown county for Kewaunee	1,264 08		
Brown county for Marinette	774 17		
Brown county for Oconto	2,059 80		
		$10,372 40	
Dodge county	$5,245 50		
Dodge county for Lincoln	499 55		
Dodge county for Oconto	1,883 65		
Dodge county for Shawano	338 30		
Dodge county for Washington	3,838 66		
Dodge county for state at large	196 96		
		$11,502 62	
Dane county	$7,790 57		
Dane county for Pierce	495 18		
		$8,285 75	
Dunn county	$3,583 92		
Dunn county for Barron	527 57		
Dunn county for Burnett	215 71		
Dunn county for Chippewa	1,368 54		
Dunn county for Douglas	324 86		
Dunn county for Eau Claire	1,448 29		
Dunn county for Jackson	285 00		
Dunn county for Pepin	398 14		
Dunn county for Pierce	630 29		
Dunn county for St. Croix	2,688 42		
Dunn county for Taylor	812 15		
Dunn county for Washburn	201 71		
Dunn county for state at large	1,961 14		
		$14,445 74	
Columbia county	$3,837 19		
Columbia county for Adams	831 51		
Columbia county for Clark	537 07		
Columbia county for Jackson	177 65		
Columbia county for Marathon	168 57		

"A."—General Fund Disbursements for 1894.

Columbia county for Marquette	$842 41	....	....
Columbia county for Portage	448 04	....	....
Columbia county for Waushara.....	796 87	....	....
Columbia county for state at large..	4,802 2?	....	....
		$11,936 03	....
Fond du Lac county	$6,094 84	....	....
Fond du Lac county for Douglas ...	404 0?	....	....
Fond du Lac county for Marquette..	1,210 5?	....	....
Fond du Lac county for Marinette..	588 1?	....	....
Fond du Lac county for Price	499 2?	....	....
Fond du Lac county for Portage ...	691 2?	....	....
Fond du Lac county for Waupaca..	185 2?	....	....
Fond du Lac county for Green Lake	1,876 77	....	....
		$11,549 54	....
Grant county.....................	$4,841 14	....	....
Grant county for Barron...........	335 64	....	....
Grant county for Crawford	3,237 75	....	....
Grant county for La Fayette	1,046 29	....	....
Grant county for Richland	1,973 92	....	....
		$11,484 74	....
Green county.....................	$4,078 70	....	....
Green county for Buffalo...........	505 85	....	....
Green county for Eau Claire........	2,224 73	....	....
Green county for Jackson..........	907 94	....	....
Green county for La Fayette.......	3,858 05	....	....
Green county for Polk	1,061 48	....	....
		$12,636 25	....
Jefferson county..................	$5,954 85	....	....
Jefferson county for Burnett.......	1,185 67	....	....
Jefferson county for Eau Claire	173 84	....	....
Jefferson county for Juneau	5,337 01	....	....
Jefferson county for state at large ..	184 28	....	....
		$12,835 15	....
Iowa county	$3,795 27	....	....
Iowa county for Buffalo....	362 40	....	....
Iowa county for Jackson	515 54	....	....
Iowa county for Pierce	623 75	....	....
Iowa county for Polk	2,471 38	....	....
Iowa county for Trempealeau	746 53	....	....
Iowa county for Waukesha	4,886 05	....	....
Iowa county for state at large......	983 18	....	....
		$14,384 05	....
La Crosse county	$4,344 44	....	....
La Crosse county for Barron	484 36	....	....
La Crosse county for Buffalo	1,959 01	....	....
La Crosse county for Clark.........	1,297 5?	....	....
La Crosse county for Jackson......	1,230 60	....	....
La Crosse county for Monroe.......	72 00	....	....
La Crosse county for Trempealeau..	1,119 63	....	....
La Crosse county for state at large..	2,139 82	....	....
		$12,647 45	....

"A."—*General Fund Disbursements for 1894.*

Manitowoc county	$4,910 36		
Manitowoc county for Marathon....	2,573 53		
Manitowoc county for Marinette ...	168 63		
Manitowoc county for Ozaukee	2,881 92		
Manitowoc county for Waupaca....	758 46		
Manitowoc county for state at large.	1,145 65		
		$12,438 55	
Milwaukee county	$51,272 29		
		$51,272 29	
Outagamie county	$4,397 18		
Outagamie county for Calumet....	2,149 71		
Outagamie county for Door	1,479 48		
Outagamie county for Kewaunee...	1,065 15		
Outagamie county for Langlade....	185 18		
Outagamie county for Oconto.....	780 80		
Outagamie county for Shawano....	837 45		
Outagamie county for Waupaca....	2,720 81		
		$13,115 76	
Portage county, erroneous charge for maintaining Marinette county patient in Vernon county asylum.	$260 89		
		$260 89	
Racine county	$5,317 92		
Racine county for Eau Claire	1,995 36		
Racine county for Kenosha	4,618 44		
Racine county for state at large....	474 31		
		$12,406 03	
Rock county	$6,770 35		
		$6,770 35	
Sauk county	$3,499 04		
Sauk county for Trempealeau	1,453 86		
		$4,953 80	
Sheboygan county	$6,523 93		
Sheboygan county for Calumet.....	1,010 06		
Sheboygan county for Chippewa....	674 31		
Sheboygan county for Washington.	446 27		
		$8,654 57	
Walworth county	$4,311 73		
Walworth county for Chippewa....	1,356 08		
Walworth county for Pepin	512 23		
Walworth county for Richland.....	1,026 40		
Walworth county for Waukesha...	2,048 77		
		$9,255 21	
Vernon county	$2,902 36		
Vernon county for Buffalo	6 74		
Vernon county for Chippewa......	2,259 28		
Vernon county for Crawford	763 29		
Vernon county for Marinette	171 89		
Vernon county for Monroe	2,387 84		

"A."—*General Fund Disbursements for 1894.*

Vernon county for Portage.........	$172 17	....	....
Vernon county for Richland........	642 86	....	....
Vernon county for Trempealeau....	1,046 44	....	....
Vernon county for Wood...........	171 49	........'....	....
Vernon county for state at large....	4,556 54	....	....
		$15,080 85	....
Winnebago county	$4,425 78	....	....
Winnebago county for Portage.....	70 20	....	....
		$4,495 98	....
George Krebs, transferring inmates.	$46 35	....	....
		$46 35	....
Total......................	....	....	$270,780 80

DEAF MUTE INSTRUCTION — CITIES AND VILLAGES.

City of La Crosse..................	$1,688 54	....	....
City of Manitowoc...	934 73	....	....
City of Wausau	1,501 12	....	....
City of Milwaukee.................	5,190 98	....	....
		$9,315 87	....

BOUNTY.

Bounty on wild animals	$13,068 00	....	....
		$13,068 00	....

CIRCUIT COURT REPORTERS.

H. A. Bush........................	$430 00	....	....
F. S. Bradford....................	740 00	....	....
C. A. Cross	1,000 00	....	....
Joseph Cover.....................	685 00	....	....
Geo. Hart	565 00	....	....
Alfred Harrison...................	835 00	....	....
F. C. Grant.....................	700 00	....	....
W. C. Kimball....................	430 00	....	....
Chas. Orton........	630 00	....	....
Jas T. Parkes....................	640 00	....	....
F. W. Spencer....	340 00	....	....
J. A. Sawyer......................	820 60	....	....
T. H. Wolford	930 00	....	....
Chas. H. Welsh	840 00	....	....
Chas W. Fiske...................	565 00	....	....
Albert Kavalage...................	10 00	....	....
		$10,160 60	....

COUNTY AGRICULTURAL SOCIETIES.

Adams County Agricultural Society	$220 50	....	....
Arcadia Agricultural and Driving Pk. Assn....	391 92	....	....
Burnett County Agricultural Society	200 00	....	....
Blakes Prairie Agricultural Society.	892 00	....	....

"A."—General Fund Disbursements for 1894.

Boscobel Agricultural and Driving P*. Assn....	$450 80	....	....
Brown County Fair and Park Assn.	677 58	....	....
Buffalo County Agricultural So- ciety................ ...	595 13	....	....
Barron County Agricultural Society.	328 60	....	....
Calumet County Agricultural So- ciety....	346 40	....	....
Clark County Agricultural Society.	450 98	....	....
Columbia County Agricultural So- ciety	744 32	....	....
Crawford County Agricultural So- ciety	200 00	....	....
Cumberland Agricultural and Driv- Park Assn	314 80	....	....
Dodge County Fair Assn...........	1,029 96	....	....
Dunn County Agricultural Society.	531 20	....	....
Eastern Monroe County Agricultural Society	313 18	....	... .
Grant County Agricultural Society.	542 72	....	....
Green County Agricultural Society..	708 40	....	....
Iowa County Agricultural Society..	784 48	....	....
In ustrial Assn. of Manitowoc County ......:......	765 00	....	....
Jackson County Agricultural Society	580 03	....	....
Jefferson County and Rock River Agr. Society	745 00	....	....
Juneau County Agricultural Society	348 20	....	....
Kewaunee County Agricultural So ciety....	200 00	....	....
La Crosse Inter-State Fair Assn....	1,200 00	....	....
La Crosse County Agricultural So ciety.	542 00	....	....
La Fayette County Agricultural So- ciety	692 20	....	....
Langlade County Agricultural So- ciety.	839 80	....	....
Lake Superior Agr.,Ind.and Fine Art Society	200 00	....	....
Little Karaboo Valley Agricultural Society	323 76	....	....
Lodi Union Agricultural Society....	359 82	....	....
Marathon County Agricultural So ciety.	248 20	....	....
Marquette County Agricultural So- ciety....	305 10	.... : ...	....
Monroe County Agricultural Society	200 00	....	...
Outagamie County Agricultural So ciety........	383 62	....	....
Ozaukee County Agricultural So- ciety.	587 30	....	....
Pepin County Agricultural Society.	842 40	....	....
Portage County Agricultural Society	200 00	....	....
Price County Agricultural Society..	200 00	....	....
Pierce County Central Fair Assn....	468 04	....	....
Richland County Agricultural So ciety.	613 20	....	....
Rock County Agricultural Society..	707 90	....	....

"A."—General Fund Disbursements for 1894.

St. Croix County Agricultural Society	$407 00	....	....
Sauk County Agricultural Society..	659 52	....	....
Seymour Fair and Driving Park Assn.	364 85	....	....
Southwestern Ind Assn.......	887 00	....	....
Sheboygan Driving Park and Exp. Assn	479 50	... .	....
Trempealeau Ind., Agr. and Driving Park Assn......	425 50	....	....
Trempealeau County Agricultural Society	528 60	....	....
Taylor County Agricultural Society.	243 70	....	....
Vernon County Agricultural Society	536 90	....	....
Walworth County Agricultural Society...	1,200 00	....	....
Washington County Agricultural Society	413 10	....	....
Waukesha County Agricultural Society...........	878 20	....	....
Waupaca County Agricultural Society......	342 20	....	....
Waushara County Agricultural Society................	374 20	....	....
		$27,874 30	....
SPECIAL APPROPRIATIONS.			
Agricultural Institutes, chapter 62, Laws of 1887	$18,000 00	....	....
Board of Normal regents, teachers' institutes	1,726 95	....	....
Callaghan & Co., annotated statutes	126 00	....	....
Fifth Normal School, chapter 364, Laws of 1885................. ..	10,000 00	....	. .....
Industrial School for Girls..........	2,500 00	... .	
Milwaukee Journal, advertising for Marquette statue......	22 40	....	....
Northern Hospital for Insane for roofing, chapter 152, Laws of 1893	1,000 00	....	....
State Agricultural Society...... ..	4,000 00	....	....
State Prison, tailor and knitting shop. chapter 280, Laws of 1880...	10,000 00	....	....
State Firemen's Association, chapter 58, Laws of 1893................	500 00	....	....
State Horticultural Society, chapter 117, Laws of 1893	1,500 00	....	....
State Prison, warden's residence, chapter 152, Laws of 1893........	1,000 00	....	....
State Prison, kitchen, hospital, etc., chapter 152, Laws of 1893........	15,000 00	....	....
Stone school house, Ind. Sch. for boys, chapter 152, Laws of 1893...	11,500 00	....	....
State University, 1 per cent. license tax, chapter 282, Laws of 1889 ...	24,642 00	....	....
State University, appropriation, ch. 280, Laws of 1893................	140,000 00	....	....

"A."—General Fund Disbursements for 1894.

School for Blind, heating app., etc., chapter 152, Laws 1893.	$5,600 00	....
School for Deaf, chapter 152, Laws of 1893............................	33 25	....
Evening Wisconsin, printing World's Fair Com........................	1,114 48	....
World's Fair Commission, chapter 140, Laws 1893.	8,415 85	....
O. E. Wells, codifying school laws, chapter 178, Laws 1893...........	2,142 84	....
Wisconsin Veterans' Home, chapter 248, Laws of 1893..............	5,000 00	....
Wisconsin Dairymen's Assn., chapter 240, Laws of 1893	2,000 00	....
Wisconsin Cranberry Growers Assn. chapter 263, Laws of 1893........	250 00	....
Total	....	$266,073 84

MISCELLANEOUS.

Andrew S. Brown, sheriff's fees, service to state....................	$115 26	....
Binner Engraving Co., illus. rep. St Hist. Soc'y	26 50	....
T. J. Cunningham, libr'n congress, fees............................	3 00	....
E. E. Bryant, compiling election laws............................	350 00	....
Dictionaries, state superintendent...	1,869 00	....
C. M. Foresman, services land commissioner......................	25 00	....
Germantown Farmers' Mutual Ins. Co., excess license fees refunded..	14 93	....
T. J. Cunningham, refunded corporation fee........................	5 00	....
F. C. Lorenz, clk. circuit court, Milwaukee Co., certified copies	31 90	....
Milwaukee Litho. & Engr. Co., cuts for election law pamphlets........	2 00	....
Marquette Co., erroneous charge of state hospital	51 50	....
Normal school regents, transfer from gen'l fund in lieu of $\frac{1}{10}$ mill tax for normal schools not levied in '93.	32,700 00	....
T. B. Pray, service state supt	150 00	....
Refunded pen. and adv., Francis Gotschy............................	10 21	....
H. W. Skinner, witness fees, insuran cases........................	21 50	....
C. KeePier, sec'y Soldiers' Orphans Home..........................	21 31	....
Wisconsin Veterans' Home, maintaining inmates...................	39,107 99	....

"A."—General Fund Disbursements for 1894.

Chas. H. Welch, services land commissioner	$10 94		
Treasurer, indemnity fund transfer for receipts 1892	6,140 08		
State treasurer, purchase of McFetridge mortgage on state fair grounds	47,782 08		
Carl Heden, refunded patent fees	50		
		$128,438 65	
Total general fund disbursements			$1,711,889 94

"A."—School Fund Receipts for 1894.

SCHOOL FUND.

RECEIPTS.		
Sales of lands..............................	$2,316 50	....
Dues on certificates of sales.....................	8,444 87	....
Loans..	56,627 16	....
Penalties..	6 78	....
Fines..	22,444 69	....
United States, 5 per cent. sales public lands......	9,164 95	....
Loan to Barron county	2,000 00	....
Loan to Brown county	4,350 00	....
Loan to Iron county.........................	108 49	....
Loan to Jackson county.....................	2,000 00	....
Loan to Lincoln county.....................	4,198 50	....
Loan to Oneida county...	1,488 26	....
Loan to Price county......................	4,000 00	....
Loan to Vilas county	2,297 04	....
Loan to Washburn county....	2,154 80	....
Loan to city of Berlin.......................	2,000 00	....
Loan to city of New London.....................	2,000 00	....
Loan to city of Merrill.........................	1,180 00	....
Loan to city of Rice Lake.....................	800 00	....
Loan to city of Wausau.......................	2,000 00	....
Loan to town of Arcadia......................	1,666 67	....
Loan to town of Arthur.........................	600 00	....
Loan to town of Arena.........................	100 00	....
Loan to town of Ashland......................	1,075 50	....
Loan to town of Crandon......................	200 00	....
Loan to town of Cleveland......................	96 43	....
Loan to the town of Clinton......................	200 00	....
Loan to the town of Day.......................	350 00	....
Loan to the town of Gillett	100 00	....
Loan to the town of Hixon	660 00	....
Loan to the town of Millston.....................	666 67	....
Loan to the town of Moscow.....................	757 00	....
Loan to the town of Mineral Point...............	1,000 00	....
Loan to the town of Maine	250 00	....
Loan to the town of Mosinee.....................	200 00	....
Loan to the town of Pleasant Valley	766 48	....
Loan to the town of Rolling.....................	100 00	....
Loan to the town of Russell....	500 00	....
Loan to the town of Richfield......................	275 00	....
Loan to the town of St. Croix Falls...............	250 00	....
Loan to the town of Spooner	3,500 00	....
Loan to the town of Shell Lake..................	3,333 33	....
Loan to the town of Weston	170 00	....
Loan to the town of Waldwick..................	850 00	....
Loan to the town of Wood.....................	1,000 00	....
Loan to the village of Bloomer..................	200 00	....
Loan to board of education, city of Madison.....	5,000 00	....

"A."—School Fund Disbursements for 1894.

Marathon county bonds..........................	$8,000 00	....
Marathon county bonds premium................	278 16	....
Oconomowoc city bonds........................	2,000 00	....
Ripon city bonds.............................	1,500 00	....
Superior city bonds premium....................	3,184 17	....
Elkhorn school bonds	2,000 00	....
Mineral Point city bonds......................	1,000 00	....
Milwaukee city bonds.........................	37,000 00	....
Total receipts..........................	....	$207,911 45

DISBURSEMENTS.

School District Loans—

School district No. 2, town of Loyal, Clark county...	$1,500 00	....
School district No. 4, town of Union, Eau Claire county........	900 00	....
School district No. 5, town of Russell, Lincoln county......................	500 00	....
School district No. 3, town of Walworth, Walworth county....	2,000 00	....
School district No. 3, town of Carson, Portage county.......................	500 00	....
School district No. 4, town of Elk Mound, Dunn county	500 00	....
School district No. 7, town of Alma, Jackson county...........................	650 00	....
School district No. 4, town of Unity, Clark county	300 00	....
School district No. 4, town of Armenia, Juneau county	150 00	....
School district No. 2, town of Rolling, Langlade county	300 00	....
School district No. 2, town of Byron, Monroe county..........	150 00	....
School district No. 15, town of Big Bend, Chippewa county....	400 00	....
School district No. 2, town of Wittenburg, Shawano county	250 00	....
School district No. 4, town of Springdale, Dane county.......................	800 00	....
School district No. 1, town of Spring Lake, Pierce county	600 00	....
School district No. 8, town of Oconto, Oconto county	300 00	....
School district No. 2, town of Georgetown, Polk county	400 00	....
School district No 1, town of Northfield, Jackson county	250 00	....
School district No. 12, town of Middleton, Dane county	2,000 00	....
School district No. 9, town of Ogema, Price county......................	300 00	....
School district No. 5, town of Norwood, Langlade county......	500 00	....
School district No. 5, town of Washington, Shawano county...	500 00	....

"A."—School Fund Disbursements for 1894.

*School District Loans—*Continued.

School district No.11, town of Stockton, Portage county	$100 00	....
School district No. 4, town of Eau Plaine, Marathon county	450 00	....
School district No. 1, town of Spence, Oconto county	400 00	....
School district No. 2, town of Pine Creek, Taylor county	700 00	....
School district No. 1, town of Lincoln, Trempealeau county	4,000 00	....
School district No. 1, town of Kronenwetter, Marathon county	500 00	....
Jt. school district No. 1, towns of Blanchard, La Fayette county and Moscow. Iowa county	700 00	....
Jt. school district No 1, towns of Moscow, Iowa county; Perry. Dane county; York, Green county	500 00	....
Jt. school district No. 1, towns of Wood and city of Pittsville, Wood county	500 00	....
Jt. school district No. 9, towns of Forest, Richland county and Liberty, Vernon county	2,845 00	... .
Jt. school district No. 1, towns of Shell Lake and Bashaw, Washburn county	2,500 00	....
Jt. school district No. 4, town of Lincoln and village of Amery	2,850 00	....
Jt. school district No. 1, city of Medford, Taylor county	8,000 00	....
School district No. 6, town of Carson	400 00	....
School district No. 10, town of Edson, Chippewa county	850 00	....
School district No. 1, village of Nekoosa	1,200 00	....
School district No. 2 town of Pensaukee	1,200 00	....
School district No. 2, town of Colfax, Dunn Co.	200 00	. ...
School directors Nebagamain, Douglas county	1,495 00	....
School directors Minocqua, Oneida county	8,600 00	....
School directors Eagle River. Vilas county	8,000 00	....
School directors Veazie, Washburn county	1,000 00	....
School directors Washburn, Bayfield county	10,000 00	....
School directors Iron River, Bayfield county	8,000 00	....
School directors Brule, Douglas county	500 00	....
School directors Minong, Washburn county	500 00	....
School directors Merrill, Lincoln county	1,500 00	....
Jt. school district No 1. Warner, Eaton and city of Greenwood, Clark county	1,500 00	....
Joint school district No. 1, town and city of Medford, Taylor county	1,500 00	....
Joint school district No. 4. towns of Colfax, Grant. Otter Creek and Tainter, Dunn county.	300 00	....
Joint school district No. 3, Harrison and Plover, Marathon county	400 00	....
Joint school district No. 4, towns of Wien and Cassell, Marathon county	545 00	....
Joint school district No. 4, towns of Sullivan and Concord, Jefferson county	1,000 00	....
Joint school district No. 8, towns of Byron and Lincoln, Monroe county	75 00	....
Joint school district No. 8, towns of Arcadia, Trempealeau Co., and Glenco, Buffalo county.	450 00	....

"A."—School Fund Disbursements for 1894.

*School District Loans—*Continued.

School district No. 7, town of Oak Grove, Dodge county......	$2,500 00	....
School district No 2, town of Egg Harbor, Door county....	500 00	....
School district No. 4, town of Colfax, Dunn county........	300 00	... ...
School district No. 4, town of Lucas, Dunn county......	400 00	....
School district No. 5, town of Stanton, Dunn county	400 00	... .
School district No. 6, town of Arthur, Chippewa county	400 00	....
School district No. 2, town of Withee, Clark county	500 00	....
School district No. 2, town of Hewett, Clark county	500 00	....
School district No. 5, town of Hanley, Crawford county	150 00	....
School district No. 1, town of Bayfield, Bayfield county	20,000 00	....
School district No. 2, town of Eau Plaine, Marathon county......	350 00	....
School district No. 1, town of Amberg, Marinette county......	750 00	....
School district No. 3, town of Granville, Milwaukee county......	4,000 00	... .
School district No. 5, town of Wauwatosa, Milwaukee county......	8,000 00	....
School district No. 7, town of Twin Bells, Pierce county	1,200 00	... .
School district No. 3, town of Union, Pierce county...	1,300 00	....
School district No. 2, town of Johnson, Polk county......	700 00	....
School district No. 4, town of Alden, Polk county	550 00	....
School district No 1, town of Richland, Shawano county......	475 00	....
School district No. 3, town of Green Valley, Shawano county...	700 00	....
School district No. 3, town of Grover, Taylor county	400 00	....
School district No. 1, town of Sumner, Trempealeau county......	1,100 00	....
School district No. 2, town of Spring Green, Sauk county......	1,500 00	....
School district No. 7, town of Christiana, Vernon county......	1,800 00	....
Total school district loans......	....	$119,485 00
Special Loans—		
Loan to city of Menasha......	$12,000 00	....
Loan to city of Chippewa Falls.....	15,000 00	....
Loan to city of Oconto....	35,000 00	....
Loan to Oneida county......	30,000 00	....
Refunded Carl Heden......	50 00	....
		$92,050 00
Total disbursements	... .	$211,535 00

"A."—School Fund Income Receipts for 1894.

SCHOOL FUND INCOME.

RECEIPTS.		
Interest on land certificates and loans...........	$24,092 87	... .
Interest on certificates of indebtedness	109,616 83	....
Mill tax...	654,943 00	....
Interest on school fund in banks	8,582 06	....
Interest on Chippewa Falls city bonds...........	1,000 00	....
Interest on Madison city bonds	3,000 00	....
Interest on Oshkosh sewer bonds.................	247 50	....
Interest on Stoughton city bonds............	1,500 00	....
Interest on Wausau city bonds..........	1,500 00	....
Interest on Ashland city bonds..................	1,250 00	....
Interest on Ashland county bonds	1,000 00	....
Interest on Chilton town bonds	788 00	....
Interest on Chilton city bonds.......	342 00	....
Interest on Eau Claire city bonds...............	1,350 00	....
Interest on Elroy city bonds	285 75	....
Interest on Mineral Point bonds.................	300 00	....
Interest on Milwaukee city bonds..	15,120 00	....
Interest on Milwaukee school bonds.............	2,400 00	....
Interest on Marathon county bonds	1,321 84	....
Interest on Fond du Lac city bonds	1,500 00	....
Interest on Oconomowoc city bonds........ ...	120 00	....
Interest on Oshkosh city bonds..................	2,796 00	....
Interest on Ripon city bonds	300 00	... .
Interest on Superior city bonds.................	11,815 83	....
Interest on Elkhorn school bonds................	500 00	....
Interest on loan to Brown county	2,958 00	....
Interest on loan to Barron county	700 00	....
Interest on loan to Jackson county......	560 00	....
Interest on loan to Oneida county..............	1,091 67	....
Interest on loan to Price county................	1,400 00	....
Interest on loan to Washburn county	75 42	....
Interest on loan to Winnebago county	170 00	....
Interest on loan to Chippewa county	30 00	....
Washburn county for non-payment of amount on special loans due 1892...	661 12	....
Washburn county for non-payment of school district loans due 1892	316 56	....
Interest on loan to city of Berlin	$300 00	....
Interest on loan to city of Chippewa Falls...... .	427 50	....
Interest on loan to city of Green Bay............	1,575 00	....
Interest on loan to city of New London..	860 00	....
Interest on loan to city of Neenah	150 00	....
Interest on loan to city of Oconto...............	1,166 66	... .
Interest on loan to city of Rice Lake	105 00	....
Interest on loan to city of Menasha.............	521 65	....
Interest on loan to city of Wausau	140 00	....
Interest on loan to board of education, city of Madison....................................	750 00	... .

"A."—School Fund Income Disbursements for 1894.

Interest on loan to town of Arcadia	$700 00	....
Interest on loan to town of Ashland.............	165 62	....
Interest on loan to town of Arena....	28 00	....
Interest on loan to town of Chilton.............	24 00	....
Interest on loan to town of Crandon........... .	60 00	....
Interest on loan to town of Day	24 50	....
Interest on loan to town of Gillett...............	5 00	....
Interest on loan to town of Moscow	264 95	....
Interest on loan to town of Mosinee.............	28 00	....
Interest on loan to town of Mineral Point........	70 00	....
Interest on loan to town of Maine	128 00	....
Interest on loan to town of Rolling...	14 00	....
Interest on loan to town of Richfield....	77 00	....
Interest on loan to town of Russell	210 00	....
Interest on loan to town of Pleasant Valley......	76 65	....
Interest on loan to town of Spooner.............	175 00	....
Interest on loan to town of St. Croix Falls.... ..	52 50	....
Interest on loan to town of Waldwick........,....	595 00	....
Interest on loan to town of Wood............ ...	210 00	....
Refunded by town of Farmington, La Crosse Co.	67 85	....
Washburn Co., penalty for non-payment of state tax, 1892	110 08	....
Total receipts..............................	....	$862,716 40

DISBURSEMENTS.

Apportionment to Counties—

Adams	$3,525 48	....
Ashland...................................	6,695 43	....
Barron....................................	8,996 91	....
Bayfield	3,198 02	....
Brown.	21,751 35	....
Buffalo...................................	8,241 06	....
Burnett...................................	2,695 00	....
Calumet.........	9,849 73	....
Chippewa	12,822 29	....
Clark.....................................	10,124 57	....
Columbia..................................	12,884 72	....
Crawford	8,279 05	....
Dane......................................	27,505 03	....
Dodge.....................................	21,448 74	....
Door......................................	9,078 33	....
Douglas...................................	7,477 07	....
Dunn.....................................	11,689 19	....
Eau Claire	14,787 22	....
Florence	1,042 17	....
Fond du Lac	21,603 44	....
Forest.....................................	397 60	....
Grant.....................................	17,761 77	....
Green	10,212 78	....
Green Lake	7,474 35	....
Iowa......................................	10,892 63	....
Iron......................................	1,681 82	....
Jackson	8,239 70	....
Jefferson	16,107 59	....
Juneau....................................	8,965 69	....

"A."—*School Fund Income Disbursements for 1894.*

Apportionment to Counties—Continued.

Kenosha	$7,459 42	
Kewaunee	9,568 20	
La Crosse	19,040 06	
La Fayette	9,497 64	
Langlade	4,471 80	
Lincoln	6,714 48	
Manitowoc	20,435 99	
Marathon	17,911 04	
Marinette	10,667 37	
Marquette	5,007 83	
Milwaukee	128,612 38	
Monroe	11,942 95	
Oconto	8,857 13	
Oneida	2,053 14	
Outagamie	21,152 91	
Ozaukee	8,314 83	
Pepin	3,563 48	
Pierce	11,021 55	
Polk	7,405 14	
Portage	13,370 52	
Price	2,604 08	
Racine	17,491 73	
Richland	9,214 03	
Rock	20,249 15	
St. Croix	11,808 61	
Sauk	15,211 97	
Sawyer	725 99	
Shawano	10,910 28	
Sheboygan	28,382 46	
Taylor	3,837 59	
Trempealeau	10,880 84	
Vernon	13,232 10	
Vilas	664 98	
Walworth	10,630 73	
Washburn	1,472 84	
Washington	12,058 30	
Waukesha	14,248 49	
Waupaca	13,863 10	
Waushara	7,082 18	
Winnebago	25,374 54	
Wood	10,412 26	
Refunded	64 92	
Total disbursements		$868,063 42

"A."—University Fund for 1894.

UNIVERSITY FUND.

RECEIPTS.		
Sales of land	$139 95	....
Dues on certificates of sales	1,067 00	....
Loans	275 00	....
Loan to Shawano county	1,500 00	....
Loan to city of Menomonie	2,000 00	....
Vernon county bonds	4,000 00	....
Tomahawk city bonds	1,500 00	....
Total receipts.	....	$10,481 95

DISBURSEMENTS.		
Loan to town of Florence, Florence county	$2,000 00	....
Loan to village of Thorp, Clark county	4,000 00	....
Greenwood city bonds	5,000 00	....
Total disbursements	....	$11,000 00

"A."—University Fund Income for 1894.

UNIVERSITY FUND INCOME.

RECEIPTS.		
From 9-40 mill tax....	$147,362 18	....
U. S. treasurer, appropriation for agricultural experimental station...................	15,000 00	....
Secretary board of regents, students' fees, etc....	48,738 72	....
One per cent. of railroad and other license fees...	24,642 67	....
Appropriation, chap. 280, laws 1893	140,000 00	....
Appropriation for agricultural institute.........	18,000 00	....
Transfer from ex-state treasurers' judgment fund.	41,936 32	....
U. S. appropriation, agricultural college..... ..	20,000 00	....
Washburn Co., penalty non payment of taxes 1892	22 81	....
Interest on land certificate loans	799 46	....
Interest on certificates of indebtedness..........	7,781 10	....
Interest on university funds in banks............	775 57	....
Interest on Jackson bequest..................	25 00	....
Interest on Eau Claire county bonds.............	500 00	....
Interest on Manitowoc county bonds.............	1,200 00	....
Interest on Vernon county bonds.......	1,000 00	....
Interest on Stoughton city bonds.................	150 00	....
Interest on Tomahawk city bonds........	536 76	....
Interest on loan to Winnebago county...........	340 00	....
Interest on loan to Shawano county.	630 00	....
Interest on loan to city of Menomonie..	100 00	....
Interest on loan to town of Florence.............	62 77	....
Interest on loan to board of education, city of Ripon.......................................	42 71	....
Interest on loan to village of Thorp..............	18 75	....
Interest on Platteville city bonds	240 00	....
Interest on Greenwood city bonds...	75 00	....
Total receipts............................	.. ..	$470,073 72
DISBURSEMENTS.		
Treasurer state university transfer..............	$470,089 40	....
Refunded	34 32	....
Total disbursements	....	$470,073 72 .

"A."—Agricultural College Fund for 1894.

AGRICULTRUAL COLLEGE FUND.

RECEIPTS.		
Sales of land	$29 12	....
Dues on certificates of sales	1,329 00	....
Loan to city of Merrill	1,000 00	....
Loan to town of Hancock	1,000 00	....
Board of education, city of Neenah bonds	3,000 00	....
Eau Claire city bonds premium	58 32	....
Grand Rapids city bonds	1,000 00	....
Platteville city bonds	1,600 00	....
Manitowoc county bonds	10,000 00	....
New Richmond city bonds	500 00	....
Total receipts	....	$19,511 44
DISBURSEMENTS.		
Loan to town of Colburn, Chippewa Co	$2,000 00	....
Loan to town of Minong	2,000 00	....
Loan to town of Day, Marathon Co.	1,400 00	....
Loan to city of Waupaca	7,000 00	....
Loan to Manitowoc Co	10 000 00	....
Total disbursements	....	$22,400 00

"A."—Agricultural College Fund Income for 1894.

AGRICULTURAL COLLEGE FUND INCOME.

RECEIPTS.		
Interest on land certificates and loans..........	$4,302 60	......:......
Interest on certificates of indebtedness.........	4,248 11	....
Interest on agricultural college funds in bank...	135 17	....
Interest on Eau Claire county'bonds.....	500 00	....
Interest on Black River Falls bonds.	1,000 00	....
Interest on Manitowoc county bonds............	2,120 00	....
Interest on New Richmond city bonds...........	100 00	....
Interest on Eau Claire city bonds...............	696 68	....
Interest on Grand Rapids city bonds	300 00	....
Interest on bd. of education,city of Neenah bonds	150 00	....
Interest on Madison city refunding bonds.......	125 00	....
Interest on Milwaukee city bonds	1,500 00	....
Interest on Platteville city bonds................	250 00	....
Interest on Tomahawk city bonds................	330 00	....
Interest on loan to town of Colburn............	133 33	....
Interest on loan to town of Day, Marathon Co ...	28 70	....
Interest on loan to town of Hancock...........	150 00	....
Interest on loan to town of Minong.............	54 44	....
Interest on loan to city of Waupaca.............	250 88	....
Interest on loan to city of Merrill	350 00	....
Interest on loan to Manitowoc Co..	655 0u	....
Interest on loan to Winnebago Co............. ..	170 00	. ...
Washburn Co., penalty non payment of tax.....	62	....
Ex-state treasurers judgment fund transfer......	10,278 48	....
Total receipts...........	....	$27,828 96
DISBURSEMENTS.		
Treasurer state university transfer..............	$27,822 13	....
Refunded	6 83	....
Total disbursements	....	$27,828 96

"A."—Normal School Fund for 1894.

NORMAL SCHOOL FUND.

RECEIPTS.		
Sales of lands	$12,860 22	....
Dues on certificates of sales	811 00	....
Loans	1,787 50	....
Centralia bridge bonds	1,000 00	....
Oshkosh city bonds	10,000 00	....
Eau Claire city bonds premium	85 28	....
Plymouth school bonds	2,000 00	....
Richland Center city bonds	1,000 00	....
Viroqua school district No. 5 bonds	4,100 00	....
Viroqua village bonds	2,000 00	....
Waushara county bonds	1,000 00	....
Taylor county bonds	1,000 00	....
Ashland city bonds premium	56 20	....
Edgerton city bonds	1,000 00	....
Milwaukee city bonds	24,000 00	....
Indemnity fund transfer one-half indemnity fund	6,772 65	....
Loan to Brown county	2,500 00	....
Loan to Dunn county	5,000 00	....
Loan to Florence county	3,000 00	....
Loan to Manitowoc county	15,000 00	....
Loan to Washburn county	4,000 00	....
Loan to city Chippewa Falls	3,000 00	....
Loan to city Columbus	1,000 00	....
Loan to city Menasha	2,500 00	....
Loan to city Phillips	666 67	....
Loan to city Waupaca	1,000 00	....
Loan to town of Grover	900 00	....
Loan to town of Waupaca	1,000 00	....
Loan to town of Worcester	500 00	....
Loan to village of Osceola	200 00	....
Loan to village of Whitefish Bay	600 00	....
Total receipts	....	$110,239 52
DISBURSEMENTS.		
Loan to the village of Boyd	$3,000 00	....
Loan to the board of education, city of Madison	40,000 00	....
Loan to the town of Pine River	1,500 00	....
Loan to Washburn county	10,000 00	....
Loan to Lincoln county	10,000 00	....
Loan to the village of Bloomer, Chippewa county	4,500 00	....
Loan to Chippewa county	17,000 00	....
Loan to city of Cumberland	5,900 00	....
Loan to board of education, city of Whitewater	10,000 00	....
Loan to dist. No. 1. Bayfield, Bayfield county	5,000 00	....
Total disbursements	....	$106,900 00

"A."—Normal School Fund Income Receipts for 1894.

NORMAL SCHOOL FUND INCOME.

RECEIPTS.		
Interest on land certificates and loans............	$1,340 42	....
Interest on certificates of indebtedness..........	36,151 05	... .
Interest on Ashland county bonds	2,250 00	....
Interest on Ashland city bonds.......	1,043 80	....
Interest on Beaver Dam city bonds..............	720 00	....
Interest on Waupaca city bonds	187 50	....
Interest on Centralia city bonds................	145 00	... .
Interest on Chippewa Falls city bonds	1,750 00	....
Interest on Columbus school bonds..............	900 00	....
Interest on Durand city bonds..................	150 00	....
Interest on Eau Claire city bonds.	464 72	....
Interest on Edgerton school bonds	750 00	....
Interest on Greenwood city bonds................	300 00	....
Interest on Hudson city bonds	1,980 00	....
Interest on Kenosha city bonds	5,000 00	....
Interest on La Crosse city bonds	500 00	....
Interest on Madison city bonds	5,062 50	....
Interest on Milwaukee city bonds	12,300 00	....
Interest on Milwaukee school bonds.............	4,150 00	....
Interest on Manitowoc county bonds.............	2,800 00	....
Interest on Oshkosh city bonds.	2,891 25	....
Interest on Portage county bonds................	960 00	...·........
Interest on Plymouth city bonds.................	550 00	....
Interest on Richland Center city bonds..........	300 00	....
Interest on Viroqua village bonds.........	124 50	....
Interest on Viroqua school district No. 5 bonds ..	287 00	....
Interest on Waushara county bonds	250 00	... .
Interest on Glenwood town bonds...............	300 00	....
Interest on Taylor county bonds	50 00	....
Interest on loan to Brown county	1,225 00	....
Interest on loan to Chippewa county............	306 95	....
Interest on loan to Dunn county................	2,700 00	....
Interest on loan to Florence county	300 00	....
Interest on loan to Jackson county	900 00	....
Interest on loan to Lincoln county..............	416 13	....
Interest on loan to Manitowoc county...........	400 00	....
Interest on loan to Oneida county..............	137 89	....
Interest on loan to Washburn county............	1,342 78	....
Interest on loan to Winnebago county	1,870 00	....
Interest on loan to city of Chippewa Falls........	405 00	....
Interest on loan to city of Cumberland..........	87 50	....
Interest on loan to bd. education city of Madison	1,706 25	....
Interest on loan to city of Menasha	837 50	....
Interest on loan to city Mineral Point	400 00	....
Interest on loan to city of Phillips..............	433 35	....
Interest on loan to city of Waupaca.............	575 00	....
Interest on loan to town of Grover	90 00	....
Interest on loan to town of Pine River..........	84 25	....
Interest on loan to town of Waupaca...........	100 00	....
Interest on loan to town of Worcester	70 00	....
Interest on loan to village of Whitefish Bay......	570 00	....

"A."—Normal School Fund Income Disbursements for 1894.

Interest on loan to village of Boyd..............	$20 50	....
Interest on loan to village of Bloomer..........	76 87	....
Interest on loan to village of Osceola...	42 00	....
General fund for fifth normal	10,000 00	... .
General fund transfer 1-20 mill tax for new normal school..........	32,700 00	....
Interest on normal school fund deposit in banks.	5,739 83	....
B. Goldsmith, regent Milwaukee normal, tuition, etc..............	837 25	....
F. B. Ainsworth, regent River Falls normal, tuition. etc...............	2,416 56	....
D. J. Gardner, regent Platteville normal, tuition, etc...............	1,984 15	....
E. M. Johnson, regent Whitewater normal, tuition, etc..............................	2,088 49	....
John H. Hume, regent Oshkosh normal, tuition, etc.............	5,018 29	....
Interest on loan to Light Horse Squadron	1,320 00	....
W. J. Turner, regent Milwaukee normal, tuition.	923 86	....
Interest on loan to board of education, city of Whitewater..........................	190 28	....
W D. Parker, refunded	2 47	....
Bernard Goldsmith, refunded...................	150 00	. ...
Washburn county, penalty non-payment of tax, 1892....................	5 21	....
Total receipts........	....	$162,131 08

DISBURSEMENTS.

Treas. board of normal school regents, transfer..	$162,114 80	....
Refunded G W. McCarthy......................	6 80	.. ..
Refunded Anne F. Smith.......................	1 60	....
Refunded G. P. Vinning.......................	7 88	....
Total disbursements	....	$162,131 08

13—Sec'y.

"*A.*"—*Drainage Fund Receipts and Disbursements for 1894.*

DRAINAGE FUND.

RECEIPTS.		
Interest on land certificates......................	$4,004 48	....
Sales of lands	10,743 86	....
Dues on certificates of sales.......	115 00	....
Gen'l fund transfer one half indemnity fund....	6,772 64	....
Total receipts......................	....	$21,635 98

DISBURSEMENTS.		
Apportionment to Counties:		
Adams....................................	$186 12	....
Ashland..................................	675 85	....
Barron............................	17 42	....
Bayfield..................................	1,499 75	....
Brown....	78 48	....
Buffalo..................................	405 12	... .
Burnett..	399 20	....
Calumet..................................	19 84	....
Chippewa................................	773 50	....
Clark.	139 54	....
Columbia................................	245 18	....
Crawford................................	176 67	....
Dane....................................	235 21	....
Dodge	232 63	....
Door....................................	123 59	....
Douglas.................................	1,097 04	....
Dunn....................................	670 04	....
Eau Claire...............................	142 91	....
Florence........... :	405 00	....
Fond du Lac........	82 84	....
Forest..................................	3,158 36	....
Grant...	4 06	....
Green...	39 23	....
Green Lake..............................	53 86	....
Iron....................................	50 00	....
Jackson.................................	114 55	....
Jefferson................................	259 85	....
Juneau..................................	135 97	....
Kenosha.................................	8 70	....
Kewaunee...............................	56 13	....
La Crosse...............................	712 94	....
Langlade................................	4,158 87	....
Lincoln.................................	1,802 19	....
Manitowoc..............................	201 58	....
Marathon....	183 12	....

"A."—Drainage Fund Disbursements for 1894.

Apportionment to Counties—Continued.

Marinette.	$599 97	....
Marquette	303 20	....
Monroe	212 68	....
Oconto	565 64	....
Oneida	3,472 20	....
Outagamie	177 27	....
Pepin	193 53	....
Polk	89 25	....
Portage	477 04	....
Price.	2,053 26	....
Racine	4 35	....
Richland	187 50	....
Rock	82 48	....
Sauk.	204 97	....
Shawano	255 40	....
Sheboygan	39 23	....
Taylor	350 00	....
Trempealeau	153 95	....
Vernon	197 25	....
Vilas	150 00	....
Walworth	143 86	....
Washburn	550 00	....
Washington	74 20	....
Waukesha	21 30	....
Waupaca	521 45	....
Waushara	216 96	....
Winnebago	168 11	....
Wood	231 78	....
Refunded Dan Crowley	81 00	....
Total disbursements	....	$30,272 0

"A."—Delinquent Tax Fund Receipts and Disbursements for 1894.

DELINQUENT TAX FUND.

RECEIPTS.		
Taxes on state lands...........................	$8,393 92	....
Total receipts...	....	$8,393 92
DISBURSEMENTS.		
Apportionment to Counties:		
Adams...	$66 17	....
Ashland..	367 89	....
Barron.......................................	23 86	....
Bayfield...........................	132 60	....
Brown.......................................	11 77	... .
Buffalo	70 57	....
Burnett..	58 10	....
Chippewa....................................	300 30	....
Clark.......................................	27 54	....
Columbia	46 08	....
Crawford..................................	54 63	....
Door..	17 95	....
Douglas.....................................	229 86	....
Dunn	46 27	....
Eau Claire..................................	68 83	....
Florence..	77 72	....
Forest	143 82	....
Grant......................................	10 67	....
Iron.......................................	593 42	....
Jackson....................................	76 21	....
Juneau	122 58	....
La Crosse..................................	11 01	....
La Fayette.................................	5 37	... .
Langlade...................................	124 38	....
Lincoln	1,147 61	....
Manitowoc..................................	27 88	....
Marathon	173 16	....
Marinette	329 25	....
Marquette..................................	24 86	....
Monroe.....................................	61 89	....
Oconto	427 15	....
Oneida	49 40	.. ..
Outagamie.................................	92 66	....
Pepin......................................	39 80	....
Pierce.....................................	56·81	....
Polk	164 84	....
Portage	87 90	....
Price......................................	40 54	....
Richland...................................	22 45	....
Rock	3 96	....
St. Croix..................................	98 20	....

"A."—Delinquent Tax Fund Disbursements for 1894.

*Apportionment to Counties—*Continued.

Sauk	$21 34	....
Sawyer	60 04	....
Shawano	376 68	....
Taylor	1,690 88	....
Trempealeau	35 18	....
Vernon	53 68	....
Washburn	132 88	....
Waukesha	8 79	....
Waupaca	55 84	....
Waushara	27 98	....
Wood	92 71	....
Refunded Geo. B. Burrows	1 56	....
Refunded E. P. Sherry	4 77	....
Total disbursements	....	$8,096 74

DEPOSIT FUND.

DISBURSEMENTS.		
Charles Pressentin, surplus	$82 74	....
A. F. Geraghty	15 31	....
Henry I. Bliss	40 18	....
Total disbursements	....	$138 23

WISCONSIN FARM MORTGAGE LAND CO. FUND.

DISBURSEMENTS.		
Caroline Oberkircher; third dividend, paid	$17 50	....
		$17 50

"A."—Ex-State Treasurers' Judgment Fund for 1894.

INDEMNITY FUND.

RECEIPTS.		
Sales of land.	$7,405 21	....
Transfer from general fund sales 1892...........	6,140 08	....
Total receipts	....	$13,545 29
DISBURSEMENTS.		
Transfer to normal school fund..................	$6,772 65	....
Transfer to drainage fund	6,772 64	....
Total disbursements.........................	....	$13,545 29

EX·STATE TREASURERS' JUDGMENT FUND.

RECEIPTS.		
On Richard Guenther judgment by Philetus Sawyer	$80,000 00	....
On. H. B. Harshaw judgment...................	175,590 01	....
Total receipts.................................	....	$250,590 01
DISBURSEMENTS.		
Treas. board regents normal schools	$47,785 20	....
Treas. university fund income	41,986 32	....
Treas. agricultural college fund income.........	10,278 48	....
Treas. general fund	327,902 55	....
Total disbursements........................	....	$427,902 55

Swamp Land, Indemnity, Redemption, etc., Funds, for 1894.

MANITOWOC AND CALUMET SWAMP LAND FUND.

RECEIPTS.		
Calumet county..................................	$19 34	....
Manitowoc county...........	201 58	....
Total receipts	....	$220 92
DISBURSEMENTS.		
Calumet county...........	$405 79	....
Manitowoc county.............................	2,611 05	....
Total disbursements...........................	....	$3,016 84

COLUMBIA AND SAUK COUNTY INDEMNITY FUND.

RECEIPTS.		
Columbia county..............................	$245 13	....
Sauk county	204 97	... .
Total receipts	....	$450 10

REDEMPTION FUND.

RECEIPTS.		
Advertising, interest, penalties and fees.........	' $113 14	....
Total receipts........................ ...	....	$113 14

ST. CROIX & LAKE SUPERIOR RAILROAD TRES-PASS FUND.

DISBURSEMENTS.		
To treasurer general fund....	$2,067 46	....
Total disbursements..................	....	$2,067 64

"B."—*Relative Value of Real and Personal Property.*

APPENDIX B—*Statement showing the value of real and personal property subject to tax ation in the several counties of the State of Wisconsin as determined and assessed by the State Board of Assessment for the year 1894.*

COUNTIES.	HORSES.			NEAT CATTLE.		
	Number	Per head.	Assessed value.	Number.	Per head.	Assessed value.
Adams.............	3,175	$50 00	$158,750	8,088	$15 00	$121,245
Ashland...........	990	50 00	49,500	1,147	15 00	17,205
Barron.............	4,092	50 00	204,600	11,197	15 00	167,955
Bayfield...	1,117	50 00	55,850	747	15 00	11,205
Brown	6,285	50 00	314,250	12,235	15 00	183,525
Buffalo	6,560	50 00	328,000	20,621	15 00	309,315
Burnett	960	50 00	48,000	4,434	15 00	66,510
Calumet......... ...	5,413	50 00	270,650	16,081	15 00	241,215
Chippewa..........	5,924	50 00	296,200	10,979	15 00	164,685
Clark..............	5,436	50 00	271,800	15,501	15 00	232,515
Columbia	12,839	50 00	641,950	29,000	15 00	435,000
Crawford..........	7,078	50 00	353,900	17,054	15 00	255,810
Dane............ ...	22,087	50 00	1,104,350	62,083	15 00	931,245
Dodge.............	13,281	50 00	664,050	40,100	15 00	601,500
Door..............	3,753	50 00	187,650	11,191	15 00	167,865
Douglas	820	50 00	41,000	291	15 00	4,365
Dunn	7,877	50 00	393,850	18,774	15 00	281,610
Eau Claire.....	6,270	50 00	313,500	12,241	15 00	183,615
Florence ......- ..	355	50 00	17,750	75	15 00	1,125
Fond du Lac. .	13,102	50 00	655,100	35,877	15 00	538,155
Forest............-	148	50 00	7,400	199	15 00	2,985
Grant.............	19,024	50 00	951,200	53,953	15 00	809,295
Green	10,952	50 00	547,600	43,936	15 00	659,040
Green Lake.........	5,917	50 00	295,850	12,813	15 00	192,195
Iowa..............	10,361	50 00	518,050	43,569	15 00	653,535
Iron..............	215	50 00	10,750	383	15 00	5,745
Jackson............	5,089	50 00	254,450	12,740	15 00	191,100
Jefferson	9,352	50 00	467,600	35,191	15 00	527,865
Juneau...	5,355	50 00	267,750	11,531	15 00	172,965
Kenosha...........	5,504	50 00	275,200	15,876	15 00	238,140
Kewaunee..........	5,502	50 00	275,100	18,390	15 00	275,850
La Crosse........ ...	6,498	50 00	324,900	15,000	15 00	225,000
La Fayette.........	9,505	50 00	475,250	36,848	15 00	552,720
Langlade...........	1,507	50 00	75,350	3,518	15 00	52,770
Lincoln	1,451	50 00	72,550	2,255	15 00	33,825
Manitowoc	10,114	50 00	505,700	27,317	15 00	409,755
Marathon..........	5,852	50 00	292,600	18,145	15 00	272,175
Marinette..........	2,091	50 00	104,550	2,059	15 00	30,885
Marquette..........	4,053	50 00	202,650	10,056	15 00	150,840
Milwaukee	16,966	50 00	848,300	11,942	15 00	179,130
Monroe	9,289	50 00	464,450	21,239	15 00	318,585
Oconto............	3,573	50 00	178,650	7,783	15 00	116,745
Oneida.............	598	50 00	29,900	397	15 00	5,955
Outagamie	7,514	50 00	375,700	21,524	15 00	332,860
Ozaukee....:......	5,002	50 00	250,100	14,931	15 00	223,965
Pepin	2,714	50 00	135,700	6,355	15 00	95,825

"B."—Relative Value of Real and Personal Property.

APPENDIX B.—*Statement showing the value of real and personal property for 1894.—*
Continued.

COUNTIES.	HORSES.			NEAT CATTLE.		
	Number	Per head.	Assessed value.	Number.	Per head.	Assessed value.
Pierce	7,118	$50 00	$355,900	16,128	$15 00	$241,920
Polk	4,035	50 00	201,750	14,602	15 00	219,080
Portage	5,756	50 00	287,800	10,051	15 00	150,765
Price........... ...	796	50 00	39,800	1,370	15 00	20,550
Racine	6,982	50 00	349,100	17,219	15 00	258,285
Richland........	8,159	50 00	407,950	20,270	15 00	304,050
Rock...............	17,811	50 00	890,550	36,586	15 00	548,790
St. Croix...........	7,137	50 00	356,850	16,354	15 00	245,810
Sauk.	11,310	50 00	565,500	27,539	15 00	413,085
Sawyer.............	257	50 00	12,850	422	15 00	6,330
Shawano...........	5,172	50 00	258,600	15,585	15 00	233,775
Sheboygan	10,303	50 00	515,150	35,494	15 00	532,410
Taylor......	1,101	50 00	55,050	2,852	15 00	42,780
Trempealeau	7,862	50 00	393,100	27,913	15 00	418,695
Vernon	11,809	50 00	590,450	25,911	15 00	388,665
Vilas...............	165	50 00	8,250	215	15 00	3,225
Walworth..........	12,930	50 00	646,500	34,501	15 00	517,515
Washburn..........	432	50 00	21,600	1,024	15 00	15,360
Washington........	8,742	50 00	437,100	23,322	15 00	349,830
Waukesha	12,144	50 00	607,200	26,053	15 00	390,795
Waupaca	9,188	50 00	459,400	19,727	15 00	295,905
Waushara..........	6,386	50 00	319,300	14,443	15 00	216,645
Winnebago........	9,026	50 00	451,300	22,578	15 00	338,670
Wood..............	3,233	50 00	161,650	9,252	15 00	138,780
Total........	459,414		$22,970,700	1,195,072		$17,926,080

"B."—Relative Value of Real and Personal Property.

APPENDIX B.—Statement showing relative value of real and personal property for 1894.—Continued.

COUNTIES.	MULES AND ASSES.			SHEEP AND LAMBS.			SWINE.		
	Number.	Per head.	Value.	Number.	Per head.	Value.	Number.	Per head.	Value.
Adams	92	$50 00	$4,600	6,455	$1 50	9,682 50	1,788	$2 00	$3,576
Ashland	2	50 00	100				94	2 00	188
Barron	113	50 00	5,650	8,760	1 50	13,140 00	2,009	2 00	4,018
Bayfield	6	50 00	300				112	2 00	224
Brown	10	50 00	500	5,217	1 50	7,825 50	2,378	2 00	4,756
Buffalo	105	50 00	5,250	12,162	1 50	18,243 00	7,889	2 00	15,778
Burnett	13	50 00	650	1,558	1 50	2,337 00	533	2 00	1,066
Calumet	25	50 00	1,250	7,771	1 50	11,656 50	4,771	2 00	9,542
Chippewa	200	50 00	10,000	6,680	1 50	10,020 00	3,512	2 00	7,024
Clark	68	50 00	3,400	10,997	1 50	16,495 50	2,743	2 00	5,466
Columbia	67	50 00	3,350	46,223	1 50	69,334 50	12,458	2 00	24,916
Crawford	96	50 00	4,800	10,619	1 50	15,973 50	7,194	2 00	14,888
Dane	93	50 00	4,650	37,861	1 50	56,791 50	26,901	2 00	53,802
Dodge	67	50 00	3,350	34,185	1 50	51,277 50	11,009	2 00	22,018
Door	38	50 00	1,900	7,288	1 50	10,857 50	2,926	2 00	5,852
Douglas	13	50 00	650	18	1 50	27 00	137	2 00	274
Dunn	196	50 00	9,800	18,294	1 50	27,441 00	8,393	2 00	16,786
Eau Claire	64	50 00	3,200	6,760	1 50	10,140 00	3,600	2 00	7,200
Florence	4	50 00	200						
Fond du Lac	57	50 00	2,850	61,516	1 50	92,274 00	11,339	2 00	22,678
Forest	11	50 00	550	2	1 50	3 00	21	2 00	42
Grant	134	50 00	6,700	15,397	1 50	23,095 50	34,948	2 00	69,896
Green	72	50 00	3,600	18,477	1 50	27,715 50	17,755	2 00	35,510
Glen Lake	32	50 00	1,600	35,878	1 50	53,817 00	6,080	2 00	12,160
Iowa	90	50 00	4,500	9,438	1 50	14,157 00	13,264	2 00	26,528

"B."—Relative Value of Real and Personal Property.

Iron	5	50 00	250	8	1 50	12 00	45	2 00	90
Jackson	51	50 00	2,550	6,812	1 50	10,218 00	3,104	2 00	6,328
Jefferson	75	50 00	8,750	16,574	1 50	24,861 00	10,528	2 00	21,056
Juneau	61	50 00	8,050	7,985	1 50	11,902 50	3,589	2 00	7,178
Kenosha	56	50 00	2,800	29,497	1 50	44,245 00	8,704	2 00	17,412
Kewaunee	41	50 00	2,050	8,388	1 50	12,582 00	4,549	2 00	9,098
La Se.	65	50 00	8,250	7,748	1 50	11,623 00	6,457	2 00	12,914
La Fayette	117	50 00	5,850	12,573	1 50	18,959 50	20,190	2 00	40,380
Langlade	46	50 00	2,800	871	1 50	556 50	764	2 00	1,528
Lin	15	50 00	750	964	1 50	1,446 00	445	2 00	890
Marathon	38	50 00	1,650	11,109	1 50	16,663 50	7,079	2 00	14,158
Marinette	55	50 00	2,750	10,389	1 50	15,583 50	4,332	2 00	8,664
Me.	35	50 00	1,750	814	1 50	471 00	454	2 00	908
Milwaukee	35	50 00	1,750	15,077	1 50	22,615 50	3,119	2 00	6,238
Monroe	58	50 00	2,900	1,097	1 50	1,645 00	2,475	2 00	4,950
Oto	81	50 00	4,050	23,065	1 50	34,597 50	6,335	2 00	12,670
Wa.	57	50 00	2,850	3,182	1 50	4,778 00	1,960	2 00	3,920
	4	50 00	200				102	2 00	204
Outagamie	48	50 00	2,400	18,964	1 30	20,946 00	7,053	2 00	14,104
Ozaukee	49	50 00	2,450	2,260	1 50	3,390 00	2,560	2 00	5,120
Pepin	49	50 00	2,450	4,798	1 50	7,169 50	3,124	2 00	6,248
Pierce	120	50 00	6,004	25,248	1 50	37,864 50	6,322	2 00	12,644
Polk	76	50 00	3,800	8,915	1 50	13,373 50	2,260	2 00	4,520
Portage	90	50 00	4,500	6,996	1 50	10,389 00	4,468	2 00	8,996
Price	34	50 00	1,700	16	1 50	22 50	191	2 00	383
Racine	57	50 00	2,850	21,156	1 50	31,734 00	4,080	2 00	8,160
Richland	180	50 00	6,500	27,862	1 50	41,793 00	9,404	2 00	18,808
Rock	108	50 00	5,150	34,980	1 50	52,470 00	19,684	2 00	89,868
St Cr.	101	30 00	5,050	14,977	1 50	22,465 50	4,891	2 00	9,782
Sauk	113	50 00	5,650	28,876	1 50	35,814 00	12,508	2 00	25,012
Sawyer							96	2 00	192
Shawano	76	50 00	3,800	10,881	1 50	16,321 50	6,215	2 00	12,480
Sheboygan	83	50 00	4,100	10,274	1 50	15,411 00	6,823	2 00	18,644
Taylor	18	50 00	900	501	1 50	751 50	242	2 01	484
Trempealeau	111	50 00	5,550	15,947	1 50	28,920 50	5,904	2 00	11,808
Vernon	90	50 00	4,500	36,403	1 50	54,604 50	10,935	2 00	21,870

"B."—Relative Value of Real an

APPENDIX B.—Statement showing relative value of real and personal property for 1894—Continued.

COUNTIES.	MULES AND ASSES.			SHEEP AND LAMBS.			SWINE.		
	Number.	Per head.	Value.	Number.	Per head.	Value.	Number.	Per head.	Value.
Vilas	1	$50 00	$50				37	$2 00	$74
..th	49	50 00	2,450	45,623	$1 50	$68,434 50	13,105	2 00	26,210
Washburn	5	50 00	250	118		177 00	79	2 00	158
Washington	125	50 00	6,250	15,649	1 50	28,473 50	8,383	2 00	16,766
Waukesha	61	50 00	3,050	52,961	1 50	79,441 50	8,271	2 00	16,542
Waupaca	120	50 00	6,000	15,801	1 50	23,701 50	5,459	2 00	10,918
Waushara	80	50 00	4,000	15,025	1 50	22,537 50	4,780	2 00	9,460
Wi..o	42	50 00	2,100	23,851	1 50	35,776 50	5,922	2 00	11,844
Wood	40	50 00	2,000	3,586	1 50	5,379 00	1,296	2 00	2,592
Total	4,428	......	$221,400	948,226	......	$1,422,339 00	420,785	......	$840,370

APPENDIX B.—*Statement showing relative value of real and personal property for 1894—Continued.*

COUNTIES.	WAGONS, CARRIAGES AND SLEIGHS.			WATCHES.		
	Number.	Each.	Assess'd value.	Number.	Each.	Assessed value.
Adams...	1,494	$25 00	$37,350	106	$20 00	$2,120
Ashland............	898	25 00	22,450	181	20 00	3,620
Barron.............	2,963	25 00	74,075	205	20 00	4,100
Bayfield............	873	25 00	21,825	159	20 00	3,180
Brown.............	4,264	25 00	106,600	315	20 00	6,800
Buffalo............	2,275	25 00	56,875	188	20 00	3,760
Burnett............	920	25 00	23,000	25	20 00	500
Calumet...........	3,498	25 00	87,450	200	20 00	4,000
Chippewa...	3,175	25 00	79,375	277	20 00	5,540
Clark	3,693	25 00	92,325	173	20 00	3,460
Columbia...	5,855	25 00	146,875	934	20 00	18,680
Crawford...........	2,024	25 00	50,600	169	20 00	3,380
Dane...............	10,375	25 00	259,375	1,487	20 00	29,740
Dodge..............	7,195	25 00	179,875	380	20 00	7,600
Door...............	3,378	25 00	84,450	321	20 00	6,420
Douglas............	555	25 00	13,875	76	20 00	1,520
Dunn...............	4,373	25 00	109,325	294	20 00	5,880
Eau Claire.........	3,755	25 00	93,875	483	20 00	9,660
Florence........	306	25 00	7,650	......	......	....
Fond du Lac.......	6,384	25 00	159,600	714	20 00	14,280
Forest..............	141	25 00	3,525	10	20 00	200
Grant..............	6,855	25 00	171,375	787	20 00	15,740
Green..............	4,718	25 00	117,950	933	20 00	18,660
Green Lake........	2,990	25 00	74,750	284	20 00	5,680
Iowa..............	3,981	25 00	99,525	364	20 00	7,280
Iron	220	25 00	5,500	2	20 00	40
Jackson	1,957	25 00	48,925	315	20 00	6,300
Jefferson...........	5,184	25 00	129,600	447	20 00	8,940
Juneau............	2,567	25 00	64,175	514	20 00	10,280
Kenosha...........	2,244	25 00	56,100	170	20 00	3,400
Kewaunee.........	4,556	25 00	113,900	138	20 00	2,760
La Crosse..........	3,996	25 00	99,900	524	20 00	10,480
La Fayette.........	3,084	25 00	77,100	270	20 00	5,400
Langlade...........	1,535	25 00	38,375	185	20 00	3,700
Lincoln	1,410	25 00	35,250	99	20 00	1,980
Manitowoc..........	7,890	25 00	197,250	177	20 00	3,540
Marathon...........	5,481	25 00	137,025	326	20 00	6,520
Marinette...........	1,795	25 00	44,875	53	20 00	1,060
Marquette..........	1,342	25 00	33,550	157	20 00	3,140
Milwaukee...... ..	13,794	25 00	344,850	2,999	20 00	59,980
Monroe	3,400	25 00	85,000	341	20 00	6,820
Oconto	2,592	25 00	64,800	122	20 00	2,440
Oneida.............	510	25 00	12,750	......	......	....
Outagamie..........	4,639	25 00	115,975	410	20 00	8,200
Ozaukee.......... ..	3,599	25 00	89,975	120	20 00	2,400

"B."—Relative Value of Real and Personal Property.

APPENDIX B.—*Statement showing relative value of real and personal property for 1894 · Continued.*

COUNTIES.	WAGONS, CARRIAGES AND SLEIGHS.			WATCHES.		
	Number.	Each.	Assess'd value.	Number.	Each.	Assessed value.
Pepin..............	1,456	$25 00	$36,400	74	$20 00	$1,480
Pierce.............	2,984	25 00	73,850	351	20 00	7,020
Polk..............	2,674	25 00	66,850	179	20 00	3,580
Portage.	3,180	25 00	79,500	330	20 00	6,600
Price.............	883	25 00	22,075	10	20 00	200
Racine	3,402	25 00	85,050	253	20 00	5,060
Richland...	2,422	25 00	60,550	362	20 00	7,240
Rock..............	8,793	25 00	219,825	1,760	20 00	35,200
St. Croix...........	3,763	25 00	94,075	466	20 00	9,320
Sauk..............	6,097	25 00	152,425	895	20 00	17,900
Sawyer........	266	25 00	6,650	3	20 00	60
Shawano...........	4,543	25 00	113,575	118	20 00	2,360
Sheboygan..........	8,964	25 00	224,100	778	20 00	15,560
Taylor.............	1,428	25 00	35,700	51	20 00	1,020
Trempealeau........	2,973	25 00	74,325	326	20 00	6,520
Vernon.......	3,473	25 00	86,825	223	20 00	4,460
Vilas	154	25 00	3,850	30	20 00	600
Walworth...........	6,124	25 00	153,100	1,577	20 00	31,540
Washburn..........	470	25 00	11,750	16	20 00	320
Washington.........	6,627	25 00	165,675	229	20 00	4,580
Waukesha..........	8,753	25 00	218,825	660	20 00	13,200
Waupaca	6,456	25 00	161,400	359	20 00	7,180
Waushara...	2,725	25 00	68,125	222	20 00	4,440
Winnebago.........	6,214	25 00	155,350	877	20 00	17,540
Wood..............	2,610	25 00	65,350	151	20 00	3,020
Total...........	256,121	......	$6,403,025	26,784	......	$534,680

"B."—Relative Value of Real and Personal Property.

APPENDIX B.—*Statement showing relative value of real and personal property for 1894—Continued.*

COUNTIES.	PIANOS, ORGANS AND MELODEONS.			BANK STOCK.	
	Number	Each.	Assessed value.	Statistics of value.	Assessed value.
Adams.............	163	$75 00	$12,225	$1,820	$1,820
Ashland............	181	75 00	13,575	365,000	365,000
Barron.............	342	75 00	25,650	9,994	9,994
Bayfield............	108	75 00	8,100	15,309	15.309
Brown.............	517	75 00	38,775	191,000	191,000
Buffalo.............	277	75 00	20,775	2,617	2,617
Burnett............	62	75 00	4,650	....	....
Calumet............	253	75 00	18,975	10,850	10,850
Chippewa..........	279	75 00	20,925	164,500	164,500
Clark.	327	75 00	24,525	61,300	61,300
Columbia...........	1,169	75 00	87,675	138,695	138,695
Crawford..........	269	75 00	20,175	16.798	16,798
Dane...............	1,797	75 00	134,775	333,600	333,600
Dodge..............	636	75 00	47,700	106,480	106,480
Door...............	347	75 00	26,025	24,608	.24,608
Douglas............	147	75 00	11,025	371,100	371,100
Dunn..............	512	75 00	38,400	15,560	15,560
Eau Claire.........	523	75 00	39,225	208,094	208,094
Florence...........	13	75 00	975	3,000	3,000
Fond du Lac.......	955	75 00	71,625	210,200	210,200
Forest.............	14	75 00	1,050	....	....
Grant..............	996	75 00	74,700	43,371	43,371
Green..............	693	75 00	51,975	253,100	253,100
Green Lake........	299	75 00	22,425	46,000	46,000
Iowa...............	575	75 00	43,125	51,387	51,387
Iron...............	9	75 00	675	4,832	4,832
Jackson............	335	75 00	25,125	38,200	38,200
Jefferson...........	745	75 00	55,875	253,680	253,680
Juneau.............	447	75 00	33,525	3,625	3,625
Kenosha............	314	75 00	23,550	54,600	54,600
Kewaunee..	134	75 00	10,050	32,540	32,540
La Crosse..........	967	75 00	72,525	495,729	495,729
La Fayette.........	552	75 00	41,400	40,451	40,451
Langlade......... ..	216	75 00	16,200	9,250	9,250
Lincoln	119	75 00	8,925	160,000	160,000
Manitowoc	525	75 00	39,375	55,400	55,400
Marathon..........	433	75 00	32,475	193,477	193,477
Marinette.........	199	75 00	14.925	142,950	142,950
Marquette	250	75 00	18,750	6,435	6,435
Milwaukee..	5,607	75 00	420,525	432,960	432,960
Monroe............	517	75 00	38,775	22,850	22,850
Oconto.........	187	75 00	14,025	56,700	56,700
Oneida.............	66	75 00	4,950	33,354	33,354
Outagamie.........	422	75 00	31,650	292,055	292,055
Ozaukee...........	207	75 00	15,525	7,000	7,000

"B."—Relative Value of Real and Personal Property.

APPENDIX B.—*Statement showing relative value of real and personal property for*
1894—Continued.

COUNTIES.	PIANOS, ORGANS AND MELODEONS.			BANK STOCK.	
	Number	Each.	Assessed value.	Statistics of value.	Assessed value.
Pepin	174	$75 00	$13,050	$10,065	$10,065
Pierce..............	537	75 00	40,275	101,086	101,086
Polk.......	184	75 00	13,800	15,086	15,086
Portage...........	527	75 00	39,525	36,834	36,834
Price..............	52	75 00	3,900	13,200	13,200
Racine.	427	75 00	32,025	70,515	70,515
Richland......	552	75 00	41,400	31,503	31,503
Roc	1,465	75 00	109,875	435,995	435,995
St. Croix..........	616	75 00	46,200	92,975	92,975
Sauk........... ...	925	75 00	69,375	94,100	94,100
Sawyer............	8	75 00	600	6,000	6,000
Shawano...........	169	75 00	12,675	15,155	15,155
Sheboygan. ...:...	921	75 00	69,075	232,000	232,000
Taylor.	79	75 00	5,925	5,045	5,045
Trempealeau......	334	75 00	25,050	11,660	11,660
Vernon	399	75 00	29,925	35,286	35,286
Vilas	27	75 00	2,025	1,835	1,835
Walworth..........	1,286	75 00	96,450	292,000	292,000
Washburn.........	72	75 00	5,400	....	....
Washington........	345	75 00	25,875	68,525	68,525
Waukesha.	1,017	75 00	76,275	238,025	238,025
Waupaca...........	676	75 00	50,700	62,120	62,120
Waushara..........	464	75 00	34,800	2,800	2,800
Winnebago.	1,204	75 00	90,300	854,485	854,485
Wood.............	317	75 00	23,775	59,740	59,740
Total....	36,482	....	$2,736,150	$7,766,456	$7,766,456

"B."—Relative Value of Real and Personal Property.

APPENDIX B.—Statement showing relative value of real and personal property for 1894—Continued.

COUNTIES.	MERCHANTS' AND MANUFACTURERS' STOCK.		MONEYS, ACCOUNTS, BONDS, CREDITS, NOTES AND MORTGAGES.		ALL OTHER PERSONAL PROPERTY.	
	Statistics of Value.	Assessed Value.	Statistics of Value.	Assessed Value.	By Local Assessors.	By State Board.
Adams	$10,176	$10,176	$1,805	$1,805	$25,916	$25,916
Ashland	255,885	255,885	7,258	7,258	461,661	461,661
Barron	162,274	162,274	4,085	4,085	B4,410	134,410
Bayfield	362,543	362,543			348,019	348,019
Brown	542,047	542,047	122,695	122,695	265,898	265,898
Buffalo	91,682	91,682	20,601	20,601	88,481	88,481
Burnett	47,192	47,192	480	480	18,955	18,955
Calumet	185,350	B5,350	52,475	52,475	222,804	222,804
Chippewa	392,777	892,777	82,850	82,850	439,655	439,655
Clark	152,972	152,972			113,871	113,871
Columbia	421,652	421,652	89,575	89,575	704,829	704,829
Crawford	99,935	99,935	6,300	6,300	102,586	102,586
Dane	955,320	955,320	1,602,920	1,602,920	647,626	647,626
Dodge	291,294	291,294	14,400	14,400	477,991	477,991
Door	170,296	170,296	45,495	45,495	196,303	196,308
Douglas	329,981	329,981			195,075	195,075
Dunn	516,333	516,333	115,005	115,005	150,304	150,304
Eau Claire	633,676	633,676	94,575	94,575	833,113	833,113
Florence	97,040	97,040			9,640	9,640
Fond du Lac	598,705	598,705	175,316	175,316	627,459	627,459
Forest	2,290	2,290			20,906	20,906
Grant	279,184	279,184	314,086	314,086	97,576	97,576
Green	344,142	344,142			1,887,284	1,887,284
Green Lake	159,736	159,736	70,848	70,848	228,206	228,206

"B."—Relative Value of Real and Personal Property.

APPENDIX B.—Statement showing relative value of real and personal property for 1894—Continued.

COUNTIES.	MERCHANTS' AND MANUFACTURERS' STOCK.		MONEYS, ACCOUNTS, BONDS, CREDITS, NOTES AND MORTGAGES.		ALL OTHER PERSONAL PROPERTY.	
	Statistics of Value.	Assessed Value.	Statistics of Value.	Assessed Value.	By Local Assessors.	By State Board.
Iowa	$151,169	$151,169	$43,711	$43,711	$204,334	$204,334
Iron	178,257	178,257			88,480	88,480
Jackson	158,537	158,537	6,730	6,730	109,882	109,882
Jefferson	360,971	360,971	19,300	19,300	618,027	618,027
Juneau	183,348	183,818	22,480	22,480	82,886	82,886
Kenosha	218,023	218,023	82,887	82,887	416,897	416,897
Kewaunee	186,559	186,559	75,869	75,869	104,117	104,117
La Crosse	1,482,872	1,482,872	774,740	774,740	208,223	208,223
La Fayette	98,261	98,261	82,651	82,651	155,068	155,068
Langlade	56,541	56,541			68,300	68,300
Lincoln	522,129	522,129			228,494	228,494
Manitowoc	888,997	888,997	173,181	173,181	240,795	240,795
Marathon	814,298	814,298	18,707	18,707	505,260	505,260
Marinette	389,547	389,547			1,059,625	1,059,625
Marquette	39,986	39,986	500	500	35,313	35,313
Milwaukee	12,181,532	12,181,532	6,545,420	6,545,420	3,426,210	3,426,210
Monroe	167,879	167,879	5,598	5,598	139,694	139,694
Oconto	193,664	193,664	250	250	370,656	370,656
Oneida	353,151	352,151			17,171	17,171
Outagamie	442,991	442,991	84,900	84,900	244,936	244,936
Ozaukee	129,410	129,410	62,845	62,845	309,059	309,059
Pepin	44,690	44,690	12,574	12,574	38,717	38,717
Pierce	175,487	175,487	15,018	15,018	248,919	248,919
Polk	85,724	85,724	20,228	20,228	94,575	94,575

"B."—*Relative Value of Real and Personal Property.*

Portage	220,285	220,285			94,415	9415
Price	265,540	265,540	5,449	5,449	68,778	68,778
Racine	1,053,307	1,053,307	30,000	30,000	1,511,299	1,511,299
Richland	158,754	158,754	18,175	18,175	203,069	203,069
Rock	817,342	817,342	26,390	26,390	1,790,092	1,790,092
St. Croix	207,861	207,861	39,040	39,040	307,941	307,941
Sauk	339,056	339,056	31,305	31,305	686,525	686,525
Sawyer	10,590	10,590	31,109	31,109	83,589	83,589
Shawano	180,514	180,514			87,887	87,887
Sheboygan	654,707	654,707	1,225	1,225	750,258	750,258
Taylor	53,043	53,043	365,870	365,870	24,875	24,875
Trempealeau	147,169	147,169			219,348	219,348
Vernon	136,128	136,128			238,178	238,178
Vilas	20,988	20,988	57,278	57,278	82,200	82,200
Walworth	395,605	395,605			1,512,834	1,512,834
Win.	79,510	79,510	187,165	187,165	76,852	76,852
Washington	210,095	210,095	100	100	451,995	451,995
Waukesha	868,409	868,409	197,345	197,345	1,562,650	1,562,650
Waupaca	248,583	343,583	114,878	114,878	138,658	138,658
Waushara	60,657	60,657	51,659	51,659	74,786	74,786
Winnebago	1,294,970	1,291,870	9,000	9,000	452,319	452,319
Wood	222,835	222,835	564,440	564,440	35,760	35,760
			9,374	9,374		
Total	$33,086,253	$33,086,253	$12,557,540	$12,557,540	$27,129,124	$27,129,124

"B."—Relative Value of Real and Personal Property.

APPENDIX B.— *Statement showing relative value of real and personal property for 1894 — Continued.*

COUNTIES.		LANDS.		CITY AND VILLAGE LOTS.	
	No. Acres.	Valuation by local assessors.	Valuation by state board.	Valuation by local assessors.	Valuation by state board.
Adams........	360,506	$789,912	$1,161,734	$21,729	$25,000
Ashland......	650,179	1,308,584	961.818	5,662,798	3,743,240
Barron	550,427	997,577	1,416,049	273,074	452,000
Bayfield......	641,183	2,191,259	2,895.445	510,894	580,000
Brown........	301,990	3,004,447	2,787,329	3,475,613	3,154,000
Buffalo.......	433,908	1,482,535	1,653,623	262,382	320,000
Burnett	308,137	431,118	648,660	61,275	50,000
Calumet......	202,106	4,729,691	4,081,282	344,180	374,000
Chippewa	1,176,915	4,428,328	3,586,449	2,482,053	2,444.000
Clark.........	760,882	3,417,430	3,364,851	568,689	560,000
Columbia.....	492,613	6,558,494	5,715.968	2,158,077	2,180,000
Crawford.....	356 981	1,299,216	1,372,355	366,348	360.000
Dane.	756,310	12,918,824	13,194,805	7,126,310	7,100,000
Dodge........	547,311	10,417,822	14,181,515	1,841,407	2,530,000
Door.........	293,005	1,318,501	667,279	568,977	500,000
Douglas......	705,783	8,863,948	4,453,108	16,583,134	12,500,000
Dunn	525,974	2,421,966	2,829,706	651,611	740,000
Eau Claire....	381,837	2,447,195	1,130,127	4,546,119	3,650,000
Florence	296,130	1,186,670	1,011,620	83,732	81,000
Fond du Lac..	449,160	10,475,309	9,316,758	4,208,198	4,200,000
Forest........	786,162	1,481,028	1,951,049	105,055	105,000
Grant	699,852	5,889,538	7,603,832	1,156,567	1,510,000
Green........	365,294	5,920,129	5,408.423	1,603,616	1,630,000
Green Lake ..	221,502	2,893,175	3,086,783	799,837	800,000
Iowa.........	480,168	4,657,061	4,492,709	736,091	900,000
Iron..........	436,592	1,918,936	1,538,369	338,354	330,000
Jackson......	516,984	1,376,685	1,777,705	325,446	300,000
Jefferson.....	324,449	6,426,896	7,743,475	2,467,650	2,480,000
Juneau	444,958	1,182,289	1,594,386	482,617	488 000
Kenosha......	171,450	4,031,124	4,227,245	1,284,104	1,600,000
Kewaunee....	217,092	2,671,432	2,385,525	555,603	500,000
La Crosse....	295,735	2,292,620	1,317.845	9,553,043	7,110,000
La Fayette ...	396,785	4,488,142	5,211,614	590,189	600,000
Langlade.....	521,641	687,347	1,090,130	299,060	440,000
Lincoln	546,810	979,804	1,409,821	1,288,810	1,076,000
Manitowoc ...	370,897	7,312,409	7,208.536	2,216,555	1,900,000
Marathon.....	981,468	2,728,655	1,270,465	2,456,260	1,550,000
Marinette.....	856,641	2,032,793	2,238,454	2,274,004	2,300,000
Marquette....	294,662	1,048,071	1,168,283	167,648	150,000
Milwaukee ...	130,515	11,184,864	10,790,597	112,490,390	89,811,000
Monroe.......	542,227	1,891,491	2,100,096	417,288	750,000
Oconto	605,406	1,477,003	1,193.527	808,794	630,000
Oneida.......	445,796	849,186	870,365	340,250	280,000
Outagamie ...	837,599	4,696,196	3,695,283	4,617,472	4,531,000
Ozaukee......	146,881	5,233,148	4,649,761	624,573	557,000

"B."—Relative Value of Real and Personal Property.

APPENDIX B.— *Statement showing relative value of real and personal property for 1894 — Continued.*

COUNTIES.	LANDS.			CITY AND VILLAGE LOTS.	
	No. Acres.	Valuation by local assessors.	Valuation by state board.	Valuation by local assessors.	Valuation by state board.
Pepin	146,087	$636,333	$594.112	$190,272	$187,000
Pierce........	365,027	2 824,613	2,423,516	664,521	668,000
Polk	567,777	1,830,997	1,652,690	155,324	157,000
Portage	492,813	1,355,275	1,469,002	947,901	957,000
Price........	696,949	1,168,894	2,046,858	156,432	170,000
Racine	206,980	5 806,716	8,795.440	8,229,706	7,908 000
Richland......	369,834	2,363 635	2,054,053	601,491	575,000
Rock.	447,095	10,412.324	12,294 303	5,280,118	5,452,000
St. Croix	456,750	3 988,331	3,819,865	1,305,545	1,298,000
Sauk.........	529,789	5,297,865	4,583,449	1,927,297	1,819,000
Sawyer.	720,640	1,281,391	1,696,189	52,635	52,000
Shawano ....:	528,927	2,206,393	1,807,733	433,186	390,000
Sheboygan....	320,325	10,084,676	10,248,215	5,751,328	4,790,000
Taylor........	614,879	705,454	808,927	49,315	56,000
Trempealeau...	469,260	2,329,513	2,190,854	. 325,375	325,000
Vernon.......	506,474	2,399,886	2,661,830	316,121	325,000
Vilas.........	455,124	883.483	1.072,903	68,036	72,000
Walworth....	348,481	9 575 233	9,612,196	2,835,302	2,835,000
Washburn....	452,024	543,614	588,523	43,513	43,000
Washington..	271,453	8,713,941	7,570,491	1,011,249	1,007,000
Waukesha....	347,225	10,881,002	10,241,709	4,061,287	3,925,000
Waupaca. ...	447,206	2,284,503	2,016,826	1,093,285	1,100,000
Waushara ...	388,377	1,751,676	1,366,450	164,634	168,000
Winnebago...	261,385	2,627,205	4,410,605	8,569,965	8,491,000
Wood	491,323	1,018,349	1,449,745	689,849	870,000
Total.......	32,229,051	$261,399,147	$254,946,643	$244,719,013	$211,509,340

"B."—Relative Value of Real and Personal Property.

APPENDIX B.— *Statement showing relative value of real and personal property for 1894—Continued.*

COUNTIES.	Personal property.	Land.	Lots.	Total.
Adams...............	$389,266	$1,161,734	$25,000	$1 6,
Ashland............	1,196,442	931,318	8,748.240	5 ,57₁,
Barron.............	809.951	1,416,049	452,000	2,578,
Bayfield...........	826,555	2,895,445	580,000	4,302,
Brown..............	1,783,671	2,787,329	3,151,000	7, ,
Buffalo............	961,377	1,653,623	320,000	2, ,
Burnett............	213,340	648,660	50,000	,
Calumet............	1,065,7.8	4,081,282	374,000	5, ,
Chippewa...........	1,673,551	3,586,449	2,444,000	7, ,
Clark.............	978,149	3,364,851	560,000	4, 3,
Columbia...........	2,782,082	5,715,968	2,180,000	10,678,000
Crawford...........	944,645	1,373,355	360,000	2,648,000
Dane...............	6,114,193	18,194,805	7,100,000	26,409,000
Dodge..............	2,467,485	14,181,515	2,530,000	19,179,000
Door	929,721	667,279	500,000	2,097,000
Douglas............	968,892	4,453,108	12,500,000	17,922,000
Dunn...............	1,680,294	2,829,706	740,000	5,250,000
Eau Claire.........	2,429,873	1,130,127	3,650,000	7,210,000
Florence...........	137,880	1,011,620	81,000	1,230,000
Fond du Lac........	3,163,242	9,316,758	4,200,000	16,680,000
Forest.............	88,951	1,951,049	105,000	2,095,000
Grant..............	2,856,168	7,603,832	1,510,000	11,970,000
Green..............	3,446,577	5,480,423	1,630,000	10,485,000
Green Lake.........	1,163,267	3,086,733	800,000	5,050,000
Iowa...............	1,817,291	4,493,709	900,000	7,210,000
Iron	294,631	1,538,369	330,000	2,163,000
Jackson............	858,295	1,777,705	300,000	2,936,000
Jefferson..........	2,486.525	7,743,475	2,480,000	12,710,000
Juneau	863,664	1,594,336	488,000	2,946,000
Kenosha............	1,383,755	4,227,245	1,600,000	7,210,000
Kewaunee...........	1,050,475	2,385,525	500,000	3,936,000
La Crosse..........	3,722,155	1,317,845	7,110,000	12,150,000
La Fayette.........	1,543,386	5,311,614	600,000	7,455,000
Langlade...........	319,870	1,090,130	440,000	1,850,000
Lincoln............	1,066,179	1,409 821	1,076,000	3,552,000
Manitowoc..........	2,046,464	7,203,536	1,900,000	11,150'000
Marathon...........	2,299,535	1,270,465	1,550,000	5,120,000
Marinette..........	1,741,546	2,238,454	2,300,000	6,280,000
Marquette..........	521,717	1,168,283	150,000	1,840,000
Milwaukee..........	24,898,403	10.790,597	89,811,000	125,000,000
Monroe	1,300,904	2,100,096	750,000	4,151,000
Oconto.............	1,009,473	1,193,527	630,000	2,833,000
Oneida............	456,635	870,365	280,000	1,607,000
Outagamie..........	1,906.717	3,695,283	4,531,000	10,133.000
Ozaukee............	1,101,239	4,649,761	557,000	6,308,000
Pepin..............	403,888	594,112	187,000	1,185,000
Pierce.............	1,315,484	2,423,516	668,000	4,407,000
Polk...............	748,310	1,652,690	157,000	2,552,000
Portage............	994,998	1,469,002	957,000	3,371,000

"B." —Relative Value of Real and Personal Property.

APPENDIX B.—*Statement showing relative value of real and personal property for 1894—Continued.*

COUNTIES.	Personal property.	Land.	Lots.	Total.
Price................	$461,142	$2,046,858	$170,000	$2,678,000
Racine	3,425,560	3,795,440	7,906,000	15,127,000
Richland	1,302,947	2,054,053	575,000	3,932,000
Rock............	5,013,697	12,294,303	5,452,000	22,760,000
St. Croix	1,429,135	3,819,865	1,298,000	6,547,000
Sauk......	2,435,551	4,583,449	1,819,000	8,838,000
Sawyer........	126,811	1,696,189	52,000	1,875,000
Shawano....	938,267	1,807,733	390,000	3,136,000
Sheboygan	3,391,785	10,248,215	4,790,000	18,430,000
Taylor	225,073	808,927	56,000	1,090,000
Trempealeau	1,337,146	2,190,854	325,000	3,853,000
Vernon	1,648,170	2,661,830	325,000	4,635,000
Vilas.................	73,097	1,072,903	72,000	1,218,000
Walworth............	3,929,804	9,612,196	2,835,000	16,377,000
Washburn.......	211,477	588,523	43,000	843,000
Washington....	1,957,509	7,570,491	1,007,000	10,535,000
Waukesha....	3,689,291	10,241,709	3,925,000	17,856,000
Waupaca....	1,506,174	2,016,826	1,100,000	4,623,000
Waushara............	826,550	1,366,450	169,000	2,361,000
Winnebago...........	4,268,395	4,410,605	8,491,000	17,170,000
Wood................	780,255	1,449,745	870,000	3,050,000
Total.............	$133,544,117	$254,946,643	$211,509,240	$600,000,000

"C."—*Valuation of Taxable Property.*

APPENDIX C.— *Statement of the valuation of the taxable property of the several counties of the state of Wisconsin, as determined by the State Board of Assessment for 1898, and the apportionment of the state tax and special charges for said year.*

COUNTIES.	Valuation by State Board.	State tax .001557676 per cent.	SPECIAL CHARGES.		
			State Hospital for Insane.	Northern Hospital for Insane.	Industrial School for Boys.
Adams..	$1,765,000	$2,749 23	$517 86	....	....
Ashland......	6,500,000	10,124 89	....	$1,896 24	$184 42
Barron	3,000,000	4,678 02	1,508 01	....	158 42
Bayfield.....	4,760,000	7,414 47	....	719 12	.. ...
Brown	8,455,000	13,170 08	....	3,193 72	266 15
Buffalo......	3,291,000	5,126 28	1,280 20	.. ..	....
Burnett	1,028,000	1,601 22	474 55	....	....
Calumet... ...	6,200,000	9,657 58	....	917 44	....
Chippewa	8,635,000	13,450 50	78 21	1,744 70	209 85
Clark........	5,500,000	8,567 21	560 77	432 30	120 43
Columbia.....	11,851,000	18,459 98	1,227 26	....	78 14
Crawford.....	3,000,000	4,678 03	1,162 70	....	103 71
Dane........	29,581,000	46,082 33	5,062 73	.... ..	167 28
Dodge...	21,487,000	33,469 79	78 21	2,188 28	195 42
Door., ...	2,395,000	3,730 61	....	1,044 10	52 14
Douglas......	20,000,000	31,153 52	. ...	1,604 50	95 71
Dunn	5,857,000	9,123 28	805 42	....	27 43
Eau Claire...	8,033,000	12,512 82	745 18	1,213 97	20 14
Florence.. ..	1,480,000	2,305 35	....	311 15	27 14
Fond du Lac .	18,576,000	28,935 43	....	1,675 26	326 43
Forest	2,566,000	3,996 96	....	10 79	....
Grant........	13,300,000	20,717 09	2,873 06	....	192 14
Green..	11,746,000	18,296 46	1,364 92	....	133 71
Green Lake...	5,744,000	8,947 30	....	1,112 86	108 85
Iowa.........	8,000,000	12,461 41	1,058 67	....	4 43
Iron.........	2,500,000	3,894 18	....	8 57	....
Jackson	3,288,000	5,121 62	1,227 75	....	60 71
Jefferson	4,134,000	22,016 25	....	2,129 34	110 43
Juneau.	3,265,000	5,085 78	1,472 01	15 00	52 14
Kenosha.....	8,086,000	12,595 39	....	649 18	151 57
Kewaunee	4,300,000	6,698 89	....	1,120 77	....
La Crosse.....	13,540,000	21,090 91	2,268 00	....	195 85
La Fayette...	8,388,000	13,065 77	1,650 25	....	46 28
Langlade.....	2,065,000	3,216 58	....	677 18	49 56
Lincoln	3,978,000	6,196 39	....	950 69	....
Manitowoc ...	12,394,000	19,305 88	....	1,859 85	281 57
Marathon	5,615,000	8,746 31	....	2,184 18	83 57
Marinette.....	7,000,000	10,903 73	....	1,474 18	188 00
Marquette ...	2,066,000	3,218 16	....	754 41	....
Milwaukee ...	125,000,000	194,709 50	....	44 07	619 28
Monroe.......	4,650,000	7,243 20	1,970 19	....	136 28
Oconto	3,175,000	4,945 62	....	1,306 43	365 57
Oneida.......	1,800,000	2,803 82	....	402 90	....

"C."—Valuation of Taxable Property.

APPENDIX C.— *Statement of the valuation of the taxable property of the several counties of the State of Wisconsin, as determined by the State Board of Assessment for 1898.* —Continued.

COUNTIES.	Valuation by State Board.	State tax .001557676 per cent.	SPECIAL CHARGES.		
			State Hospital for Insane.	Northern Hospital for Insane.	Industrial School for Boys.
Outagamie ...	$11,350,000	$17,679 60	....	$1,361 62	$551 56
Ozaukee	7,063,000	11,001 90	....	1,281 62	. ...
Pepin	1,328,000	2,068 55	$506 81	....	....
Pierce........	4,935,000	7,687 06	1,918 97	... .	126 85
Polk..........	2,859,000	4,453 84	1,290 31	....	51 43
Portage	3,772,000	5,875 50	....	2,088 17	9 43
Price	3,000,000	4,673 03	....	664 42	35 14
Racine	16,800,000	26,168 95	... .	1,067 26	34 28
Richland.....	4,504,000	7,015 76	1,147 72	....	52 14
Rock.. ...	25,498,000	39,717 65	3,132 95	....	102 85
St. Croix.....	7,333,000	11,422 40	1,671 80	....	156 57
Sauk	9,900,000	15,420 98	1,061 27	....	261 28
Sawyer... ..	2,100,000	3,271 11	501 45	....	....
Shawano.....	3,512,000	5,470 53	....	851 59	52 14
Sheboygan ...	20,500,000	31,932 36	....	2,201 68	156 43
Taylor........	1,110,000	1,729 00	....	433 04	133 28
Trempealeau .	4,314,000	6,719 78	1,914 56	....	... .
Vernon.......	5,100,000	7,944 15	1,863 27	....	159 71
Vilas........	1,592,000	2,479 82	....	....	....
Walworth....	17,200,000	26,792 06	1,509 11	....	109 71
Washburn	943,000	1,468 72	321 18	....	50 85
Washington..	11,803,000	18,385 29	....	1,169 97	104 28
Waukesha....	20,000,000	31,153 52	77 75	2,208 88	260 00
Waupaca.....	5,094,000	7,934 79	....	2,039 46	190 71
Waushara....	2,644,000	4,118 50	....	827 18	32 43
Winnebago...	18,388,000	28,564 71	....	3,949 26	523 71
Wood.......	3,411,000	5,313 17	....	1,413 72	144 00
Total.....	$654,000,000	$1,018,720 00	$43,802 50	$53,149 05	$8,055 53

"C."—Valuation of Taxable Property.

APPENDIX C. — *Statement of the valuation of the taxable property of the several counties of the state of Wisconsin, as determined by the State Board of Assessment for 1893, and the apportionment of the state tax and special charges for said year.*

COUNTIES.	SPECIAL CHARGES.					Grand Total.
	Care Chronic Insane.	Total tax and Special Charges.	Special Loans.	School District Loans.	Tax and Penalty 1892.	
Adams ...	$175 08	$3,441 67	....	$473 13	....	$3,914 80
Ashland..	....	12.205 55	$1,241 12	3,343 50	... .	16,789 17
Barron ...	700 23	7,039 68	3,329 00	1,37.) 40	....	11,789 08
Bayfield..	....	8,133 59	... . ..	6.660 83	....	14,793 92
Brown....	....	16,629 95	12,608 00	142 04	....	29,379 99
Buffalo...	1,501 69	7.908 17	....	72 35	....	7,980 52
Burnett ..	751 08	2,826 80	....	245 44	....	3,072 24
Calumet .	1,678 70	12,248 72	....	....	....	12,248 72
Chippewa	3,044 73	18,527 99	4,235 00	1,663 59	....	24,426 58
Clark. ...	970 80	10.651 51	830 00	1,36) 67	....	12,851 18
Columbia.	....	19.760 38	....	106 00	....	19,866 38
Crawford.	2,172 76	8,112 20	....	599 00	....	8,711 20
Dane.....	....	51,812 34	6,425 00	720 87	....	58,458 21
Dodge....	... .	35 931 70	....	....	....	35,931 70
Door......	877 26	5,704 11	....	586 47	....	6,290 58
Douglas...	398 25	33,251 98	....	1,192 00	....	34,443 98
Dunn.....	....	9,956 13	9,800 00	1,186 22	....	20,942 35
Eau Claire	3,097 43	17,589 49	843 13	3,789 43	....	22,222 05
Florence..	....	2,648 64	3,300 00	... .	....	5,943 64
F'd du Lac	....	30,937 12	....	... .	....	30,937 12
Forest....	....	4,007 75	260 00	331 00	....	4,598 75
Grant	....	23.282 29	.. ..	820 00	....	24,102 29
Green	....	19,795 09	... .	878 84	....	20,673 93
Gr'n Lake	1,018 76	11,187 77	2,300 00	....	....	13,487 77
Iowa.....	....	13.524 51	4,064 95	179 20	....	17,768 66
Iron	....	3.902 75	108 49	....	....	4,011 24
Jackson...	1,672 87	8,083 95	4,126 67	804 73	....	13,014 35
Jefferson..	....	24.256 02	....	....	....	24,256 20
Juneau...	2,864 59	9,489 52	....	405 82	....	9,895 34
Kenosha .	2,470 02	15,866 16	....	... ...	....	15,866 16
Kewaunee	1,251 86	9,071 02	....	240 00	....	9,311 02
La Crosse	....	23,554 76	....	132 60	.....	23,687 86
LaFayette	2,638 92	17,401 22	....	973 50	....	18,374 72
Langlade.	106 97	4,050 29	114 00	425 60	... ...	4,589 89
Lincoln...	265 55	7,413 63	7,551 85	1,129 43	....	16,093 91
Manitow'c	....	21,897 25	15,400 00	....	....	36,797 25
Marathon.	1,464 52	12,477 58	2,838 93	2,047 78	... . ..	17,364 29
Marinette.	1,179 86	13,745 77	....	903 05	....	14,647 82
Marquette	1,122 12	5,094 69	....	105 00	....	5,199 69
Milw'kee..	....	195,372 85	1,170 00	....	....	196,542 85
Monroe ..	1,353 06	10.702 73	... .	826 36	....	11,529 09
Oconto....	2,252 82	8,870 44	105 00	1,451 83	....	10,427 27
Oneida....	....	3.206 72	1,636 15	2,154 00	....	6,986 87

"C."—Valuation of Taxable Property.

APPENDIX C.—Statement of the valuation of the taxable property of the several counties of the state of Wisconsin, as determined by the State Board of Assessment for 1893. —Continued.

COUNTIES.	Care Chronic Insane.	SPECIAL CHARGES.				Grand Total.
		Total tax and Special Charges.	Special Loans.	School District Loans.	Tax and Penalty 1892.	
Outag'mie	....	$19,592 78	$373 00	$8,654 90	......	$28,620 68
Ozaukee ..	$1,507 06	13,790 58	....	....		13,790 58
Pepin.....	482 66	3,058 02	....	133 15	....	3,191 17
Pierce....	922 94	10,655 82	....	262 00	....	10,917 82
Polk......	1,876 85	7,671 93	544 50	1,137 37	....	9,353 80
Portage ..	756 50	8,679 60	... .	1,299 48		9,979 08
Price.....	274 68	5,647 27	7,070 00	254 00	....	12,971 27
Racine....		27,270 49	....	....		27,270 49
Richland.	1,932 25	10,197 87	....	266 09		10,463 96
Rock . ..	....	42,953 45	....	2,356 20		45,309 65
St. Croix..	1,401 21	14,651 98	....	2,946 00		17,597 98
Sauk.....	....	16,743 53	....	2 20	....	16,745 73
Sawyer...	....	3,772 56	....	....		3,772 56
Shawano..	367 40	6,741 66	2,130 00	1,758 65		10,630 31
Sheboyg'n	....	84,290 47	....	......		84,290 47
Taylor....	421 07	2,716 39	990 00	673 20	...:..	4,379 59
Tr'mp'le'u	2,803 95	10,938 29	2,366 67	1,204 79	....	14,509 75
Vernon ...	....	9,967 18	....	962 85	....	10,929 98
Vilas.....	....	2,479 82	2,297 04	1,100 00		5,876 86
Walworth	....	28,410 88	....	420 40	....	28,831 28
Washb'rn.	108 35	1,944 05	4,927 40	2,195 32	15596 18	24,662 95
Wash'gt'n	2,260 87	21,919 91	....	... .		21,919 91
Waukesha	3,650 85	37,351 00	....	....		37,351 00
Waupaca.	1,933 71	12,098 67	5,535 00	354 74	....	17,988 41
Waushara	483 59	5,411 70	1,150 00	1,124 84	....	7,686 54
Win'bago.	....	33,037 68	1,875 00	1,480 00		36,392 68
Wood	93 28	6,964 17	1,582 00	1,461 53	... ...	9,987 70
Total...	$55,796 10	$1,179,523 18	$113,097 90	62374 89	15596 18	$1,370,592 15

"C."—Valuation of Taxable Property.

APPENDIX C.—*Statement of the valuation of the taxable property of the several counties of the state of Wisconsin, as determined by the State Board of Assessment for 1894, and the apportionment of the tax and special charges for said year.*

COUNTIES.	Valuation by State Board.	State Tax .0004 per cent.	SPECIAL CHARGES.		
			State Hospital for Insane.	Northern Hospital for Insane.	Industrial School for Boys.
Adams	$1,576,000	$630 40	$578 95	....	....
Ashland......	5,871,000	2,348 40	....	$2,410 91	$227 13
Barron.......	2,678,000	1,071 20	1,075 85	....	163 43
Bayfield......	4,302,000	1,720 80	....	901 56	11 71
Brown	7,675,000	3,070 00	....	2,963 03	314 00
Buffalo	2,985,000	1,174 00	811 11	....	....
Burnett	912,000	364 80	435 23	....	....
Calumet	5,521,000	2,208 40	....	920 18	57 72
Chippewa ...	7,704,000	3,081 60	78 81	2,299 68	257 00
Clark	4.903,000	1,961 20	804 11	223 41	17 86
Columbia....	10,678,000	4,271 20	1,556 19	....	126 28
Crawford.....	2,678,000	1,071 20	1,227 09	....	62 00
Dane.........	26,409,000	10,563 60	5,533 98	....	375 00
Dodge........	19,179,000	7,671 60	78 21	2,141 67	250 56
Door	2,097,000	838 80	....	813 37	31 57
Douglas	17,922,000	7,168 80	....	2,168 14	147 02
Dunn	5,250,000	2,100 00	1,854 88	....	....
Eau Claire....	7,210,000	2,884 00	1,182 80	720 92	52 14
Florence	1,230,000	492 00	....	484 08	....
Fond du Lac..	16,680,000	6,672 00	....	1,703 42	95 71
Forest	2,095,000	838 00	....	....	....
Grant........	11,970,000	4,788 00	2,819 37	....	208 56
Green........	10,485,000	4,194 00	1,634 79	....	162 85
Green Lake...	5,050,000	2,020 00	....	1,257 62	87 14
Iowa	7,210,000	2,884 00	921 69	....	....
Iron	2,163,000	865 20	....	278 82	....
Jackson......	2,936,000	1,174 40	1,179 72	....	96 86
Jefferson.....	12,710,000	5,084 00	....	2,508 23	81 29
Juneau	2,946,000	1,178 40	1,821 27	....	52 14
Kenosha......	7,210,000	2,884 00	....	638 70	86 57
Kewaunee....	3,936,000	1,574 40	....	1,030 79	91 43
La Crosse....	12,150,000	4,860 00	1,685 06	....	356 27
La Fayette ...	7,455,000	2,982 00	1,457 46	....	....
Langlade.....	1,850,000	740 00	....	434 34	103 43
Lincoln	3,552,000	1,420 80	....	777 19	....
Manitowoc....	11,150,000	4,460 00	....	1,205 07	186 71
Marathon ...	5,120,000	2,048 00	....	1,515 86	104 58
Marinette	6,280,000	2,512 00	....	1,818 07	58 71
Marquette....	1,840,000	736 00	....	737 54	....
Milwaukee ...	125,000,000	50,000 00	....	....	388 27
Monroe.......	4,151,000	1,660 40	1,980 98	....	236 28
Oconto..	2,883,000	1,133 20	....	1,497 08	329 71
Oneida.	1,607,000	642 80	....	585 92	....
Outagamie ...	10,133,000	4,053 20	....	1,784 01	412 99
Ozaukee	6,308,000	2,523 20	....	1,306 51	....

"C."—Valuation of Taxable Property.

APPENDIX C.— *Statement of the valuation of taxable property of the several counties of the state, etc., for 1894.* — Continued.

COUNTIES.	Valuation by State Board.	State Tax .0004 per cent.	SPECIAL CHARGES.		
			State Hospital for Insane.	Northern Hospital for Insane.	Industrial School for Boys.
Pepin........	$1.185,000	$474 00	$553 62	....	....
Pierce........	4.407,000	1,762 80	2,063 55	....	$150 57
Polk.	2,558,000	1,021 20	1,093 43	....	35 29
Portage......	8,871,000	1,848 40	....	$1,864 95	39 43
Price........	2,678,000	1,071 20	....	813 20	....
Racine	15,127,000	6,050 80	....	1,242 38	45 43
Richland.....	8,932,000	1,572 80	1,135 97	....	143 43
Rock..... ..	22,760,000	9,104 00	3,880 45	..........'.	96 44
St. Croix	6,547,000	2,618 80	2,207 60	33 53	188 99
Sauk	8,838,000	3,535 20	1,192 92	....	383 98
Sawyer	1,875,000	750 00	479 52	....	....
Shawano.....	8,136,000	1,254 40	... .	945 29	32 43
Sheboygan ...	18,430,000	7,872 00	....	2,295 75	152 14
Taylor	1,090,000	436 00	.. ..	467 10	118 15
Trempealeau .	8,853,000	1,541 20	1,440 25	....	52 86
Vernon	4,635,000	1,854 00	1,613 70	....	209 86
Vilas........	1,218,000	487 20	....	....	....
Walworth ...	16,377,000	6,550 80	1,343 72	... .	188 42
Washburn ...	843,000	337 20	208 63	....	....
Washington..	10,535,000	4,214 00	....	985 46	58
Waukesha ...	17,856,000	7,142 40	....	2,565 57	311 71
Waupaca.....	4,623,000	1,849 20	....	1,571 58	120 57
Waushara....	2,361,000	944 40	....	778 16	2 86
Winnebago...	17,170,000	6,868 00	64 47	2,840 91	316 86
Wood........	3,050,000	1,220 00	....	979 35	66.71
Total.....	$600,000,000	$240,000 00	$44,540 38	$52,453 29	$7,724 63

"C."—Valuation of Taxable Property.

APPENDIX C.— *Statement of the valuation of taxable property of the several counties of the state, etc., for 1894.— Continued.*

COUNTIES.	SPECIAL CHARGES.				Grand Total.
	Care of Chronic Insane.	Total Tax and Special Charges.	Special Loans.	School District Loans.	
Adams........	$251 28	$1,460 58	....	$187 25	$1,647 83
Ashland	....	4,986 44	$765 75	3,155 00	8,907 19
Barron.......	1,234 49	3,544 97	3,451 00	1,806 12	8,802 09
Bayfield......	17 14	2,651 21	....	10,062 33	12,713 54
Brown	....	6,347 03	12,259 00	135 23	18,741 26
Buffalo	1,776 82	3,761 93	....	63 19	3,825 12
Burnett......	825 17	1,625 20	....	66 77	1,691 97
Calumet	1,780 79	4,967 04	....	....	4,967 04
Chippewa....	3,402 47	9,119 56	7,235 00	1,719 62	18,074 18
Clark	1,370 53	4,376 11	675 00	1,733 67	6,784 78
Columbia	....	5,953 67	....	100 00	6,053 67
Crawford	2,601 83	4,962 12	....	421 50	5,383 62
Dane..... ...	....	16,472 58	7,300 00	1,261 74	25,034 32
Dodge	....	10,142 04	....	600 00	10,742 04
Door	1,088 68	2,772 42	....	489 57	3,261 99
Douglas.	251 09	9,785 05	....	2,064 80	11,799 85
Dunn........	....	3,454 88	9,475 00	1,804 21	14,234 09
Eau Claire....	3,294 49	8,134 35	804 80	4,112 29	13,051 44
Florence.....	....	976 08	5,150 00	....	6,126 08
Fond du Lac..	....	8,471 13	125 00	....	8,596 13
Forest	....	838 00	250 00	314 00	1,402 00
Grant........	....	7,315 93	....	697 25	8,013 18
Green........	89 63	6,081 27	....	619 08	6,700 35
Green Lake ..	890 15	4,254 91	2,200 00	....	6,454 91
Iowa	....	3,805 69	2,875 46	243 06	6,924 21
Iron.........	....	1,144 02	... .	....	1,144 02
Jackson	1,706 79	4,157 77	3,320 00	964 38	8,442 15
Jefferson.....	....	7,623 52	....	50 00	7,673 52
Juneau..	2,805 22	5,857 08	....	395 28	6,252 31
Kenosha	2,368 73	5,978 00	....	....	5,978 00
Kewaunee. ..	1,412 08	4,108 70	... .	....	4,108 70
La Crosse	....	6,901 33	....	126 75	7,028 08
La Fayette ...	3,444 55	7,884 01	....	1,178 88	9,062 39
Langlade.....	248 12	1,525 89	107 00	573 18	2,206 07
Lincoln	606 88	2,804 87	4,209 04	1,274 84	8 288 75
Manitowoc ...	....	5,851 78	9,500 00	....	15,351 78
Marathon	1,016 93	4,685 87	648 00	2,017 42	7,350 79
Marinette	1,043 66	5,422 44	....	1,100 72	6,523 16
Marquette....	946 00	2,419 54	....	100 00	2,519 54
Milwaukee ...	....	50,838 27	555 00	600 00	51,498 27
Monroe	1,466 98	5,294 64	....	811 00	6,105 64
Oconto	2,492 06	5,452 05	3,512 50	1,873 82	10,838 37
Oneida.......	....	1,178 72	3,469 91	1,248 50	5,897 13
Outagamie. ..	....	6,250 20	358 00	3,440 00	10,048 20
Ozaukee......	1,414 90	5,244 61	....	....	5,244 61

"C."—*Valuation of Taxable Property.*

APPENDIX C.—*Statement of the valuation of taxable property of the several counties of the state, etc., for 1894.*— Continued.

COUNTIES.	SPECIAL CHARGES.				Grand Total.
	Care of Chronic Insane.	Total Tax and Special Charges.	Special Loans.	School District Loans.	
Pepin	$609 10	$1,635 72	....	....	$1,635 72
Pierce........	1,049 94	5,026 86	....	$481 60	5,458 46
Polk..........	2,242 07	4,391 99	$513 00	1,511 33	6,416 32
Portage	1,233 72	4,485 50	....	1,398 47	5,883 97
Price	373 83	2,258 23	6,721 67	636 00	9,615 90
Racine	....	7,388 61	....		7,388 61
Richland.....	2,262 49	5,114 69	....	378 20	5,492 89
Rock	....	12,580 89	....	2,449 10	15,029 99
St. Croix	1,418 84	6,462 75	....	2,476 45	8,939 20
Sauk.........	....	5,062 10	....	188 81	5,200 91
Sawyer......	92 39	1,321 91	... .	....	1,321 91
Shawano	554 24	2,786 36	2,025 00	1,764 65	6,576 01
Sheboygan...	....	9,819 89	....		9,819 89
Taylor...	419 02	1,440 27	945 00	1,753 66	4.188 93
Trempealeau .	2,532 54	5,506 85	2,250 00	1,371 56	9,188 41
Vernon......	....	8,677 56	....	960 27	4.637 83
Vilas........	....	487 20	....	5,730 00	6,217 20
Walworth ...	....	8,077 94	2,400 00	404 00	10,881 94
Washburn....	85 81	726 64	5,937 50	2,679 24	9,343 38
Washington..	2,605 97	7,896 01	....	....	7,806 01
Waukesha ...	8,662 94	13,682 62	... .	... .	13,682 62
Waupaca ...	2,730 49	6,271 84	6,070 00	347 58	12,689 42
Waushara....	379 03	2,104 45	1,100 00	1,069 47	4,273 92
Winnebago...	....	10,090 24	5,900 00	1,430 00	17,420 24
Wood	621 19	2,887 25	1,472 75	1,825 86	5,685 86
Total ...	$62,719 02	$407,437 32	$113,580 38	$74,667 20	$595,684 90

"D."—Abstract of Assessment Rolls.

APPENDIX D.—*Abstract of the assessment rolls of the several counties in the state of Wisconsin as returned to the secretary of state for the year 1833, under the provision of section 1067 of the Revised Statutes.*

COUNTIES.	HORSES.			NEAT CATTLE.		
	Number	Value.	Av. value.	Number.	Value.	Av. value.
Adams........	3,175	$84,211	$26 52	8,083	$65,044	$8 05
Ashland.......	950	60,230	60 74	1,147	24,494	21 35
Barron........	4,092	108,448	22 20	11,197	83,998	7 52
Bayfield......	1,117	60,059	53 76	747	15,532	20 80
Brown.........	6,285	243,971	38 81	12,235	142,519	10 01
Buffalo........	6,560	205,351	31 30	20,621	150,357	7 24
Burnett.......	960	39,548	41 10	4,434	42,565	9 60
Calumet.......	5,413	231,025	42 69	16,031	172,368	10 72
Chippewa.....	5,924	256,366	43 27	10,979	105,521	9 61
Clark.........	5,436	153,330	28 02	15,501	121,597	7 84
Columbia.....	12,839	452,865	35 27	29,000	276,309	9 53
Crawford.....	7,078	214,702	30 33	17,054	140,707	8 25
Dane..........	22,087	944,555	42 79	62,083	713,459	11 50
Dodge.........	13,281	453,653	34 15	40,100	401,574	10 01
Door..........	3,753	156,775	41 79	11,191	132,970	11 80
Douglas.......	820	34,612	42 21	291	5,320	18 28
Dunn.........	7,877	234,065	30 00	18,774	130,784	6 97
Eau Claire....	6,270	329,498	52 55	12,241	· 124,151	10 14
Florence... ...	355	14,155	40 00	75	1,135	15 13
Fond du Lac..	13,102	512,856	39 14	35,877	408,016	11 37•
Forest..... .	148	5,470	37 00	199	2,538	11 83
Grant........	19,024	462,922	24 38	53,953	421,162	7 81
Green........	10,952	386,884	35 33	43,936	564,009	12 61
Green Lake...	5,917	155,391	26 26	12,813	103,446	8 07
Iowa.........	10,361	320,980	30 97	43,569	478,238	10 86
Iron..........	215	16,147	75 10	383	7,705	20 12
Jackson......	5,089	200,007	39 28	12,740	116,613	9 15
Jefferson.....	9,352	330,525	35 34	35,191	436,935	12 39
Juneau.......	5,355	127,870	23 87	11,531	74,984	6 49
Kenosha......	5,504	201,026	36 52	15,876	203,607	12 12
Kewaunee....	5,502	177,521	32 25	18,390	147,114	8 00
La Crosse.....	6,498	323,734	49 82	15,000	159,199	10 61
La Fayette....	9,505	242,559	25 52	36,848	301,106	8 12
Langlade	1,507	37,882	24 80	3,518	32,443	9 22
Lincoln.......	1,451	61,380	42 37	2,255	25,771	11 43
Manitowoc....	10,114	357,313	35 33	27,317	310,635	11 37
Marathon......	5,852	214,555	36 66	18,145	148,686	8 19
Marinette.....	2,091	95,290	45 59	2,059	18,582	9 02
Marquette.....	4,053	121,036	29 94	10,056	75,129	7 47
Milwaukee....	16,966	949,317	55 95	11,942	184,743	15 47
Monroe........	9,289	193,242	20 80	21,239	127,579	6 00
Oconto........	3,578	120,032	33 60	7,783	54,829	7 04
Oneida........	598	21,545	36 02	397	5,112	12 89
Outagamie....	7,514	243,369	32 38	21,524	198,878	9 24
Ozaukee.......	5,002	212,020	42 39	14,931	172,467	11 55
Pepin	2,714	78,469	28 91	6,855	41,803	6 49
Pierce........	7,118	307,168	41 74	16,128	143,220	8 20

"D."—Abstract of Assessment Rolls.

APPENDIX D—*Abstract of the assessment rolls of the several counties in the state of Wisconsin for 1898—Continued.*

COUNTIES.	HORSES.				NEAT CATTLE.		
	Number	Value.	Av. value.		Number.	Value.	Av. value.
Polk..........	4,085	$135,442	$36 04		14,602	$116,016	$7 89
Portage........	5,756	191,400	33 25		10,051	88,009	8 75
Price..........	796	36,508	45 81		1,370	19,428	14 18
Racine........	6,982	251,735	36 05		17,219	280,990	13 42
Richland......	8,159	288,101	35 18		20,270	176,096	8 68
Rock	17,811	658,890	37 00		36,586	435,794	11 91
St. Croix..... .	7,137	318,224	44 59		16,354	147,892	8 40
Sauk..........	11,310	465,297	41 14		27,589	280,464	10 18
Sawyer.... ...	257	13,255	51 57		422	9,096	21 55
Shawano......	5,172	162,692	31 45		15,585	125,291	8 04
Sheboygan.....	10,308	466,114	45 24		35,494	484,644	13 65
Taylor.........	1,101	30,896	28 07		2,852	27,465	9 63
Trempealeau..	7,862	281,109	35 75		27,913	204,265	7 22
Vernon........	11,809	334,717	28 84		25,911	196,627	7 58
Vilas	165	5,275	32 00		215	3,251	15 12
Walworth.....	12,930	559,524	43 27		34,501	587,806	15 29
Washburn.....	432	12,460	29 00		1,024	16,290	15 90
Washington...	8,742	342,453	38 02		23,322	263,821	11 31
Waukesha.....	12,144	460,263	37 9		26,053	332,464	12 76
Waupaca......	9,188	263,665	28 26		19,727	140,907	7 14
Waushara.....	6,386	196,776	30 81		14,443	133,470	9 24
Winnebago....	9,026	426,463	49 46		22,578	272,478	12 07
Wood........	3,233	72,525	22 43		9,252	65,581	7 09
Total.........	459,414	$16,727,208	$35 43		1,195,072	$12,117,048	$10 14

15—Secy.

"D."—Abstract of Assessment Rolls.

APPENDIX D. — *Abstract of the assessment rolls of the several counties in the state of Wisconsin for 18?3.*— Continued.

COUNTIES.	MULES AND ASSES.			SHEEP AND LAMBS.		
	Number	Value.	Av. value.	Number.	Value.	Av. value.
Adams	92	$2,188	$24 00	5.455	$6,684	$1 03
Ashland.......	2	15	7 50	....	....	...
Barron	113	2,303	20 38	8,760	9,497	1 08
Bayfield.......	6	140	23 33	....	....	
Brown	10	585	53 50	5,217	6,178	1 18
Buffalo	105	2,445	23 28	12,162	12,821	1 05
Burnett........	13	411	31 61	1,558	1,859	1 19
Calumet	25	1,040	41 60	7,771	9,981	1 28
Chippewa	200	2,648	13 20	6,680	7,826	1 17
Clark.	68	1,855	19 93	10,997	12,147	1 10
Columbia	67	1,573	23 48	46,223	70,423	1 52
Crawford.....	96	2,800	29 17	10,649	17,250	1 62
Dane..	93	3,365	36 18	37,861	75,474	1 99
Dodge.	67	1,817	27 12	34,185	42,336	1 24
Door.........	38	1,038	27 33	7,238	10,485	1 45
Douglas	13	500	38 46	18	25	1 33
Dunn..	196	5,284	26 96	18,294	22,045	1 20
Eau Claire.....	64	1,825	28 51	6,760	10,636	1 57
Florence.	4	100	25 00	....	....	
Fond du Lac...	57	2,475	43 42	61,516	86,297	1 40
Forest.	11	435	39 55	2	4	2 00
Grant........	134	3,015	23 50	15,397	24,029	1 56
Green	72	1,970	25 97	18,477	37,009	2 00
Green Lake ..	32	800	25 00	35,878	39,423	1 09
Iowa..........	90	2,675	29 66	9,438	22,964	2 42
Iron	5	140	28 00	8	12	1 50
Jackson	51	1,447	28 41	6,812	8,766	1 40
Jefferson......	75	2,090	27 87	16.574	24,416	1 41
Juneau......	61	1,108	18 16	7,935	8,070	1 00
Kenosha.......	56	1,730	30 00	29,497	42,107	1 43
Kewaunee.....	41	681	16 16	8,388	12,184	1 45
La Crosse.....	65	2,865	44 08	7,748	12,159	1 57
La Fayette. ...	117	2,588	22 12	12,573	21,968	1 74
Langlade. ...	46	833	18 11	371	352	95
Lincoln	15	350	23 33	964	931	91
Manitowoc ...	33	519	15 78	11,109	16,134	1 45
Marathon......	55	1,210	22 00	10,389	11,174	1 07
Marinette.....	35	1,163	33 23	314	322	1 03
Marquette....	35	810	23 14	15,077	17,392	1 15
Milwaukee	58	2,080	35 86	1,097	2,344	2 18
Monroe	81	1,292	15 95	23,065	24,243	1 05
Oconto	57	1,540	27 02	3,182	3,587	1 12
Oneida	4	150	37 00	....	....	
Outagamie	48	1,695	35 31	13,964	17,239	1 23
Ozaukee.... ..	49	1,383	28 22	2,260	4,469	1 98
Pepin	49	1,045	21 33	4,793	4,940	1 03

"D."—Abstract of Assessment Rolls.

APPENDIX D. — *Abstract of the assessment rolls of the several counties in the state of Wisconsin for 1893* —Continued.

COUNTIES.	MULES AND ASSES.			SHEEP AND LAMBS.		
	Number	Value.	Av value	Number.	Value.	Av. value.
Pierce.......	120	$3,459	$28 75	25,243	$34,958	$1 38
Polk......... ..	76	1,650	21 71	8,915	10,219	1 15
Portage:.......	90	1,586	17 62	6,926	6,969	1 00
Price	34	880	25 88	15	15	1 00
Racine	57	1,247	21 88	21,156	33,314	1 56
Richland	130	4,470	38 38	37,862	57,810	1 53
Rock	103	4,595	44 61	24,980	46,435	1 86
St. Croix.. ..	101	3,420	33 86	14,977	21,354	1 42
Sauk	113	3,544	31 36	23,876	40,425	1 69
Sawyer	....	....	....	....	....	
Shawano	76	1,723	22 67	10,881	12,492	1 15
Sheboygan	82	2,448	29 75	10,274	22,024	2 14
Taylor. ..	18	290	16 11	501	624	1 24
Trempealeau ..	111	3,570	32 16	15,947	22,797	1 43
Vernon........	90	2,414	26 82	36,403	47,266	1 30
Vilas	1	25	25 00	....	....	
Walworth.....	49	2,085	42 55	45,623	83,530	1 81
Washburn.....	5	86	17 20	118	113	96
Washington ...	125	4,172	53 37	15,649	29,933	1 91
Waukesha.....	61	1,615	26 47	52,961	81,242	1 53
Waupaca......	120	3,297	27 47	15,801	16,761	1 06
Waushara	80	2,030	25 37	15,025	16,140	1 07
Winnebago....	42	1,560	37 14	23,851	37,595	1 58
Wood	40	698	17 4	3,586	2,855	99
Total.......	4,428	$120,335	$27 40	948,226	$1,383,023	$1 46

"D."—Abstract of Assessment Rolls.

APPENDIX D.—*Abstract of the assessment rolls of the several counties for 1893.—*
Continued.

COUNTIES.	SWINE.			WAGONS, CARRIAGES AND SLEIGHS.		
	Number	Value.	Aver-age value	Number	Value.	Aver-age value.
Adams.............	1,788	$4,662	$2 61	1,494	$13,051	$8 74
Ashland.............	94	288	3 06	898	16,274	18 12
Barron.............	2,009	4,288	2 18	2,963	22,100	7 46
Bayfield.............	112	430	3 84	873	12,479	14 27
Brown.............	2,378	4,245	1 78	4,264	66,788	15 67
Buffalo...........	7,889	14,488	1 83	2,275	18,555	8 16
Burnett.............	533	1,814	2 46	920	8,108	8 81
Calumet.............	4,771	9,752	2 04	3,498	41,262	11 79
Chippewa.............	3,512	9,255	2 54	3,175	44,708	14 08
Clark	2,743	5,186	1 86	3,693	31,654	8 57
Columbia	12,458	61,853	4 97	5,855	71,794	12 26
Crawford.............	7,194	19,287	2 68	2,024	25,542	12 61
Dane........	26,901	117,644	4 37	10,875	164,840	15 88
Dodge.............	11,009	29,292	2 66	7,195	81,166	11 28
Door	2,926	6,106	2 09	3,378	38,104	11 28
Douglas.........	187	385	2 81	555	14,480	26 09
Dunn.............	8,393	20,10-	2 39	4,373	42,533	9 73
Eau Claire	3,600	12,127	3 37	3,755	73,652	19 61
Florence	.....	.....	.....	306	4,058	13 26
Fond du Lac.........	11,839	40,763	3 59	6,384	105,263	16 49
Forest.............	21	85	4 19	141	1,171	8 30
Grant.............	34,948	80,890	2 32	6,855	64,075	9 35
Green	17,755	93,601	5 27	4,718	64,716	13 76
Green Lake	6,080	12,763	2 09	2,990	30,343	10 15
Iowa......	13,264	55,599	4 19	3,981	43,753	10 99
Iron.	45	227	5 04	220	5,532	23 79
Jackson.............	3,164	7,463	2 35	1,957	24,892	12 72
Jefferson....	10,528	41,620	3 95	5,184	76,449	14 75
Juneau.	3,589	5,919	1 65	2,567	22,399	8 73
Kenosha.............	8,706	14,005	1 61	2,244	27,728	12 35
Kewaunee	4,549	6,725	1 48	4,556	38,634	8 48
La Crosse.............	6,457	20,265	3 14	3,996	88,535	24 66
La Fayette.........	20,190	45,087	2 23	3,084	28,781	9 33
Langlade.	764	1,390	1 82	1,535	12,280	8 00
Lincoln	445	935	2 10	1,410	18,683	13 25
Manitowoc.............	7,079	14,635	2 06	7,890	86,574	19 72
Marathon	4,332	8,022	1 85	5,481	59,882	10 93
Marinette	454	1,129	2 49	1,795	36,217	20 18
Marquette.............	3,119	9,354	2 99	1,342	14,430	10 75
Milwaukee.............	2,475	7,418	2 99	13,794	807,919	58 57
Monroe.............	6,335	12,994	2 05	3,400	28,807	8 47
Oconto.............	1,960	3,331	1 70	2,592	32,200	12 43
Oneida.............	102	246	2 41	510	5,693	11 16
Outagamie	7,052	14,279	2 03	4,639	59,121	12 74
Ozaukee.............	2,560	6,694	2 61	3,599	52,752	14 66
Pepin.............	3,124	7,696	2 46	1,456	12,124	8 33

"D."—Abstract of Assessment Rolls.

APPENDIX D.—*Abstract of the assessment rolls of the several counties for 1893.—*
Continued.

COUNTIES.	SWINE.			WAGONS, CARRIAGES AND SLEIGHS.		
	Number	Value.	Average value.	Number	Value.	Average value.
Pierce....	6,322	$16,846	$2 68	2,964	$42,051	$14 33
Polk	2,260	5,243	2 32	2,674	21,949	8 21
Portage	4,468	8,344	1 88	3,180	38,623	12 11
Price................	191	814	4 24	883	8,827	10 00
Racine..............	4,080	13,871	3 40	3,402	60,762	17 86
Richland............	9,404	33,048	3 51	2,422	31,391	12 96
Rock.	19,684	111,369	5 68	8,793	141,659	16 11
St. Croix............	4,891	17,168	3 51	3,763	46,653	12 40
Sauk	12,506	54,370	4 34	6,097	89,670	14 71
Sawyer..............	96	272	2 83	266	4,085	15 36
Shawan ᛁ............	6,215	8,179	1 31	4,543	39,100	8 61
Sheboygan	6,822	27,343	4 01	8,964	133,317	14 87
Taylor	242	483	2 00	1,428	11,027	7 72
Trempealeau........	5,904	21,167	3 58	2,973	31,195	10 88
Vernon..............	10,935	28,315	2 59	3,473	37,484	9 93
Vilas	37	51	1 38	154	1,965	12 76
Walworth	13,105	70,506	5 38	6,124	118,137	19 27
Washburn........ ..	79	184	2 33	470	3,881	8 15
Washington....	8,383	24,036	2 87	6,627	84,509	12 74
Waukesha...........	8,271	29,312	3 54	8,753	110,695	12 64
Waupaca............	5,459	9,828	1 80	6,456	61,091	9 46
Waushara...........	4,780	10,002	2 11	2,725	28,415	10 43
Winnebago.........	5,922	24,804	4 19	6,214	136,638	21 99
Wood...	1,296	1,775	1 37	2,614	21,166	8 09
Total.........	420,185	$1,351,670	$3 21	256,121	$3,944,285	$19 12

"D."—Abstract of Assessment Rolls.

APPENDIX D.—*Abstract of the assessment rolls of the several counties for 1893—Continued.*

COUNTIES.	WATCHES.			PIANOS, ORGANS AND MELODEONS.		
	Number.	Value.	Av. value	Number.	Value.	Av. value.
Adams...............	106	$733	$6 91	163	$1,954	$12 00
Ashland	181	4,317	23 85	181	18,127	10 01
Barron..............	205	1,491	7 27	342	5,856	17 11
Bayfield	159	3,172	20 00	108	6,513	60 30
Brown..............	815	7,851	23 83	517	36,091	69 81
Buffalo	189	1,371	7 29	277	6,001	21 66
Burnett.............	25	375	15 00	62	1,542	23 26
Calumet............	200	1,836	9 02	253	8,211	32 45
Chippewa...........	277	5,265	19 01	279	12,593	45 14
Clark	173	1,876	10 84	327	7,024	21 48
Columbia...........	934	13,314	14 25	1,169	35,487	30 44
Crawford...........	169	2,198	13 00	269	7,866	29 24
Dane	1,487	20,847	14 02	1,797	84,397	46 96
Dodge...............	380	5,692	14 94	636	15,636	24 58
Door	321	4,924	15 33	347	18,455	53 19
Douglas............	76	1,920	25 26	147	15,245	103 70
Dunn...	294	3,655	12 43	513	11,824	23 19
Eau Claire.........	483	9,013	18 66	523	29,329	56 08
Florence	......	......	....	23	550	42 30
Fond du Lac........	714	9,487	13 29	955	33,286	34 85
Forest	10	180	13 00	14	360	25 71
Grant..............	787	7,014	8 92	996	24,497	24 54
Green	938	9,795	10 48	693	21,290	30 73
Green Lake.........	284	2,747	9 67	299	7,078	23 65
Iowa	361	4,112	11 30	575	12,319	21 25
Iron	2	30	15 00	9	555	61 66
Jackson............	315	3,717	11 80	335	8,520	25 43
Jefferson...........	447	5,174	11 57	745	19,015	25 52
Juneau.............	514	4,949	9 62	447	8,929	20 00
Kenosha............	170	2,752	16 19	314	7,694	24 50
Kewaunee..........	138	2,081	15 08	134	6,127	45 72
La Crosse	524	10,821	20 65	987	72,344	74 81
La Fayette.........	270	2,190	8 11	553	7,340	13 37
Langlade	183	1,863	10 29	216	4,978	23 05
Lincoln	99	1,685	17 02	119	6,265	52 65
Manitowoc....	177	2,319	13 10	525	16,995	32 35
Marathon...........	326	5,321	16 32	433	21,670	50 05
Marinette	53	1,755	32 74	199	16,837	84 60
Marquette.........	157	1,230	7 87	250	4,145	16 58
Milwaukee..........	2,999	85,841	28 62	5,607	635,604	11 84
Monroe	341	3,216	9 43	517	10,382	20 81
Oconto.............	122	2,680	21 97	187	7,684	41 91
Oneida	......	......	... ..	66	2,838	42 88
Outagamie..........	410	5,447	13 28	422	17,857	42 30
Ozaukee............	120	1,680	14 00	207	6,740	32 56

"D."—Abstract of Assessment Rolls.

APPENDIX D.—*Abstract of the assessment rolls of the several counties for 1893.—*
Continued.

COUNTIES.	WATCHES.			PIANOS, ORGANS AND MELODEONS.		
	Number.	Value.	Av. value.	Number.	Value.	Av. value.
Pepin........	74	$501	$6 28	174	$5,281	$30 35
Pierce..............	351	3,879	11 05	587	13,419	24 90
Polk...	179	1,835	10 25	184	4,155	22 58
Portage............	380	3,754	13 88	527	14,240	27 02
Price	10	146	14 60	52	1,186	22 81
Racine......	253	6,760	26 72	427	20,800	47 54
Richland..........	362	3,659	10 11	552	15,120	27 39
Rock..............	1,760	25,472	14 47	1,465	61,004	41 64
St. Croix..........	466	4,764	10 22	616	15,244	24 74
Sauk	895	9,996	11 17	925	25,597	27 66
Sawyer............	3	55	18 33	8	240	30 00
Shawano	118	1,294	10 96	169	5,657	34 07
Sheboygan....	778	7,423	9 54	921	36,178	39 28
Taylor.............	51	479	9 39	79	2,028	35 80
Trempealeau........	326	2,661	8 16	334	7,391	22 10
Vernon.............	223	1,410	6 32	399	6,739	16 89
Vilas..............	30	275	9 17	27	1,200	44 44
Walworth....	1,577	21,127	13 39	1,286	53,496	40 04
Washburn..........	16	319	19 94	72	1,891	26 26
Washington........	229	3,168	13 66	345	12,715	38 96
Waukesha..........	660	10,586	16 03	1,017	37,133	36 51
Waupaca...........	359	3,857	17 43	676	14,649	21 67
Waushara..........	222	1,976	8 90	464	8,835	19 04
Winnebago.........	877	17,392	19 80	1,204	53,616	44 53
Wood..............	151	1,408	8 09	317	6,891	21 74
Total...........	26,734	$401,552	$15 02	36,482	$1,728,189	$47 03

"D."—Abstract of Assessment Rolls.

APPENDIX D.—Abstract of the assessment rolls of the several counties in the state of Wisconsin for 1891–Continued.

COUNTIES.	SHARES OF BANK STOCK.		Value of merchants' and manufacturers' stock.	Am't of money, accounts, bonds, credits, notes and mortgages.	Value of all other personal property.	Total value of all personal property.
	Number.	Value.				
Adams.....	......	$1,890	$10,176	$1,805	$25,916	$218,244
Ashland.....	......	365,000	255,885	7,258	461,661	1,213,549
Barron.....	......	9,994	162,274	4,085	134,410	548,744
Bayfield.....	19	15,809	362,543	....	348,019	824,196
Brown	......	191,000	542,047	122,695	265,398	1,628,763
Buffalo.....	......	2,617	91,682	20,601	88,481	614,770
Burnett.....	......	....	47,192	480	18,955	162,349
Calumet.....	5	10,850	135,850	52,475	222.304	896,404
Chippewa...	......	164,500	392,777	82,850	489,655	1,523,964
Clark.......	761	61,800	152,972	....	118,871	662,312
Columbia...	......	188,695	421,652	89,575	704,829	2,338,369
Crawford ...	....	16,798	99,935	6,300	102,586	655,971
Dane........	3,841	833,600	955,820	1,602,920	647,626	5,664,047
Dodge	250	106,430	291,294	14,400	477,991	1,921,281
Door.......	6	24,608	170,296	45,495	198,303	807,559
Douglas.....	1,237	871,100	329,981	....	195,075	968,643
Dunn.......	......	15,560	516,388	115,005	150,304	1,267,500
Eau Claire..	......	208,094	633,676	94,575	833,113	2,859,689
Florence....	......	3,000	97,040	....	9,640	129,678
Fond du Lac	1,101	210,200	593,705	175,316	627,459	2,805,123
Forest.......	..	....	2,390	....	20,906	38,889
Grant.......	1,946	43,871	279,184	314,036	97,576	1,821,771
Green.......	450	253,100	344,142	....	1,387,284	3,163,790
Green Lake.	1,300	46,000	159,736	70,848	228,206	856,776
Iowa........	31	51,887	151,169	48,711	204,324	1,386,131
Iron........	......	4,832	178,257	....	88,480	301,917
Jackson.....	647	38,900	158,537	6,730	109,832	684,724
Jefferson....	3,950	253,680	360,971	19,300	613,027	2,183,202
Juneau......	20	3,625	188,848	22,480	82,886	547,017
Kenosha....	910	54,600	218,023	32,887	416,397	1,222,556
Kewaunee ..	......	32,540	136,559	75,869	104,117	740,152
La Crosse..	4,850	495,729	1,482,872	774,740	208,223	3,651,486
La Fayette..	......	40,451	98,261	32,651	155,063	978,085
Langlade....	....	9,250	56,541	....	63,300	220,612
Lincoln. ...	1,600	160,000	522,129	....	228,424	1,026,562
Manitowoc..	......	55,400	388,997	173,181	240,795	1,663,497
Marathon...	10	193,477	814,298	18,707	505,260	2,002,263
Marinette...	202	142,950	339,547	....	1,059,625	1,713,397
Marquette. .	......	6,435	39,936	500	35,313	325,710
Milwaukee..	Ves'ls	432,960	12,131,532	6,545,420	3,426,210	25,211,383
Monroe.....	250	22,850	167,879	5,593	189,634	737,711
Oconto......	......	55,700	198,664	250	870,656	847,158
Oneida......	......	33,854	352,151	....	17,171	438,260
Outagamie..	462	292,055	442,991	34,900	244,936	1,572,767
Ozaukee....	.... ..	7,000	129,410	62,845	309,059	966,519

"D."—Abstract of Assessment Rolls.

APPENDIX D.—*Abstract of the assessment rolls of the several counties in the state of Wisconsin for 1898*—Continued.

COUNTIES.	SHARES OF BANK STOCK.		Value of merchants' and manufacturers' stock.	Am't of money, accounts, bonds, credits, notes and mortgages.	Value of all other personal property.	Total value of all personal property.
	Number.	Value.				
Pepin.......	250	$10,065	$44,690	$12,574	$38,717	$257,405
Pierce.......	659	101,086	175,487	15,018	248,9'9	1,105,510
Polk	......	15,086	85,724	20,223	95,575	513,117
Portage....	......	36,834	230,285	5,449	94,415	709,908
Price......	......	13,200	265,540	30.0 0	68.773	440,312
Racine......	......	70,515	1,063,307	18.175	1,511,299	3,272,275
Richland....	10	31,503	153,754	26.330	203,069	1,024,351
Rock	1,121	435,995	817,342	139,040	1,720,092	4,598.187
St. Croix....	.....	92,975	207,861	31,305	307.941	1,214,301
Sauk........	1,250	94,100	339,056	31,109	686,525	2,120 153
Sawyer	2	6,000	10,590	....	83,539	127,132
Shawano...	273	15,155	180.514	1,225	87 837	641,159
Sheboygan..	3,000	232,000	654,707	365,370	750.258	3,181,826
Taylor... ..	1	5,045	53,043	....	24,375	155,755
Trempealeau	220	11,660	147,169	.. ..	219,348	952,332
Vernon. ...	10	35,286	136,128	57,278	238,178	1,121,842
Vilas	......	1,835	20,988	....	32,200	67,065
Walworth...	3,150	292,000	395.605	187,165	1,512 834	3,883,815
Washburn. .	......	.. ..	79,510	100	76,852	191,636
Washington.	......	68,525	210,095	197,845	451,995	1,692.767
Waukesha ..	......	238,025	368,409	114,878	1,562,650	3,347,271
Waupaca ...	1,001	62,120	243,533	51,659	133,658	1,005,025
Waushara...	......	2,800	60,657	9,000	74,786	544,887
Winnebago .	3,299	854,185	1,291,370	564,440	452,219	4,136,060
Wood......	......	59,740	222,835	9 374	35,76	500,608
Total....	38,094	$7,766,456	$33,036,253	$12,557,540	$27,129,124	$115,262,683

"D."—Abstract of Assessment Rolls.

APPENDIX D — *Abstract of the assessment rolls of the several counties in the state o Wisconsin for 1893.*—Continued.

COUNTIES.	LAND.		Aver age value.	Value of city and village lots.	Total value of real estate.	Total value of all property.
	No. acres.	Value.				
Adams ...	360,506	$789,912	$2 19	$21,729	$811.641	$1.029,885
Ashland..	650,179	1,3 3,584	2 00	5,663,798	6.916.882	8,179.931
Barron ...	550,427	997,577	1 81	278,074	1.270.651	1.819.395
Bayfield..	641,182	2,191,259	3 42	510,894	2.702.153	3 526 349
Brown ...	301,990	3,004,447	9 95	3,475,613	6.486.060	8.108.823
Buffalo...	433,908	1,482,535	3 42	262,882	1,744,917	2,359,687
Burnett ..	308,137	431,118	1 40	61,275	492.898	654.742
Calumet..	2, 2,106	4,749,691	23 40	344,180	5.073.871	5,970.275
Chippewa	1,176,915	4,425,828	3 61	2,482,058	6 910,881	8 434.345
Clark. ..	760,382	3,417,480	4 49	563,689	3.986,119	4.648 431
Columbia.	492,613	6,558,494	13 11	2,158,077	8.716.571	11 054 940
Crawford.	356,941	1,299,216	3 64	366,348	1.665.564	2.321.535
Dane	756,310	12,913,824	17 01	7,125,810	20.040.134	25 704.181
Dodge ...	547,311	10,417,822	19 03	1,841,407	12,259,229	14,180.510
Door ...	293,005	1,318,501	4 81	568,977	1.837,478	2,695.037
Douglas ..	705,783	8,803,948	12 55	16,583,134	25 447.082	26.415.725
Dunn ...	525,974	2,421,966	4 60	651,611	3.073.577	4.341,077
Eau Claire	381,337	2,447,195	6 42	4,546,119	6.993.814	9,353.003
Florence..	296,130	1,186,670	4 01	83,732	1.270.402	1.400.080
F. du Lac.	449,160	10,475,309	23 32	4,208,198	14.683.507	17.488.680
Forest ...	786,16	1,48,028	1 88	105,055	1,586.088	1,619 472
Grant	699,852	5,389,586	7 70	1,156,567	6.566 103	8 367.874
Green .	365,294	5,920,129	16 21	1,603.616	7.523,705	10 687 495
G. Lake...	221,502	2,893,175	13 06	799,837	3.693.175	4 549.951
Iowa	480,168	4,657,061	9 69	736,091	5.893 152	6 779.283
Iron	436,592	1,913,936	4 39	338,354	2,257,290	2,559.207
Jackson ..	516,984	1,376,685	2 66	325,446	1 702.131	2,386.855
Jefferson .	324,449	6,426,396	19 81	2,467,650	8.894 046	11.077.248
Juneau ...	444,958	1,132,259	2 54	482,617	1.605,685	2.152,702
Kenosha..	171,450	4,081,124	23 39	1,284.104	5.815.228	6 537.784
Kewaunee	217,092	2,671,483	12 31	555,603	3.227.035	3,967.187
La Crosse.	295,735	2,292,620	7 75	9,553,043	11.845.663	15,497.149
La Fayet'e	396,785	4,478,142	11 31	590,189	5,078 831	6.056.416
Langlade.	531,641	677.347	1 32	299,060	986,408	1,207,020
Lincoln ..	546,310	979,804	1 79	1,288,810	2,268.614	3,295.176
Manitow'c	370.897	7,312,409	19 71	2,216,555	9.528 964	11,192,461
Marathon	981,463	2,728,655	2 78	2,456,260	5.184 915	7,187.177
Marinette	856,641	2,032,793	2 49	2,374,004	4.306.796	6.020,193
Marquette	294,662	1,048,071	3 59	167,648	1,215.722	1,541,432
Milwauk'e	130,515	11,184,364	85 70	112,490,390	123.674.754	148 886,137
Monroe...	542,227	1,891,491	3 49	417,238	2.644.092	3.381.808
Oconto ...	605,406	1,477,003	2 44	808,794	2,285.798	3 182.951
Oneida ...	445,796	849,106	1 90	340,250	1,189.486	1.627.696
Outag'mie	337,599	4,696,196	13 91	4,617,472	9.313.668	10.886.435
Ozaukee..	146,881	5,233,148	35 63	624,578	5.857.721	6,824.240
Pepin.....	146,087	636,338	4 36	190,272	826.605	1,084,010
Pierce ...	365,027	2,824,613	7 74	664,521	3,489,134	4,594,644

"D."—Abstract of Assessment Rolls.

APPENDIX D.— *Abstract of the assessment rolls of the several counties in the state of Wisconsin for 1893.*—Continued.

COUNTIES.	LANDS.		Average value.	Value of city and village lots.	Total value of real estate.	Total value of all property.
	No. acres.	Value.				
Polk	567,777	$1,880,997	$8 22	$155,324	$1,986,321	$2,499.488
Portage .	492,818	1,355,275	2 79	947,901	2,303,176	3,013.084
Price ...	696,949	1,168,894	1 77	156,432	1,325,326	1,765.688
Racine ...	206,980	5,806,716	28 05	8,229,706	14,036,422	17,308.697
Richland .	369,334	2,863,635	6 40	601,491	2,965,126	3,989.477
Rock. ...	447,095	10,412,324	23 07	5,280,118	15,692,442	20,290.629
St. Croix.	456,750	3,983,331	8 72	1,305,545	5,288,876	6,503.177
Sauk	529,739	5,297,865	10 00	1,927,297	7,225,162	9,345,815
Sawyer...	720,640	1,281,391	1 78	52,685	1,334,026	1,461,158
Shawano..	528,937	2,206,393	4 17	433,186	2,639,579	3,280,738
Sheboyg'n	320,325	10,084,676	31 48	5,751,328	15,836,004	19,017,830
Taylor....	614,879	705,454	1 15	49,315	754,769	910.524
Trem'leau	469,260	2,329,513	4 96	325,375	2,654.888	3,607.220
Vernon ..	506,474	2,399,886	4 74	316,121	2,716,007	3,837,849
Vilas	455,124	888,483	1 95	68.086	956,519	1,023.584
Walworth	348,483	9,575,233	27 47	2,835.302	12,410.535	16,244,350
Washbu'n	452,024	543,614	1 20	43,513	587,127	778.763
Washin'n	271,453	8,713,941	32 10	1,011,249	9,725,190	11,417.957
Waukes'a.	347,225	10,881,002	31 05	4,061,287	14,942,289	18,269,560
Waupaca	447,206	2,234,503	5 00	1,093,285	3,327,788	4 332,813
Wausha 'a	388,377	1,751,676	4 51	164,634	1,916.310	2,461,197
Winneb'o	261,385	5,627,205	2 15	8,569,965	14,197,170	18,833,230
Wood	491,323	1,018,349	2 07	689,349	1,707,698	2,208,806
Total...	32,229,051	$261,399,147	......	$244,719,013	$506,444,430	$624,707,113

"E."—*Valuation of all Property in the State.*

APPENDIX E.—*Valuation of all property in the state as fixed by the county boards of supervisors and town assessors, and the amount of state, county, town, city and village taxes levied for 1893.*

COUNTIES.	Valuation of all property.	Current expenses.	School purposes.	Support of poor.
Adams	$1,029,821 00	$2,874 74	$7,116 84	....
Ashland	8,287,609 80	79,881 78	35,794 49	....
Barron	1,821,429 90	14,234 18	82,558 17	$1,988 50
Bayfield	4,918,827 30	50,146 00	89,485 00	7,919 08
Brown	8,113,588 00	31,577 45	82,646 10	5,608 08
Buffalo	2,363,616 00	8,519 00	18,751 00	805 00
Burnett	657,187 00	2,578 85	7,726 30	1,164 28
Calumet	5,997,270 00	7,789 28	16,877 98	1,567 75
Chippewa	8,113,538 00	41,478 52	56,207 90	....
Clark	4,668,658 85	18,786 84	42,380 90	1,574 85
Columbia	11,071,091 00	27,104 92	87,859 18	....
Crawford	2,556,882 00	4,418 40	15,830 75	....
Dane	25,823,788 50	77,031 86	101,689 26	1,252 77
Dodge	14,497,864 00	36,318 04	51,900 53	2,045 45
Door	2,647,622 58	7,990 00	18,337 77	646 00
Douglas	26,416,517 00	348,559 00	149,784 00	....
Dunn	4,858,904 55	25,488 67	38,766 65	1,500 00
Eau Claire	9,820,856 00	138,180 90	74,703 78	1,585 91
Florence	1,402,820 00	5,500 12	11,782 28	....
Fond du Lac	17,463,581 00	68,857 61	52,336 18	7,662 88
Forest	1,658,902 00	5,580 00	5,100 00	....
Grant	8,015,205 00	15,948 01	57,593 48	2,548 15
Green	10,711,500 00	22,612 07	40,313 26	....
Green Lake	4,533,978 00	11,507 90	15,608 83	4,060 00
Iowa	6,993,464 00	17,493 17	34,447 28	943 08
Iron	2,555,246 00	28,760 00	17,076 00	12,000 00
Jackson	2,390,869 00	9,784 48	19,848 72	2,151 49
Jefferson	11,599,780 00	14,625 70	51,197 80	3,152 62
Juneau	2,049,173 25	12,072 80	25,469 86	44 17
Kenosha	6,543,644 00	82,466 83	81,915 61	6,100 00
Kewaunee	8,975,762 62	14,578 23	13,055 17	669 28
La Crosse	15,602,068 00	162,270 39	68,391 83	17,090 68
La Fayette	6,120,048 00	9,535 22	87,360 84	1,922 26
Langlade	1,284,588 89	5,289 14	24,579 81	371 00
Lincoln	8,392,133 00	18,390 00	82,218 07	....
Manitowoc	11,176,265 00	21,067 67	40,838 11	2,974 59
Marathon	7,226,444 00	59,960 63	47,800 89	2,278 67
Marinette	1,533,829 00	41,588 63	89,345 11	4,500 00
Marquette	1,624,718 00	8,076 48	8,489 04	525 00
Milwaukee	155,056,728 00	2,035,843 88	284,227 81	....
Monroe	8,256,265 14	19,679 54	29,546 10	20 48
Oconto	8,158,319 00	21,884 52	20,340 79	4,058 69
Oneida	1,680,096 00	9,722 87	18,484 66	150 00
Outagamie	10,922,815 00	92,785 74	64,880 46	11,305 18
Ozaukee	6,814,475 00	12,052 43	25,083 89	500 00
Pepin	1,155,686 85	2,962 57	8,898 85	704 00
Pierce	4,579,041 60	11,194 23	28,930 77	1,087 83
Polk	2,504,001 00	9,096 28	22,903 92	1,899 24
Portage	8,016,806 30	28,841 22	50,464 84	8,725 00

"E."—*Valuation of all Property in the State.*

APPENDIX E.— *Valuation of all property in the state as fixed by the county boards of supervisors for 1898 — Continued.*

COUNTIES.	Valuation of all property.	Current expenses.	School purposes.	Support of poor.
Price..............	$1,719,137 85	$11,632 51	$34,532 93	$2,600 00
Racine	17,180,074 00	8,908 28	53,880 61	658 99
Richland..........	8,438,717 00	12,251 32	20,187 40	....
Rock..............	20,274,182 00	40,280 05	88,455 78	....
St. Croix.	6,577,207 00	21,857 96	44,848 87	....
Sauk.	9,338,802 00	19,810 78	48,623 42	....
Sawyer...........	1,461,185 00	10,000 00	9,000 00	....
Shawano...... ..	2,590,919 45	10,009 36	20,192 86	1,390 00
Sheboygan	19,029,553 00	38,161 07	62,340 97	1,000 00
Taylor............	919,801 50	8,152 36	21,950 56	....
Trempealeau	8,630,605 00	9,171 70	24,516 82	3,350 00
Vernon...........	8,885,892 00	13,631 08	25,851 24	....
Vilas......	1,028,658 00	12,800 00	13,450 00	400 00
Walworth........	16,524,987 00	37,997 28	61,085 04	....
Washburn........	728,069 60	9,230 68	16,123 08	400 00
Washington	11,451,559 00	7,298 08	34,823 17	140 00
Waukesha........	18,281,292 00	13,403 36	50,906 15	2,000 00
Waupaca.........	4,889,546 50	20,719 25	30,091 91	1,541 71
Waushara........	3,184,561 00	5,089 53	14,692 45	1,761 16
Winnebago.......	18,325,588 00	129,993 40	73,166 81	8,710 11
Wood	2,300,745 83	16,750 64	24,904 26	....
Total........	$628,796,249 86	$4,174,357 48	$2,774,317 49	$143,988 82

"E."—Valuation of all Property in the State.

APPENDIX E.—*Valuation of all property in the state as fixed by the county boards of supervisors for 1898 — Continued.*

COUNTIES.	Roads, bridges and poll tax.	Other purposes.	Total town, city and village taxes.	Total county taxes, exclusive of town and city and vil. taxes.	Total town, city, village and county taxes.
Adams....	$5,848 42	$475 50	$16,315 50	$9,134 10	$25,449 60
Ashland.	17,478 43	145,011 43	278,166 08	167,184 00	445,350 08
Barron...	22,903 37	14,087 38	85,716 55	38,737 59	124,454 14
Bayfield..	13,878 34	47,056 51	158,484 93	32,094 94	190,529 87
Brown ...	46,945 41	48,861 90	165,638 89	95,284 49	260,923 38
Buffalo...	15,489 00	2,561 00	46,125 00	29,700 00	75,825 00
Burnett ..	8,149 48	....	19,613 41	11,161 41	30,774 82
Calumet..	17.672 96	4,458 55	48,316 47	20,317 58	68,634 05
Chippewa	43,013 46	9,243 86	149,943 74	74,615 00	224,558 74
Clark.....	34,485 95	10,962 70	103,190 74	37,784 68	140,975 42
Columbia.	25,336 97	15,159 62	105,460 69	48,302 00	153,762 69
Crawford.	13,905 94	603 68	34,258 77	32,362 87	66,621 64
Dane.....	71,427 79	47,175 52	298,576 70	119,503 33	418,080 03
Dodge	34,552 64	10,357 16	135,173 82	86,243 53	221,417 35
Door.....	11,461 39	2,008 05	35,443 21	21,895 69	57,838 90
Douglas ..	33,221 04	561,169 48	1,087,683 52	142,543 56	1,230,227 08
Dunn	23,864 76	5,663 34	95,283 42	36,567 71	131,851 13
Eau Claire	25,266 53	24,089 02	258,826 14	54,222 38	313,048 52
Florence..	7,318 79	....	24,601 19	10,644 17	35,245 36
F'd du Lac	34,764 97	17,191 23	180,312 82	71,222 46	251,535 28
Forest...	....	3,378 62	14,058 62	10,500 00	24,558 62
Grant	49,449 20	26,899 34	152,433 13	58,988 00	211,371 13
Green....	26,843 41	6,451 19	96,219 93	51,812 87	148,032 80
Gre'n L'ke	12,242 84	1,828 86	45,247 93	21,276 61	66,524 54
Iowa.....	12,710 55	15,924 68	81,518 76	32,458 39	113,977 15
Iron	15,210 75	9,462 25	77,509 00	45,000 00	122,509 00
Jackson ..	15,641 59	4,145 33	51,531 61	38,716 39	90,248 00
Jefferson.	37,163 38	36,972 62	143,112 12	62,315 94	205,428 06
Juneau...	12,787 99	7,096 74	57,471 06	21,964 52	89,435 58
Kenosha..	20,798 69	27,530 45	118,811 08	24,486 64	143,297 72
Kewa'nee.	22,229 66	8,420 98	58,948 27	28,153 50	87,101 77
La Crosse	42,075 29	3,861 34	293,689 53	79,484 25	373,173 78
La Fay'tte	27,736 63	20,188 02	96,742 97	49,669 97	146,412 94
Langlade.	11,035 55	20,824 81	62,100 31	30,565 01	92,665 32
Lincoln...	13,800 69	41,925 52	101,424 28	37,246 85	138,671 13
Manito w'c	50,920 13	6,445 08	122,245 58	87,938 32	210,183 90
Marathon	39,793 50	6.292 51	155,620 40	98.624 28	254,244 68
Marinette.	16,578 29	2,890 22	98,852 25	61,897 70	160,749 95
Marquette	7,953 91	1,528 83	21,523 21	18,041 95	39 565 16
Milwa'kee	70,432 44	8,239 72	2,398,743 35	613,086 80	3,011,830 15
Monroe ...	17,626 60	25,105 56	91,978 28	42,800 00	134,778 28
Oconto....	18,806 12	36,309 30	100,849 42	69,048 85	169,898 27
Oneida....	7,892 50	35,416 49	71,666 52	42,550 00	114,216 52
Out'gamie	33,919 96	11,261 37	213,102 71	76,058 60	289,161 31
Ozaukee..	11,653 75	3,205 36	52,494 93	20,172 23	72,667 16
Pepin	6,848 52	1,060 08	19,968 47	9,530 36	29,498 83

"E,"—Valuation of all Property in the State.

APPENDIX E.— *Valuation of all property in the state as fixed by the county boards of supervisors for 1898 — Continued*

COUNTIES.	Roads, bridges and poll tax	Other purposes.	Total town. city and village taxes.	Total county taxes, exclusive of town and city and vil. taxes.	Total town, city, village and county taxes.
Pierce ..	$26,409 19	$4,990 37	$72,612 88	$26,128 88	$98,736 26
Polk	25,958 52	6,096 92	65,954 88	18,068 76	84,023 64
Portage ..	21,372 28	8,323 17	107,726 01	58,389 28	166,115 29
Price. ...	22,013 26	13,109 88	83,888 58	47,456 02	131,344 60
Racine. ..	16,543 35	109,184 21	189,120 59	57,920 17	247,040 56
Richland..	22,493 37	2,265 34	57,197 43	33,555 89	90,752 82
Rock. ...	38,338 23	56,986 33	224,060 34	91,699 43	315,759 77
St. Croix..	25,018 58	15,315 51	107,065 42	51,532 11	158,597 53
Sauk.	48,951 59	12,800 89	130,186 68	58,720 31	188,906 99
Sawyer...	2,000 00	....	21,000 00	36,326 65	57,326 65
Shawano.	25,522 22	8,451 76	65,566 20	31,505 02	97,071 22
Sheboyg'n	63,608 37	107,899 04	273,009 45	77,621 56	250,631 01
Taylor. ..	21,495 05	7,213 01	58,810 98	37,295 04	96,106 02
Tremp'l'u.	23,135 97	15,878 10	76,052 59	24,048 69	100,101 28
Vernon...	28,436 42	4,815 19	72,723 93	45,042 64	117,766 57
Vilas. ..	4,200 00	22,571 00	53,421 00	27,700 00	81,121 00
Walworth	33,143 99	55,818 86	188,044 67	41,999 39	230,044 06
Washb'rn.	6,961 10	19,302 48	52,017 34	16,500 00	68,517 34
Wash'ton.	37,523 00	2,644 94	82 469 19	39,637 58	122,106 77
Wa'kesha.	40,066 62	17,792 96	124,169 09	79,728 92	203,898 01
Waupaca.	20,834 12	20,129 90	93,316 89	42,754 74	136,071 63
Waushara	11,911 58	9,372 71	42,777 43	18,088 87	60,866 30
Win'bago.	119,912 60	78,022 85	409,805 27	96,752 66	506,557 93
Wood ...	16,057 90	19,056 82	76,769 62	32,901 77	109,671 39
Total...	$1,803,134 89	$1,956,912 89	$10,852,711 07	$3,873,228 40	$14,725,939 47

"F."—Purposes for which County Tax was Expended.

APPENDIX F.—*Statement showing purposes for which the county tax was expended in the several counties for the year ending December, 1893.*

Counties.	Support of poor.	County buildings.	Railroad aid.	Roads and bridges.	Salaries of county officers.	Court expenses.
Adams....	$3,000 00				$2,250 00	$1,000 00
Ashland..	11,874 76	$1,791 07	$6,750 00	$312 00	14,891 21	13,317 46
Barron...	1,509 66	184 25		2,685 00	6,254 43	2,615 79
Bayfield..	1,533 86	12,500 00		4,025 49	4,100 00	4,531 00
Brown...	1,701 57	2,000 00	7,755 00	700 00	7,200 00	7,608 34
Buffalo...	1,448 00			2,650 00	3,280 00	963 00
Burnett...	130 00	100 00			1,825 00	232 20
Calumet..	1,454 52	290 16			8,900 00	1,815 09
Chippewa	5,814 66	1,502 40		5,059 37	9,037 50	1,467 26
Clark....	2,715 04			7,150 60	4,700 00	5,551 37
Columbia	14,000 00	5,500 00			6,150 00	539 28
Crawford.	3,805 08	700 00		702 58	5,600 00	2,212 42
Dane.....	12,393 75	36,793 39			11,793 33	9,169 70
Dodge....	1,646 00	5,000 00		6,685 00	9,855 00	7,000 00
Door.....	1,120 74	784 80			3,450 00	1,861 19
Douglas..	17,680 75			20,500 00	13,813 70	27,264 60
Dunn....	1,233 17	6,279 85		2,437 50	5,000 00	2,711 56
Eau Claire	2,519 75				5,750 00	11,809 57
Florence.	525 24			55 00	3,710 00	474 40
Fond du L	1,617 47	559 89			7,640 00	833 90
Forest....	751 43	549 00		1,500 00	3,286 98	450 06
Grant....	521 04	607 13		9,700 00	6,075 00	7,028 80
Green...	13,000 00	2,000 00			4,250 00	5,582 23
Green Lke	734 96	111 72			3,000 00	1,138 17
Iowa.....		105 00			4,350 50	1,961 48
Iron.....						
Jackson..	2,552 11	174 02		3,427 00	4,100 00	1,950 96
Jefferson.	6,800 00	1,915 00		2,500 00	5,300 00	2,000 00
Juneau...	3,290 58	139 32			4,958 64	2,487 80
Kenosha..	932 55	290 25			8,050 00	2,878 57
Kewaunee	2,745 50	176 00			3,500 00	1,834 60
La Crosse	4,000 00		7,000 00	8,000 00	6,000 00	13,000 00
LaFayette	3,120 27	1,799 03		10,491 75	5,200 00	4,113 58
Langlade.	1,465 80	844 17			4,401 64	4,174 55
Lincoln..	4,147 00	800 00		1,667 44	6,160 00	7,171 47
Manitow'c	1,700 00	4,500 00		2,000 00	7,300 00	3,094 35
Marathon.	1,587 53	10,000 00		6,230 98	8,850 00	8,919 24
Marinette.	5,120 49	1,382 26		4,040 80	5,594 83	1,793 24
Marquette	800 00				3,150 00	941 48
Milwauk'e	53,816 55	182,870 01		996 09	145,914 20	25,852 56
Monroe..	4,500 00				5,050 00	3,500 00
Oconto....	1,013 27	2,290 00			4,685 00	3,896 56
Oneida....	3,127 94			7,510 35	5,914 80	5,423 29
Outag'mie	3,972 81	8,000 00	4,000 00	1,700 00	8,000 00	4,747 90
Ozaukee..		1,000 50			4,450 00	2,250 00
Pepin...	252 25				2,050 00	794 04
Pierce....	2,615 55	161 00	326 50	600 00	4,800 00	1,345 22

"F."—Purposes for which County Tax was Expended.

APPENDIX F.—*Statement showing purposes for which the county tax was expended in the several counties for the year ending December, 1893.* —Continued.

Counties.	Support of poor.	County buildings.	Railroad aid.	Roads and bridges.	Salaries of county officers.	Court expenses.
Polk......	$500 00	$400 00	....	$625 00	$2,450 00	$1,000 00
Portage ..	1,723 66	15,600 00	$9,000 00	1,000 00	4,500 00	5,000 00
Price	....	....	....	6,800 00	5,200 00	3,000 00
Racine ...	4,076 57	21,269 02	....	3,870 76	8,830 00	4,430 00
Richland..	3,363 39	5,500 00	....	....	3,500 00	1,999 11
Rock......	8,285 19	533 58	....	3,450 26	13,831 60	16,117 54
St Croix..	5,681 78	....	....	3,260 00	3,950 00	5,791 43
Sauk......	14,982 00	3,500 00	....	7,100 00	5,800 00	3,830 43
Sawyer...	2,334 19	115 85	....	3,773 04	3,705 01	464 66
Shawano..	1,069 17	44 00	....	625 50	4,940 00	950 23
Sheboyg'n	4,532 32	....	....	....	8,800 00	3,600 00
Taylor....	4,614 62	14,713 40	....	2,840 80	4,405 00	2,165 90
Tr'mp'le'u	1,652 89	....	....	....	4,150 00	1,030 00
Vernon...	3,821 24	100 00	5,700 00	5,380 00	3,500 00	1,561 26
Vilas.. ..	69 58	10,480 50	....	1,843 12	2,117 12	....
Walworth	10,643 31	....	....	....	5,200 00	4,422 71
Washburn	500 00	100 00	....	5,000 00	3,250 00	572 00
W'shingtn	1,691 00	6,900 00	....	....	3,950 00	1,274 00
Waukesha	7,174 53	....	....	....	7,450 00	5,263 05
Waupaca.	3,020 27	1,065 95	....	1,720 00	4,825 00	3,355 72
Waushara	725 76	1,350 00	....	....	3,019 00	1,909 94
Win'ebago	6,000 00	500 00	....	1,482 00	10,000 00	8,190 36
Wood	4,941 47	957 48	....	....	5,950 00	3,967 20
Total...	299,688 59	371.859 00	$40,531 50	161,995 78	527,407 54	304,737 82

16—Sec'y.

"F."—Purposes for which County Tax was Expended.

APPENDIX F.—*Statement showing purposes for which the county tax was expended in the several counties for the year ending December, 1893.*—Continued.

Counties.	Sheriff's accounts.	Jail expenses.	Miscellaneous.	All other county expenses.	Total taxes expended.
Adams. ...	....	....	....	$2,500 00	$7,750 00
Ashland ...	$3,771 64	$5,005 05	$1,793 18	13,209 80	7£,716 17
Barron.....	5,044 92	1,536 32	....	18,398 76	38,179 18
Bayfield....	4,935 37	594 10	....	9,897 83	42,117 15
Brown.,....	3,578 96	2,500 00	....	39,850 88	72,894 75
Buffalo. .	1,294 00	273 88	2,840 00	8,429 92	21,173 80
Burnett....	400 00	5 00	600 00	2,800 00	6,092 20
Calumet....	488 62	138 73	....	2,881 01	10,498 13
Chippewa..	7,528 68	1,479 49	.......,..	33,681 82	65,570 68
Clark.. ..	2,167 51	657 90	....	12,699 45	35,641 27
Columbia..	2,878 17	500 00	..,......	4,237 55	33,805 00
Crawford .	2,438 95	....	400 00	12,824 67	28,683 65
Dane......	4,589 36	7,427 74	.. ..	13,209 88	95,375 64
Dodge.....	5,363 40	5,477 60	....	44,216 53	85,243 53
Door	933 76	258 93	....	2,889 89	11,294 81
Douglas....	19,758 37	....	....	87,416 07	136,432 49
Dunn	2,552 86	250 00	16,429 06	4,561 74	41,455 74
Eau Claire..	7,334 88	408 01	3,580 00	22,820 17	54,222 38
Florence ...	749 89	414 50	....	2,970 83	8,899 86
Fond du Lac	7,758 25	3,348 02	....	49,459 93	71,222 46
Forest.....	1,484 91	767 38	....	2,260 83	11,050 59
Grant......	4,821 55	1,000 00	1,665 00	10,319 42	41,637 44
Green.....	901 00	500 00	23,523 28	2,056 36	51,812 87
Green Lake.	2,158 64	150 00	800 00	2,788 94	10,832 43
Iowa......	1,522 45	....	....	12,000 00	19,939 43
Iron.......	....	....	....	....	.. ...
Jackson....	2,038 19	400 00	....	5,125 90	19,768 18
Jefferson...	6,500 00	....	....	37,770 94	62,815 94
Juneau.....	3,577 67	769 36	1,280 00	4,529 22	21,037 59
Kenosha ...	....	32 63	475 66	6,866 07	19,025 72
Kewaunee .	1,411 12	356 20	....	5,470 20	15,493 62
La Crosse ..	9,000 00	....	....	3,200 00	50,200 00
La Fayette.	1,964 00	....	2,485 00	6,727 49	35,901 12
Langlade...	3,313 96	104 60	874 25	19,965 08	26,144 05
Lincoln ..	2,632 61	621 89	2,750 00	... .	26,000 41
Manitowoc..	2,363 62	350 00	....	24,000 00	45,807 97
Marathon ..	4,280 89	300 00	1,119 59	37,042 22	78,330 45
Marinette ..	5,069 69	3,150 00	....	8,740 53	34,891 40
Marquette..	400 00	200 00	....	5,789 52	10,781 00
Milwaukee..	7,479 18	41,891 31	....	199,935 19	658,755 09
Monroe....	3,500 00	700 00	....	9,600 00	26,850 00
Oconto.....	3,024 15	1,195 99	...i......	26,873 79	42,477 76
Oneida....	2,181 29	3,244 92	....	15,928 26	43,330 35
Outagamie..	3,374 21	1,374 39	....	33,126 36	63,295 67
Ozaukee....	1,650 50	1,500 00	1,149 00	....	12,000 00
Pepin	516 01	68 80	....	781 00	4,412 10
Pierce	1,721 55	923 12	10,132 00	1,907 04	24,581 98

"F."—Purposes for which County Tax was Expended.

APPENDIX F.—*Statement showing purposes for which the county tax was expended in the several counties for the year ending December, 1893.—*Continued.

Counties.	Sheriff's accounts.	Jail expenses.	Miscellaneous.	All other county expenses.	Total taxes expended.
Polk........	$4,200 00	$100 00	....	$791 25	$10,066 25
Portage	3,500 00	....	....	4,167 93	44,491 59
Price.......	....	....	....	33,339 00	48,339 00
Racine	2,599 88	....	....	17,835 59	62,911 82
Richland....	1,864 12	....	....	18,061 19	29,287 81
Rock.......	3,412 02	736 72	$2,870 15	27,479 46	76,716 52
St. Croix....	3,021 14	....	....	9,355 81	31,060 16
Sauk.......	1,185 93	725 80	3,000 00	503 15	39,577 31
Sawyer	4,679 83	820 90	....	7,261 18	23,154 66
Shawano ...	1,006 35	374 56	800 00	10,176 96	19,986 77
Sheboygan..	2,800 00	5,123 75	....	11,238 32	36,094 39
Taylor......	1,939 56	226 50	372 93	9,312 25	40,590 96
Trempeale'u	869 77	....	1,000 00	1,829 74	10,032 40
Vernon.....	2,760 10	400 00	13,177 02	8,693 02	45,042 64
Vilas.......	2,011 33	135 28	....	12,097 27	28,753 20
Walworth..	5,844 52	....	5,850 47	....	31,461 01
Washburn..	1,565 25	300 00	1,175 30	....	12,462 55
Washington	1,650 54	....	316 57	3,787 89	19,570 00
Waukesha..	10,045 15	659 11	14,296 00	39,706 62	84,593 46
Waupaca...	7,401 88	238 75	....	16,127 22	42,754 74
Waushara ..	1,232 81	....	....	3,267 93	11,505 44
Winnebago.	9,438 49	....	2,489 51	45,531 72	83,582 08
Wood	3,574 77	....	668 58	10,077 15	80,136 65
Total.....	$237,058 17	$99,712 22	$117,362 55	$1,097,160 24	$3,257,512 91

"G."—Indebtedness of Counties.

APPENDIX G.—*Statement showing the bonded and other indebtedness of the several counties in the state December 31st, 1898, as appears by the reports under sec. 1017, R. S.*

COUNTIES.	BONDED INDEBTEDNESS.				
	Railroad aid.	Bridges.	Other purposes.	Interest unpaid.	Total bonded indebtedness.
Adams ...	....	....	$345,505 72	$6,468 75	$351,974 47
Ashland...	....	....	8,400 00	....	19,900 00
Barron....	$11,500 00	....		....	19,900 00
Bayfield...	45,222 25	....	....	....	45,222 25
Brown ...	42,714 43	$40,000 00	15,773 00	6,430 41	104,917 84
Buffalo....	7,623 00	....	1,300 00	....	8,923 00
Burnett...	....	....	....	....	....
Calumet...	51,000 00	....		....	51,000 00
Chippewa.	....	2,070 00	109,306 17	....	111,376 17
Clark ...	....	11,600 00	9,660 52	137 67	21,398 19
Columbia.	....	....	24,650 00	1,062 00	25,712 00
Crawford..	775 00	....	....	....	775 00
Dane	153,500 00	140 00	131,000 00	....	284,640 09
Dodge	5,250 00	....	33,010 00	325 50	38,585 50
Door	16,000 00	....	....	....	16,000 00
Douglas...	....	50,000 00	2,118,244 22	....	2,168,244 22
Dunn	16,061 00	....	....	109 28	16,170 28
Eau Claire.	....	101,900 00	166,332 96	80 00	268,312 96
Florence ..	....	....	....	....	....
F'nd du L'c	90,000 00	....	6,000 00	250 00	96,250 00
Forest.....	....	....	1,200 00	....	1,200 00
Grant	....	80 00	15,000 00	31 50	15,111 50
Green	....	....	....	....	....
Green Lake	....	....	20,000 00	....	20,000 00
Iowa......	9,000 00	300 00	6,521 95	820 00	16,641 95
Iron	....	....	27,000 00	1,700 00	28,700 00
Jackson...	....	500 00	21,750 00	....	22,250 00
Jefferson..	11,706 76	....	13,380 00	669 00	25,755 76
Juneau....	6,000 00	1,915 00	6,630 25	200 00	14,745 25
Kenosha ..	170,000 00	....	....	....	170,000 00
Kewaunee.	56,000 00	....	....	2,440 00	58,440 00
La Crosse..	45,000 00	155,000 00	190,000 00	....	390,000 00
La Fayette	12,500 00	....	....	750 00	13,250 00
Langlade..	....	....	6,337 01	280 00	6,617 01
Lincoln...	....	28,000 00	30,000 00	3,374,00	61,374 00
Manitowoc	47,000 00	30,000 00	10,000 00	....	87,000 00
Marathon..	1,000 00	4,434 39	91,056 43	240 00	96,730 82
Marinette..	....	24,000 00	53,000 00	....	77,000 00
Marquette.	....	....	....	....	....
Milwaukee	....	595,000 00	4,674,000 00	....	5,269,000 00
Monroe....	....	7,000 00	....	....	7,000 00
Oconto....	....	....	....	....	....
Oneida ...	....	....	....	....	....
Outagamie	3,000 00	36,100 00	20,000 00	1,380 00	60,480 00
Ozaukee...	....	2,200 00	....	....	2,200 00
Pepin.....	....	....	....	....	....

"G."—Indebtedness of Counties.

APPENDIX G.—*Statement showing the bonded and other indebtedness of the several counties in the state December 31st, 1898—Continued.*

COUNTIES.	BONDED INDEBTEDNESS.				
	Railroad aid.	Bridges.	Other purposes.	Interest unpaid.	Total bonded indebtedness.
Pierce.....	....	....	$27 91	....	$27 91
Polk......	$2,350 00	$112 20	600 00	$64 00	3,126 20
Portage...	24,900 00	....	....	....	24,900 00
Price......	1,000 00	....	....	600 00	1,600 00
Racine....	....	13,000 00	212,000 00	....	225,000 00
Richland..	....	....	16,500 00	800 00	17,300 00
Rock......	43,500 00	6,300 00	6,500 00	....	56,300 00
St. Croix..	....	2,800 00	25,900 00	23 33	28,723 33
Sauk......	....	27,800 00	52,803 46	3,790 20	84,393 66
Sawyer....	....	....	....	....	....
Shawano..	....	....	1,742 95	....	1,742 95
Sheboygan	50,000 00	35,000 00	150,688 42	....	235,688 42
Taylor.....	....	....	8,800 00	....	8,800 00
Trempeal'u	12,366 67	500 00	....	35 00	12,901 67
Vernon....	....	....	12,000 00	75 00	12,075 00
Vilas......	....	....	7,000 00	245 00	7,245 00
Walworth.	59,000 00	....	....	3,950 00	62,950 00
Washburn.	....	....	1,000 00	....	1,000 00
Wash'ton..	....	....	4,000 00	....	4,000 00
Waukesha.	....	....	30,000 00	....	30,000 00
Waupaca..	19,357 22	6,000 00	3,750 00	1,714 50	30,821 72
Waushara.	21,999 75	....	....	165 00	22,164 75
Win'bago..	91,250 00	60,000 00	169,567 60	8,412 50	329,230 10
Wood......	....	15,000 00	....	....	15,000 00
Total....	$1,126,576 08	$1,256,751 59	$8,857,933 57	$46,622 64	$11,287,883 88

"G."—Indebtedness of Counties.

APPENDIX G.—*Statement showing the bonded and other indebtedness of the several counties in the state December 31st, 1893—* Continued.

COUNTIES.	Indebtedness of sch'l district or for school purposes.	All other indebt'dness of towns, cities and villages.	Total indebtedness of towns, cities and villages.	Valuation of county as fixed by the county board.
Adams..				$987,035 00
Ashland	$13,466 98	$2,576 59	$368,018 04	8,00,000 00
Barron	4,533 35		24,433 35	1,928,686 00
Bayfield	35,300 00		80,522 25	4,920,512 70
Brown	51,800 00	2,500 00	159,217 84	7,160,552 00
Buffalo	8,157 00		17,080 00	2,571,645 00
Burnett	3,230 97		3,230 97	614 352 35
Calumet			51,000 00	6,702,581 00
Chippewa	17,648 05		129,024 22	9,751,270 00
Clark	1,860 00	1,021 32	24,279 51	2,864,182 00
Columbia		1,085 00	26,797 00	9 658,572 00
Crawford	11 66	8,613 61	9,400 27	2,135,298 35
Dane	34,300 00	150 00	319,090 00	24,727,307 00
Dodge	1,890 00	325 00	40,8 0 50	13,034,153 00
Door	1,126 95		17,126 95	2,139,572 00
Douglas	228,500 00		2,396,744 22	26,418,122 00
Dunn	1,036 25		17,206 53	5,135,174 00
Eau Claire	834 15		269,147 11	8,9 00 0 00
Florence				730, 00 00
Fond du Lac	12,000 00	3,800 00	112,050 00	16,740,333 00
Forest	500 00		1,700 00	1,800,000 00
Grant	3,089 06		18,200 56	6,441,150 00
Green	1,800 00		1,800 00	
Green Lake		1,800 00	21,8 0 00	4,067,941 00
Iowa	8,480 00	17,600 00	42,721 95	6,462,730 00
Iron	3,139 49	5,822 76	37,662 25	2,500,000 00
Jackson	283 91	200 00	22,733 91	1,951,121 00
Jefferson	8,100 00		33,855 76	10,894,911 50
Juneau	15,725 42		30,470 67	2,255,767 00
Kenosha			170,000 00	5,499.678 00
Kewaunee	40 00	52 66	58,532 66	3,568,000 00
La Crosse	80,200 00		470,200 00	10,474,240 00
La Fayette	1,500 00	12,100 00	26,850 00	5,871,758 00
Langlade	15,535 60	36 00	22,517 61	
Lincoln	8,336 19	16,277 00	85,987 19	3,985,00 00
Manitowoc		17,100 00	104,100 00	10,97,542 00
Marathon	5,535 61	975 26	103,241 69	5,143,804 00
Marinette	19,30 00		96,030 00	6,400,000 00
Marquette	150 00		150 00	1,635,342 00
Milwaukee	22,000 00	55,000 00	5,346,0 00 00	84,6 0,000 00
Monroe	7,500 00		14,500 00	3,254,0 00 00
Oconto	10,110 86	2,351 79	12,462 65	
Oneida				1,500,000 00
Outagamie	3,150 00		63,630 00	8,718,10 00
Ozaukee	14,000 00		16,200 00	5,837,504 00
Pepin		3,000 00	3,000 00	1,163,656 20

"G."—Indebtedness of Counties.

APPENDIX G.—*Statement showing the bonded and other indebtedness of the several counties in the state December 31st, 1898—Continued.*

COUNTIES.	Indebtedness of sch'l district or for school purposes.	All other indebt'dness of towns, cities and villages.	Total indebtedness of towns, cities and villages.	Valuation of county as fixed by the county board.
Pierce............	$6,900 00	$695 00	$7,622 91	$3,314,352 25
Polk.............	1,011 81	74 50	4,212 51	2,320,865 75
Portage	38,250 00	9,826 75	72,976 75	4,044,69 • 87
Price............	9,918 00	7,978 92	19,496 92	2,045,437 08
Racine	....	....	225,000 00	10,000,000 00
Richland........	3,000 00	....	20,300 00	3,433,717 00
Rock............	33,205 16	8,9 0 00	98 405 16	18,000,000 00
St. Croix........	38,818 16	24,773 52	92,315 01	5,547,478 00
Sauk............	9,250 00	1,910 41	95,554 07	6,577,737 62
Sawyer	....	....	....	1,461,158 00
Shawano........	5,858 15	1,827 83	9,428 93	....
Sheboygan	14,400 00	7,000 00	2 57,083 42	14,200,000 00
Taylor	510 56	2,790 00	12,100 56	1,000,000 00
Trempealeau....	4,713 68	....	17,615 35	3,306,703 00
Vernon..........	11,561 59	2,325 00	25,961 59	4,355,725 00
Vilas............	15,000 00	3,553 54	25,798 54	1,024,301 00
Walworth........	25,700 00	....	88,650 00	15,269,762 00
Washburn	1,933 33	9,500 00	12,433 33	755,212 00
Washington......	14,625 00	1,100 00	19,725 09	5,649,000 00
Waukesha.......	27,500 00	....	57,500 00	13,232,000 00
Waupaca	9,*03 00	3,000 00	42,824 72	4,255,000 00
Waushara........	1,091 75	13 10	23,269 60	1,*56,820 00
Winnebago	24,400 00	6,741 60	360,371 70	15,584,000 00
Wood.	13,997 00	4,988 02	33,985 02	2,075,000 00
Total....	$954,548 69	$249,714 18	$12,492,146 75	$485,918,811 67

"*H.*"—*Indebtedness of Counties.*

APPENDIX H —*Statement showing the bonded and other indebtedness of the several counties in the state December 31, 1893, as appears by the reports under Chapter 236, Laws of 1881.*

COUNTIES.	BONDED INDEBTEDNESS.				
	Railroad aid.	Roads and bridges.	Interest unpaid.	Miscellaneous.	Other purposes.
Adams......					
Ashland......	$75,000 00				$60,000 00
Barron......				$10,700	
Bayfield......					6,800 00
Brown........	137,450 00				2,000 00
Buffalo......					12,000 00
Burnett......				10,000 00	
Calumet.....					
Chippewa....		$4,000 00			75,000 00
Clark					
Columbia....					10,000 00
Crawford.....					
Dane.......					
Dodge........				5,000 00	
Door........	6,000 00				
Douglas.... ..					
Dunn				65,000 00	
Eau Claire...					20,000 00
Florence.....				9,000 00	
Fond du Lac.					
Forest.......					5,000 00
Grant........					
Green.......					26,000 00
Green Lake..					
Iowa........					
Iron.........					
Jackson......	18,000 00			8,000 00	
Jefferson.....				3,500 00	
Juneau.......			$210 00	3,000 00	
Kenosha.....					
Kewaunee....					
La Crosse....					
La Fayette....					
Langlade.....				7,000 00	
Lincoln					6,000 00
Manitowoc ...	177,000 00				
Marathon				32,000 00	80,000 00
Marinette					20,000 00
Marquette ..					
Milwaukee...					285,000 00
Monroe.......					
Oconto.......					22,500 00
Oneida.......					
Outagamie..					80,000 00
Ozaukee.....					

"H."—Indebtedness of Counties.

APPENDIX H.- *Statement showing the bonded and other indebtedness of the several counties in the state December 31, 1893—Continued.*

COUNTIES.	BONDED INDEBTEDNESS.				
	Railroad aid.	Roads and bridges.	Interest unpaid.	Miscellaneous.	Other purposes.
Pepin					
Pierce					
Polk					
Portage	$200,000 00				
Price				$2,800 00	$20,000 00
Racine					
Richland					
Rock					120,000 00
St. Croix					
Sauk					
Sawyer					
Shawano					
Sheboygan					
Taylor					24,000 00
Trempealeau					
Vernon				30,000 00	
Vilas					15,000 00
Walworth					
Washburn					8,000 00
Washington					12,000 00
Waukesha				40,000 00	
Waupaca					18,000 00
Waushara					5,000 00
Winnebago				60,000 00	
Wood					
Total	$613,450 00	$4,000 00	$210 00	$286,000 00	$869,800 00

"H."—Indebtedness of Counties.

APPENDIX H.—*Statement showing the bonded and other indebtedness of the several counties in the state December 31, 1898—Continued.*

COUNTIES.	Total bonded indebtedness.	All other indebtedness.	Miscellaneous.	Total indebtedness of counties.
Adams				
Ashland	$135.000 00			$135.000 00
Barron	10,700 00			10,700 00
Bayfield	6 800 00			6.800 00
Brown	189.450 00			189.450 00
Buffalo	12.000 00			12,000 00
Burnett	10,000 00			10,000 00
Calumet				
Chippewa	79,000 00			79,000 00
Clark				
Columbia	10,000 00			10,000 00
Crawford				
Dane				
Dodge	5.000 00			5,000 00
Door	6,000 00			6,000 00
Douglas				
Dunn	65,000 0			65.000 00
Eau Claire	20.000 00			20.000 00
Florence	9,000 00			9,000 00
Fond du Lac				
Forest	5,000 00			5,000 00
Grant				
Green	26,000 00			26,000 00
Green Lake				
Iowa			$30,000 00	30,000 00
Iron				
Jackson	26.000 00			26.000 00
Jefferson	3.500 00			3,500 00
Juneau	8,210 00			8,210 00
Kenosha				
Kewaunee				
La Crosse	70,000 00			70,000 00
La Fayette				
Langlade	7.000 00			7 000 00
Lincoln	6 000 00			6.000 00
Manitowoc	177 000 00			177 000 00
Marathon	112.000 00			112.000 00
Marinette	20,000 00			20,000 00
Marquette				
Milwaukee	235,000 00		40,000 00	275,000 00
Monroe				
Oconto	22,500 00			22,500 00
Oneida		$7,891 52		7,891 52
Outagamie	80,000 00			80,000 00
Ozaukee				
Pepin				
Pierce				
Polk				

"H."—Indebtedness of Counties.

APPENDIX H.—*Statement showing the bonded and other indebtedness of the several counties in the state December 31, 1898—Continued.*

COUNTIES.	Total bonded indebtedness.	All other indebtedness.	Miscellaneous.	Total indebtedness of counties.
Portage	$200,000 00	$30,000 00	....	$230,000 00
Price.	22,800 00	....		22,800 00
Racine	77,000 00	....		77,000 00
Richland	....	....		....
Rock................	120,000 00	20,000 00	....	140,000 00
St. Croix	....	....		....
Sauk.	17,500 00	....		17,500 00
Sawyer.......	....	....		....
Shawano....	....	....		....
Sheboygan	....	46,000 00		46,000 00
Taylor	24,000 00	....		24,000 00
Trempealeau	....	....		....
Vernon	30,000 00	....		30,000 00
Vilas.	15,000 00	....	$10,096 55	25 096 55
Walworth.............	... .	....		....
Washburn.......	8,000 00	6,600 00	....	14,600 00
Washington....	12,000 00	....	....	12,000 00
Waukesha....	40,000 00	....	....	40,000 00
Waupaca....	18,000 00	....	....	18,000 00
Waushara.............	5,000 00	... .	....	5,000 00
Winnebago............	60,000 0	... .	....	60,000 00
Wood	....	....	....	....
Total.............	$1,937,960 00	$110,491 52	$80,096 55	$2,128,548 07

"I."—Statement of Principal Farm Products.

APPENDIX I.— *Statement of principal farm products grown in 1898, as ascertained and compiled pursuant to provisions of section 1010, R. S.*

COUNTIES.	NUMBER OF BUSHELS.					
	Wheat.	Corn.	Oats.	Barley.	Rye.	Potatoes.
Adams......	19,874	250,917	165,015	1,156	105,675	221,570
Ashland......	354	615	8.946	152	466	12,430
Barron.......	20,464	33,080	153,101	3,750	9,403	128,209
Bayfield.... ..	20	68	48	6	....	3,688
Brown	167,806	48,544	747.787	42,626	72.807	142,262
Buffalo	419,476	464,470	654,457	58,891	21,791	72,528
Burnett	8,884	9,010	35,970	119	4,098	89,051
Calumet.....	287,981	134,807	588.267	448,302	22,638	70,071
Chippewa	33,805	107,488	475.476	30,108	36,655	133,154
Clark........	31,718	84,576	257.442	4.915	35,059	105,405
Columbia	231,971	1,420,261	1,653.249	360,287	117,623	421,587
Crawford.....	181,204	475,438	562,669	8.452	41,833	81,996
Dane.........	306,267	2,304,690	2,988,175	352.489	37.278	206,179
Dodge	381,286	1,256,864	1,189,660	1,795.907	56,448	191,761
Door..........	76,166	12,597	150,270	11,648	34,751	102,680
Douglas	15	580	590	....	....	10,880
Dunn	75,845	372,889	664.140	27,597	74,483	143,719
Eau Claire....	79,159	187,812	478.617	46,618	67,779	112,786
Florence	....	....	1,500	....	....	10,986
Fond du Lac..	297,252	854,654	1,508,480	1,287,402	10,972	316,814
Forest........	22	106	1,776	20	10	3,871
Grant........	85,879	1,635,679	1,266,808	8,764	45,238	118,355
Green	31,319	1,360,694	1,785,335	10,598	31,292	62,632
Green Lake...	170,301	613,510	780,057	178,841	55,192	139,234
Iowa.........	74,950	975,809	1,346,802	4,488	46,295	76,467
Iron..........	....	120	400	....	....	8,800
Jackson......	128,896	208,392	1,084,526	12,756	32,672	48,947
Jefferson	380,802	1,021,181	1,044,885	848,072	101,426	117,576
Juneau.......	70,761	275,597	435,173	5,709	47,634	189,156
Kenosha.....	11,458	382,517	504,075	84 388	5,205	51,286
Kewaunee....	168,850	3,051	301.071	47,561	70,753	65,611
La Crosse....	155,412	462,088	588 057	75,470	28.375	180,793
La Fayette...	12,792	1,454,367	1,825,223	4,465	14,395	59,286
Langlade.....	1,520	3,387	21,551	1,941	2,857	27,874
Lincoln	1,405	449	22.780	890	3,123	80,031
Manitowoc ...	276,083	21,992	703,953	238,729	131,582	148,576
Marathon.....	43,286	14,161	301,077	20,082	86,295	182,819
Marinette.....	6,484	8,942	72,116	1,592	4,885	85,927
Marquette....	32,037	479,449	168,150	755	125,472	184,851
Milwaukee ...	42,086	164,990	404,765	128,029	89,691	259,814
Monroe	191,647	810,640	521,356	81,471	84,897	130,905
Oconto	34,867	86,464	189,991	8,187	14,412	72,814
Oneida	....	....	1,000	....	....	5,370
Outagamie ...	375,260	300,897	864,555	100,214	24,186	136,364
Ozaukee......	85,406	70,502	336.337	348,457	57,835	107,016
Pepin	55,636	158,941	218.327	65,038	16,021	27,428
Pierce........	176,555	298,221	546,520	282,194	96,330	99,981

"I."—*Statement of Principal Farm Products.*

APPENDIX I.— *Statement of principal farm products grown in 1898, as ascertained and compiled pursuant to provisions of section 1010, R. S.*— Continued.

COUNTIES.	NUMBER OF BUSHELS.					
	Wheat.	Corn.	Oats.	Barley.	Rye.	Potatoes.
Polk	79,605	108,359	301,418	18.418	80,018	115 608
Portage	19,597	294,257	370,563	2,688	92,062	917,436
Price	894	305	6,869	70	431	26,205
Racine	34,480	483,182	620,196	63,819	25,224	142,241
Richland	189,837	776,040	474,505	2,404	19,453	67,436
Rock	54,504	1,848,180	1,181,924	318,269	72,509	125,180
St. Croix.....	218,504	163,296	1,497.928	79,131	111,296	187.938
Sauk	444,780	983,586	1,168,090	7,789	97,459	239,704
Sawyer.......	....	200	4.000	....	....	20,000
Shawano	163,107	67,061	235,838	13,098	40,591	67.931
Sheboygan ...	208,228	579,661	826 197	682.898	113,494	208,844
Taylor.	104	190	5.679	374	1,382	25 019
Trempealeau..	185,012	1,200,893	1,035.477	31,713	34,838	82,903
Vernon.......	273,212	527,771	885,775	65,148	13,932	132,419
Vilas	....	....	....	....	....	....
Walworth....	89,219	1,515,940	1,048.312	883,265	19,150	105,180
Washburn....	749	1,976	5 547	....	241	15,116
Washington..	262,618	334,702	545,456	685,051	67,671	193,784
Waukesha....	184,269	513,527	921,408	497,388	78.017	239,577
Waupaca	183,554	210,752	418,154	10.061	52,857	689,113
Waushara...	58,114	400,056	1,057.446	1,097	99.626	729 205
Winnebago ..	278,497	606,930	1,019,283	160.974	40,655	203,204
Wood	8,633	39,703	76 158	3,423	25,283	61,879
Total	8,063,627	28,941,418	41,161,26 ?	9,455,599	2,845,965	9,652,947

"I."—Statement of Principal Farm Products.

APPENDIX I.— *Statement of principal farm products grown in the several counties in 1893.—Continued.*

COUNTIES.	NUMBER OF BUSHELS.						
	Root crops.	Cran berries.	Apples.	Strawberries.	Raspberries.	Blackberries.	Currants.
Adams	315	185	563	157	46	23	22
Ashland	5,525	600	40	133	60	....	76
Barron	4,983	....	95	38	....	....	12
Bayfield	151	... .	6	20	....	....	8
Brown	47,013	....	4,339	781	100	50	50
Buffalo	97	....	203	1	17	....	12
Burnett	2,105	91	31				
Calumet	1,887	....	11,028	110	9	....	2
Chippewa	2,366	16	45	411			
Clark	6,339	....	572	63	37	....	
Columbia	5,420	....	6,152	841	584	188	30
Crawford	752	....	7,354	35	34	24	11
Dane	10,784	....	4,190	1,505	429	143	38
Dodge	35,466	12	7,489	628	389	185	16
Door	13,950	7	1,055	42	....	....	2
Douglas	2,965	....	....	16			
Dunn	5,863	15	434	425	148	147	12
Eau Claire	1,913	....	492	363	556	52	12
Florence	1,687						
Fond du Lac	17,965	15	17,779	3,068	3,870	5,992	411
Forest	1,415	....	2	....	1	....	1
Grant	1,770	....	6,037	419	272	219	....
Green	5,005	....	1,299	156	124	30	16
Green Lake	1,781	1,112	1,982	231	58	115	28
Iowa	805	....	2,946	16	4	10	....
Iron	2,450						
Jackson	4,420	24,965	833	64	24	6	6
Jefferson	35,855	72	2,543	273	74	30	33
Juneau	6,075	15,106	1,042	542	39	84	
Kenosha	2,450	....	3,158	2,915	212	9	
Kewaunee	2,126		2,858				
La Crosse	4,549	....	4,842	1,272	191	115	197
La Fayette	100	....	1,183	42	7	1	12
Langlade	15,659	....	217	13	11	....	7
Lincoln	5,242	....	49	15	4	....	
Manitowoc	6,201	....	9,738	250	16	4	... .
Marathon	19,068	....	256	76	100	....	
Marinette	8,077	800	807	4,100	2,400	3	100
Marquette	515	459	1,891	113	10	16	2
Milwaukee	46,152	....	4,401	8,540	1,283	86	1,047
Monroe	6,785	7,263	3,176	2,735	1,300	2,144	154
Oconto	16,361	1	1,171	117	28	....	2
Oneida	3,935						
Outagamie	13,788	... ...	5,091	115	61	129	18
Ozaukee	8,985	....	6,511				
Pepin	228	....	109	80	35	8	... .

"I."—Statement of Principal Farm Products.

APPENDIX I.— *Statement of principal farm products grown in the several counties in 1893.* Continued.

COUNTIES.	NUMBER OF BUSHELS.						
	Root Crops.	Cran- berries.	Apples.	Straw- berries.	Rasp- berries	Black- berries.	Cur- rants.
Pierce	8,945	.....	848	441	125	45	....
Polk ...	8,841	438	28	12	4	15	5
Portage	1,000	55	931	825	199	45	58
Price	5,852	5	29	15	......	....	....
Racine	12,481	. ....	1,487	12,756	63	2	45
Richland....	2,140	......	7,616	171	493	253	8
Rock	8,985	....	1,168	2,027	1,411	210	77
St. Croix. ..	11,452	....	122	765	149	21	....
Sauk.	7,995	....	7,012	2,869	2,262	230	41
Sawyer	8,455		....	... ..	... ..		
Shawano.....	16,028	....	1,411	10	....	....	....
Sheboygan ..	28,020	2	51,974	1,691	513	681	122
Taylor. ...	1,468		21	33	......	....	....
Trempealeau.	1,071	....	42	805	345	302	202
Vernon ...	5,402	93	14,676	388	124	85	4
Vilas	... ..	.		... ..	... ..		
Walworth...	8,180	....	1,756	1,010	127	28	14
Washburn...	7,086	....		.. ..			
Washington .	23,965	....	7,441	258	81	4	48
Waukesha ..	25,837	27	7,119	5,712	378	213	124
Waupaca. ...	1,270	411	5,531	485	128	365	10
Waushara...	2,727	6,459	8,640	220	146	270	1
Winnebago	20,406	5.500	11 840	4,721	8,029	2,218	146
Wood	7,258	38,960	638	38	14	....	....
Total......	8,474,161	97,119	1,063,798	64,925	22,024	14,745	8,227

"I."—*Statement of Principal Farm Products.*

APPENDIX I.—*Statement of the principal farm products grown in the several counties in 1898.*—Continued.

COUNTIES.	NUMBER OF BUSHELS.			NO. OF ACRES FOR SEED.		NO. OF POUNDS.	
	Grapes.	Clover Seed.	Tim'th Seed. y	Clover.	Tim'thy	Flax.	Hops.
Adams......	13	12,605	82	5,783	18	....	29,195
Ashland.....	....	250	20	21	42	....	......
Barron......	....	15	9	7	......	....	2,665
Bayfield.....	....	....	....	......	......	....	......
Brown.	18	769	5	430	......	....	33
Buffalo.....	4,407	1,114	580	936	295	....	......
Burnett......	....	....	....	......	......	....	..
Calumet	3	14,816	....	6,525	......	....	......
Chippewa...	....	48	337	33	58	....	......
Clark........	75	....	2	....	1	....	....
Columbia....	356	6,508	4,797	4,288	1,090	84,755	34,958
Crawford....	47	3,648	295	1,441	217	951	......
Dane........	6,770	10,835	8,843	4,209	474	312	....
Dodge	65	11,807	508	7,557	129	13,438	800
Door	17	73	....	67	....	....	25
Douglas.....	....	....	....	......	10	....	......
Dunn.	11	584	212	358	30	....	....
Eau Claire...	2	214	43	1,119	117	....	5
Florence.....	....	....	....	......	......	....	......
Fand du Lac.	614	6,981	1,318	3,837	80	13,686	....
Forest	....	....	....	......	......	....	......
Grant.......	400	8,328	1,987	4,868	358	900	......
Green.......	5,012	975	1,219	1,060	555	4	....
Green Lake,.	128	5,661	3,334	3,281	1,214	148,733	5,500
Iowa	177	4,156	3,221	2,675	1,122	5,600	......
Iron........	....	....	....	......	......	....	......
Jackson.....	7	2,478	121	1,475	51	1	3,101
Jefferson....	984	1,716	213	1,182	93	... .	23,300
Juneau......	30,502	5,124	449	2,209	360	......	131,584
Kenosha....	15	892	529	580	75	121,191	......
Kewaunee...	....	1,965	386	1,194	175	87	......
La Crosse,..	594	3,065	182	1,168	44	......	3,200
La Fayette...	290	1,866	4,070	1,001	293	....	......
Langlade ...	....	....	....	......	......	....	......
Lincoln.....	5	....	....	......	......	....	......
Manitowoc..	....	8,779	162	3,976	36	......	....
Marathon....	....	....	147	....	......	....	......
Marinette....	....	39	......	27	1	1	......
Marquette...	150	8,175	14	4,394	3	2	75
Milwaukee...	360	843	59	529	1	655	40,000
Monroe......	5	7,200	121	3,579	29	67	5,400
Oconto......	2	53	....	60	3	....	......
Oneida	....	2	161	....	....	....	......
Outagamie..	43	779	69	989	173	1	... ..

"I."—Statement of Principal Farm Products.

APPENDIX I.—*Statement of the principal farm products grown in the several counties in 1893.—Continued.*

COUNTIES.	NUMBER OF BUSHELS.			NO. OF ACRES FOR SEED.		NO. OF POUNDS.	
	Grapes.	Clover Seed.	Tim'thy Seed.	Clover.	Tim'thy	Flax.	Hops.
Ozaukee. ...	......	6,689	149	4,458	60	19	......
Pepin........	....	702	50	541	26	......	....
Pierce.......	40	1,805	766	1,762	227	45,582	....
Polk	2	18	6	31	......	5	....
Portage	6	2,135	233	1,541	124	....	126,500
Price	....	......	......	....	....	....	....
Racine.....	56	764	193	394	38	169,214	......
Richland ...	475	1,204	141	738	68	....	3,000
Rock	2,884	2,950	5,155	2,178	1,060	... ..	....
St. Croix	6	856	2,617	690	624	138,818	....
Sauk ......:	1,019	6,994	383	4,117	163	1,600	79,025
Sawyer......	......	......	......	....	....	....	....
Shawano ...	191	2,989	45	1,439	45	200	....
Sheboygan ..	338	7,802	199	4,061	34	....	....
Taylor... ...	....	....	....	....	....	....	....
Trempealeau.	155	4,974	1,079	2,379	184	4,800	....
Vernon......	123	4,718	327	2,435	99	11,885	2,706
Vilas	......	....	....	....	....	....	....
Walworth...	405	2,502	4,246	2,075	896	21,150	....
Washburn...	....	....	....	....	....	....	....
Washington.	12	17,203	153	9,280	6	1,400	... .
Wau‹esha...	525	968	448	1,180	165	113	19,800
Waupaca....	1,045	4,300	19	2,673	2	....	5,200
Waushara...	16	7,636	106	4,301	31	....	....
Winnebago..	1,614	2,037	82	883	261	700	....
Wood........	......	14	80	....	80	....	....
Total......	59,979	211,066	44,952	117,659	11,340	785,320	515,572

17—Sec'y.

"I."—Statement of Principal Farm Products.

APPENDIX I.—*Statement of the principal farm products grown in the several counties in 1894. — Continued.*

COUNTIES.	Number of Pounds of Tobacco.	Number of Tons of Cultivated Grasses.	Number of Pounds of Butter.	Number of Pounds of Cheese.
Adams	6,400	6,978	256,596	7,590
Ashland	4	1,525	3,200	
Barron		22,365	436,695	38,111
Bayfield		517	5,480	
Brown		36,363	503.195	540,803
Buffalo		38,800	479,462	166,640
Burnett		1,728	96,157	1,150
Calumet		33,740	525,109	1,872,306
Chippewa	25	23,849	317,357	
Clark		32,504	713,143	60,726
Columbia	1,252,195	40,764	2,165,936	106,415
Crawford	431,249	24,430	376,005	10,800
Dane	10,041,524	109,282	3,888,865	816,765
Dodge	12,150	64,394	2,138,565	8,330,622
Door	584	15,480	218,692	476,961
Douglas		510	6,585	
Dunn		26,849	451,987	17,960
Eau Claire		16,758	363,967	22,423
Florence		819	2,385	
Fond du Lac	115	98,104	1,699,785	2,144,362
Forest		202	2,735	
Grant	16,725	50,573	662,083	373,815
Green	565,931	65,719	567,530	4,171,849
Green Lake	54	15,847	383,385	156,752
Iowa		59,377	966,856	1,888,345
Iron		310	3,000	
Jackson	501	11,537	553,943	
Jefferson	2,678,809	61,202	5,028,487	1,205,533
Juneau	17,800	15,135	223,424	380,803
Kenosha		37,119	1,153,692	
Kewaunee	581	28,334	281,493	1,678,081
La Crosse	1,700	31,962	933,560	14,280
La Fayette	65,874	50,787	679,206	1,175,621
Langlade		4,188	60,766	100
Lincoln		4,504	65,660	
Manitowoc		45,293	781,164	8,625,588
Marathon	200	28,809	308,254	35,826
Marinette		6,870	83,401	750
Marquette	360	3,549	435,532	420
Milwaukee		49,771	509,618	109,390
Monroe	22,500	96,942	513,403	319,800
Oconto		14,870	289,682	
Oneida				
Outagamie		35,660	719,402	2,423,297
Ozaukee		35,815	401,470	1,030,930
Pepin		6,450	168,860	800
Pierce	7,950	24,160	346,727	61,703
Polk		16,472	444,261	26,475
P				

"I."—Statement of Principal Farm Products.

APPENDIX I.—*Statement of the principal farm products grown in the several counties in 1898.*—Continued.

COUNTIES.	Number of Pounds of Tobacco.	Number f Tons ofo Cultivated Grasses.	Number of Pounds of Butter.	Number of Pounds of Cheese.
Portage......	....	13,741	319,182	61,920
Price............	....	8,657	47,555	250
Racine	28,900	48,135	2,745,180	162,930
Richland......	....	39,055	508 095	2,571,388
Rock..................	7,417 423	62,780	1,962,187	182,506
St. Croix..............	....	31,079	496,242	464,410
Sauk.	....	52,652	945,604	525,875
Sawyer................	....	1,900	1,500	....
Shawano............	....	17,668	298,872	136,794
Sheboygan	....	72,882	596,001	6,508,118
Taylor..	....	5,325	55,671	1,250
Trempealeau	....	31,657	1,808,400	2,694
Vernon ....:...	1,070,444	28,692	556,815	41,840
Vilas................	....	....	....	....
Walworth.............	12,800	70,425	2,540,843	2,468,700
Washburn............	....	1,911	11,480	....
Washington...........	....	39.699	917,026	808,950
Waukesha	78,400	59.140	1,390,205	48,429
Waupaca	....	22,476	565,828	329,486
Waushara	8	22,865	624,460	1,427,072
Winnebago...........,.	....	49,198	998,344	1,462,288
Wood	....	10,409	149,165	55,824
Total............	23,725,201	2,076,446	48,104,565	45,588,490

"I."—Statement of Principal Farm Products.

APPENDIX. I.—*Statement of principal farm products growing in the several counties at time of making the annual assessment for 18ด4, as ascertained and compiled pursuant to provisions of Section 1010, R. S.*

COUNTIES.	NUMBER OF ACRES.							
	Wheat.	Corn.	Oats.	Barley.	Rye.	Potatoes.	Root Crops.	Cranberries.
Adams ...	1,984	18,199	9,775	120	12,183	6.207	14	17
Ashland..	375	247	1,582	141	267	4,819	2,614	24
Barron ...	3,232	2,923	16,955	423	2,446	3,854	146	....
Bayfield..	20	68	48	6	......	3,758	154	....
Brown ...	18,056	2,038	30,572	2,331	5,591	3,968	311	....
Buffalo ...	27,114	20,328	36,479	4,989	2,815	1,445	3	....
Burnett ..	1,103	752	.1,704	26	778	2,860	65	7
Calumet..	11,245	4,827	20,595	21,528	1,240	909	41	.....
Chippewa	3,461	6,868	30,373	1,249	4,374	2,628	76	16
Clark	2,523	3,122	12,327	360	3,263	1,998	88	....
Columbia	9,990	49,055	60,771	14,744	9,028	6,449	58	6
Crawford.	7,809	36,220	29,206	656	2,468	1,284	8	....
Dane.....	14,287	85,538	102,074	14,264	2,603	3,672	59	......
Dodge....	18,452	27,274	42,865	71,639	8,348	2,635	121	10
Door......	6,487	977	10,002	950	3,024	1,886	214	9
Douglas..	2	38	20	....	......	575	89	....
Dunn	6,770	31,436	36,680	1,782	8,544	5,159	65	......
Eau Claire	6,218	9,856	23,197	2,499	6,092	6,314	14	......
Florence .	....	......	218	6	....	254	35	......
F. du Lac.	14,705	24,505	52,846	53,780	760	4,019	108	.....
Forest....	18	5	217	9	1	117	27	......
Grant	8,957	46,497	52,585	463	3,748	2,056	9	1
Green....	1,686	45,946	41,802	449	2,930	1,446	20	......
Gr'n Lake	9,056	16,548	26,122	6,191	4.087	1,708	22	19
Iowa......	4,001	67,079	52,538	387	3,536	1,608	11	......
Iron......	3	84	42	10	....	201	84	......
Jac son ..	7,261	9,677	26,285	424	4,014	867	88	.....
Jefferson .	10,595	28,998	29,855	12,845	7,180	1,987	68	17
June u ..	8,152	10,717	19,192	250	5,665	3,688	82	1,683
Kenosha .	724	14,175	17,890	1,665	392	918	7	......
K'waunee	12,198	416	18.501	3,492	4.644	1.249	68	......
La Crosse.	10,534	23,331	26,040	5,386	8,871	3,002	59	......
LaFayette	758	51,560	58,924	248	1,663	1,735	1	......
Langlade.	132	157	1,792	160	319	341	180	......
Lincoln ..	187	23	2,805	80	434	613	116	......
Manit'woc	17,087	2,051	36,543	19,674	9,161	2,419	67	......
Marathon.	4,787	1,460	22,058	1,848	4,205	5,832	238	......
Marinette.	698	561	4,185	172	384	1,147	78	400
Marquette	2,884	18,095	9.308	......	14,347	4,107	16	133
Milwa'kee	9,797	9,252	87,467	7,806	5,375	17,690	3,483	....
Monroe...	11,870	11,854	23.298	2,026	2,467	2,340	67	173
Oconto...	8,224	1,677	10,100	225	1,493	1,725	144	1
Oneida ...	....	5	115	....	17	146	90	...
Out'gamie	15,540	15,322	32,743	5,988	2,145	2,790	114	....

"I."—Statement of Principal Farm Products.

APPENDIX I.—*Statement of the principal farm products growing in the several counties in 1894.*—Continued.

COUNTIES.	NUMBER OF ACRES.							
	Wheat.	Corn.	Oats.	Barley.	Rye.	Pota-toes.	Root Crops.	Cran-ber-ries.
Ozaukee..	8,954	8,058	13,269	17,415	3,424	1,587	33	......
Pepin	3,789	7,027	7,349	4,469	2,034	487	23	......
Pierce ...	22,843	14,997	24,344	18,406	8,972	1,980	105	1
Polk.....	2,271	4,651	16,766	1,014	4,087	2,856	215	15
Portage..	1,484	10,089	24,936	138	12,298	21,816	47	250
Price	13	11	816	4	29	350	92	......
Racine....	1,861	14,354	23,161	2,863	1,486	2,312	42	......
Richland.	11,347	25,845	21,404	188	1,740	948	6	......
Rock.....	2,499	68,771	54,404	15,458	6,306	2,930	38	......
St. Croix..	17,313	13,408	79,465	4,225	9,821	3,546	52	......
Sauk.....	19,904	34,276	42,296	370	7,976	4,321	29	......
Sawyer...	......	...	300	......	......	200	105	......
Shawano..	10,799	8,696	16,492	1,410	3,606	2,057	179	1
Sheboyg'n	11,213	13,164	27,856	28,396	6,093	2,676	204	......
Taylor....	12	6	756	35	182	842	44	1
Tremp'le'u	11,002	18,402	51,069	1,555	4,759	1,765	25	... ...
Vernon...	15,003	25,841	42,755	6,257	1,394	2,731	21	......
Vilas......	......	......	......	......	......	......	... ...	......
Walworth	8,125	40,886	35,793	16,618	1,226	1,937	19	......
Washburn	19	169	547	......	20	158	22	... ...
Wash'gt'n	12,609	12,121	22,174	33,583	4,962	2,266	129	......
Waukesha	6,060	19,948	33,044	20,594	3,992	3,790	98	205
Waupaca.	10,620	11,324	27,472	952	7,388	17,777	6	62
Wausbara	2,427	17,603	19,367	52	11,380	16,902	9	632
Win'bago.	8,975	19,637	34,815	6,697	1,873	3,001	66	410
Wood.....	993	2,486	11,361	1,780	3,195	1,578	88	2,517
Total...	464,512	1,076,426	1,744,200	443,049	259,043	223,973	11,059	6,110

"I·"—Statement of Principal Farm Products.

APPENDIX I.—*Statement of the principal farm products growing in the several counties in 1894—Continued.*

COUNTIES.	NUMBER OF ACRES.			MILCH COWS.	
	Tobacco.	Cultivat'd grasses.	Growing timber.	Number	Value.
Adams...	4	7,565	18,622	3,132	$49,186 00
Ashland..........	3	932	1,256	454	6,568 00
Barron............	....	21,740	24,198	4,652	61,605 00
Bayfield..........		671	....	406	4,830 00
Brown............	.. -	31,312	14,449	8,806	126,724 00
Buffalo...........	....	20,756	48,083	9,483	114,411 00
Burnett..	....	1,667	....	1,648	16,658 00
Calumet..........	....	26,959	22,432	12,130	176,434 00
Chippewa	....	27,648	3,596	4,777	.62,308 00
Clark.............	1	25,350	66,041	6,936	69,987 00
Columbia	890	47,363	56,630	14.065	282,258 00
Crawford........	297	19,546	85,574	6.481	95.894 79
Dane.............	8,729	98,284	94,286	36,280	518.722 00
Dodge............	8	39,534	32,297	31,180	456.848 00
Door.............	3	21,186	11,865	6,292	75,281 00
Douglas..........	....	350	....	282	5.085 00
Dunn.............	....	27.661	55,298	8,762	82,750 00
Eau Claire.......	....	20,002	11,095	5,114	50,718 00
Florence..	....	987	143,480	168	2,342 00
Fond du Lac	....	51,144	29,349	22,969	336.771 00
Forest...........	....	242	1,908	92	1,868 00
Grant....	18	50,178	66,434	17,839	185,286 00
Green	184	64,894	35,622	27.325	482.162 00
Green Lake	....	15,496	19,268	6,820	103 2,8 00
Iowa.............	....	46,569	61,436	17,837	241,551 00
Iron..............	....	1,080	8,210	217	6,*90 00
Jackson..........	5	16,599	10,856	5,689	60,821 00
Jefferson.........	385	26,975	21,190	27,031	395.775 00
Juneau...........	17	14,636	45,708	5,897	82.885 00
Kenosha..........	....	26,597	11,784	12,319	284.058 00
Kewaunee	....	22,310	13,512	10.866	100,891 00
La Crosse........	....	25,981	36,481	9.791	201.886 00
La Fayette......	26	53,187	24,542	16,910	232,671 00
Langlade........	....	3,083	7,839	933	12,922 00
Lincoln	....	5,094	....	1,105	13,143 00
Manitowoc.......	.. -	49,468	33,878	20,022	253,806 00
Marathon	1	33,750	254,059	8,718	72,323 00
Marinette	....	7,311	240,458	2,780	29,345 00
Marquette.......	20	5,680	41,180	3,797	45,6,6 00
Milwaukee	....	36,217	11,180	9,879	149.811 00
Monroe..........	22	23,171	28,884	7,608	86,818 00
Oconto	....	12,268	53,237	3,474	36,256 00
Oneida........ ..	....	234	....	134	4,020 00
Outagamie...	....	31,726	26,157	14,961	168,058 00
Ozaukee	....	25,901	14,487	10,859	147 096 00
Pepin............	....	4,884	11,271	2,269	27,539 00
Pierce...........	7	21,045	36,237	7,886	83,115 00

"I."—Statement of Principal Farm Products.

APPENDIX I.— *Statement of the principal farm products growing in the several counties in 1894—Continued.*

COUNTIES.	NUMBER OF ACRES.			MILCH COWS.	
	Tobacco.	Cultivat'd grasses.	Growing timber.	Number	Value.
Polk..............	....	13,670	43,019	6,476	$56,786 50
Portage	....	17,517	43,669	5,166	78,491 00
Price........	....	2,653	4,712	447	7,536 00
Racine.	6	31,206	11,535	11.308	190,423 00
Richland.........	....	39,088	77,600	16.959	121,925 00
Rock	5,851	60,147	32,435	19,904	375,319 00
St. Croix........	....	35,018	11,389	8,881	114,955 04
Sauk	... .	33,573	57,335	14,178	245 422 00
Sawyer	....	1,520	....	78	1,950 00
Shawano........	....	17,664	21,463	6,743	75,033 00
Sheboygan	....	56,626	38,559	23,276	362,825 00
Taylor.	....	3,845	....	971	10,720 00
Trempealeau	....	33,002	44,359	12,918	176,700 00
Vernon	852	40,079	78,854	8,474	153,367 00
Vilas....	....	....	....	....	....
Walworth.......	29	46,699	34,354	24,802	561 902 00
Washburn	....	1,440	....	313	3,338 00
Washington......	....	25,850	39,981	14,331	221,772 00
Waukesha	2	38,403	32,625	16,827	263.625 25
Waupaca	....	23,484	39,696	10,409	118,131 00
Waushara.......	....	18,300	49,332	7,864	114,330 00
Winnebago	....	32,995	15,430	14,870	249.698 00
Wood............	....	10,933	9,387	3,904	35,918 00
Total..	17,360	1,696,740	2,509,747	663,099	$9,573,352 58

"I."—*Statement of Principal Farm Products.*

APPENDIX I.—*Statement of principal farm products growing in 1894, as ascertained and compiled pursuant to provisions of section 1010, R. S.*—Continued

COUNTIES.	APPLE ORCHARDS.		NUMBER OF ACRES.						
	No. of acres.	No. of bearing trees.	Straw-berries.	Rasp-berries.	Black-berries.	Cur-rants.	Grapes.	Flax.	Hops.
Adams....	51	1,532	18½	4¾	1¾	1½	2	......	105½
Ashland...	3	144	4½	10	3	6	......	......	......
Barron....	13	704	4	......	......	½	......	......	4
Bayfield...	......	......	25	......	......	3¼	......	......	......
Brown.....	731	12,474	12	2	2	2	......	......	......
Buffalo....	15	1,086	......	......	......	......	......	......	......
Burnett....	13	179	......	......	......	......	......	......	......
Calumet....	539	20,288	1	1	1	......	......	......	......
Chippewa..	9	337	17	5	5	......	......	......	......
Clark.....	64	2,179	1	......	......	......	......	......	......
Columbia...	908	27,916	46¼	32¼	19¾	6¾	5¼	97	97
Crawford..	769	19,134	14	9	7	4	6	37	......
Dane.......	2,032	51,259	50¾	28½	7	2¾	27½	40	......
Dodge.....	1,141	36,219	14⅞	8	3½	½	1¾	35¼	2
Door.......	535	15,077	2	......	......	......	¼	......	......
Douglas....	......	......	16	......	......	......	......	......	......
Dunn.......	58	2,706	47	4	5	......	......	......	......
Eau Claire..	......	1,934	160⅛	20⅞	20	⅛	......	3	......
Florence....	6	115	......	......	......	......	......	......	......
Fond du Lac	1,624	39,216	45	51⅛	128½	42¾	14	35	......
Forest......	......	15	½	25	25	86	......	......	......
Grant......	811	24,232	22¾	18	20	......	449¾	3	......
Green......	966	30,146	9	9½	3¾	½	8⅝	......	......
Gr'n Lake..	416	9,762	13¼	3½	8¼	1¾	2¼	302	8
Iowa......	508	14,894	2	4	2	2	22	58	......
Iron........	......	2	2	......	......	......	......	......	......
Jackson....	86	2,022	14½	9	3½	40	¼	4	11
Jefferson...	3,735	45,572	25	9⅛	¾	2½	48⅛	......	33¼
Juneau.....	60	6,634	13¼	14⅝	14¾	1	12	......	231¼
Kenosha,...	1,624	41,295	48½	5⅝	⅛	......	2	350	......
Kewaunee..	36,830	18,549	1	......	......	......	......	......	......
La Crosse..	98	5,873	100	18	31	9	27	11	32
La Fayette..	529	15,386	3	3	2¼	½	3	110	⅛
Langlade...	23	556	3	½	1	⅛	......	......	......
Lincoln.....	16	626	1	......	......	......	......	......	......
Manitowoc.	1,588	41,418	5	2	½	......	......	......	......
Marathon...	16	4,687	7	......	......	......	......	2	......
Marinette...	206	5,950	16	1½	1	2	......	......	......
Marquette..	478	4,771	24¼	5¼	2	......	2¾	1	2
Milwaukee..	2,916	65,866	559¾	280½	......	172½	350	71½	4
Monroe.....	190	8,280	134	88½	104	5⅝	½	65	14
Oconto.....	447	9,558	1½	½	¼	......	......	......	......
Oneida.....	......	12	1	......	......	......	......	......	......
Outagamie.	548	16,534	17	7	4	1	......	1	......
Ozaukee....	1,008	33,806	......	......	......	......	......	1	......

"I."—*Statement of Principal Farm Products.*

APPENDIX I.—*Statement of principal farm products growing in 1894, as ascertained and compiled pursuant to provisions of section* 1010, *R. S.*— Continued.

COUNTIES.	APPLE ORCHARDS.		NUMBER OF ACRES.						
	No. of acres.	No. of bearing trees.	Straw-berries.	Rasp-berries.	Black-berries.	Cur-rants.	Grapes.	Flax.	Hops.
Pepin	......	2,169	8	1¼	⅜	......	2	......	......
Pierce	135	3,445	30	15	2	......	......	276	......
Polk	....	654	.. ..	......	.....	......	......	......	......
Portage	61	1,723	8½	12	2½	½	2½	......	333
Price	......	41	5	......	......	......	......	......	.....
Racine	1,806	57,437	113	8¼	1⅜	2	1⅜	990	......
Richland ...	817	16,915	10¼	18⅜	4½	¾	11¾	......	6
Rock	3,847	53,838	48½	39¼	10½	5⅞	5½	......	......
St. Croix...	11	1,677	69½	18	8⅛	.....	.. ..	887	......
Sauk	679	25,842	103	135	45	2	32	48	81
Sawyer	....	. ...	..	.....	......	......	......	......	......
Shawano ...	176	7,718	50	1	1	......	.....	2	.. ...
Sheboygan .	2,511	108,693	10	14	8	1	2	......	......
Taylor	2	91	......	......	.....	......	......	......	......
Trempeale'u	11	1,795	25⅜	9⅝	22¼	2	2⅜	16¾	......
Vernon	612	17,992	10⅛	17⅝	10	⅜	3½	60	......
Vilas	......	... ...	......	.....	......	.....	. ...	......	......
Walworth ..	1,910	43,007	22⅛	15¾	¼	1⅛	9	63	......
Washburn ..	.....	31	.....	......	......	.....	......	......	......
Washington	2,158	56,733	2⅛	......	......	½	....	......	......
Waukesha ..	6,525	64,820	47	11¾	5½	10	10¼	3	4
Waupaca ...	350	13,743	23	15	14	......	¼	.....	3
Waushara ..	203	6,545	10½	2	5¾	.....	......	.....	......
Winnebago.	804	34,507	87	113	58	6	20	10	......
Wood	38	1,613	¼	¼	..	. ..	......	......	......
Total.....	34,266	1,159,974	2,182	1,079½	626¾	427	1,087¾	3,527½	972⅛

"J."—Reports of Industrial and Agricultural Societies.

APPENDIX J.—*Synopsis of annual reports of industrial*

NAME OF SOCIETY.	RECEIPTS.		
	From State.	Member- ship.	Admission Fee.
Adams County Agrl. Society........ ...	$200 00	$11 00	$345 98
Arcadia Agrl and Driving Association	385 50	....	625 30
Barron County Agrl. Society..	276 48	....	327 85
Boscobel Agrl. and Driving Park Asso ciation	384 90	....	1,433 30
Brown County Fair and Park Associa tion	843 54	....	2,684 80
Buffalo County Agrl. Society..........	470 94	810 00	195 82
Burnett County Agrl. Society.	200 00	....	41 25
Blake's Prairie County Agrl. Society ..	392 00	....	502 95
Calumet County Agrl. Society	330 00	....	936 80
Clark County Agrl. Society...........	391 06	....	726 00
Columbia County Agrl. Society.......	339 95	10 00	973 00
Crawford County Agrl. Society......	200 00	135 00	203 15
Cumberland Agrl. and Driving Park Association... ....;	330 60	....	369 45
Dodge County Fair Association........	884 50	30 00	2,422 68
Dunn County Agrl. Society.	461 08	490 00	1,089 10
Eastern Monroe County Agrl. Society.	325 18	....	385 70
Grant County Agrl. Society...........	513 30	10 00	1,365 45
Green County Agrl. Society...........	787 90	....	1,819 55
Iowa County Agrl. Society	651 30	862 00	880 50
Industrial Assn of Manitowoc County.	733 10	....	1,667 15
Jackson County Agrl. Society...... ..	563 96	... .	905 15
Jefferson County and Rock River Val ley Agrl. Society.	900 96	10 00	2,418 10
Juneau County Agrl. Society.........	367 76	....	517 20
Kewaunee County Agrl. Society.......	200 00	112 50	259 25
La Crosse County Agrl. Society... ...	496 20	451 00	615 40
La Crosse Inter-State Fair Association.	1,200 00	80 00	6,415 85
La Fayette County Agrl. Society......	625 40	....	1,011 05
Langlade County Agrl. Society........	339 80	129 00	267 75
Little Baraboo Valley Agrl. Fair So- ciety	341 04	....	486 85
Lodi Union Agrl. Society......	358 30	....	722 50
The Lake Superior Agrl , Industrial and Fine Art Society......	181 40	....	465 67
Marathon County Agrl Society........	200 00	35 00	125 75
Marquette County Agrl. Society.......	352 20	....	402 75
Monroe County Agrl. Society	261 93	....	109 25
Outagamie County Agrl. Society......	351 19	....	750 00
Ozaukee County Agrl. Society........	444 82	179 00	597 65
Pepin County Agrl. Society	328 16	200 00	837 00
Pierce County Central Fair............	265 90	....	594 75
Portage County Agrl. Society.........	200 00	....	227 90
Price County Agrl. Society............	200 60	36 00	126 00
Richland County Agrl. Society........	590 16	10 00	1,333 90

"J."—Reports of Industrial and Agricultural Societies.

and county agricultural societies for the year 1892.

RECEIPTS.				Cash on hand at last report.	Total.
Entries.	Subscription	Other Sources.	Total Receipts.		
$168 51	.. ..	$244 83	$970 32	$2 05	$972 37
306 92	....	427 90	1,745 62	22 .08	1,767 65
275 00	$81 00	98 62	1,008 95	....	1,008 95
602 00	....	499 97	2,920 17	53 62	2,973 79
1,696 00	....	1,768 72	6,983 06	402 91	7,385 97
451 00	11 39	302 78	2,241 98	197 58	2,439 46
7 00	181 00	9 00	438 25	301 96	740 21
329 40	328 26	189 50	1,694 11	2 85	1,694 96
304 50	21 00	126 47	1,718 27	414 79	2.133 06
890 41	221 10	1,028 50	2,757 07	....	2,757 07
272 00	....	1,165 65	2,765 60	2 13	2,767 73
141 65	....	78 55	758 35	45 86	803 71
262 50	....	212 79	1,175 34	....	1,175 34
660 00	466 00	1,595 00	6,058 18	100 02	6,158 20
242 00	49 00	513 80	2,844 98	....	2,844 98
80 60	....	379 87	1,171 35	.. ..	1,171 35
501 60	....	484 25	2,874 60	140 56	3,015 16
446 00	....	1,217 87	4,221 32	168 25	4,384 57
946 95	60 00	460 00	3,360 75	.....	8,360 75
566 50	....	1,993 82	4,960 57	24 90	4,985 47
537 20	....	287 00	2,293 81	744 84	3,038 15
494 25	215 00	1,266 94	5,805 25	3 82	5,809 07
202 50	....	97 50	1,184 96	....	1,184 96
13 45	... .	888 51	978 71	179 16	1,152 87
198 70	.. ....	178 00	1,934 80	....	1,934 80
1,875 00	319 40	8,544 84	13,485 09	21 64	13,456 73
828 80	61 00	2,346 49	4,372 74	....	4,372 74
130 00	41 45	189 00	1,097 00	17 45	1,114 45
275 00	....	80 75	1,188 14	132 75	1 315 89
207 50	....	403 88	1,692 18	5 22	1;697 40
....	....	275 92	922 99	88 13	1,011 12
21 00	....	1,913 46	2,295 21	58 23	2,353 44
185 00	3 50	54 00	947 45	2 48	949 93
75 00	....	42 25	488 43	....	488 43
114 17	....	679 40	1,894 76	4 45	1,899 21
246 50	210 25	327 60	2,005 32	....	2,005 32
260 20	2 50	474 00	2,101 76	....	2.101 76
721 00	....	557 75	2,188 90	479 86	2,618 76
19 00	30 00	176 61	658 51	12 53	666 04
10 00	....	200 00	572 00	143 18	715 18
145 00	....	971 60	3,055 66	54 53	3,110 19

"J. "—Reports of Industrial and Agricultural Societies.

APPENDIX J.—*Synopsis of annual reports of industrial*

NAME OF SOCIETY.	RECEIPTS.		
	From State.	Member-ship.	Admission Fee.
Rock County Agrl. Society	$732 90	... .	$938 85
St. Croix County Agrl. Society........	428 60	$358 50	847 70
Sauk County Agrl. Society............	675 40	80 00	1,299 75
Seymour Fair and Driving Park Association...	353 45	....	584 60
Sheboygan Exposition and Driving Park Association........	479 50	... .	1,170 58
South Western Wis. Industrial Association . ...,......	803 10	287 00	1,887 65
Taylor County Agrl Society...	201 00	....	158 50
Trempealeau County Agrl. Society ..	444 60	525 00	849 01
Trempealeau County Ind'l., Agrl. and Driving Park Association.	415 00	....	635 55
Vernon County Agrl. Society.........	626 46	4 00	1,489 67
Walworth County Agrl. Society.......	1,200 00	976 00	2,395 95
Waushara County Agrl. Society......	350 60	....	928 25
Washington County Agrl. Society....	894 90	..••......	636 80
Waukesha County Agrl. Society......	787 08	....	1,990 25
Waupaca County Agrl. Society.......	362 00	....	820 70
Total............................	$26,084 50	$5,231 00	$54,327 76

"J."—Reports of Industrial and Agricultural Societies.

and county agricultural societies for the year 1893—Continued.

	RECEIPTS.			Cash on hand at last report.	Total.
Entries.	Subscription	Other Sources.	Total Receipts.		
$101 00	....	$2,612 33	$4,385 08	$2 03	$4,387 11
192 50	....	616 90	1,954 20	78 95	2,033 15
174 00	$531 00	2,036 00	4,746 15	6 65	4,752 80
239 88	....	300 93	1,478 86	14 78	1,493 64
552 75	... .	996 91	3,199 69	214 34	3,414 03
749 66	130 00	661 95	4,469 36	1,035 54	5,504 90
178 75	....	349 75	888 00	5 11	893 11
....	292 50	350 73	2,461 84	498 30	2,960 14
350 17	180 00	1,082 20	2,662 92	8 19	2,671 11
424 03	....	543 03	3,087 19	12 50	3,099 69
906 50	....	2,808 55	8,287 00	756 59	9,043 59
....	100 00	42 81	1,421 66	296 63	1,718 29
250 00	....	875 75	2,157 45	808 11	2,965 56
949 50	....	1,059 04	4,785 87	....	4,785 87
214 23	....	110 60	1,507 53	....	1,507 53
$19,932 78	$3,485 35	$41,645 87	$150,707 26	$7,559 95	$158,267 21

"J."—Reports of Industrial and Agricultural Societies.

APPENDIX J.—*Synopsis of annual reports of industrial*

NAME OF SOCIETY.	DISBURSEMENTS.		
	Premiums	Trials of speed.	Fair expenses.
Adams County Agrl Society..........	$494 08	$250 00	$107 72
Arcadia Agrl. and Driving Association..	479 80	550 00	266 93
Barron County Agrl. Society	321 50	500 00	74 20
Boscobel Agrl and Driving Park Ass'n.	627 00	953 69	322 08
Brown County Fair and ark Ass'n....	1,193 95	2,927 50	1,630 22
Buffalo County Agrl Society..........	762 84	775 00	626 86
Burnett County Agrl. Society	119 90	....	37 00
Blake's Prairie County Agrl Society....	480 00	585 00	171 81
Calumet County Agrl. Society..........	366 00	1,002 50	248 35
Clark County Agrl Society............	627 45	779 22	522 48
Columbia County Agrl. Society.........	1,360 79	500 00	582 53
Crawford County Agrl. Society........	469 90	....	158 33
Cumberland Agrl. and Driving Park Ass'n....	332 00	455 00	63 55
Dodge County Fair Ass'n............ ...	2,074 90	1 325 00	1,804 11
Dunn County Agrl. Society...........	828 00	537 50	698 11
Eastern Monroe County Agrl. Society..	282 95	518 00	114 01
Grant County Agrl. Society..........	856 81	910 00	232 15
Green County Agrl. Society...........	1,271 00	871 17	1,015 11
Iowa County Agrl. Society	1,461 20	780 00	260 00
Industrial Association of Manitowoc Co.	1,412 50	1,215 00	756 50
Jackson County Agrl Society......	950 05	887 50	546 53
Jefferson County and Rock River Valley Agrl. Society....	1,362 50	1,154 00	88 97
Juneau County Agrl. Society	370 50	500 00	89 00
Kewaunee County Agrl. Society	328 56	106 00	152 96
La Crosse County Agrl. Society........	875 00	480 00	461 42
La Crosse Inter State Fair Ass'n..... .	3,032 75	4,420 00	2,133 12
La Fayette County Agrl. Society	1,230 50	585 00	328 46
Langlade County Agrl Society.......	414 50	485 00	171 49
Little Baraboo Valley Agrl. Fair Society.	809 40	621 50	219 42
Lodi Union Agrl Society	424 55	475 00	246 97
The Lake Superior Agrl., Industrial and Fine Art Society	404 95	....	533 22
Marathon County Agrl. Society.... ...	585 50	85 00	189 02
Marquette County Agrl Society	262 75	500 00	81 65
Monroe County Agrl Society	75 50	200 00	58 12
Outagamie County Agrl. Society.......	959 05	....	693 15
Ozaukee County Agri Society	978 25	490 00	558 52
Pepin County Agrl. Society	356 00	508 40	881 00
Pierce County Central Fair	670 10	525 00	464 39
Portage County Agrl Society	241 00	68 25	138 95
Price County Agrl Society	198 75	160 00	101 20
Richland County Agrl. Society..........	1,033 00	880 50	704 80
Rock County Agrl Society	1,269 75	545 00	1,048 00
St. Croix County Agrl. Society.........	542 50	475 00	269 88
Sauk County Agrl. Society.............	1,148 80	500 00	511 64

"J."—*Reports of Industrial and Agricultural Societies.*

and county agricultural societies for the year 1893.

	DISBURSEMENTS.			Cash on hand.	Total.	Indebtedness.
Secretary's office.	Improvements.	Other purposes.	Total disbursements			
$25 00	$16 68	$78 53	$967 01	$5 36	$972 37	.... ..
25 00	....	424 00	1,745 73	21 92	1,767 65	....
18 60	8 31	55 36	977 97	30 98	1,008 95	....
85 49	617 09	887 95	2,993 30	... .	2,993 30	$19 51
....	176 07	608 23	6,535 97	850 00	7,385 97	....
28 00	444 94	111 12	2,748 26	....	2,748 26	308 80
85 50	....	172 79	865 19	375 02	740 21	....
87 55	280 00	91 10	1,694 96	....	1,694 96	....
50 00	26 61	426 75	2,115 21	17 85	2,133 06	....
15 70	218 07	508 85	2,671 77	85 28	2,757 07	....
115 50	....	198 75	2,752 57	15 16	2,767 73	....
59 08	54 05	42 67	784 03	19 68	803 71	....
15 00	98 97	210 82	1,175 34	....	1,175 34	....
100 00	191 69	596 61	6,092 31	65 89	6,158 20	....
75 00	423 39	277 28	2,889 28	5 70	2,844 98	....
60 00	9 70	186 69	1,171 35	....	1,171 35	....
150 65	524 59	20 00	2,694 20	320 96	3,015 16	....
51 97	366 50	800 00	4,375 75	8 82	4,384 57	....
148 60	300 00	410 95	3,360 75	....	3,360 75	....
176 88	201 47	1,222 82	4,985 47	....	4,985 47	....
50 00	75 00	579 07	3,038 15	....	3,038 15	579 07
206 10	1,069 02	1,433 48	5,309 07	....	5,309 07	....
25 00	....	200 46	1,184 96	....	1,184 96	....
12 00	50 00	346 70	991 22	161 65	1,152 87	....
100 45	118 09	288 49	2,823 45	....	2,323 45	889 15
662 93	442 96	2,703 88	13,395 64	61 09	13,456 73	....
91 15	59 65	2,065 99	4,360 75	11 99	4,372 74	....
30 40	....	50 00	1,101 39	13 06	1,114 45	....
....	....	....	1,150 32	165 57	1,315 89	....
75 00	231 68	243 77	1,696 97	43	1,697 40	....
....	....	....	938 17	72 95	1,011 12	....
... .	....	1,507 32	2,316 84	36 60	2,353 44	....
10 00	83 20	57 00	944 60	5 33	949 93	. ....
....	....	42 25	375 87	112 56	488 43	....
65 00	50 00	131 26	1,898 46	75	1,899 21	....
128 20	161 72	644 31	2,961 00	....	2,961 00	....
15 90	556 91	281 93	2,100 14	1 62	2,101 76	....
....	400 36	546 00	2,605 85	12 91	2,618 76	....
50 00	153 00	14 84	666 04	....	666 04	....
25 00	192 00	.... ..	676 95	88 23	715 18	....
87 00	342 73	72 66	3,110 19	....	3,110 19	....
36 51	500 00	847 67	4,246 93	140 18	4,387 11	....
23 15	166 20	....	1,476 23	556 92	2,033 15	....
56 25	1,688 16	813 81	4,668 66	84 14	4,752 80	....

"J."—Reports of Industrial and Agricultural Societies.

APPENDIX J.—*Synopsis of annual reports of industrial*

NAME OF SOCIETY.	DISBURSEMENTS.		
	Premiums	Trials of speed.	Fair expenses.
Seymour Fair and Driving Park Ass'n...	$410 88	$508 75	$282 10
Sheboygan Exposition and Driving Park Ass'n	698 75	1,241 25	170 20
Southwestern Wis. Industrial Ass'n.....	1,592 50	1,250 00	962 73
Taylor County Agrl. Society	163 25	446 00	61 00
Trempealeau County Agrl. Society .. .	821 50	1,025 00	334 39
Trempealeau County Industrial, Agrl. and Driving Park Ass'n	568 75	500 00	438 77
Vernon County Agrl. Society..........	842 25	690 25	579 78
Walworth County Agrl. Society	8,052 65	2,020 00	2,410 48
Waushara County Agrl. Society.	485 50	640 00	37 00
Washington County Agrl. Society	532 75	583 00	313 75
Waukesha County Agrl. Society	1,695 50	1,409 00	712 60
Waupaca County Agrl. Society.........	₂57 00	498 50	181 43
Total..	$44,958 06	$40,797 48	$26,336 41

"J."—Reports of Industrial and Agricultural Societies.

and county agricultural societies for the year 1898—Continued.

| | DISBURSEMENTS. | | | | | |
Secretary's office.	Improvements.	Other purposes.	Total disbursements	Cash on hand.	Total.	Indebtedness.
$50 00	$259 67	$115 49	$1,626 89	....	$1,626 89	$133 25
104 07	29 16	691 10	2,934 58	$479 50	3 414 08	....
199 00	161 83	1,338 84	5,504 90	....	5,504 90	....
7 50	25 00	173 00	875 75	17 86	893 11	....
40 00	....	739 25	2,960 14	....	2,960 14	. .....
....	925 46	243 01	2,670 99	12	2,671 11	....
75 00	257 44	662 89	3,107 56	....	3,107 56	7 87
848 00	358 30	390 88	8,580 26	463 88	9,043 59	.. ..
55 00	423 85	126 94	1,718 29	....	1,718 29	....
52 50	813 28	314 23	2,609 50	356 06	2.965 56	....
376 16	213 57	379 04	4,785 87	.... .	4,785 87	....
136 87	94 80	88 29	1,351 89	155 64	1,507 53	....
$4,467 66	$13,801 17	$24,950 06	$155,310 84	$4,770 63	$160,081 47	$1,437 65

18—Sec'y.

"K."—Abstract of Marriages, Births and Deaths.

APPENDIX K.—*Abstract of marriages, births and deaths reported, recorded and indexed in the department of state for the years ending December 31, 1892, and December 31, 1893.*

COUNTIES.	1892.			1893.		
	Marriages.	Births.	Deaths.	Marriages.	Births.	Deaths.
Adams	39	58	37	56	94	35
Ashland	344	38	2	226	39	6
Barron...............	116	265	60	189	207	58
Bayfield...............	87	137	5	78	147	11
Brown	366	1,085	282	321	943	138
Buffalo	143	216	73	161	257	69
Burnett	34	77	23	28	65	30
Calumet	114	227	41	88	208	22
Chippewa...	184	222	76	287	357	80
Clark	156	95	14	146	117	21
Columbia............	236	223	108	258	282	114
Crawford............	152	276	130	184	215	81
Dane...............	433	899	171	483	833	142
Dodge...............	324	521	184	337	528	161
Door	80	138	37	95	153	25
Douglas	479	464	89	402	391	117
Dunn	210	266	112	169	300	76
Eau Claire............	295	507	42	331	449	23
Florence	67	98	6	53	75	20
Fond du Lac........	868	878	278	359	603	295
Forest	5	2	1	5	3	1
Grant	392	725	240	390	528	137
Green............	247	184	99	258	193	57
Green Lake..........	110	18	17	123	14	19
Iowa....	135	116	45	120	132	61
Iron	....	....	....	49	79	91
Jackson............	120	204	98	128	248	75
Jefferson............	282	890	160	318	498	197
Juneau	193	144	65	117	264	74
Kenosha............	482	296	162	546	388	93
Kewaunee.......	137	208	71	126	294	50
La Crosse............	436	889	208	470	982	255
La Fayette	170	354	155	153	297	107
Langlade............	91	100	44	73	84	31
Lincoln	115	288	26	133	327	25
Manitowoc............	325	1,055	432	244	728	328
Marathon	267	886	155	298	879	137
Marinette	206	421	286	342	539	294
Marquette............	64	59	41	97	59	24
Milwaukee............	3,011	7,971	5,472	3,085	8,551	5,156
Monroe............	185	93	38	172	62	37
Oconto..	115	159	163	136	192	112
Oneida..	79	100	14	89	99	250
Outagamie	299	662	188	318	1,157	191
Ozaukee	105	204	33	92	196	89
Pepin...............	73	71	30	85	56	12

"K."—Abstract of Marriages, Births and Deaths.

APPENDIX K.—*Abstract of marriages, births and deaths, reported, recorded and indexed in the department of state for the years ending December 31, 1892, and December 31, 1893.* —Continued.

COUNTIES.	1892.			1893.		
	Mar-riages.	Births.	Deaths.	Mar-riages.	Births.	Deaths.
Pierce................	203	7	4	180	24	2
Polk..................	109	107	61	117	103	39
Portage	443	309	88	286	240	49
Price.	62	113	18	68	178	31
Racine..............	596	1,114	536	498	1,117	464
Richland.............	197	347	185	162	397	176
Rock	588	477	173	576	542	262
St. Croix.............	528	328	102	477	273	88
Sauk........	257	340	150	243	374	142
Sawyer...............	23	61	17	24	49	5
Shawano.............	162	319	44	144	165	68
Sheboygan...........	434	1,290	458	383	1,180	401
Taylor...............	86	83	32	70	72	21
Trempealeau..	148	303	101	161	239	95
Vernon..............	181	209	46	184	128	60
Vilas...	....	....	....	16	7	2
Walworth............	318	315	175	284	341	160
Washburn..	34	67	18	26	79	19
Washington..........	159	359	134	170	397	126
Waukesha.......... .	318	447	206	280	460	175
Waupaca.	248	358	142	246	316	113
Waushara	107	30	10	125	59	18
Winnebago	513	1,289	863	464	1,214	1,091
Wood................	134	46	2	177	48	4
Total.....	17,664	29,539	13,558	17,514	30,504	12,968

STATE OF WISCONSIN.

REPORT

OF THE

COMMISSIONERS OF PUBLIC PRINTING.

DEPARTMENT OF STATE,
October 10, 1894.

To His Excellency, GEO. W. PECK,
Governor of the State of Wisconsin.

SIR:—In conformity to law we have the honor herewith to submit our second biennial report of the transactions in public printing, publishing, and the purchase of paper for the fiscal term from October 1st, 1892, to September 30th, 1894.

The respective amounts paid for publishing and advertising are as follows.

Publishing general laws in newspapers	$42,100 00
Publishing local laws in newspapers	478 80
Advertising sales of land	915 05
Publishing, advertising, etc	1,955 15
Publishing laws in state paper	1,461 00
Total	$46,910 00

COST OF PRINTING, BINDING, ETC.

The total cost of all printing for the legislature since the last report was $6,671.66,

The cost of printing the Blue Book was $5,594.72.

Report of the Commissioners of Public Printing.

The cost of all other printing required by the state in its several departments including reports, blanks, etc., was $47,623.67.

. The grand total being $59,890.05.

As the cost of printing for each department is given in detail in the Secretary of State's report it is unnecessary to repeat it here. A detailed statement of the cost of each job, together with a specimen of the same is filed in the Secretary of State's office and is open for inspection. For detailed statement of the cost of printing for the several departments see Secretary of State's report, pages, 61, 71, 146 and 154.

COST OF PAPER.

There has been paid for paper during the past two years the sum of $29,204.79. Of this sum $15,467.49 was for paper purchased under the contract of September 2nd, 1892.

STATE PRINTER.

During the past two years the Democrat Printing Company, of Madison, has been the State Printer; the contract having been taken at 63½ *per centum* of discount from the maximum rates established by law. The Democrat Printing Company will succeed itself as State Printer, having been awarded the contract for two years, commencing January 1st, 1895, at 61⅔ *per centum* discount from established rates.

Report of the Commissioners of Public Printing.

The following schedule shows the maximum and contract rates for 1893 and 1894:

	Maximum Rate.	Contract Price.
COMPOSITION PER 1,000 EMS.		
Plain..	$0.60	$.22
Figure work...	.90	.33
Rule and figure work................................	1.20	.44
PRESS WORK.		
Per token of 250 impressions	.60	.22
FOLDING.		
Per 100 sections of 16 pages	.10	.08667
STITCHING, TRIMMING AND COVERING PAMPHLETS.		
Per 100 copies	1.25	.45837
BINDING, INCLUDING STOCK, PER VOLUME.		
In paste-board, 16 mo. or 12 mo	.35	.12834
In cloth, 16 mo. or 12 mo	.45	.165
In full sheepskin, 16 mo. or 12 mo	.80	.29836
In full calfskin, 16 mo. or 12 mo	1.25	.45837
In Turkey Morocco, 16 mo. or 12 mo	1.50	.55
In half Turkey Morocco, 16 mo. or 12 mo	.75	.275
Flat cap or cap, half binding, sheep back	3.00	1.10
Flat cap or cap, Russia ends and bands	6.00	2.20
Medium or folio post, half binding, sheep back.....	5.00	1.8835
Medium or folio post, full sheep	9.00	3.30
Medium or folio post, Russia ends and bands	10.50	3.85
Medium or folio post, extra Russia ends and bands..	12.00	4.40
Medium or folio post, full Russia..................	18.00	6.60
BINDING BLANK BOOKS PER QUIRE, INCLUDING RULING AND STOCK FOR BINDING.		
Flat cap, half binding, sheep back	.70	.25669
Flat cap, full sheep	.90	.33
Flat cap, Russia ends and bands	1.00	3.667
Flat cap, extra Russia ends and bands	1.25	.45837
Folio post, half binding, sheep back..............	1.00	.3667
Folio post, Russia ends and bands	1.50	.55
Medium, half binding, sheep back	1.25	.45837
Medium, Russia ends and bands	1.75	.6417
Medium, extra Russia ends and bands	2.00	.7334
Medium, full Russia	3.00	1.10
Super-royal, Russia ends and bands	2.00	.7334
Super-royal, extra Russia ends and bands	2.25	.826
Super-royal, full Russia	3.50	1.28345
Paging, extra per volume..........................	1.00	.3667
Indexing, extra per quire.........................	.25	.091675
Each numbering	....	.50
Canvas cover......................................	....	1.50
RULING.		
Blanks, per quire.................................	.10	.08667

BIDS FOR PRINTING.

Pursuant to the notice of the letting of the contract for doing the Public Printing for the term of two years from the first day of January, 1895, advertised in accordance with law, the Commissioners of Public Printing met July 27th, 1894, at the office of the Secretary of State, and proceeded to publicly open and consider the bids submitted. Proposals were received as follows:

Taylor & Gleason, Madison, 48 *per centum* of discount from the maximum rates established by law.

Tracy, Gibbs & Co., Madison, 55 *per centum* of discount from the maximum rates.

M. J. Cantwell, Madison, 58½ *per centum* of discount from the maximum rates.

Democrat Printing Co., Madison, 61⅔ *per centum* of discount from the maximum rates.

King, Fowle & Co., Milwaukee, 70 *per centum* of discount from the maximum rates.

King, Fowle & Co., of Milwaukee, the lowest nominal bidder, having stipulated in its proposal that the printing should be done in Milwaukee, contrary to the law, and to the terms of the advertisement calling for bids, the Commissioners, after hearing argument by the firm's attorneys, and by counsel in opposition for the Democrat Printing Company, of Madison, the next lowest bidder, determined that the proposal of King, Fowle & Co. was irregular, and accordingly awarded the contract for doing the state printing from January 1st, 1895, to December 31st, 1896, to the Democrat Printing Company.

The *per centum* of discount from the maximum rates fixed by law under the new contract is 1⅔ per cent. less than under the previous printing contract, which was the lowest ever let under the present law. The contract, however, is a very favorable one for the state, though it will slightly increase the cost of printing for the ensuing two years.

PURCHASE OF PAPER.

There was but one general purchase of paper during the past two years. In addition to this two small purchases were made of paper not regularly carried in stock nor ordinarily needed by the state, and the quantity purchased was too small to warrant the expense of advertising.

The regular advertised purchase was February 23rd, 1894. For this purchase sealed bids were received by the Commissioners of Public Printing, as follows:

DESCRIPTION OF PAPER.	H. Niedecken Co., Milwaukee.	Standard Paper Co., Milwaukee.	C. B. Walworth, Eau Claire.	Chicago Paper Co., Chicago.	Bradner, Smith & Co., Chicago.
FIRST CLASS.	Per lb.	Per lb.	Per lb.	Per lb.	Per lb.
4,000 reams sized and calendered Book Paper, 25x38 inches, weighing 60 pounds per ream ...	$.0425	$.0449	$.0470	$.0443	$.0440
100 reams sized and calendered Book Paper, 21x32 inches, weighing 40 pounds per ream	.0425	.0449	.0470	.0443	.0440
SECOND CLASS.					
100 reams extra wove Folio Post, 17x22 inches, weighing 20 pounds per ream.....	.05	.0860	.0650	.08	.0650
150 reams extra wove Folio Post, 17x22 inches, weighing 24 pounds per ream...	.10	.1085	.09	.09	.0875
100 reams extra wove Folio Post, 17x22 inches, weighing 28 pounds per ream.	.10	.1015	.09	.09	.0875
350 reams extra wove Double Flat Cap, 17x28 inches, weighing 28 pounds per ream. .	.1080	.1064	.09	.09	.0995
200 reams extra wove Double Flat Cap, 17x28 inches, weighing 36 pounds per ream.	.0860	.0860	.09	.09	.0995
100 reams Granite Cover Paper, 20x25 inches, weighing 40 pounds per ream	.05	.0525	.0550	.0550	.0525
100 reams (either Crane's, Weston's or Parson's Record Medium, 18x23 inches, weighing 40 pounds per ream .	.17	.22	.1650	.1790	.19
10,000 sheets No. 29 Glazed Board Paper, 17x22 inches per 1,000 sheets	15.00	21.25	18.84	18.84	22.18

C. B. Walworth of Eau Claire, was the lowest nominal bidder on the second class papers, but his proposal was found to be insufficient and irregular as the accompanying

Report of the Commissioners of Public Printing.

bond contained but one surety, two being required by law. The contract for both classes of papers was accordingly awarded to H. Niedecken Co., of Milwaukee. The contract called for the delivery of the paper at the Capitol, free of all charges, on or before May 1, 1894.

The following exhibit shows the paper purchased, consumed and on hand for the past two years:

Description of Paper.	On Hand Sept. 30, 1892.		Received During Two Years.		Consumed During Two Years.		On Hand October 1, 1894.	
	Reams.	Quires.	Reams.	Quires.	Reams.	Quires.	Reams.	Quires.
Book paper, 60 lbs. per ream	918	.....	8,104	18	5,699	13	3,324	6
Book paper, 40 lbs. per ream	7	$19\frac{6}{24}$	181	19	112	15	77	$8\frac{6}{24}$
Tinted book paper, 40 lbs. per ream	.....	.....	158	5	34	8	123	17
Print paper, 40 lbs per ream	90	3	85	$16\frac{11}{24}$	85	$16\frac{11}{24}$	90	3
Record medium, 40 lbs per ream	198	1	100	.....	96	$11\frac{12}{24}$	201	$9\frac{11}{24}$
Super Royal, 54 lbs. per ream	54	15	.....	.....	4	$15\frac{11}{24}$	49	$23\frac{1}{24}$
Folio Post, 20 lbs. per ream	16	8	125	....	59	$13\frac{12}{24}$	81	$14\frac{12}{24}$
Folio Post, 24 lbs. per ream	58	8	300	.....	113	$11\frac{2}{24}$	144	$16\frac{8}{24}$
Folio Post, 28 lbs. per ream	25	14	201	.....	55	$6\frac{8}{24}$	171	$7\frac{8}{24}$
Double Flat Cap, 28 lbs. per ream	5	14	805	.....	319	$8\frac{11}{24}$	491	$5\frac{7}{24}$
Double Flat Cap, 36 lbs per ream	8	4	400	.....	223	$18\frac{11}{24}$	184	$9\frac{19}{24}$
Granite Cover, 40 lbs. per ream	88	1	245	.....	124	$12\frac{8}{24}$	203	$12\frac{12}{24}$
Bond paper, 17x22	22	$9\frac{9}{24}$	20	$16\frac{12}{24}$	23	$10\frac{11}{24}$	19	$15\frac{11}{24}$
Bond paper, 25x38	..	.....	10	$8\frac{8}{24}$	5	$18\frac{8}{24}$	4	$14\frac{6}{24}$
Card oard, sheets	3,908	.....	.....	.....	2,573	.....	1,335	.....
Tracing paper	2	$18\frac{12}{24}$	.....	.....	....	3	2	$15\frac{11}{24}$

All of which is respectfully submitted,

T. J. CUNNINGHAM, Secretary of State.
JOHN HUNNER, State Treasurer.
J. L. O'CONNOR, Attorney General.
Commissioners of Public Printing.

Report of Superintendent of Public Property.

REPORT

OF THE

SUPERINTENDENT PUBLIC PROPERTY.

MADISON, WIS., October 2nd, 1893.

To His Excellency, GEO. W. PECK, *Governor:*

I herewith submit to you the annual report of this office.

The annexed tabular statements will explain themselves.

The legislature by chapter 53 of the laws of 1893 extended the provisions of chapter 205 of the laws of 1891 so that this office has distributed in accordance with said law five copies each to Vilas and Iron county for county officers; eleven copies to town clerks of new towns and sixteen copies to the village clerks of new villages. At present there are three copies on hand for distribution. This law also appropriated money to pay for 192 copies of the S. & B. Ann. Statutes for the legislature of 1893.

By chapters 267 and 299 of the laws of 1893 I was authorized to purchase copies of the S. & B. Ann. Statutes to replace such copies as had been lost to the following named members: D. Jennings, J. W. Parkinson, S. A. Peterson, G. A. Abert, O. W. Bowe and A. A. Leissring.

Chapter 70 of the laws of 1893 authorized the purchase of Simons' Digest and Wisconsin Reports to complete sets for new counties and new courts of record, and the counties of Vilas and Iron were furnished at a cost of $284.90.

The painting and recarpeting of the two legislative

Report of Superintendent of Public Property.

---

chambers became necessary, which accounts for the heavy expenses in carpets, paint, labor and painters. Painting, $1,100; carpet in Senate chamber, $1,577.38; in Assembly chamber, $1,184.00. .

Besides this, the rooms in the basement used by the State Treasurer and Secretary of State have been furnished with steel floors and new iron shelving and filing cases thereby making the records more secure against fire and also providing for more shelf room which will soon be needed.

The cost of new brick work and resetting three boilers, with new pipe coverings over same, amounts to about $1,000.00, and about $1,050.00 were expended for new water closets and sewerage.

As to books in my charge, I have received the laws of the second extra session of 1892, the laws of 1893, and the journals of both sessions and they were distributed according to law. I have also received and distributed 250 copies each of the Supreme Court Reports, volumes 81, 82 and 83.

The sales from books in my charge amount to $399.05.

Yours very respectfully,

E. V. BRIESEN,
Superintendent Public Property.

STATIONERY PURCHASED, YEAR ENDING SEPT. 30, 1893.

191,000	Envelopes, plain	$358 37
97,000	Envelopes, lithographed	238 80
40,000	Envelopes, document	192 52
2,000	Envelopes, cloth lined	44 00
20,500	Letter heads, plain	82 86
223,500	Letter heads, lithographed	712 55
16,000	Letter heads, printed	52 00
2,000	Letter heads, embossed	17 00
14¼	Reams letter paper	30 83
15,000	Note heads, lithographed	33 75
1,500	Note heads, printed.	1 80
11	Reams note paper	13 65

Report of Superintendent of Public Property.

STATIONERY PURCHASED—Continued.

67½ Reams	legal cap paper	$158 75
64½ Reams	typewriter paper	94 13
4	Quires mimeograph stencil paper	5 95
348	Gross steel pens	192 56
277	Fountain pens	275 10
91	Ruling and shading pens	16 75
42	Gold pens and holders	79 37
247½	Dozen pen holders	78 73
100	Pen fountains	5 00
25	Pen racks	3 29
990	Dozen lead pencils	354 70
10	Dozen pencil sharpeners	20 00
180	Quarts ink	90 20
109	Bottles ink, assorted	26 19
404	Inkstands	116 70
27	Dozen bottles mucilage	36 90
3	Dozen sponge cups	1 95
878	Blank books	228 71
32	Copy books	50 83
5	Reams blotters	79 50
576	Gross rubber bands	167 61
33	Dozen rulers	60 74
60	Dozen erasers	139 64
557	Knives	526 76
317	Paper knives	71 35
7	Dozen shears	89 50
20	Dozen scissors	69 00
9	Dozen thumb tacks	14 49
3	Rolls tracing cloth	28 35
76	Dozen pyramid pins	61 38
12	Dozen card cases	48 00
2	Dozen eyelet punches and sets	51 00
4	Dozen McGill punches	9 60
40	Clips	12 52
15,000	Red seals	17 85
7	Desk baskets	4 95
8	Dozen letter files	33 30
2	Lbs. sealing wax	80
11	Dozen paper weights	27 98
50	Mailing tubes	2 50
5,000	McGill fasteners	6 16
10,000	Eyelets	2 20
75	Typewriter ribbons	46 99
1,100	Carbon	37 40
500	Manilla covers	2 13

$5,225 64

Report of Superintendent of Public Property.

STATIONERY DISBURSED, YEAR ENDING SEPTEMBER 30, 1893.

Executive office	$174 11
Secretary of state	303 24
State treasurer	141 80
Superintendent of public instruction	248 80
Railroad commissioner	32 33
Attorney general	118 95
Insurance commissioner	52 44
Board of control	174 69
Superintendent of public property	85 80
Land department	202 74
State agricultural society	120 95
Adjutant general, war record	78 40
Adjutant general, national guard	120 42
Adjutant general, pension department	92 95
Bureau of labor	66 00
Quartermaster general	90 21
Treasury agent	26 15
State prison	143 95
State veterinarian	32 91
State historical society	131 04
Supreme court	130 59
Law library	37 26
Fish and game warden	28 30
Lieutenant governor	22 15
Wisconsin assembly	2,106 60
Wisconsin senate	844 93
	$5,607 71

INVENTORY OF STATIONERY, OCTOBER 2, 1893.

145,500	Envelopes, plain	$233 55
11,769	Envelopes, document and tie	67 06
9,500	Envelopes, printed	44 63
700	Envelopes, cloth lined	14 68
22,000	Letter heads, lithographed	130 95
10,500	Letter heads, plain	21 00
6¾	Reams letter paper	17 94
21	Reams typewriter paper	25 39
1	Ream journal paper	2 80
3¼	Reams legal cap paper	10 20
2,000	Note heads, lithographed	15 00
1,000	Note heads, plain	1 30
14	Boxes note paper, embossed	18 48
151½	Quarts ink	84 59
115	Bottles ink, assorted	20 19
79	Quarts mucilage	53 72
94	Bottles mucilage	12 50
75	Inkstands	57 98
32	Sponge cups	5 18
122	Gross steel pens	69 28
32	Gold pens and holders	56 49
23	Fountain pens	29 20

INVENTORY OF STATIONERY—Continued.

25	Ruling pens	$7 73
11	Boxes quills (pens)	3 74
5	Dozen crow quill pens	1 65
22	Pen racks	3 08
44½	Dozen pen holders	18 93
278	Dozen lead pencils	121 09
46	Dozen lead pencils, colored	31 85
50	Propelling pencils	15 92
5	Automatic pencils	1 00
83	Boxes leads	4 39
65	Pencil sharpeners	7 65
1¼	Reams blotters, large	18 96
78	Packages blotters, cut	21 18
439	Blank books	70 09
41	Copy books	48 45
51	Knives	53 36
2,141	Tablets	122 93
114	Paper knives	38 61
7	Desk pads	5 25
134	Clips	25 58
43	Card cases	18 90
5	Bill books	8 35
2	Dozen finger shields	70
48	Paper weights	6 24
18	Bill stickers	2 34
25	Scissors	6 84
6	Shears	6 42
4	Desk racks	3 36
104	Rules	18 43
2¾	Sealing wax	1 10
	Boxes staples	6 80
	Staple inserters	2 25
	Eyelet punches and sets	17 04
	Boxes eyelets	12 74
	McGill punches	3 20
	Boxes McGill fasteners	8 82
	Copy bowl	23
	Copy brushes	63
	Erasers	6 88
	Dozen pyramids pins	14 82
	Catch alls	18 00
14, 34	Gilt seals	44 44
13,	Red seals	21 42
8	Boxes file bands	8 00
42	Spools tape	15 54
166	Carbons	5 65
25	Typewriter ribbons	14 88
177½	Gross rubber bands	74 65
29	Dozen thumb tacks	4 79
61	Letter files	25 38
48	Pen cups	10 56
		———
		$2,002 95

GENERAL EXPENDITURES.

Advertising, coal proposals....................	$6 00
Appropriation, chapter 53, laws 1893.............	2,088 00
Appropriation, chapter 70, laws 1893.............	284 90
Appropriation, chapter 267, laws 1893	27 00
Appropriation, chapter 299, laws 1893.............	27 00
Blacksmith work...	48 45
Capitol and park...........................	1,718 57
Carpets, matting, rugs, etc......................	4,566 81
Draying..	433 85
Electric light....	696 00
Freight..................................	217 61
Fuel	4,625 14
Furniture and repairing........................	870 40
Gas..	5,298 04
Gas fixtures....	387 43
Hardware.......................................	1,128 40
Ice...	187 50
Law books...	69 60
Lumber and mouldings.........................	835 17
Paints, oils, glass, etc.......	1,009 26
Paper and twine....	319 16
Plumbing..	1,404 41
Premium on steam boiler insurance.........	100 00
Repairing clocks, mowers, etc....................	34 80
Soaps, brooms, oil, matches, etc...	1,869 43
Sundries	145 10
Telephone rents.................................	372 00
Typewriters, exchanges and supplies............	358 56
Vault fixtures, secretary of state, state treasurer and land department........................	6,612 50
	$35,740 57

REPAIRS AND CARE OF EXECUTIVE RESIDENCE.

Furniture, carpets, curtains, crockery, etc........	$1,067 08
Fuel.....	443 86
Gas...	268 48
Hardware.......................................	86 24
Lumber and mouldings..........	50 12
Mason work....	41 80
One laborer..................................	660 00
Plumbing......	32 03
Sundries	117 10
Water, city of Madison.....	41 53
	$2,807 69

Report of Superintendent of Public Property.

EMPLOYMENT.

Clerks and storekeeper....	$3,710 00
Engineers, firemen and gas-fitter................	6,372 75
Carpenters...................................	4,767 90
Painters....................................	4,266 35
Elevator attendants.	848 00
Police and watchmen...........................	5,754 00
Janitors and messengers........................	17,736 00
Laborers	19,070 28
Women, scrubbing and washing................	2,204 80
	$63,730 08

MADISON, WIS., October 1st, 1894.

To His Excellency, GEO. W. PECK, *Governor.*

I herewith submit the report of this office for the year ending September 30th, 1894.

The accompanying statements show the purchase and distribution of stationery and also the amounts expended for labor and all expenses.

By chapter 304 of the laws of 1893, the sum of $6,000.00 was appropriated for the purchase of new desks for both chambers and new chairs for the Assembly chamber. The legislative committee (Hon. G. W. Pratt, Hon. P. Bechtner, Hon. G. A. Abert, Hon. W. H. Wheelihan, Hon. H. C. Putnam) submitted drafts and specifications under Joint Resolution No. 49 Senate. I advertised for proposals according to these plans and specifications and with consent of your excellency submitted the proposals to the committee in March. The committee recommended that the proposals for desks be rejected and that new bids for desks with a sample desk be asked for from the following parties in this state: The Phoenix Manufacturing Co. of Eau Claire, O. J. Schoenleber, The Northwestern Furniture

Report of Superintendent of Public Property.

Co., The Wollaeger Manufacturing Co. and Clement, Williams & Co., of Milwaukee. The committee met July 2nd, 1894, and recommended the purchase of desks from the Wollaeger Manufacturing Co. of Milwaukee as follows: 36 Senate desks at $32.50,—$1,170.00 and 102 Assembly desks at $24.50,—$2,499.00, and the purchase of 105 Assembly chairs from Clement, Williams & Co., of Milwaukee, at $8.50, —$892.50. The furniture is to be delivered at the capitol before December 15th, 1894.

The painting of the Assembly chamber commenced in November of 1892 was completed and I estimate the expense at $1,500.00.

New steel files were furnished in the vault of the State Treasurer and in the vault of the Adjutant General at a cost of $2,154. This was necessary in order to better utilize the room and provide more file room so that other rooms would not be necessary.

Sanborn & Berryman annotated statutes were furnished under chapter 205 of the laws of 1891, as amended, one copy each to city clerk of Rhinelander, seven village clerks, six town clerks, superior court of Douglas county, newly organized state normal school at Stevens Point, and four copies to the county officers of Price county to replace copies destroyed in recent fire at Phillips.

The session laws and revised statutes were also furnished to the county officers of Price county. But no Wisconsin Reports have yet been furnished to the county judge or clerk of the circuit court, of said county.

The amount received for books sold during the year is $327.45.

Yours very respectfully,

E. V. BRIESEN,

Superintendent of Public Property.

19—Sec'y.

STATIONERY PURCHASED, YEAR ENDING SEPT. 30, 1894.

128,000	Envelopes, plain..........................	$221 53
10,050	Envelopes, document.....................	71 36
4,050	Envelopes, cloth lined...................	92 60
5,000	Envelopes, embossed	32 50
7,000	Envelopes, lithographed...	22 40
42,000	Letter heads, plain......................	102 60
39,000	Letter heads, lithographed	168 10
3,000	Letter heads, embossed..................	30 00
1,000	Note heads, plain.......................	2 00
2	Reams note paper and envelopes, embossed	23 10
93	Reams typewriter paper..................	155 54
34	Reams legal cap..........................	87 20
5	Reams fool cap..........................	12 00
5	Reams letter paper......................	10 80
29	Reams note paper	43 46
2,000	Tablets.................................	44 51
8	Quires mimeograph stencil paper.........	11 91
76	Gross steel pens.........................	41 53
59	Fountain pens...........................	104 70
24	Gold pens and holders............	45 50
18	Ruling pens.............................	23 25
50	Dozen penholders.......................	50 22
217	Dozen pencils....	84 35
6	Pencil sharpeners.......................	1 00
42	Inkstands	53 60
355	Quarts ink.............................	144 83
18	Bottles ink............................	5 80
8	Tubes mimeograph ink...................	8 46
2	Bottles mimeograph varnish	34
84	Bottles mucilage........................	12 00
100	Sponges for sponge-cups.................	3 75
348	Blank books............................	62 65
36	Copy books.............................	42 00
164	Diaries.................................	104 34
2	Reams blotters.........................	31 50
13	Patent blotters.........................	4 54
231	Gross rubber bands	60 83
24	Rules..................................	4 25
168	Erasers.................................	14 09
144	Knives.................................	141 25
66	Paper knives...........................	23 23
12	Shears, paper..........................	12 80
72	Scissors................................	16 50
4	Gross thumb tacks	7 40
42	Card cases.............................	23 25
1	Challenge eyelet punch	2 50
59	Boxes eyelets..........................	26 42
50	Boxes McGill fasteners..................	6 16
11,000	Gold seals.............................	28 05
20	Spools silk braid.......................	87 10
15	Desk baskets...........................	14 50
7	Files..................................	1 88

Report of Superintendent of Public Property.

STATIONERY PURCHASED—Continued.

12 Copy brushes..............	$2 50
1,100 Manuscript covers........................	5 25
36 Bottles typewriter oil.....................	2 55
1,100 Carbon...................................	37 52
79 Typewriter ribbons.....................	49 52
	———— $2,523 52

STATIONERY DISBURSED, YEAR ENDING SEPT. 30, 1894.

Executive office.................................	$299 42
Secretary of State..............................	297 65
State Treasurer.................................	86 96
Superintendent Public Instruction..............	244 73
Railroad Commissioner..........................	42 51
Attorney General...............................	151 59
Insurance Commissioner.........................	77 16
Board of Control...............................	124 19
Superintendent Public Property.................	59 91
Land Department................................	88 88
State Agricultural Society......................	156 70
Adjutant General, national guard................	121 65
Adjutant General, pension department...........	18 37
Bureau of Labor................................	44 50
Quartermaster General..........................	201 62
Treasury Agent.................................	18 64
State Prison....................................	190 31
State Veterinarian.............................	23 01
State Historical Society........................	62 50
Supreme Court.................................	178 80
Law Library....................................	39 69
Fish and Game Warden	17 35
	———— $2,546 14

INVENTORY OF STATIONERY, OCTOBER 1, 1894.

184,500	Envelopes, plain..........................	$314 44
7'500	Envelopes, lithographed..................	34 71
4 100	Envelopes, cloth lined...................	93 75
9 175	Envelopes, document and tie...........	72 63
11,500	Letter heads, plain......................	27 60
21,000	Letter heads, lithographed..............	136 95
14¼	Reams note paper, plain................	20 96
2	Reams note paper, lithographed.........	15 00
3	Reams note paper, embossed...........	15 84
36	Reams typewriter paper.................	44 84
4½	Reams letter paper......................	13 08
7¾	Reams legal cap paper..................	22 83
1	Ream fools cap paper..................	2 40
2,540	Tablets.................................	94 50
352	Quarts ink..............................	159 51
50	Bottles ink.............................	8 21
52	Quarts mucilage........................	35 36
31	Bottles mucilage........................	4 57
72	Gross steel pens.......................	42 04
33	Gold pens and holders..................	57 97
22	Ruling pens.............................	12 26
3	Fountain pens..........................	3 68
228	Dozen pencils..........................	106 82
60	Automatic pencils......................	17 01
78	Boxes leads............................	3 90
45	Pencil sharpeners......................	5 55
28	Dozen pen holders.....................	31 84
21	Pen racks..............................	2 94
44	Pen cups...............................	9 68
274	Blank books............................	55 22
35	Copy books............................	42 14
¾	Ream blotters..........................	11 25
83	Packages blotters......................	20 75
7	Patent blotters.........................	2 60
67	Inkstands..............................	60 96
12	Sponge cups...........................	84
100	Sponges................................	3 75
27	Knives.................................	20 67
101	Paper knives...........................	28 82
65	Scissors................................	15 28
4	Shears	4 28
7	Desk baskets...........................	7 89
7	Desk pads..............................	5 25
4	Desk racks.............................	3 36
19	Letter files............................	8 55
8	Invoice files...........................	5 04
105	Clips	19 13
34	Card cases.............................	17 07
74	Rules..................................	18 10
40	Paper weights..........................	5 20
12	McGill punches........................	2 40
57	Boxes McGill fasteners.................	7 73

Report of Superintendent of Public Property.

INVENTORY OF STATIONERY—Continued.

3	Staple inserters...........................	$2 25
34	Boxes staples............................	6 80
6	Eyelet punches and sets................	12 78
49	Boxes eyelets...........................	20 51
98	Erasers	6 19
14	Copy brushes............................	2 94
4,000	Red seals................................	4 76
16,000	Gold seals...............................	47 66
8	Portfolio catchalls	12 00
48	Pyramids pins...........................	3 12
10	Spools red tape..........................	3 70
8	Boxes file bands........................	8 00
110	Carbon..................................	3 74
4	Quires mimeograph stencil paper........	5 96
5	Tubes mimeograph ink...................	3 80
15	Typewriter ribbons......................	8 62
500	Manuscript covers.......................	2 10
40	Dozen thumb tacks......................	6 30
167½	Gross rubber bands.....................	44 31

$1,982 69

GENERAL EXPENDITURES, YEAR ENDING SEPTEMBER 30th, 1894.

Advertising, furniture proposals................	$9 40
Appropriation, chapter 53, laws of 1893........	180 00
Blacksmith work................................	74 49
Capitol and park................................	1,078 64
Carpets, matting, rugs, etc.....................	2,307 19
Draying..	326 00
Electric light..................................	672 00
Freight..	135 18
Fuel...	6,048 59
Furniture and repairing........................	188 27
Gas...	3,684 17
Gas fixtures...................................	531 63
Hardware......................................	820 60
Ice, 15 months.................................	312 50
Law books.....................................	51 50
Lumber and mouldings.........................	634 64
Paint, oils, glass, etc..........................	1,297 36
Paper and twine...............................	325 17
Plumbing......................................	358 20
Repairing clocks, locks, mowers, etc...........	84 55
Rubber hose...................................	104 15
Soap, brooms, matches, oil, etc................	778 45
Sundries......................................	238 38
Telephone rents...............................	298 15
Typewriters, exchanges, supplies, etc..........	352 60
Vault fixtures, offices adjutant general and state treasurer...................................	2,154 00

$23,045 81

Report of Superintendent of Public Property.

REPAIRS AND CARE OF EXECUTIVE RESIDENCE.

Furniture. carpets, curtains, crockery, etc......	$297 15	
Fuel......	501 33	
Gas...	172 06	
Hardware...	122 40	
Lumber and mouldings...	41 57	
One laborer...	660 00	
Plumbing, pipe-fitting and covering...	99 87	
Sundries...	60 75	
Water, city of Madison...	42 32	
		$1,997 45

EMPLOYMENT.

Clerks and storekeeper...	$2,710 00	
Engineers, firemen and gas-fitter...	6,767 26	
Carpenters...	3,486 25	
Painters...	4,282 88	
Janitors and messengers...	17,864 00	
Laborers...	15,857 31	
Police and watchmen...	5,840 00	
Elevator attendant...	730 00	
Women, scrubbing and washing...	2,141 70	
		$59,679 40

VALUE OF BOOKS ON HAND SEPTEMBER 30th, 1894.

12	Private and local laws 1858 ...	$18 00
6	Private and local laws 1865 ...	9 00
172	Private and local laws 1871 ...	258 00
157	Private and local laws 1872 ...	117 75
149	Session laws 1836–7–8, reprint...	111 75
1	Session laws 1855, half bound...	50
24	Session laws 1856, half bound...	12 00
2	Session laws 1857, half bound...	1 00
325	Session laws 1858, half bound...	162 00
2	Session laws 1862, half bound...	1 00
1	Session laws 1865, half bound...	50
2	Session laws 1866, half bound...	1 00
212	Session laws 1867, half bound...	106 00
701	Session laws 1868, half bound...	350 50
574	Session laws 1869, half bound...	287 00
923	Session laws 1870, half bound...	461 50
1,416	Session laws 1871, half bound...	708 00
1,115	Session laws 1872, half bound...	836 25
2,641	Session laws 1873, half bound. ...	3,301 25
361	Session laws 1873, sheep bound...	577 60
1,627	Session laws 1874, half bound...	2,440 50
245	Session laws 1874, sheep bound...	453 25
1,643	Session laws 1875, half bound...	1,067 95
258	Session laws 1875, sheep bound...	258 00
2,459	Session laws 1876, volume 1, half bound...	1,229 50

Report of Superintendent of Public Property.

VALUE OF BOOKS ON HAND—Continued.

296	Session laws 1876, volume 1, sheep bound..	$251 60
2,753	Session laws 1876, volume 2, half bound...	1,376 50
309	Session laws 1876, volume 2, sheep bound..	262 50
2,226	Session laws 1877, half bound.............	1,113 00
344	Session laws 1877, sheep bound	292 40
571	Session laws 1878, half bound.............	285 50
277	Session laws 1878, sheep bound	235 45
1	Session laws 1879, half bound.............	50
141	Session laws 1879, sheep bound	119 85
223	Session laws 1880, sheep bound	189 55
12	Session laws 1881, half bound.............	6 00
297	Session laws 1881, sheep bound............	252 45
20	Session laws 1882, half bound.............	15 00
344	Session laws 1882, sheep bound	378 40
352	Session laws 1883, volume 1, half bound...	176 00
334	Session laws 1883, v lume 1 sheep bound .	283 90
6	Session laws 1883, volume 2, half bound...	4 50
1,130	Session laws 1885, volume 1, half bound...	847 50
299	Session laws 1885, volume 1, sheep bound..	328 90
281	Session laws 1885, volume 2, half bound...	281 00
1 303	Session laws 1887, volume 1, half bound...	1,303 00
304	Session laws 1887, volume 1, sheep bound..	410 40
391	Session laws 1887, volume 2, half bound...	586 50
1,344	Session laws 1889, volume 1, half bound...	1,008 00
402	Session laws 1889, volume 1, sheep bound..	442 20
564	Session laws 1889, volume 2, half bound...	423 00
2,208	Session laws 1891, volume 1, half bound...	1,656 00
39	Session laws 1891, volume 1, sheep bound..	42 90
180	Session laws 1891, volume 2, half bound...	153 00
210	Session laws 1891, volume 2, sheep bound..	232 00
2,897	Session laws 1892, first session, half bound.	869 10
277	Session laws 1892, first session, sheep bound	180 05
3,611	Session laws 1892, second session, half bound	1,083 30
266	Session laws 1892, second session, sheep bound................................	172 90
2,511	Session laws 1893, half bound.............	1,883 25
224	Session laws 1893, sheep bound...........	246 40
477	Revised Statutes 1878....................	1,431 00
589	Geological survey, volume 1	486 25
176	Geological survey, volume 3	880 00
597	Geological survey, volume 4..............	2,985 00
991	Town laws 1885.........................	991 00
78	Roster Wisconsin soldiers, volume 1......	117 00
97	Roster Wisconsin soldiers, volume 2......	145 50
		$37,218 70

Index.

INDEX.

Index.

Index.

Index.

Index.

Index.

Index.

APPENDIX.